Law and Religion

The International Library of Essays in Law and Legal Theory
Series Editor: Tom D. Campbell

Schools

Natural Law, Vols I & II *John Finnis*
Justice *Thomas Morawetz*
Law and Economics, Vols I & II *Jules Coleman and Jeffrey Lange*
Critical Legal Studies *James Boyle*
Marxian Legal Theory *Csaba Varga*
Legal Reasoning, Vols I & II *Aulis Aarnio and Neil MacCormick*
Legal Positivism *Mario Jori*

American Legal Theory *Robert Summers*
Law and Language *Fred Schauer*
Sociological Theories of Law *Kahei Rokumoto*
Rights *Carlos Nino*
Law and Psychology *Martin Levine*
Feminist Legal Theory *Frances Olsen*
Law and Society *Werner Krawietz*

Areas

Criminal Law *Thomas Morawetz*
Tort Law *Ernest Weinrib*
Contract Law, Vols I & II *Larry Alexander*
Anti-Discrimination Law *Christopher McCrudden*
Consumer Law *Iain Ramsay*
International Law *Martti Koskenniemi*
Property Law, Vols I & II *Elizabeth Mensch and Alan Freeman*
Constitutional Law *Mark Tushnet*
Procedure *Denis Galligan*
Evidence and Proof *William Twining and Alex Stein*

Administrative Law *Denis Galligan*
Child Law *Harry Krause*
Family Law, Vols I & II *Harry Krause*
Welfare Law *Peter Robson*
Medicine and the Law *Bernard Dickens*
Commercial Law *Ross Cranston*
Communications Law *David Goldberg*
Environmental Law *Michael Blumm*
Conflict of Laws *Richard Fentiman*
Law and Religion *Wojciech Sadurski*
Human Rights Law *Philip Alston*
European Community Law, Vols I & II *Francis Snyder*

Legal Cultures

Comparative Legal Cultures *Csaba Varga*
Law and Anthropology *Peter Sack*
Hindu Law and Legal Theory *Ved Nanda*
Islamic Law and Legal Theory *Ian Edge*
Chinese Law and Legal Theory *Michael Palmer*
Socialist Law and Legal Theory *W. Butler*

Japanese Law and Legal Theory *Koichiro Fujikura*
Law and Development *Anthony Carty*
Jewish Law and Legal Theory *Martin Golding*
Legal Education *Martin Levine*

Future Volumes
Labour Law, Common Law and Legal Theory, Civil Law and Legal Theory,
African Law and Legal Theory, Legal Ethics and Cumulative index.

Law and Religion

Edited by

Wojciech Sadurski

University of Sydney

NEW YORK UNIVERSITY PRESS
REFERENCE COLLECTION

First published in the U.S.A. in 1992 by
NEW YORK UNIVERSITY PRESS
Washington Square
New York NY 10003

Library of Congress Cataloging-in-Publication Data
Law and religion / edited by Wojciech Sadurski.
        p.   cm. – (The International library of essays in law and
legal theory.   Areas)
    "New York University Press reference collection."
    Includes bibliographical references and index.
    ISBN 0-8147-7953-0
    1. Religion and law.   2. Religion and state.   I. Sadurski,
Wojciech, 1950–   .   II. Series.
BL65.L33L39   1992
344′.096 s−dc20
[342.496]   92–4119

Contents

Acknowledgements

The editor and publishers wish to thank the following for permission to use copyright material.

Connecticut Law Review for the essay: Mark Tushnet (1986), 'The Constitution of Religion', *Connecticut Law Review*, **18**, pp. 701–38.

Duke Law Journal for the essay: Stephen L. Carter (1987), 'Evolutionism, Creationism, and Treating Religion as a Hobby', *Duke Law Journal*, No. 6, pp. 977–96. Copyright © Duke Law Journal.

Duke University School of Law for the essay: James Hitchcock (1981), 'Church, State and Moral Values: The Limits of American Pluralism', *Law and Contemporary Problems*, **44**, No. 2, pp. 3–21.

The Law Book Company Limited for the essay: Wojciech Sadurski (1989), 'On Legal Definitions of "Religion"', *Australian Law Journal*, **63**, pp. 834–43.

New York University Press for essays: Eric Mack, 'Liberalism, Neutrality and Rights', in J.R. Pennock and J.W. Chapman (eds), *Nomos XXX: Religion, Morality and the Law*, Chapter 2, pp. 46–70, and David A.J. Richards, 'Religion, Public Morality and Constitutional Law', in J.R. Pennock and J.W. Chapman (eds), *Nomos XXX: Religion, Morality and the Law*, Chapter 8, pp. 152–78.

Princeton University Press for the essay: Robert Audi, 'The Separation of Church and State and the Obligations of Citizenship', *Philosophy and Public Affairs*, Vol. 18, No. 3, pp. 259–96.

SLS Legal Publications (NI) for the essay: St. John A. Robilliard (1981), 'Religion, Conscience and Law', *Northern Ireland Legal Quarterly*, **32**, No. 4, pp. 358–72.

The University of Akron for the essay: Gail White Sweeney (1980), 'Conscientious Objection and the First Amendment', *Akron Law Review*, **14**, pp. 71–84.

University of California Press Journals for the essay: Phillip E. Johnson (1984), 'Concepts and Compromise in First Amendment Religious Doctrine', *California Law Review*, **72**, pp. 817–46. © Copyright 1984 by California Law Review Inc. Reprinted from California Law Review Vol. **72**, pp. 817–46 by permission.

Series Preface

The International Library of Law and Legal Theory is designed to provide important research materials in an accessible form. Each volume contains essays of central theoretical importance in its subject area. The series as a whole makes available an extensive range of valuable material which will be of considerable interest to those involved in the research, teaching and study of law.

The series has been divided into three sections. The Schools section is intended to represent the main distinctive approaches and topics of special concern to groups of scholars. The Areas section takes in the main branches of law with an emphasis on essays which present analytical and theoretical insights of broad application. The section on Legal Cultures makes available the distinctive legal theories of different legal traditions and takes up topics of general comparative and developmental concern.

I have been delighted and impressed by the way in which the editors of the individual volumes have set about the difficult task of selecting, ordering and presenting essays from the immense quantity of academic legal writing published in journals throughout the world. Editors were asked to pick out those essays from law, philosophy and social science journals which they consider to be fundamental for the understanding of law, as seen from the perspective of a particular approach or sphere of legal interest. This is not an easy task and many difficult decisions have had to be made in order to ensure that a representative sample of the best journal essays available takes account of the scope of each topic or school.

I should like to express my thanks to all the volume editors for their willing participation and scholarly judgement. The interest and enthusiasm which the project has generated is well illustrated by the fact that an original projection of 12 volumes drawn up in 1989 has now become a list of some 60 volumes. I must also acknowledge the vision, persistence and constant cheerfulness of John Irwin and the marvellous work done by Mrs Margaret O'Reilly and Mrs Sonia Bridgman.

TOM D. CAMPBELL
Series Editor
The Faculty of Law
The Australian National University

Introduction

Rightly or wrongly, the 1980s have been widely perceived as an era of significant religious revival in much of the world. One can see the reasons for such a perception: the newly acquired influence and visibility of a number of fundamentalist movements such as Moral Majority and right-wing 'televangelists' in the United States; the moves towards entrenching religious values in the legal systems in new democracies in Eastern and Central Europe (for example, reintroduction of teaching of religion in public schools and steps towards prohibiting abortion in Poland); a great resurgence of Muslim fundamentalism in much of the Arab and Muslim world (the Salman Rushdie affair has been perhaps the most clear example of this phenomenon), and the growth of political influence of orthodox religious groups in Israel. These are but some of the examples of the phenomenon of a rise of religiosity in the 1980s.

Whether this phenomenon has been accompanied by any deeper changes in individual attitudes towards religion and whether it will have any lasting effect upon the role of religion in the modern world are questions beyond the brief of this introductory essay. But one thing is certain: the rise of the public role of religious bodies, groups and churches has called for a rethinking and reinterpreting of the basic principles which govern the relationship between the law and religions (in particular the organized, powerful religions) in the modern state. Some vexed questions currently prominent are the limits of legitimate state funding of religiously-affiliated schools, the role of religious tenets in the public schools curricula, the appropriateness of legal prohibitions of behaviour (such as abortion or homosexuality) condemned by certain religious creeds, and the fairness of granting exemptions from burdensome tasks (such as military service) to religious objectors. In the midst of such controversies, it is evident that vague references to slogans such as 'freedom of religion' or 'separation of state and religion' do not furnish obvious and clear answers.

The purpose of this collection is to provide the reader with a range of texts which will aid reflection upon these issues. In conformity with the principles behind the series, these essays present a diversity of ideological and scholarly responses to questions related to the relationship of law and religion in modern societies. Some general caveats are necessary at the outset, however.

First, as the table of contents indicates, not all the major issues of the 'law and religion' relationship are covered here. Some degree of arbitrariness is perhaps inevitable in any process of selection of topics, and readers should not expect from this volume a fully comprehensive coverage of the matters which pertain to the role of law towards organized religions. For instance, the question of government regulation of religious organizations has been deliberately disregarded since this topic seems to be rather derivative of responses to more fundamental questions such as understanding the proper meaning of 'free exercise of religion' or the principle of church-state separation. Further, the question of state regulation of religious bodies seems to belong to those issues which are to a greater extent shaped by contingent, technical legal mechanisms than by general philosophical principles. In a word, this volume focuses on those issues which directly lend themselves to a discussion of the 'law and religion' relationship at a fairly high level of theoretical abstraction.

Secondly, the question of legal responses to religious phenomena and claims in society provides the centre of attention in this volume, rather than the influence of religious beliefs upon the shaping of the law. There is no point in denying that the evolution of religious beliefs has had a major impact upon the developments of legal rules, doctrines and institutions. But the historical issue is outside the theme of this volume; what matters most in present controversies is how the law should respond to already existing religious beliefs and organizations. Most particularly, a major issue in the 'law and religion' controversy is how the law should respond to religious diversity (by which I understand also the occurrence of a significant number of non-religious people and views) in modern democratic societies.

Thirdly, as the preceding remark suggests, the essays in this volume are concerned with a legal regime of religion in a society which is, and attempts to remain, democratic and pluralistic. We are not concerned here with legal aspects which issue from direct, blatant and uncontroversial violations of human conscience in non-democratic societies, such as those which either enforce religious uniformity or which punish any form of religious belief. From the point of view of legal doctrine these are, so to speak, easy cases. Difficult legal and doctrinal problems arise with regard to a society which is, by and large, committed to respect that aspect of human liberty which relates to religious or anti-religious beliefs; they arise where the controversy centres on the ways in which individual religious liberties can best be protected in conformity with general democratic principles.

Fourthly, readers may be surprised by the fact that nearly all the essays in this book have been written by American authors and largely concern American legal materials. This is not due to any deliberate attempt by the editor to focus solely on the United States; indeed, the aspiration of the volume is to provide readers with grounds for reflection which are universal in their character and which may be helpful for a discussion of the legal regime of religious liberty in Ireland as well as in India, in the Philippines and in Poland. The clear over-representation of American texts reflects a general state of affairs in the English-language literature on the subject. There may be different explanations for this fact (the sheer size of the American legal academia, the importance of a written Bill of Rights which generates an enormous quantity of jurisprudential interpretation, etc), but they are beside the point. The effect is that there have not been many significant contributions to the subject in the English language outside the United States. The reader is thus invited to use the deliberations by American authors (for instance, about the judicial doctrines of the US Supreme Court under the Religion Clauses of the First Amendment) merely as illustrations of more general issues and to try to apply these discussions, *mutatis mutandis*, to his or her own society and legal system.

One useful way of looking at the relationship between the state and religion in modern democratic nations is to view it as a matter of mutual adjustment and reconciliation between two main, governing principles: the principle of the separation of the state and religion, and the principle of freedom of religion. At first blush, it may seem that the two are coextensive, and that the former is but an institutional method of implementing the latter. Indeed, it is generally thought that if the state is fully disengaged from religious matters, citizens can freely pursue their religious plans according to their own wishes; in contrast, there is the perception that a state-established religion interferes with the free exercise of the followers of nonestablished religions. As Professor Kurland observes in an essay reprinted in Part I of this collection, the 'existence of an established church implied [in the eyes of the draftsmen of the Bill of Rights] intolerance for the nonestablished religions. The ban on a national church monopoly would factionalize the churches and thereby assure religious freedom'.[1] And yet, much of the scholarly literature and judicial arguments concerning the relationship of law and religion, especially in the United States, is about tensions between these two governing principles (see, for instance, the essay by Johnson in Part II of this book).[2]

To realize that this tension is real and significant, it suffices to reflect upon the positive, active meaning of religious liberty which calls for something more than mere non-interference by the state in the religious affairs of citizens. In numerous contexts, the principle of religious liberty demands affirmative steps by the state to accommodate the religious wishes of its citizens including, for example, exemptions from general duties when the fulfilment of those duties could impair believers' opportunities to exercise their religious preferences. But in the name of religious freedom, the demands go further than that. An author of one of the essays reproduced in this collection, James Hitchcock, believes for instance that the government has a duty to support denominational schools financially: 'If it is assumed that church-operated schools are an important exercise of religious freedom, if it is assumed that by operating schools the churches are performing a vital social service, and if it is recognized that parents who send their children to religious schools are also taxpayers, it would seem that the state has a compelling interest in seeing to it that these schools are as good as they can be and are not starved for funds'.[3]

Without entering into the merits of the argument, it illustrates one particularly controversial issue in which the postulates of the separation principle and the religious freedom principle seem to point in opposite directions. State funds for religious schools do constitute taxpayers' support for a particular religion (even if those schools also perform non-religious functions); on the other hand, failure to subsidize those schools by the government may render meaningless parents' freedom to educate their children in accordance with their own religious preferences. This consequence is seen by many as undermining those parents' religious freedom. Indeed, Professor Hitchcock himself states elsewhere in his essay that 'a judicial policy of remaining vigilant against church-state entanglement in practice often means the willingness to impose, or to allow others to impose, burdens on the free exercise of religion'.[4]

We may generalize the problem in the following way: while the principle of religious freedom calls for some degree of governmental accommodation of religion, the separation principle, in contrast, is suspicious of any such accommodation, detecting in it impermissible governmental assistance to religion. In other words, the tension between the two principles stems from the fact that the principle of religious liberty has an expanding dynamic built into it (calling, as it does, for a positive and active legal attitude towards claims to have one's religious requirements respected through legal accommodation, exemptions, privileges, subsidies, etc). This very dynamic threatens to undermine the disengagement of the state from religious matters demanded by the principle of separation.

These two general principles correspond to two constitutional clauses – the Free Exercise Clause[5] and the Non-Establishment Clause[6] – which may be found in a number of contemporary constitutions and bills of rights. To appreciate how the tension between the two general, governing principles extends into a conflict between these two constitutional clauses, it is useful to compare current judicial doctrines regarding the interpretation of the two Religion Clauses of the First Amendment of the US Constitution. As far as the construction of the Non–Establishment Clause is concerned, in a landmark decision the Court established that, in order to conform with the Clause, government action must (1) have a secular purpose, (2) have, as its primary effect, neither the advancement nor the inhibition of the religion, and (3) avoid excessive governmental entanglement with religion.[7] In contrast, the Supreme Court's interpretation of the Free Exercise Clause involves balancing the state's interests in achieving valid governmental aims and the individual's interests in exercising his or her religious objectives in an unrestrained manner.[8] The difference between the interpretations of the two clauses is clear: the former is formulated in categorical, yes-or-no terms (at least as far as the first tier of the test is concerned, regarding the secular character of the legislative purpose), while the latter calls for weighing and balancing conflicting interests, with no guarantee that individual interests in religious freedom will necessarily be given priority.

To bring this tension away from the realm of abstract judicial doctrines and closer to real life, we may envisage a number of situations which generate conflict between the two principles. For one thing, there may be situations in which implementation of the Free Exercise Clause will offend the Non–Establishment Principle: when, for instance, religion–based exemptions from military service or from work on a holy day may be seen as privileges which discriminate against non–adherents to a particular religion or to non–believers. Secondly, and conversely, there may be situations in which the claims based on the Non–Establishment Clause will be viewed as denials of Free Exercise requirements: when, typically, a state refusal to provide subsidies or other aid to a particular religion (such as to a denominational school) will be seen as inhibiting the exercise of religious freedom.

Several authors, including those whose essays are reproduced in this book, illustrate various aspects of this conflict and try to work out a strategy of resolving it. One such strategy is to postulate the priority of one principle over the other; proponents usually stipulate the priority of the Free Exercise Principle over the Non–Establishment Principle,[9] though a clear minority favour the separation of law and religion.[10] For instance Professor Katz (in an article not included in this collection) asserts that the principle of church–state separation has only a secondary and relative character, and that it should be applied only insofar as it contributes to the furtherance of religious liberty.[11] But this strategy has some obvious drawbacks. First, it goes against a constitutional mandate in those countries (including the United States and Australia) where Bills of Rights enumerate both these principles without expressly prioritizing either of them. Secondly, to subordinate the non–establishment principle to the clause of religious freedom could, in consequence, create serious threats to the liberty of non–believers and of adherents to minority non–orthodox sects and churches.

An alternative and much more promising strategy is to show that both these principles are subordinated to a higher coordinating value which both should serve. If such a higher, unifying value can be identified and defended, then it may perhaps be shown that each of these two principles has a proper place in a jurisprudence of religious freedom, and that the conflict may be solved, in each particular case, by reflecting upon the best way to promote the fundamental value.

Essays in Part I of this collection all exemplify this strategy: more specifically, they appeal to the idea of state neutrality towards religion. This is an influential strategy: it has often been thought that the idea of neutrality towards religion is the best interpretation of the complex set of rules governing the relationship of law and religion in a democratic state.[12] As Sidney Hook wrote in a small but important book, *Religion in a Free Society*, 'a genuinely democratic state, especially one which contains a plurality of religious faiths, should be neutral in matters of religion, and regard it as essentially a private matter'.[13] The US Supreme Court repeatedly asserted its commitment to 'a scrupulous neutrality by the State, as among religions, and also between religious and other activities'.[14] It should also be said that this appeal to the state's religious neutrality certainly resonates well with an important tenet in recent liberal theories which view this principle of moral neutrality as the best interpretation of a liberal state committed to the protection of individual liberties, along the lines of John Stuart Mill's 'harm to others' principle.

Be that as it may, the principle of religious neutrality of the state is neither obvious nor universally accepted. The very concept of 'neutrality' is a complex one, and difficulties in understanding are only compounded when we apply this concept to the realm of the law's attitudes towards religion. Some of the arguments in Part I attempt to distinguish between different possible understandings of 'neutrality' and to identify the most plausible ones. From this point of view, a distinction drawn by Eric Mack between 'non-interventionist', 'equal promotionist', Benthamite and 'proceduralist' types of neutrality seems to me to be particularly helpful; his plea for the 'non-interventionist' understanding of state neutrality seems to be well-grounded in his broader view about the proper role of a liberal state *vis-à-vis* morality in general, not only with respect to religion. Professor Audi's recent essay (also included in Part I of this book) is a valuable reminder that the principle of neutrality is only one possible normative basis for the doctrine of separation of church and state, and that the libertarian or egalitarian rationales for the principle of separation will yield different theoretical and practical consequences.

It is against the background of these theoretical clarifications that we can appreciate the significance of theories which call for as strict as possible a separation of state and religion, referring often to a famous metaphor by Thomas Jefferson of a 'wall of separation'. Incidentally, it is useful to keep in mind an observation by James Hitchcock in the essay reproduced in Part II that, historically, the tradition of church-state separation was a double-edged sword: it was meant not only to 'protect the public weal from the intrusion of religion' but also, as in the writings of Raymond Williams, 'to insure maximum freedom for the churches without government interference'.[15] Both these concerns seem to inform the perspectives of some of the contemporary writers (whose essays are reproduced in Part I) calling for strict separation. Jonathan Weiss believes that 'the Constitution prevents law from entering the purely private domain of religious expression and belief', which implies that 'the state can neither tamper with nor examine religious affirmations nor prescribe religious perspectives'.[16] Consequently, he would deny a number of religiously motivated exemptions and privileges, as they constitute (in his opinion) an unconstitutional breach of separation of a private sphere of religion and a public sphere of law. Similarly, Philip Kurland, who has been perhaps the most outspoken defender of the strict separation doctrine in American legal scholarship,[17] believes that, as a general principle, 'government cannot utilize religion as a standard for action or inaction' because the two Religion Clauses 'prohibit classification in terms of religion either to confer a benefit or to impose a burden'.[18] Robert Audi puts forward and defends the 'principle of secular rationale' which demands that only those laws and policies be accepted which are supported by secular reasons. And David Richards shows how the neutralist interpretation of strict church-state separation gives weight to the underlying values of tolerance, liberty and respect for persons.

However, as already mentioned, the ideal of state neutrality towards religion is far from being uncontroversial (indeed, Professor Kurland caustically observes that his own principle, quoted above, 'met with almost uniform rejection'),[19] and the essays reproduced in Part II of this collection display a range of critical attitudes towards this ideal. Briefly, the arguments against neutrality may be divided into two types: that neutrality towards religion is unattainable, and that it is not an attractive ideal. It should be said that the critics of neutrality usually resort to both arguments, but for the sake of clarity we mention these two criticisms separately.

It will perhaps come as no surprise that the critics of the ideal of neutrality usually view it as a thinly disguised form of hostility towards religion or – at best – as an attempt to belittle its importance. This charge is made explicit in the very title of Professor Carter's paper; he himself attributes to the liberal partisans of neutrality a view which 'treats religion as a hobby'. Similarly in the essay reproduced below, Mark Tushnet claims that much of the jurisprudence relating to the Supreme Court's Religion Clauses rests 'on a set of ideas that do not take religion seriously as a form of human endeavor'.[20] And recently, Michael Sandel has written that liberal interpretations of governmental neutrality towards religion, aimed at the mission of protecting individual autonomy, 'may miss the role that religion plays in the lives of those for whom the observance of religious duties is a constitutive end, essential to their good and indispensable to their identity'.[21]

In Carter's opinion, by advocating strict neutrality of law towards religion, liberals are guilty of derogating religious beliefs. Professor Carter's essay is all the more interesting as it focuses on a particularly difficult area of current controversy in the US and elsewhere – the contents of school curricula: should so-called 'creationism' be taught alongside 'evolutionism' as an equally respectable theory about the origins and growth of life on Earth?[22] But what really matters for the main themes of this book is a more general problem raised by Carter and expressed as a rhetorical question: 'Why is it that contemporary liberalism, which proclaims the freedom of individual conscience, values conscience less when an individual chooses to discover the world through faith rather than through reason? What is it about religious belief that liberalism so fears?'[23]

Indeed, what is it? And is the charge against liberals fair? Obviously, liberals such as Kurland or Richards (for all the differences between the two) do not think so, responding that the policy of strict neutrality and of 'wall of separation' does not reflect any hostility towards religion but, rather, is critical of allowing a favoured role for religion in the public forum. The evil which they perceive is not the strong role of religion in an individual's life, but an opportunity for one particular religion to impose sectarian religious views upon other cults or upon non–religious people. But this answer will hardly impress the critics of neutrality such as Carter or the other writers whose essays are reproduced in Part II below.

However, more often than not the critics of 'neutrality' believe that it is a chimerical ideal; that neutrality is unattainable. The best the law can do, they often claim, is to attain a degree of even-handedness of treatment as between particular religions, but it is incoherent (the argument goes) to hope that the law can be neutral as between religion and unbelief. This is the position taken, *inter alia*, by Professors Hitchcock (in Part IV of his essay) and Johnson. They reach this conclusion in slightly different ways: Johnson points out that the ideal of 'neutrality' presupposes a neutral starting point or baseline of already existing advantages or disadvantages, and thus is arbitrary; Hitchcock believes that, on a number of issues such as abortion, sex education or polygamy, whatever choice government takes, it will be non–neutral as it will involve moral choices which may be controversial.

Naturally, my simplistic characterizations of the views of the critics of neutrality do not do justice to the complexity of their arguments, and it is for readers to judge their weight. Nevertheless, two simple observations may be in order. One is that no answer to the doubts about the coherence (or otherwise) of the ideal of neutrality can be found in a semantic dissection of the word 'neutrality', or in seeking help from other areas where the concept of 'neutrality' has often been applied, notably in international law (as J.T. Valauri in his important article about neutrality towards religion seems to suggest).[24] It is not a matter of the word's lack of clarity which is at the root of disagreements which concern the proposed policy of 'neutrality'. Rather, the disagreements issue from the controversies about the normative weight of various purposes and ideals contained in a cluster of values shared by the liberal partisans of 'neutrality'. It is not the case that they mistakenly take that notion to have a clear meaning while it is in fact incoherent (as their critics seem often to suggest), but rather that their fundamental values about the role of the law towards religion are not the same as those of their detractors. Hence, in order to clarify the concept of 'neutrality' in this context, it is inevitable that we must first reflect upon our visions of the ideals offered in a liberal theory of a democratic, secular state. And clearly, those ideals (as illustrated by the essays in Part I of the book) are not exactly the same as those adopted by the authors in Part II. One clear area of disagreement is the question of whether a state may be protective of religion in preference to 'non–religion'. Kurland, Richards *et al.* clearly give a negative answer; Johnson and Carter seem to incline towards a positive one.

A second observation about the controversy between the views expounded in Part I and those in Part II of this book is that some writers (including Johnson, whose essay is reprinted in Part II) challenge the very use of the notion of 'neutrality' in the 'law and religion' context. They claim that it is inherently unstable: to suggest that a particular policy conforms with the neutrality requirement presupposes a baseline by reference to which any departure is to be judged as non–neutral. And yet, the argument goes, any such baseline is largely arbitrary and is often shaped by current conventional acceptance of a particular distribution of advantages and disadvantages, benefits and burdens. Change this baseline and your conclusions about the neutrality of a given policy will change – hence the alleged instability and arbitrariness of the notion.

This argument is a serious one, and it has often been made very effectively with respect to a broader notion of a state's neutrality towards moral issues. And yet we should realize that to say that a baseline presupposes an individual value judgement (by reference to which we will describe any breaches as non–neutral) does not imply that it is 'arbitrary' in a way which conclusively discredits such an act of judgement. Some departures from our baselines (those points at which we consider a state's policy to be even-handed towards relevant practices) are more reprehensible than others. To say, for instance, that it is non–neutral to grant exemptions to religious objectors but not to other serious moral objectors does indeed presuppose a certain baseline of advantages and disadvantages in a society; this baseline implicates our substantive ideals about the fairness of a particular distribution of advantages and disadvantages with respect to a given practice. But it does not follow that no sustained argument about the plausibility of that baseline can be made at all.

This last example is not coincidental, as the question of neutrality arises very clearly with respect to religion–based exemptions from common duties and standards. As is often the case, burdens and requirements which are facially impartial may have a disparate impact upon different groups, including different religious groups. Whereas for any other person compulsory military service may be a burden but not much more, for a Jehovah's Witness it may be a very drastic violation of his most fundamental principles of moral integrity. Should the law allow for such claims for exemption from common duties? These issues are illustrated by the essays in Part III, but it should be kept in mind that they are also alluded to by a number of papers in Parts I (Kurland, Weiss, Audi) and II (Hitchcock, Johnson). In particular, it has been an important implication of Kurland's principle, quoted above, that the very fact of 'religiousness' does not add any extra weight to someone's claims for exemptions or other advantages. For, as Professor Kurland says, 'to afford a privilege of freedom claimed for adherents to one religion necessarily results in aiding the religion over others or over the nonreligious'.[25] For this very reason, those American judges who took seriously the principle of neutrality and of separation of state and religion felt uneasy about endorsing religion-based conscientious objections. Criticizing the law which exempted religious objectors from military service, Justice Douglas once wrote: 'The law as written is a species of those which show an invidious discrimination in favor of religious persons and against others with like scruples'.[26]

There are, in an ascending order of generality, three neutrality-related problems raised by religion-based exemptions. First, can the law grant exemptions to some religions but not to others? In the American law of military conscientious objection, it has been established that exemptions can be granted to those who are conscientiously opposed to all war, but not to those who are opposed to a particular war which is deemed by an objector to be 'unjust'. Is not this distinction between a general and a selective opposition to war discriminatory against those religions which prohibit participation in unjust wars only? Secondly, the religion-based exemptions may be seen to discriminate against those who object to war (or any other practice in question) on profoundly moral but secular grounds. As Sidney Hook, in an already-quoted book, asserted: 'If the state is truly neutral, then no privilege can be extended to any religious group which is not open to any nonreligious group'.[27] Thirdly, these exemptions may be seen to discriminate against those who object to such duties on non-moral grounds, but which may nevertheless be of high importance to them. Consider the case of those traders who do not benefit from the religious exemptions from Sunday closing laws and who may justifiably fear economic losses.

One possible strategy to mitigate the perceived non–neutrality of religion–based exemptions would be to interpret the actual notion of 'religion' very broadly, so that a number of claims for exemptions could be allowed even if not considered truly 'religious' in conventional language. This leads us to the set of issues discussed in the essays included in Part IV of this book. Again, it has been considered in some earlier Parts of this collection as well (notably by Hitchcock, Weiss and Johnson), but the articles in Part IV deal exclusively with the problem.

The example of religious objections indicates the importance of the issue, but of course it has a much wider significance. In various contexts, different bodies or individuals may wish to have their beliefs considered as 'religious' (for instance, in order to qualify for a tax exemption or an exemption from military service) or, conversely, as 'non-religious' (for example, when a particular group wants to promote its practices in public schools, or to have its tenets included in the school curriculum).

At this stage, it is useful to return to the observation with which I opened this introductory essay concerning the two guiding principles which regulate the law–religion relationship (the principles of religious freedom and of separation of religion and state), and the inherent tension between the two. This tension informs much of the argument concerning a plausible definition of 'religion' for the purposes of the law. As I note in my own essay, reproduced in Part IV, the natural tendencies built into the two principles affect the concept of law in opposite directions. When we contemplate issues related to the freedom of religion, the natural tendency is to lean towards as broad a concept of religion as possible (in order to avoid the discriminatory consequences of a narrow definition which would leave some religions or religion-like views outside the range of justified claims for exemptions, privileges, etc). In contrast, when we consider the issues related to the separation of state and religion, there is an understandable tendency towards a narrower definition. This is because in a state committed to a wide scope of social and economic functions (as all modern states are), a broad definition of religion would necessarily invalidate a number of otherwise unobjectionable governmental activities under the separation principle.

A solution which I recommend, and defend, is to adopt a 'bifurcated' definition of religion – different for the purposes of the two principles. Whilst I am not alone in advocating such a solution (see the literature cited in footnote 44 of my essay), it has not been widely accepted. In another essay reproduced in Part IV, one of its critics, Bob Clements, lists a number of desiderata for a proper, legal definition of religion – it must be flexible, specific and uniform. His solution to the problem identified earlier is to advocate a purely 'functional' approach based not so much on the substance of a given religious position, but rather on the role religion plays in the life of its adherents. According to Clements, some of the core functions that recognized religions can play are in addressing the fundamental questions of human existence and in providing a guide for conducting one's life.

One advantage of Clements's position is that it can claim support from much of the recent jurisprudence of the US Supreme Court, especially under the Free Exercise Clause. This is not surprising; indeed, it may be viewed as a strategy by the Court to pay lip-service to the constitutional mandate (which puts 'religion' in a preferred position *vis-à-vis* other types of morality) while at the same time to avoid discrimination against non-religious moralities. But again, there are important criticisms that can be made about a 'functional' definition. Jesse Choper, for one, is not entirely satisfied with such an approach, believing that it is necessary to include at least some content-based indicia in the constitutional concept of religion. In an essay reproduced in this collection, he advocates what he calls 'the extratemporal consequences' criterion. Whatever the merits of this definition (and some important criticisms of it can be found in the contributions by Clements and by Johnson), it runs into the difficulty identified above: it may induce discrimination against those genuine and honest claims for exemptions from common duties which do not match Choper's (or anyone else's) criteria of 'religion'.

One rather extreme response to this quandary is to abandon the search for any definition of 'religion' altogether. This solution is briefly advocated in the essay by Weiss in Part I of this book: consistently with his strict neutralist position, he believes that any legally entrenched definition of faith or religion will inevitably lead to the exclusion of some religions, or articles of faith, from the privileges granted by the principle of religious freedom. Hence, Weiss says, 'religious freedom is served by allowing a completely open realm for defining religion rather than by establishing a domain or definition in which religions can freely operate'.[28] More recently, in a lengthy essay not included here but strongly recommended to any reader particularly interested in this question, Professor George C. Freeman has argued that 'religion' can never be satisfactorily defined.[29]

Whether the Freeman/Weiss position is a solution to, or an avoidance of, the problem is for the reader to decide. Just as with the other issues discussed in this volume, so in the case of the problem of the definition of religion for legal purposes, the aim of this Introduction has merely been to outline a range of theoretical responses to the problem rather than to recommend 'the correct' solution.

Notes

1 P.B. Kurland (1978), 'The Irrelevance of the Constitution: The Religion Clauses of the First Amendment and the Supreme Court', *Villanova Law Review*, **24**, 3–27, at 9 [reprinted in Part I of this book].

2 See also, generally, L.H. Tribe (1988), *American Constitutional Law*, Mineola, The Foundation Press, 2nd edition, para. 14–2.

3 James Hitchcock (1981), 'Church, State, and Moral Values: The Limits of American Pluralism', *Law & Contemporary Problems*, **44** (2) 3–21, at 12 [reprinted in Part II].

4 *Id.* at 11.

5 In the US Constitution (Amendment I): 'Congress shall make no law . . . prohibiting the free exercise [of religion]'; in the Australian Constitution (Article 116): 'The Commonwealth shall not make any law . . . for prohibiting the free exercise of any religion'. In the International Covenant on Civil and Political Rights (1966), Article 18 (1): 'Everyone shall have the right to freedom of thought, conscience and religion. This right shall include freedom to have or to adopt a religion or belief of his choice, and freedom, either individually or in community with others and in public or private, to manifest his religion or belief in worship, observance, practice and teaching.'

6 In the US Constitution (Amendment I): 'Congress shall make no law respecting an establishment of religion'; in the Australian Constitution (Article 116): 'The Commonwealth shall not make any law for establishing any religion'.

7 *Lemon v. Kurtzman* 403 U.S. 602 (1971).

8 See, e.g., *Wisconsin v. Yoder* 406 U.S. 205 (1972).

9 Prominent proponents of this position include: D.A. Gianella (1968), 'Religious Liberty, Nonestablishment, and Doctrinal Development, Part II: The Nonestablishment Principle', *Harvard Law Review*, **81**, 513–90; G. Merel (1978), 'The Protection of Individual Choice: A Consistent Understanding of Religion Under the First Amendment', *University of Chicago Law Review*, **45**, 805–43; W.G. Katz (1953), 'Freedom of Religion and State Neutrality', *University of Chicago Law Review*, **20**, 426–40; Tribe, para. 14–8. In Australian literature, this view has been defended by C.L. Pannam (1963), 'Travelling Section 116 With a U.S. Road Map', *Melbourne University Law Review*, **4**, 41–90.

10 See L. Pfeffer (1980), 'Freedom and/or Separation: The Consitutional Dilemma of the First Amendment', *Minnesota Law Review*, **64**, 561–84; P.A. Freund (1969), 'Public Aid to Parochial Schools', *Harvard Law Review*, **82**, 1680–92.

11 W.G. Katz (1953), 'Freedom of Religion and State Neutrality', *University of Chicago Law Review*, **20**, 426–40.

12 In addition to the essays referred to in this Introduction and those reproduced in Part I, some important discussions of the concept of neutrality of law towards religion can be found in: M.W. McConnell (1986), 'Neutrality under the Religion Clauses', *Northwestern University Law Review*,

81, 146–67; M.W. McConnell and R.A. Posner (1989), 'An Economic Approach to Issues of Religious Freedom', *University of Chicago Law Review*, **56**, 1–60; A.H. Loewy (1986), 'Rethinking Government Neutrality Towards Religion Under the Establishment Clause', *North Carolina Law Review*, **64**, 1049–70; Tribe, para. 14–7, and in particular J.T. Valauri (1986), 'The Concept of Neutrality in Establishment Clause Doctrine', *University of Pittsburgh Law Review*, **48**, 83–151. Valauri's article had to be excluded from this collection solely because of its length, but is strongly recommended to readers.

13   S. Hook (1967), *Religion in a Free Society*, Lincoln: University of Nebraska Press, p. 27.
14   *Roemer v. Board of Public Works*, 426 U.S. 744, 746–7 (1976). For other examples of judicial appeals to the concept of neutrality, see e.g. *Zorach v. Clauson*, 343 U.S. 306, 314 (1952); *Epperson v. Arkansas*, 393 U.S. 97, 103 (1968); *Gillette v. United Sates*, 401 U.S. 437, 449 (1971), and *Jones v. Wolf*, 443 U.S. 595, 602 (1979). But note the opinion by Rehnquist, J. (now Chief Justice of the US Supreme Court) that 'nothing in the Establishment Clause requires government to be strictly neutral between religion and irreligion, nor does that Clause prohibit Congress or the States from pursuing legitimate secular ends through nondiscriminatory sectarian means', *Wallace v. Jaffree*, 472 U.S. 38, 113 (1985).
15   Hitchcock, *op. cit.*, at 7.
16   J. Weiss (1964), 'Privilege, Posture and Protection: "Religion" in the Law', *Yale Law Journal*, **73**, 601–23, at 623 [reprinted in Part I].
17   In addition to his essay reprinted in this book, see also his (1975) *Church and State: The Supreme Court and the First Amendment*, Chicago: University of Chicago Press; (1961) 'Of Church and State and the Supreme Court', *University of Chicago Law Review*, **21**, 1–96; and (1984), 'The Religion Clauses and the Burger Court', *Catholic University Law Review*, **34**, 1–19.
18   Kurland, 'The Irrelevance of the Constitution', *op. cit.*, at 24.
19   *Id.*
20   Mark Tushnet (1986), 'The Constitution of Religion', *Connecticut Law Review*, **18**, 701–38 [reprinted in Part II].
21   M.J. Sandel (1990), 'Freedom of Conscience or Freedom of Choice?' in J.D. Hunter and O. Guinness (eds.), *Articles of Faith, Articles of Peace: The Religious Liberty Clauses and the American Public Philosophy*, Washington, D.C.: Brookings Institution, p. 89.
22   For an affirmative answer to this question, see *inter alia* Note (1978), 'Freedom of Religion and Science Instruction in Public Schools', *Yale Law Journal*, **87**, 515–70; Note (1985), 'The Myth of Religious Neutrality by Separation in Education', *Virginia Law Review*, **71**, 127–72.
23   S.L. Carter (1987), 'Evolutionism, Creationism, and Treating Religion as a Hobby', *Duke Law Journal*, 977–90, at 985–86 [reprinted in Part II].
24   Valauri, *op. cit.*, at 89–92.
25   Kurland, 'The Irrelevance of the Constitution', *op. cit.*, at 15.
26   *Gillette v. United States*, 401 U.S. 437, 469 (1971).
27   Hook, *op. cit.*, at 45.
28   Weiss, *op. cit.*, at 604.
29   G.C. Freeman, III (1985), 'The Misguided Search for the Constitutional Definition of Religion', *Georgetown Law Review*, **71**, 1519–65.

Bibliography

(Note: This Bibliography does not include the books and articles referred to in the footnotes to the Introduction above.)

Alley, R.S. (ed.) (1988), *The Supreme Court on Church and State*, New York: Oxford University Press.
Berman, H.J. (1974), *The Interaction of Law and Religion*, London: SCM Press.
Berman, H.J. (1983), 'Religious Foundations of Law in the West: An Historical Overview', *Journal of Law and Religion*, **1**, 3–43.

Boothby, L. and R.W. Nixon (1982), 'Religious Accommodation: An Often Delicate Task', *Notre Dame Lawyer*, **57**, 797–808.

Buzzard, L.R. (ed.) (1982), *Freedom and Faith: The Impact of Law on Religious Liberty*, Westchester, Ill.: Crossway Books.

Clark, R. (1979), 'The United Nations and Religious Freedom', *New York University Journal of International Law and Politics*, **11**, 197–225.

Fellman, D. (1965), *Religion in American Public Law*, Boston: Boston University Press.

Garbett, C. (1950), *Church and State in England*, London: Hodder & Stoughton.

Garvey, J.H. (1981), 'Freedom and Equality in the Religion Clauses', *Supreme Court Review*, 193–221.

Gianella, D.A. (1967 and 1968), 'Religious Liberty, Nonestablishment, and Doctrinal Development, Part I: The Religious Liberty Guarantee', *Harvard Law Review*, **80**, 1381–431; 'Part II: The Nonestablishment Principle', *Harvard Law Review*, **81**, 513–90.

Glenn, G.D. (1987), 'Forgotten Purposes of the First Amendment Religion Clauses', *Review of Politics*, **49**, 340–67.

Greenawalt, K. (1988), *Religious Convictions and Political Choice*, New York: Oxford University Press.

Hogan, M. (1981), 'Separation of Church and State: Section 116 of the Australian Constitution', *Australian Quarterly*, **53**, 214–28.

Hunter, J.D. and O. Guinness, (eds) (1990), *Articles of Faith, Articles of Peace: The Religious Liberty Clauses and American Public Philosophy*, Washington, D.C.: Brookings Institution.

Ingber, S. (1989), 'Religion or Ideology: A Needed Clarification of the Religion Clauses', *Stanford Law Review*, **41**, 233–333.

Laycock, D. (1986), 'A Survey of Religious Liberty in the United States', *Ohio State Law Journal*, **47**, 409–51.

Laycock, D. (1981), 'Towards a General Theory of Religion Clauses: The Case of Church Labor Relations and the Right to Church Autonomy', *Columbia Law Review*, **81**, 1373–1417.

Lupu, I.C. (1989), 'Where Rights Begin: The Problem of Burdens on the Free Exercise of Religion', *Harvard Law Review*, **102**, 933–90.

Manning, L.F. (1981), *The Law of Church-State Relations*, St. Paul: West Publishing Co. [Nutshell Series].

McDougal, M.S., H.D. Lasswell, and L. Chen (1976), 'The Right to Religious Freedom and World Public Order: The Emerging Norm of Nondiscrimination', *Michigan Law Review*, **74**, 865–98.

Miller, R.T. and R.B. Flowers (1982), *Toward Benevolent Neutrality: Church, State, and the Supreme Court*, Waxo, Texas: Markham Press, revised edition.

Neff, S.C. (1977), 'An Evolving International Norm of Religious Freedom: Problems and Prospects', *California Western International Law Journal*, **7**, 543–82.

Note (1980), 'Religious Exemptions Under the Free Exercise Clause: A Model of Competing Authorities', *Yale Law Journal*, **90**, 350–76.

Note (1982), 'The Sacred and the Profane: A First Amendment Definition of Religion', *Texas Law Review*, **61**, 139–74.

Note (1984), 'Reinterpreting the Religion Clauses: Constitutional Construction and Conceptions of the Self', *Harvard Law Review*, **97**, 1468–86.

Note (1987), 'Developments in the Law: Religion and the State', *Harvard Law Review*, **100**, 1606–781.

Note (1989), 'Burdens on the Free Exercise of Religion: A Subjective Alternative', *Harvard Law Review*, **102**, 1258–77.

Pennock, J.R. and J.W. Chapman (eds) (1988), *Religion, Morality, and the Law: Nomos XXX*, New York and London: New York University Press.

Pfeffer, Leo (1970), 'The Right to Religious Liberty', in N. Dorsen (ed.), *The Rights of Americans*, New York: Vintage Books, 326–47.

Richards, D.A.J. (1986), *Toleration and the Constitution*, New York: Oxford University Press.

Robertson, G. (1981), 'Blasphemy', *Public Law*, 295–303.

Robilliard, St. J. (1984), *Religion and the Law*, Manchester: Manchester University Press.

Schwartz, A. (1968), 'No Imposition of Religion: The Establishment Clause Value', *Yale Law Journal*, **77**, 692–737.

Smith, M.E. (1983), 'The Special Place of Religion in the Constitution', *Supreme Court Review*, 83–123.

Stokes, A. and L. Pfeffer (1964), *Church and State in the United States*, Westport: Greenwood Press.

Symposium (1966), 'Expanding Concepts of Religious Freedom', *Wisconsin Law Review*, 215–330.

Symposium (1981), 'Religion', *Law and Contemporary Problems*, **44** (2), 1–184.

Symposium (1984), 'The Religion Clauses', *California Law Review*, **72**, 753–921.

Symposium (1986), 'Religion and the Law', *Connecticut Law Review*, **18**, 697–853.

Symposium (1987), 'Law and Religion', *American Journal of Comparative Law*, **35**, 1–254.

Symposium (1990), 'Religious Dimensions of American Constitutionalism', *Emory Law Journal*, **39**, 1–215.

Van Alstyne, W.W. (1987), 'What Is "An Establishment of Religion"?', *North Carolina Law Review*, **65**, 909–16.

Way, F. and B.J. Burt (1983), 'Religious Marginality and the Free Exercise Clause', *American Political Science Review*, **77**, 652–65.

Weber, P.J. (ed.), (1990), *Equal Separation: Understanding the Religion Clauses of the First Amendment*, Westport: Greenwood Press.

Part I
Neutrality of Law Toward Religion

[1]

2

LIBERALISM, NEUTRALISM, AND RIGHTS

ERIC MACK

I. INTRODUCTION

In recent years the increased strength and assertiveness of socially conservative political movements have heightened public debate about the legitimate role of the state in enforcing moral prescriptions that are arguably the product of particular, sectarian, religious or moral perspectives. Social conservatives, motivated by components of their religious commitments, have not only condemned homosexual activity and abortion (to pick the two most prominent issues) but have also argued that these activities ought to be legally prohibited. In opposition to such proposals, there has been a reassertion of the liberal doctrines that political institutions must be neutral between competing moral and religious ideals, between competing conceptions of the good and that political neutrality precludes state enforcement of anyone's religious or moral program. In this essay I inquire how best to understand the doctrine of neutralism, how to assess its force against conservative proposals, e.g., legal prohibitions on abortions, and how to understand the relation between neutralism and liberalism.

Unfortunately, even at the most general level, neutralism may be construed in a variety of ways. We can distinguish between noninterventionist, equal promotionist, Benthamite, and proceduralist neutralism. Under *noninterventionist neutralism*, the state is constrained from interfering with individuals in specified ways

46

that would characteristically diminish their abilities to pursue
their own life plans or conceptions of the good even if intervention would foster acknowleged or widely affirmed values.
The emphasis in noninterventionist neutralism is on constraints
upon state action and on the insufficiency of the promotion of
the good to override these moral-political constraints. Noninterventionism is based upon the liberal, individualist idea of
private spheres of control centered on each person, which others, including state officials, may not invade except under special justifying conditions.

But, neutralism can also be conceived as requiring evenhead-
edness in state intervention. One such neutralism would mandate the equal promotion by the state of all or nearly all diverse
life plans or conceptions of the good.[1] *Equal promotionist neutralism* may be based upon either of two distinct moral outlooks.
The first is that each life plan or conception of the good is
equally worthy of being fulfilled. Here the demand for a life
plan's fulfillment flows from the moral stature of its content.
The demand for equality in fulfillment flows from the equal
stature of the content of different life plans. An alternative basis for the equal promotionist doctrine is the belief that value
resides *in the satisfaction* of life plans, whatever their content,
combined with an egalitarian commitment that this satisfaction
be equally distributed among life planners.

The third type of neutralism, viz., *Benthamite neutralism*, demands a different sort of evenhandedness. The Benthamite rejects talk about the worth, equal or otherwise, of life plans or
conceptions of the good. The good consists indiscriminately in
the satisfaction of any desire, preference, or plan of life. And
no egalitarian rider is imposed on the distribution of the good
among desirers or life planners. Rather than fostering particular life plans or conceptions of the good, state action must be
justified on the basis of its promotion of aggregate utility or
aggregate preference or life plan satisfaction. Under Benthamite neutralism, any promotion or thwarting of specific life plans
or conceptions of the good would be entirely incidental to the
social maximization of whatever forms of satisfaction are taken
to have intrinsic value.

Equal promotionism, Benthamism, and nonintervenionism are
all substantive in the sense that each specifies the social states,

the political-legal outcomes, that must obtain if neutrality is to prevail. Substantive versions of neutralism require that the state's activities actually yield the outcomes that this or that version of neutralism demands. For example, a pro-choice advocate of any of these substantive versions of neutralism would argue that true political morality requires that the state not prohibit abortion and that this represents neutrality because the political morality that requires nonprohibition precludes any weight being given to particular life plans or conceptions of the good. What is crucial is that, as he sees it, the pro-choice conclusion is implied by this substantivist's political morality. It is no part of his case against prohibition that anyone's actual prohibitionist beliefs, proclamations or policies in fact are the psychological or sociological products of a special weighing of particular life plans or conceptions of the good. Whether neutrality obtains is a matter of the way the legal-political world is, not of how it got that way.

In contrast, *procedural neutralism* formulates the demand for neutrality as a restriction on what types of beliefs can motivate legitimate political proposals and actions. If a political proposal is in fact the product of neutrality violating beliefs or, perhaps, is the sort of proposal that typically arises from such beliefs, it is to be accorded no weight in proper political debate. For instance, a pro-choice proceduralist will argue that the demand that the state prohibit abortion is to be dismissed as politically out-of-order on the basis of the type of beliefs that motivate this demand, e.g., particular, sectarian, religious beliefs. The pro-choice proceduralist does not rely on a conception of true political morality that requires nonprohibition. His only, or at least primary, defense of nonprohibition is that anti-abortion arguments or policies are all procedurally tainted.

Unfortunately, a fine line runs between substantive and procedural neutralism.[2] When the liberal attacks an advocate of legally mandatory church membership for his attempt to impose his religious vision on others, is the liberal's underlying complaint that mandated membership would infringe individual rights? Or is it that it would unequally promote different conceptions of the good? Or is it that its advocate is moved to his proposal by his own special conception of the good? In general, the argument is proceduralist whenever criticism is directed against the sort of reasons one's opponent offers or is moved by. The outcome of the reasoning is irrelevant. While the substantivist will deny that there are sufficient reasons for certain state actions, the proceduralist will decry the reasons why certain state actions are proposed. It is proceduralist neutralism that Joseph Raz seems to have in mind when he contrasts substantive noninterventionist liberalism that is based on "doctrines of basic liberties which limit the power of the state by declaring that certain areas of conduct are outside of its authority" with "principles of restraint [which] deny the appropriateness of certain reasons for political action, or for certain kinds of political action."[3]

The noninterventionist emphasizes constraints on the state's promotion of all valued ends. The equal promotionist emphasizes distributional requirements on the state's promotion of values. The Benthamite does not constrain state promotion of ends, even distributionally. But his restrictive theory-of-value precludes the state's favoring certain preference or life plan satisfactions over quantitatively similar preference or life plan satisfactions. The proceduralist seeks to block the state's pursuit of particular conceptions of the good by banning arguments and proposals that are motivated by those particular conceptions. All four have some claim to represent the liberal doctrine that the state is not to promote any particular and, hence, contentious conception of the good.

In this essay I shall argue in favor of the noninterventionist version of neutralism and against its three competitors. Arguments against the equal promotion and the Benthamite forms of neutralism are presented in section II. Proceduralist neutralism, which is the most common form of neutralism used against social conservatism in recent political debate, is criticized in section III. Finally, in section IV, I try to give an attractive explication of the noninterventionist view and, making this view less attractive to some, to show the extensive ties between this form of neutralism and liberal individualism.

II. EQUAL PROMOTIONIST AND BENTHAMITE NEUTRALISM

The equal promotionist advocates that each conception of the good or, better, each individual's pursuit of his conception of the good ought to be promoted by the state and promoted equally. This advocacy puts *all* conceptions of the good on a par. So the sadist must receive encouragement equal to that received by his more conventionally motivated victim. This collides with bedrock moral intuitions and with all neutralists' expectations about what a regime of neutrality would look like. Can the equal promotionist escape equal respect for sadists and their intended victims?[4] To do so, he must argue that some life plans, e.g., the plans of sadists, fall outside the range of plans to which neutralism applies. Here, however, we must recall the alternative bases for equal promotionism. It may be thought to rest on the value of the *satisfaction* of life plans combined with a separate egalitarian rule that these satisfactions be equally distributed. Or it may be said to rest on the equal worthiness of life plans. If the equal promotionist turns to the first of these bases, it is hard to see how he can even begin an orderly retreat from equal respect for the sadist and his intended victim. For both the sadist and his victim precisely the same thing is at stake, viz., satisfaction, and this is supposed to be equally divided.

If, on the other hand, equal promotionism is held to rest on the relative worthiness of life plans, its proponent can at least begin to argue that some life plans are beyond the pale. The argument would have to be that some pursuits can be excluded because they are so patently *less worthy* than others. But, once comparative judgments about the worth of different life pursuits are brought into political morality, there does not seem to be any mark on the worthiness-of-pursuit continuum that would allow the equal protectionist to say, *on the basis of worthiness*, that while certain pursuits are not worthy of state encouragement, the rest should receive *equal* support. Different degrees of worthiness among those pursuits meriting support would seem to call for different degrees of encouragement. Also troublesome for the equal promotionist is the fact that some of the activities that manifest unworthiness would seem to disqualify have been protected by standard demands for political neutrality. Consider typical unworthy behavior that proponents of neutralism usually take to be protected: addictive drug use, promiscuous sexual conduct, religious cult membership, the consumption of wine coolers and so on. If disvalue or unworthiness disqualifies certain life plans from equal promotion, then the resulting pol-

icy of equal promotion will protect far less than liberals generally expect when they invoke neutralism.

Note that the equal promotionist cannot avail himself of the
strategy employed by Nozick in addressing a case parallel to
our sadist-victim example. Nozick maintains that:

> Not every enforcement of a prohibition which differentially ben-
> efits people makes the state non-neutral. Suppose some men are
> potential rapists of women, while no women are potential rapists
> of men or of each other. Would a prohibition against rape be
> non-neutral ? It would, by hypothesis, differentially benefit peo-
> ple; but for potential rapists to complain that the prohibition was
> non-neutral between the sexes, and therefore sexist, would be ab-
> surd. There is an *independent* reason for prohibiting rape.[5]

For here Nozick rejects the core of equal protectionism, viz.,
that neutrality consists in equal encouragement. How a position
like Nozick's should be construed as noninterventionism is developed in section IV.

Benthamite neutralism relies on the political theory that since
"the state is an instrument for satisfying the wants that men
happen to have rather than a means of making men good,"
only "want-regarding principles" and never "ideal-regarding
principles" should determine the proper activities of the state.
Want-regarding principles are "principles which take as given
the wants which people happen to have and concentrate attention entirely on the extent to which a certain policy will alter
the overall amount of want-satisfaction."[6] The Benthamite has
his own problems with the sadist and his victim. While the equal
promotionist appears to be committed to the equal encouragement of the sadist and his victim, the Benthamite appears to be
committed to maximizing satisfaction across the sadist and his
victim. As much sadism is to be allowed, indeed fostered, as
brings the sadist more satisfaction than it brings dissatisfaction
to the victim. Similarly, as much and only as much freedom in
pursuit of one's conception of the good is to be permitted as
will yield satisfaction for one greater than the dissatisfaction
this pursuit will yield for others, e.g., those who despise one's
conception of the good. True, Benthamism precludes any status for the *worth* of the sadist's conception of the good in making it right that he enjoy himself at the expense of his victim.

Similarly, it precludes any place for the *worth* of the teetotaler's conception of the good in making prohibition justified. The quality of the sadist's or the teetotaler's desires plays no justificatory role. Instead, everything depends on the range and intensity of the preferences expressive of the competing conceptions—on how many individuals subscribe to them and how fervently. It is clear, though, that the view that only want-regarding considerations should count, and count aggregatively, in determining political right and wrong implies nothing like what the liberal has in mind when he invokes neutralism against conservative proposals for, e.g., the suppression of immoral life plans.

Once again, the obvious alternative for the principled rejection of the demands of the sadist, the teetotaler, etc., for political support is noninterventionist neutralism. For it is not the disvalue of their plans, nor their demand for more than equal support, nor any insufficiency in the range or intensity in their desires that shows that these proposals should be rejected. Rather, what fundamentally condemns them is their invasiveness of others' privileged spheres of choice and control. And, it is interventionist neutralism that specifies state neutrality in terms of respect for private spheres of choice and the moral side-constraints defined by, or defining, them.

A final and common problem confronts equal protectionist and Benthamite neutralism. Neither is responsive to the real challenge posed by social conservatives. That challenge is to reconcile a moral realism that affirms that some life plans are morally superior and others are to be morally condemned with a refusal to permit the state to promote the valuable or to suppress the defective. The most extensive recent public debate about the state's role in promoting good and vanquishing evil occurred during the 1984 elections when the conservatives attacked Catholic political leaders who both endorsed state neutrality and condemned many of the practices that neutrality would allow. The main charge was that Catholics like Mario Cuomo and Geraldine Ferraro were inconsistent in morally condemning most abortions while maintaining that it would be wrong for the state to prohibit these evils. So, one of the key parameters of recent debate about neutrality is the presumption that important sound judgments can be made about the comparative value of different ways of life and different conceptions of the good. This presumption of moral realism sets the stage for the conservative demand that some good explanation be given why the state is not to be guided by these admittedly sound judgments. Both the equal promotionist and the Benthamite fail to address this challenge because they do not share this presumption of moral realism. Rather both equal promotionism and Benthamism put all, or almost all, conceptions of the good on a moral par. The former affirms the equal worth of each life plan (or each within a set of minimally acceptable plans). The latter affirms the moral irrelevance of what is qualitatively distinct about particular life plans.[7] In these ways both the equal promotionist and the Benthamite rely upon moral scepticism about our ability to make significant comparative judgments of different conceptions of the good. In contrast, the two remaining versions of neutralism, proceduralism and noninterventionism, do attempt to accommodate the liberal rejection of the state as moral disciplinarian with moral realism.

III. PROCEDURALIST NEUTRALISM

The noninterventionist reconciles moral realism and systematic restraint on the state's activity by insisting upon a fundamental distinction between two branches of morality. The first branch is the theory of the good, which specifies valuable ends and the means to those ends and allows us to evaluate life plans and conceptions of the good in terms of their worth. The second branch is the theory of rights, the theory of moral side-constraints on the means that any agent may employ in the pursuit of any end no matter (or, perhaps, almost no matter) how valuable that end be. For the noninterventionist, these rights define or at least predominantly characterize enforcible public morality. Activities that do not violate these side-constraints are not subject to prohibition even if they are strongly condemned by the theory of the good. And activities that do violate these side-constraints are to be suppressed even if they produce valuable results. It can be *consistent* to condemn abortions while denying that they are appropriately subject to state suppression. And it can be *consistent* to acknowledge the overall good of vigilante suppression of abortions while insisting that this use of coercion is morally impermissible and itself properly subject to state prohibition. Because of the noninterventionist's separation of judgments generated by the theory of the good from the dictates of political morality, no degree of realism about values, about our capacity to rank alternative life plans, seriously threatens to justify an expansion of the state's mandate for action.

Contemporary liberals are, however, understandably reluctant to accept the noninterventionist insistence that political morality is at least predominantly a matter of respecting and enforcing moral side-constraints on the pursuit of goals and the narrow role for the state that this political morality seems to imply. They do not want to surrender the vision of the state as a promoter of value. The problem, then, if moral realism is embraced, is to explain why the state should promote certain acknowledged values while not promoting other equally acknowledged values. The problem is "to find any reason for supporting politically some elements of a conception of the good and not others that are admitted to be valid and valuable."[8] Yet no explanation seems possible in terms of discrepancies in value between equally acknowledged goods. And arguments that invoke the impermissible invasiveness of certain promotions of values by the state would be to noninterventionist in spirit. The solution advanced by the liberal proceduralist is that certain sound judgments about worthy and unworthy pursuits are, nevertheless, inadmissible in political debate and in the motivation of political policy.

An address by New York Governor Mario Cuomo, given at the University of Notre Dame during the 1984 campaign, is a characteristic statement of the proceduralist position.[9] As one would expect, the central illustrative issue is abortion—more specifically, the compatibility of Cuomo's moral condemnation of most abortion with his rejection of its prohibition by the state. Cuomo makes two suggestions, which he wisely does not pursue. The first is that his oath of office requires him to uphold "the Constitution that guarantees this [abortion] freedom."[10] But this basically proceduralist argument needs the premise that the Supreme Court is currently *correct* about what the Constitution requires (perhaps, because the Supreme Court *must* be correct about the Constitution). Yet this premise will be dis-

puted by almost anyone who sees many or most abortions as
instances of morally unjustified manslaughter, a perspective that
Cuomo himself presumably shares! Moreover, even if sound,
this argument in no way indicates that either Cuomo or anyone
else should hestitate to bring about an anti-aboration constitutional amendment. Cuomo next proposes the "truth" that "to
assure our freedom we must allow others the same freedom,
even if occasionally it produces conduct by them which we hold
to be sinful."[11] But this is an argument for noninterventionism,
not for proceduralism; and it is an argument with a crucial unstated premise about who is to be included among the others
who must be granted equal freedom.

In contrast to these preliminary suggestions, Cuomo's central
argument cites both the religious origins of anti-abortion judgments and the absence of consensus about the prohibition of
abortion. Usually it seems that the argument is supposed to turn
on the absence of consensus, which is to be *accounted for* by the
influence of diverse religious perspectives. The key passage de-
clares that:

> Our public morality, then, the moral standards we maintain for
> everyone, not just the ones we insist on in our private lives, de-
> pends on a consensus view of right and wrong. The values de-
> rived from religious belief will not, and should not, be accepted
> as part of the public morality unless they are shared by the plu-
> ralistic community at large, by consensus.[12]

Yet why should correct, enforcible public morality depend on
consensus? Is it only right, e.g., to prohibit slavery when there
is a consensus in favor of this prohibition? And is *anything* pol-
iticially right if there is a consensus in its favor? Cuomo replies
to this objection by identifying the rightness of a political program with its political feasibility. According to Cuomo, since
the "legal interdicting of abortion . . . is not a plausible possibility and even if it could be obtained, it would not work,"[13] it
is contrary to political morality to interdict abortion. In parallel
fashion, Cuomo maintains that the failure of the American
Catholic bishops to condemn slavery in the pre-Civil War period was justified because such a condemnation would have been
ineffective or counterproductive.[14] But, clearly, even if these

factual claims are correct, they do not establish that an anti-abortion crusade now is wrong or that an antislavery crusade then would have been wrong. And even less do these facts establish the rightness of allowing and protecting abortion or allowing and protecting slavery.[15] By identifying political virtue with political pragmatism, Cuomo's argument disarms the liberal who wants to argue and campaign against legal enforcement of any item of the current moral consensus.

Cuomo might have placed more emphasis on the specifically religious sources of anti-abortion sentiment. And he does seem implicitly to appeal to these sources when he repeatedly condemns the imposition of some people's "religious values" on others, even while he acknowledges that these values may also have a fully secular basis.[16] Indeed, liberal opponents of the conservative program commonly invoke the specifically *religious* coloration or source of anti-aboration sentiment and try to argue that these judgments should not be part of anyone's public morality. Yet there seems to be a simple dilemma facing this downgrading of political arguments that rely upon religious premises. Either the use of religious premises should be rejected because of their falsity, or their use should be rejected independently of their truth or falsity. No doubt the proposed exclusion of religious or religiously based propositions from legitimate political debate is often based on the substantive idea, implicitly endorsed by those notorious "secular humanists," that no religious or religiously based beliefs are true or worthy of being acted upon. Yet, however true this judgment about religious propositions, it is not a judgment that the opponents of conservatism are willing to assert as part of their political argument. Nor would even a blanket and valid dismissal of all religious routes to pro-prohibition conclusions justify the dismissal of those conclusions. Moreover, this denial of the truth value of religious premises would not be a proceduralist maneuver. It would not be an instance of showing why certain ordinarily good reasons for action were not good or admissible reasons in political discourse.

On the other hand, how can one downgrade the significance of conclusions arrived at by means of religious premises if one does not discount the verity of those premises? Why should the adherent to, e.g., an anti-abortion argument that employs some religious premise, find it plausible that this argument and its conclusion has any less political validity than an argument he equally endorses that arrives without the aid of religious premises at the conclusion that killing burdensome cripples should be forbidden? It is difficult to see what quality might be thought to inhere especially in the religious premises, other than falsity, that would justify this discounting.

However, perhaps a type of contractarian argument can be formulated that relies upon a contingent fact about such religious premises, viz., their contentiousness within religiously and culturally pluralistic societies. The argument goes something like this: Even advocates of religiously based prescriptions must acknowledge that each of many conflicting religiously based views will, from the inside, seem so vitally correct that no compromise with any conflicting view will, from the inside, seem tolerable. Moreover, any person, including any participant in such religiously based views, can recognize the intransigence with which such views are held. So there is little prospect of non-coerced conversion of religiously based disputants. This intransigence, insofar as it is not merely pathological, is due to the lack of any common authority for people's diverse religiously based norms. One person appeals to his holy text, another to his church tradition, and a third to his revelatory experience. In addition, it follows from the fact of conflict among these religiously based beliefs that, from the outside, any one of them is quite likely to be false. Given this, the argument proceeds, it seems reasonable for anyone recognizing these general facts, including individuals who themselves participate in such religiously based beliefs, mutually to accept a ban on appeals to private authorities in their common debate about public policy. It is rational for each to agree to put forward only contentions that appeal to public, objective, and secular arguments and, hence, to bracket as inappropriate to the political realm prescriptions that proceed upon religious commitment.

This argument is not at all loony. But major problems arise with its application. For one thing, it presumes a line between idiosyncratic, subjective, religious bases for moral belief and public, objective, secular bases. The line must be bright, and perception of it must not depend upon the observer's substantive position on the issue under debate. But whether or not the basis for someone's beliefs is perceived to be idiosyncratic or subjective will very much depend upon who is scrutinizing that basis. And, of course, the rational theologian and ethicist will argue that he has perfectly public and objective, if not secular, grounds for his theological commitments and their associated ethical precepts. Worse yet, in many cases of hot dispute about public policy—abortion is a perfect example—disputants on the allegedly religious based side can easily be found who argue in unquestionably public, objective, and secular terms. The contractarian argument will not banish *these* anti-abortion arguments. And, of course, even if all actually offered arguments for a given prohibition are banished, this hardly establishes that the prohibition would be improper. One need only recall the example of a prohibition on slavery in a society where all antislavery opinion is significantly colored by religious conviction.

If the proceduralist wants to avoid the objection that it is hard to discriminate between religious and some nonreligious premises within policy arguments and that many avowedly nonreligious supporters can be found for supposedly religiously inspired conclusions, he must broaden his characterization of the premises that are, because they are deeply contentious, to be banished from legitimate political dialogue in pluralistic societies. If the ban is sufficiently broadened it will, perhaps, become plausible to hold that every argument any sane person might actually use in defending certain conservative prohibitions utilizes at least one tainted premise. The argument for this broader ban would run something like this: Commitments expressive of people's personal moralities are intransigent and beyond the scope of objective public debate. Moreover, insofar as anyone can step outside these personal commitments, anyone can see that his own most cherished values are quite likely to be objectively mistaken or without truth value.[17] So it is rational for people to agree to exclude personal commitments from political debate. Exclusion may take the form of a procedural principle to the effect that when there is some fundamental division among the members of the political community expressive of divergent personal moral commitments—with, perhaps, the divergence itself being the evidence of the merely "personal" status of the commitments—those commitments should have no weight in the determination of public policy.

Unfortunately, this argument for a more encompassing ban on personal commitments is in danger of being either self-destructive or question-begging. It is self-destructive if it impartially includes all moral premises—and aren't they all contentious?—within the tainted personal commitment category. For then, in general, no premises will be left to justify any public morality and, in particular, there will be no available non-tainted arguments against the conservative's political demands. It will be question-begging if only the premises needed to justify the conservative's favored prohibitions turn out to be matters of intransigent personal commitment while the liberal's political morality, perhaps including the premises needed for his favored prohibitions, survive this screen. Certainly it is conceivable that the proceduralist's proposal be neither self-destructive nor question-begging; some principled reasons might be found for identifying certain premises and, perhaps, all the relevant possible premises for certain conclusions, as personal commitments of the sort that it is reasonable for us mutually to agree to ban from political debate. However, it is not even clear how one would go about developing such principled reasons.[18]

These two contractarian arguments, formulated in terms of what contentious beliefs it is reasonable for individuals mutually to agree should have no political significance, involve a nonstrategic sense of rationality. Each person is thought to recognize that it would be unreasonable to expect others to convert; albeit each also insists that others recognize that it would be unreasonable to expect him to convert. The threat these reasonable people seek to avoid is the threat of their making unreasonble demands upon others, given others' moral perceptions, and of others' making unreasonable demands upon them, given their moral perceptions. However, one can also construct contractarian arguments that employ a more strategic sense of rationality. On this construction, an individual does not really care about what is reasonable for himself or for others to expect or believe. Rather, each individual is worried about the ways in which clashing and intransigent views threaten social peace. It is strategically rational for each to give up any chance for the enforcement of his contentious views, if, by doing so, he can secure similar concessions from others. The proceduralist version of this argument's conclusion is that it is strategi-

cally rational for individuals in a pluralistic society to agree to
a set of "gag rules" for political debate that prohibit invocation
of religious or all personal commitments in arguments for public policy. The substantive version of this argument's conclusion
is that it is strategically rational for individuals to agree to "pri-
vatize" the areas of choice over which intransigent dispute exists by declaring these areas within the protected private spheres
of individuals.[19] By excluding these areas from the state's
legitimate purview, battles over who will capture and use the
state's authority are avoided. The substantive version of the
strategic argument is, then, an argument for noninterventionist
neutralism.

The procedural version of the strategic argument will face
the same problems already noted for proceduralism:

> What beliefs are to be subject to the gags?; How can these
> beliefs be specified in a non-self-defeating and non-ques-
> tion-begging way?; and Why believe that a non-self-defeat-
> ing and non-question-begging specification of beliefs to be
> subject to gag rules will guarantee that all arguments for
> conservative prohibitions will include some banned prem-
> ises?

But, the strategic argument has one advantage over the nonstrategic. If I genuinely believe that God will punish any society
that allows homosexuality, it is difficult to see how it can be
reasonable for me to bracket this belief simply because others
reject it along with many other of my cherished beliefs. But it
is not difficult to see how it might be strategically rational for
me to agree not to invoke this belief in exchange for others'
not invoking their belief that God only smiles on those societies
that require everyone to engage in some homosexual activities.
This example, however, employs a highly contrived countervailing belief. In reality, if I have this belief about God's hatred
for even tolerance of homosexuality, it is very likely that, as I
see it, I have more to lose by agreeing not to invoke this belief
in debate than I have to gain by others' agreeing not to invoke
certain of their religious or personally moral beliefs. In most
cases, the strategic contractarian argument will give the religious prohibitionist *some* reason, but not at all a decisive reason,

for abandoning his prohibitionist program. The example of the crusading homophobe brings out another weakness in the strategic contractarian argument. Mutually agreed to gag rules or privatizations of areas of choice that heighten the prospects of social peace are only strategically, mutually attractive to those who, because their worldviews are already sufficiently alike, prefer peace partially on their opponents' terms to going to war for their own terms.

Finally, in this critique of proceduralist neutralism, we should note that part of the attractiveness of proceduralist restraint derives from the intuition that restraints of some sort must be valid if a pluralistic social order is to thrive. But the proceduralist as proceduralist has no right to draw support for his position from the independent attractiveness of pluralism. The proceduralist can associate himself with pluralism only insofar as he establishes the rationality of restraints on what may properly motivate political discourse and policy and these restraints would foster pluralism. The noninterventionist has a far stronger claim to invoke the pluralist image of individuals and associations of individuals freely pursuing their diverse conceptions of the good—whatever their ultimate true worth—and restricted only by the enforcement of social rules that support the freedoms needed for these varied pursuits.

IV. NONINTERVENTIONIST NEUTRALISM

The proceduralist wants to affirm a rich theory of value and he wants to maintain that considerations of value determine political right and wrong. But he does not want to give political effect to all of his favored theory of value. Unhappily, it is difficult for him to find a principled basis for reserving political significance for only that part of his theory of value that he wants to give political effect, and it is difficult to argue for the political nonsignificance of the other part while still genuinely affirming it as part of his full theory of value. The noninterventionist avoids this problem by denying that political right or wrong is a matter of the state's promoting or thwarting even what the most correct and rich theory of value identifies as the good or the bad. The noninterventionist need not hold that there is no theoretical connection between his theory of value

and his basic principles of political morality. But the connection
will be sufficiently indirect that the principles of politics will be
structurally unlike the principles of value theory. In particular,
the principles of politics will contain, or entirely consist in, moral
side-constraints that apply both to how individuals may treat
one another and how the state may treat those under its sway.
These side-constraints define, or are defined by, private spheres'
interference with which is impermissible, absent, extraordinary,
justifying conditions; and the basic role of the state is to prevent such interference.[20]

Connected to the dual affirmation of a theory about what life
pursuits are valuable, worthy, etc., and a side-constraint conception of political morality is the idea that actions or ways of
life can be wrong in two radically different ways. An action can
be wrong by virtue of being invasive of the sphere rightfully
inhabited or controlled by another, and this type of wrong is
not, or not simply, a matter of the disvalue associated with that
action or the way of life that gave rise to it. State actions to
suppress such wrongs are entirely compatible with neutrality,
since what justifies these actions is the prevention, or nullifica-
tion, of side-constraint violations, not the value of the suppression or the disvalue of the actions suppressed. In light of the
distinction between value and side-constraint reasons for moral
condemnation, Nozick speaks far too generally when he says
that the suppression of rape is consistent with neutrality because "There is an *independent* reason for prohibiting rape." The
more precise point for the noninterventionist is that there is a
side-constraint reason for condemning the rape that is quite
separate from any view about the value or disvalue of the prohibited action's particular consequences. The prohibition is
compatible with neutrality because it does not need to be vindicated by any conception of the good.

In contrast, actions can be wrong solely because in their performance agents diverge from valuable or rational goals or ways
of life. If actions are wrong only in this second fashion, their
political suppression would itself violate side-constraints. And
suppression of merely disvaluable or unworthy actions would
violate neutrality because it would not be justified by the con-
tra-value, side-constraint, dimension of morality. It is liberal individualism of this sort that best accommodates an idea crucial

to moral realists who also demand state neutrality, viz., the idea that one can have a right to do wrong. One can both be doing wrong and have every right to do what one does.

At least implicit in the liberal individualist structure of private rights is the belief that an agent's failure, even his knowing failure, to prevent another's loss of a rightfully held object or condition does not constitute that agent's violating the other's right to that object or condition. Of course, if this agent has a special obligation to the other to prevent this loss, his failure to act violates the other's right to that prevention. We may sometimes think poorly of an agent for standing aside when he could prevent another's loss, but standing aside remains significantly morally different from invading the other's rights, from *imposing* the loss upon the other. This liberal individualist belief in a significant distinction between *allowing* and *producing* is essential to any coherent doctrine of neutralism. For, if state neutrality is to be possible, it must be possible for the state to *stand aside* even when it can intervene and determine a given outcome. State neutrality when the state cannot, in any case, determine the outcome does not merit demanding. Consider state neutrality with regard to Pushkin versus pushpin. Suppose that if the state does not impose severe penalties on the playing of pushpin the craze for this game will result in the complete cessation of Pushkin reading while rather severe penalties on pushpin playing will lead to a resurgence in Pushkin reading. The state's decision not to intervene to prevent the demise of Pushkin reading cannot be described as neutrality if this nonintervention itself is thought of as being morally on a par with causing the demise of Pushkin appreciation.

The state can be described as neutral vis-à-vis competing social alternatives only if its allowing one of the alternatives to triumph, or gain an edge, is not thought of as being the moral, equivalent of its intervening to cause the other alternative to triumph, or gain an edge. In short, and on reflection not surprisingly, the demand for neutrality presupposes that significant nonintervention is possible. And this means that it must be possible knowingly to allow an outcome, even an undesirable one, without being to blame for that outcome in the way one would be, had one straightforwardly brought it about. Those who wish to advocate state neutrality and to maintain coher-

ence of their arguments will have to eschew the many arguments in current political philosophy that morally equate knowingly allowing some disvaluable outcome with causing that
outcome and, hence, morally equate the state's forcing individuals to prevent untoward outcomes with the state's forcing individuals not to cause those outcomes. The neutralist will have
to avoid, e.g., the many variations on the argument that the
able should be forced to aid the needy because to allow the able
to escape this responsibility would be to allow them to be responsible for the suffering of the needy. A careful avoidance
of such arguments will tend to make the neutralist more classically, and less contemporarily, liberal.

Of course, the fact that it must be possible for the state to
stand aside if the demand for neutrality is to be coherent does
not mean that the state displays neutrality whenever it stands
aside. The state does *not* display neutrality when it stands aside
and allows the rapist to proceed with his crime if the rapist's
victim has a right to protection from that state. Given that right,
the state would be violating moral side-constraints in failing to
protect the victim. Given that right to protection, the state's
nonintervention would at least approach moral parity with the
assailant's intervention. But if victims do not have rights to protection by a given state as, for example the Spanish Loyalist's
did not have rights to protection by the United States government, then it is neutrality when that government merely stands
aside neither aiding the criminal aggressors nor the victims.

What about actions by the state that do not involve the use
of force, at least in a comparably direct way, but which predictably influence the outcome of some social competition? For instance, what of the choice of the state to include knowledge of
Pushkin, but not skill in the game of pushpin, on state employment exams or within the curriculum of state schools? Or what
of the curricular choice of evolutionary theory over creationism, or "values clarification" over good old biblical ethics, in
public schools? The noninterventionist answer continues to be
that neutrality is violated whenever the state's influence on contested social issues is a product of moral side-constraint violation. So, for example, religious and social conservatives are correct in charging that often state education violates neutrality by
fostering "secular humanism" over this or that religious vision

if, but only if, it is correct to judge the state's coercive funding of this education, its compulsory attendance laws and the like as illegitimate infringements upon moral side-constraints.

What about the inclusion of Pushkin but not pushpin on state employment exams, which predictably fosters Pushkin over pushpin? In such a case, one would have to reach further to argue for non-neutrality. One possible line of argument might focus on whether or not illegitimate state restrictions on non-governmental employment improperly forced people to turn to the state for employment. Another, quite different, possible line of argument would introduce an additional sort of neutrality that could especially be demanded of the state. This would be the neutrality of not fostering particular values except as the by-product of efficiently carrying out its legitimate functions. If testing aspiring bureaucrats on their knowledge of Pushkin is a good way of enhancing the efficient legitimate functioning of the state, the inclusion of Pushkin does not violate this neutral-ity. Otherwise it does.

Coherent advocacy of state neutrality is tied to the type of substantive political theory that I have labeled "individualistic liberalism," which adheres to a basic structure of private rights that plays at least a very prominent role in the definition of enforcible political morality. Neutrality is a matter of action and policy in accordance with this sort of political morality, in con-trast with action and policy justifiable only on the basis of the promotion of particular values. But I have also tried to indicate how specific judgments about whether or not neutrality is vio-lated depends upon particular judgments about what people's rights are—about what moral side-constraints exist. Thus, the coherent advocacy of neutrality is not tied, or not at all tightly tied, to any specific version of individualistic liberalism. Indi-vidualistic liberals may differ about the precise definition of persons' private rights, about the boundaries of persons' pri-vate spheres, and even about who possesses such rights. There may be disputes about who has what sort of private rights over natural resources or over ideas, or about whether the imposi-tion of certain psychic costs counts as an illicit invasion of oth-ers' private spheres. Thus, it is helpful to distinguish between the noninterventionist *concept* of neutrality and specific nonin-terventionist *conceptions* of neutrality which result from adherence to the concept and also to a set of particular judgments about who has precisely what private rights.

This distinction is important for understanding the inadequacy of another common liberal response to conservative proposals in the recent abortion debate. This inadequacy reflects a final attempt at pulling the substantive rabbit, the illegitimacy of prohibitions on abortion, out of a procedural or, in any case, formal hat. The liberal argument that is put to the anti-abortion conservative is: Surely even you prohibitionists acknowledge that there is a distinction between private and political morality; surely you are not prepared to hold that the state should force people to be virtuous. All we are saying, as pro-choice advocates, is that choices about private morality ought not to be determined by the state.

This sort of argument is rhetorically effective to the extent that it fosters the impression that the anti-abortionist is committed to challenging the private morality/public morality distinction and to rejecting the ideal of the neutral state in favor of a state that presses a particular conception of the good upon its populace. The liberal hopes to appeal to all those who are not willing to entrust the state with the task of "soulcraft"—and this includes most of those favoring the prohibition of abortion. His method is to claim a monopoly on neutralism for the pro-choice position. But this confuses a claim to represent a particular conception of neutrality with a claim to represent neutrality as such. The liberal's particular conception of neutrality is a function of his judgment about what particular rights pregnant women have and fetuses lack. But the anti-abortionist may lay claim to another particular conception of neutrality which is a function of his different judgment about what particular rights the parties to abortions have. On the anti-abortionist's view, there are side-constraint reasons against abortion, perhaps absent special countervailing conditions. So, on his view, abortion and the protection of it violates neutrality—as much as state's sanctioning of other forms of unjustified manslaughter.

This is a substantive dispute between this prohibitionist and the pro-choice advocate, and no appeal to the ideal of state neutrality or to the beauty of the private morality/public morality distinction can settle this dispute. What matters is who is right—and right about where the rights lie. Only a sound appeal to specific rights can supply the state with justifications for its coercive activity that neither depend upon comparative evaluations of life plans or their components, which would render the state's activity non-neutral, nor depend upon justifications that make it difficult to sustain moral realism and to arrive at the specific restraints on the state's activity that the invocation of neutralism normally connotes.

What happens if there is no sound appeal to specific rights? What happens if, as is sometimes suggested about the abortion controversy, the moral arguments by the prohibitionist and the pro-choice advocate, which center on rights asserted and denied, are comparably plausible?[21] This moral indeterminacy would favor neither side. The common argument that, given moral uncertainty, one should opt for tolerance and against state prohibition works no better on behalf of those seeking abortions than on behalf of those engaged in the vigilante suppression of them. If there is no sound appeal to specific rights, state neutrality would consist in standing aside and letting the prohibitionists and the pro-choice advocates fight it out in the streets and in the back alleys. Or state neutrality would consist in enforcing the terms of the armistice these contending parties would enter into, should there be armistic terms that they both prefer over the fortunes of social warfare.[22]

NOTES

1. Equal promotionist neutralism is exemplified in the second and third principles of neutralist restraint formulated by Joseph Raz. Joseph Raz, "Liberalism, Autonomy, and the Politics of Neutral Concern", in *Midwest Studies in Philosophy VII* (1982) ed. Peter A. French et al. pp. 92–93.
2. An alternative mapping would describe both substantive and procedural interpretations of noninterventionist, equal protectionist and Benthamite neutralism. But it would not be fruitful to spell out procedural interpretations of these three types of neutralism since what would be most significant about those three interpretations would be what they had in common, viz., proceduralism.
3. Raz, "Liberalism, Autonomy," pp. 89–90. Subsequently, in specifying variants on the principles of restraint route, he uses the formula, "No political action may be undertaken or justified on the ground that . . ." This, again, seems to be a proceduralist restric-

tion to the effect that political action or argument is invalidated insofar as it proceeds from certain beliefs—insofar as it has a certain causal history. Raz is not himself an advocate of "the doctrine of neutral political concern." See p. 116.

4. We leave aside all the obvious, but very vexing, questions about what would constitute equal promotion, e.g., does equal promotion require that everyone's "expected life plan fulfillment" be equalized?; or is it a matter of equal additions to each person's "expected life plan fulfillment" given some inegalitarian baseline?; how can equality in life-plan fulfillment be characterized or measured across qualitatively different life plans? And, of course, any program for equal promotion of life pursuits has to take account of scarcity of resources that require constant choices between the promotion of this or that pursuit.

5. Robert Nozick, *Anarchy, State and Utopia* (New York: Basic Books, 1974), pp. 272–73. Interestingly, Nozick then heads in the direction of a proceduralist interpretation of his noninterventionist neutralism. "That a prohibition thus independently justifiable works out to affect different persons differently is no reason to condemn it as nonneutral, *provided it was instituted or continues for (something like) the reasons which justify it, and not in order to yield differential benefits.*" (Emphasis added.) However, he then seems to recognize and be dubious of the idea that a policy's neutrality is a matter of its causal history. For he adds, "(How should it be viewed if it *is* independently justifiable, but actually is supported and maintained because of its differential benefits?)"

6. Brain Barry, *Political Argument* (London: Routledge and Kegan Paul, 1965); quoted by Raz, "Liberalism, Autonomy," p. 98. Barry's characterization of want-regarding principles continues so as to allow a distributional component, viz., "or in the way in which the policy will affect the distribution among people of opportunities for satisfying wants." In the text I have omitted this last clause in order, among other reasons, to maintain a strong contrast between the distributionally oriented equal promotionist and the aggregation oriented Benthamite.

7. More precisely, one route to equal promotionism affirms the equal worth of all, or nearly all, life plans while the other route to equal promotionism joins Benthamism in denying the moral significance of the content of life plans.

8. Raz, "Liberalism, Autonomy," p. 100.

9. Mario Cuomo, "Religious Belief and Public Morality: A Catholic Governor's Perspective," *Notre Dame Journal of Law, Ethics and Public Policy* 1 (1984).

10. Ibid., 16.

11. Ibid., 16.
12. Ibid., 18.
13. Ibid., 24–25.
14. Ibid., 23.
15. While from the absence of consensus against abortion Cuomo infers both that a crusade to prohibition abortion would be wrong and that it is right for abortion to be allowed and protected, he does not infer from the previous absence of a consensus against slavery that slavery ought to have been allowed and protected. But he should be making this inference.
16. Cuomo, "Religious Belief," 17.
17. Here we see the tension between this contractarian argument and moral realism. The case for its being reasonable not to favor imposition of one's moral judgment consists in downgrading the truth value of that judgment. This is nicely illustrated in Geraldine Ferraro's book. See Geraldine Ferraro, *Ferraro, My Story* (New York: Bantam Books, 1985), p. 215ff. She begins by asserting her belief in the wrongness of abortion but explains her defense of allowing abortion by unwittingly recounting how her anti-abortion views came to be downgraded to the status of a personal (dis)taste conditioned by her religious background. She does not merely reject prohibitions on abortion. She does not expect those with different conditioning backgrounds to share her "moral" distaste. She rejects abortion in the way in which I reject frog legs.
18. Ronald Dworkin, "Neutrality, Equality and Liberalism" in *Liberalism Reconsidered,* eds., Douglas MacLean and Claudia Mills. (Totowa, N.J.: Rowman and Allanheld, 1983), p. 3. Ronald Dworkin formulates procedural neutralism upon an egalitarian base—or, more specifically, upon a right of people to be treated with equal concern and respect. In proceduralist fashion, Dworkin maintains that the government, "must impose no sacrifice or constraint on any citizen *in virtue of an argument* that the citizen could not accept without abandoning his sense of equal worth." But his neutralism provides the citizen with no protection against systematic interference with his private choices based upon other arguments, e.g., arguments about the great benefits these inroads allow others to enjoy, or against gratuitous interference motivated by no arguments at all. In addition, Dworkin's neutralism provides no protection at all for the citizen who already lacks a sense of his own worth. The self-esteeming prostitute receives more immunity than the self-condemning prostitute.
19. Stephen Holmes discusses what I call the strategic argument in his historical essay, "Jean Bodin: the Paradox of Sovereignty and the Privatization of Religion" (this volume). He does not distinguish

between a proceduralist version with its emphasis on the idea of a "gag rule" and a substantivist version with its emphasis on "rights [that] define a nonpolitical sphere withdrawn from the jurisdication of public authorities."

20. I presume throughout the legitimacy of some set of institutions that use coercion to enforce certain social rules. This legitimate "state" may or may not fit standard definitions of the state.

21. Joan Callahan, "Religion, Abortion, and Public Policy" in typescript, portions of which appear as idem, "The Fetus and Fundamental Rights," *Commonweal* 11 (April 1986).

22. This essay was written during the tenure of a summer research grant from the Murphy Institute for Political Economy of Tulane University.

[2]

ROBERT AUDI

The Separation
of Church and State
and the Obligations
of Citizenship

The issue of separation of church and state has great moral, legal, and political importance, and the subject currently holds special interest. An unprecedented number of people are injecting religion into politics; pressures are mounting both to have religious observances in public schools and to support sectarian education through tax revenues; and the United States Supreme Court may soon be reinterpreting constitutional constraints on the relation between religion and public life. In this article I approach the separation of church and state from a conceptual and moral standpoint. My broadest aim is to build a framework that clarifies certain moral, legal, and political questions about religion and civil life. My specific purpose is to develop a theory of separation of church and state that serves two major ends. The first is to clarify the traditional separation doctrine as usually understood—as addressed above all to governmental institutions. The second aim is wider and has not so far received substantial treatment in the literature: it is to ascertain what restrictions on individual conduct should, in a free and democratic society, accompany a commitment to separation of church and state.[1] Part I interprets the

This article was completed under a grant from the University of Nebraska College of Law, Center for the Teaching and Study of Applied Ethics. An earlier version was delivered at a conference on separation of church and state at the College in October 1986, and I benefited much from comments by the other speakers: Robert Crosby, Fr. James Dawson, Bette Evans, Stephen Kalish, Paul Pines, Darlene Rischling, John Snowden, and Otis Young. I have also profited from comments by Elizabeth Bilynskyj, Stephen Bilynskyj, Patrick Francken, James Gustafson, Robert Haller, R. Scott Harnsberger, Joseph Mendola, Nelson Potter, James Sennett, the Editors of *Philosophy & Public Affairs*, and, especially, William Frankena and Craig Lawson.

1. A notable exception to the general neglect of this topic is Kent Greenawalt's recent *Religious Convictions and Political Choice* (Oxford: Oxford University Press, 1988). I discuss the central thesis very briefly in Part VI. For a variety of recent perspectives, see *National Forum* 68, no. 1 (1988), a special issue devoted to church-state controversies.

separation doctrine. Part II considers its basis. Part III applies the doctrine to some important current issues. Parts IV and V introduce the second phase of my theory, concerning the obligations of citizens in a free and democratic society; here I propose principles of separation for individual conduct. The concluding sections apply the principles of individual conduct and explore the connections among religion, morality, and democracy.

I. The Content of the Separation Doctrine

The doctrine of separation of church and state antedates the United States Constitution[2] and goes well beyond what is implicit in the Constitution's establishment clause, which says that "Congress shall make no law respecting an establishment of religion, or prohibiting the free exercise thereof."[3] There is a vast legal literature on the doctrine, including many pertinent court decisions. Philosophers, theologians, and others have also addressed the subject. In speaking of the *separation doctrine*, then, I am not referring to something codified for our scrutiny, but to the general view that in a free and democratic society the state should neither establish a church nor impair religious liberty. This formulation is intentionally vague; I want to begin with a statement encompassing a

2. An interesting case in point (though it did not protect non-Christians) is the Maryland Act of Toleration, passed, but also repealed, in the 1640s. It said, "no person . . . professing to believe in Jesus Christ shall from henceforth be in any ways troubled, molested or discountenanced for or in respect to his or her religion, nor in the free exercise thereof within this province . . . nor in any way compelled to the belief or exercise of any other religion." For the full text, see *The Proceedings and Acts of the General Assembly of Maryland* (Baltimore, 1883), pp. 244ff. An abridgment is contained in *Church and State in American History*, ed. John W. Wilson (Boston: D.C. Heath, 1965). This collection contains other indications of preconstitutional concern with separation of church and state, including a statement by Samuel Davies, fourth president of the College of New Jersey (Princeton) on behalf of dissenters in Virginia (pp. 38–42).

3. Article 1 of the first ten amendments (ratified in 1791) reads, "Congress shall make no law respecting an establishment of religion, or prohibiting the free exercise thereof; or abridging the freedom of speech, or of the press; or the right of people peaceably to assemble, and to petition the government for redress of grievances." Various accounts have been offered to explain the relation between the establishment and free exercise clauses, which have played distinct roles in Supreme Court decisions. For a useful discussion of this problem, see Paul G. Kauper, *Religion and the Constitution* (Baton Rouge: Louisiana State University Press, 1964), esp. chap. 3. My account of the basis of the separation doctrine suggests how the two clauses might be unified philosophically, but the account may at best reflect the thinking of *some* of the framers.

261 *The Separation
of Church and State*

commitment shared by both the framers of the Constitution and most others who support a separation of governmental and religious institutions in the interest of religious liberty—including the freedom to reject religious views.[4] In refining this formulation, my aim will be not to satisfy specific legal or historical demands, but to provide a series of principles that clarify the issues to which the separation doctrine is plausibly applied.

The establishment clause seems explicitly addressed to the state, and historically, at least in the United States, the separation doctrine has been conceived mainly, though by no means entirely, as restricting what the state may do vis-à-vis the church, that is, in relation to religious institutions—'church' here is a generic term.[5] Let us call the doctrine so construed *the institutional separation doctrine.* By this I mean the doc-

4. In this connection it is noteworthy that James Madison not only supported Jefferson's Virginia Statute of Religious Freedom, passed in 1786, which stated that "our civil rights have no dependence on our religious opinions, any more than our opinions in physics and geometry," but also defended the nontheist, arguing that our freedom implies the right to have no religious beliefs. A vivid recent statement of the view is Justice Jackson's in his dissenting opinion in *Zorach v. Clauson,* 343 U.S. 306 (1952): "The day that this country ceases to be free for irreligion it will cease to be free for religion—except for the sect that can win political power. The same epithetical jurisprudence used by the Court today to beat down those who oppose pressuring children into some religion can devise as good epithets tomorrow against those who object to pressuring them into a favored religion." Cf. the citation in note 11.

5. This dominating interest arises largely from the historical centrality, prominent in the thinking of the framers, of the concern to prevent the state's abridging religious freedom. It is apparent not only in the general literature, but in Supreme Court decisions. See, for example, the pertinent decisions in *The Supreme Court on Church and State,* ed. Joseph Tussman (New York: Oxford University Press, 1962). A vivid statement of concern with institutional relations between church and state is Chief Justice Burger's in *Larkin v. Grendel's Den* (103 U.S. 505, 1982). Striking down a law prohibiting Grendel's Den from serving liquor near a church, he said that it "substitutes the unilateral and absolute power of a church for the reasoned decisionmaking of a public legislative body acting on evidence and guided by standards, on issues with significant economic and political implications. The challenged statute thus enmeshes churches in the processes of government . . . few entanglements could be more offensive to the spirit of the Constitution." The term 'enmesh' recalls the threefold test laid down by the Court in *Lemon v. Kurtzman* in 1971 (402 U.S. 602): to satisfy the establishment clause a statute "first . . . must have a secular legislative purpose; second, its principal or primary effect must be one that neither advances nor inhibits religion . . . finally, the statute must not foster 'an excessive government entanglement with religion' " (pp. 612–13, citations omitted). The reference to entanglement recalls Justice Felix Frankfurter's statement that "the public school must keep scrupulously free from entanglement in the strife of sects" (*McCullom v. Board of Education,* 333 U.S. 203, 1948).

trine of separation of church and state as applied to governmental institutions in relation to religious ones and taken to imply that the state
should not interfere with the church, and (though this is usually given
lesser emphasis) the church should not interfere with the state. The separation doctrine is also intended to apply to the state in relation to religious individuals who are not affiliated with any church. Such cases are
not often discussed, but they are important and will be implicitly covered
by my treatment of the general subject.

There are at least three basic strands in the institutional doctrine.
These are bound together by the ideal of religious liberty as a central
element in a free society; but other ideals, such as those of equality of
persons regardless of their religious affiliation, unfettered democratic
participation, and social pluralism, can also unify and support the various
elements in the institutional doctrine. Throughout what follows I leave
open whether the normative principles I formulate are moral. I argue
only that they are appropriate *given* a commitment to a free and democratic society; but if (as seems likely) there is an adequate moral basis
for preferring such a society, then the principles may also express (prima
facie) moral obligations. For if a free and democratic society is morally
preferable to its alternatives, then there is a prima facie moral obligation
to adhere to principles that are known, or at least justifiedly believed, to
be required for the realization of such a society. Let me describe, in turn,
the basic strands in the institutional doctrine of separation of church and
state.

First of all, the institutional doctrine requires that the state permit the
practice of any religion, within certain limits. Call this *the libertarian
principle*. Both the relevant limits, and indeed, religion itself, are difficult
to characterize. I shall not propose definitions, but some examples will
help. Imagine a religion that permitted sacrificing young girls to appease
its gods. A government's outlawing this practice would not violate the
separation of church and state. The freedom of religion it guarantees is
limited by certain basic human rights, such as the rights of life, liberty,
and the pursuit of happiness. But there are difficult cases. For instance,
is a proper separation of church and state violated by the prohibition of
religiously sanctioned polygamy? At least two lines of argument support
a negative answer. One is that the prohibition does not violate a proper
separation, because polygamy breaches certain important rights, such as
the right not to be legally bound in an exploitive marriage, and these

263   *The Separation*
                              of Church and State

rights must be respected even at the cost of limiting the separation of church and state. This answer may be thought to be objectionably parentalistic, since it presupposes that consenting adults cannot adequately judge their own welfare. One might, however, argue the point without any suspect parentalism, on the ground that polygamous marriages are a serious moral wrong through injustice to the children of such marriages, who may be subject to damaging jealousies, or in any case may have a poor chance of adequate parenting. By contrast, one might argue that prohibiting religiously sanctioned polygamy *does* violate a proper separation of church and state, since it abridges religious liberty without a compelling reason, such as protection of life. Clearly, we are already in an area where the application of the institutional doctrine is controversial.[6]

The second strand in the institutional doctrine is perhaps less difficult to interpret. It is the principle that the state may not give preference to one religion over another. Call this *the equalitarian principle.* It not only rules out an established church—the existence of which might be plausibly argued to be consistent with the libertarian principle—but also precludes such things as requiring a certain religious affiliation, say that of the majority, as a condition for public office.[7] This principle goes well beyond the libertarian principle; for in theory, at least, a state can allow virtually unlimited religious freedom and still treat some religious groups preferentially. The framers clearly accepted both principles, and it is a vexed question whether such practices as requiring Sunday closings, say of liquor stores, and declaring national holidays on Christian feast days, must violate at least the equalitarian principle. One relevent consideration is whether other religious holidays are *respected*, for instance by employees' having leave to observe them; another is whether the Christian feast days are observed as national holidays because a great majority of the people want them to be, and not because a majority *religion* does. Presumably, the principle would allow that, provided everyone's religious

6. In speaking of polygamy, we should note that if one man's having two or more wives is permissible, one woman's having two or more husbands should be also. In the latter case, the woman's children might be fated to wonder which husband is their father and the husbands to wonder which, if any, of the children are theirs. The troubles this might cause can be exaggerated, but they do not depend on religious considerations.

7. In Lebanon, for example, it has long been an unwritten requirement that the president be a Maronite Christian and the prime minister a Sunni Moslem. As this illustrates, there can be *degrees of establishment*, nor need it be restricted to one religion.

holidays are (within reason) respected, it is not preferential treatment of the religious majority as such to have national holidays coincide with its main feasts. But this is debatable, and even if correct it does not by itself square forced Sunday closings with the equalitarian principle.

The third strand in the institutional doctrine is less commonly recognized, but it belongs to any full-blooded interpretation of separation of church and state.[8] What I have in mind might be called *the neutrality principle*: the state should give no preference to religion (or the religious) *as such*, that is, to institutions or persons simply because they are religious. One could of course derive this requirement from the equalitarian principle *provided* one construed being nonreligious as having a religious stance and thereby deserving equal treatment with the various other religious positions. But surely someone might be nonreligious through mere indifference or through ignorance of the alternatives, and hence not have any *stance* on the matter. It is also more perspicuous to distinguish the neutrality requirement from the requirement of equal treatment of the various religious elements in a society; there are differences in the ideals underlying the two requirements, and distinguishing the principles provides a better basis for concrete assessments of church-state relations.

The neutrality principle would go against requiring periods of prayer or even of silent religious observance in public schools; for even assuming that no one religion is favored by the practice, it tends to favor the interests of the religious over those of the nonreligious. It is difficult to say whether the neutrality principle prohibits allowing conscientious objector status only to people with appropriate religious objections to war, and not on moral grounds alone. That practice can certainly result in better treatment of the religious than of the nonreligious. But it could also be argued to be permissible in preservation of religious liberty, and hence justified by the libertarian principle. (This does not imply that the libertarian principle cannot be overridden, for example when on religious grounds too many citizens object to fighting for a nation in a self-defensive war; but no simple rule determines when that point is reached.)

Prima facie, one would expect anyone committed to freedom and democracy to want to be governed by the libertarian and equalitarian prin-

---

8. Some relevant points concerning constitutional interpretation are indicated in note 3. General reasons drawn from ethics and political philosophy will be offered in the text.

The Separation
of Church and State

ciples. But the neutrality principle might seem desirable only for a society committed to fostering *pluralism*, and optional for one which, though upholding ideals of freedom and democracy, sees itself as religious. Granted, supporting liberty does not entail fostering, as opposed to protecting, pluralism. But clearly fostering pluralism tends both to protect liberty and to contribute to its substantive exercise. In any case, the neutrality principle must be distinguished from what we might call *the principle of pluralism*, the principle that (within certain limits) the state should foster pluralism. The former principle bears more directly on freedom and appears reasonable for a free and democratic society even if it is *not* committed to fostering any more pluralism than is implied by the exercise of liberty, and so not *directly* committed to fostering pluralism at all. The latter principle could be rejected by proponents of minimal government even if they heartily embrace the former. This point will be developed as we explore all three strands in the separation doctrine in relation to its underlying grounds.

II. Some Normative Grounds for Separation
of Church and State

Supposing the institutional doctrine of separation of church and state comprises mainly the three principles I have described, why should a free and democratic society endorse the doctrine? This is a large question, and I shall cite only the most general supporting grounds. I take the principles in turn.

It is plain that a society without religious liberty is simply not adequately free. Moreover, freedom is required for democracy, at least in any sense of 'democracy' relevant here.[9] Thus, if one's ideal is a free and democratic society, one wants a social (presumably constitutional)

---

9. It would be a mistake, however, to identify a democratic society with a free one, as some have tended to do. Freedom surely does not entail democracy. Moreover, even if, by definition, political power in a *democracy* is exercised freely, it remains possible for a people freely to vote away a great deal of liberty, thus creating an unfree society. Pervasive restrictions of liberty that can be undone by democratic vote are still coercive. The ideals of freedom and democracy are distinct, as the possibility of freedom under anarchy or benevolent oligarchy shows, and it is best not to run the two ideals together. Equal treatment is yet another ideal, for reasons indicated in the text; and a constitutional case can be made for both the equalitarian and the neutrality principles by appeal to the equal protection clause of the Fourteenth Amendment.

framework to guarantee at least this: (1) freedom of religious belief, understood to prohibit the state or anyone else from inculcating religious beliefs in the general population, where this is taken to exclude or restrict cultivation of competing religious beliefs; (2) freedom of worship, involving, minimally, a right of peaceable religious assembly, as well as a right to offer prayers by oneself; and (3) freedom to engage in (and to teach one's children) the rites and rituals of one's religion, provided these practices do not violate certain basic moral rights. Clearly, then, a free and democratic society should adopt the libertarian principle. Without the freedom it guarantees, there would be inadequate protection against governmental *coercion*.

The case for the equalitarian principle is more complicated. The (or a) central premise is that if the state prefers one or more religions, people might well find it hard to practice another, or would at least feel *pressure* to adopt the (or a) religion favored by the state. The degree of pressure would tend to be proportional to the strength of governmental preference. The pressure might be as great as requirement of a certain religious affiliation as a condition for holding a government job, or as minor as inviting clergy from just one religion to officiate at certain ceremonies. Any governmental preference, however, creates some tendency for greater power to accrue to the preferred religion, particularly if it is that of the majority. Such concentrations of power easily impair democracy, under which citizens should have equal opportunities to exercise political power on a fair basis, even if certain disproportionate powers do not actually (or at least do not directly) restrict anyone's liberty. Moreover, when a state establishes or prefers a given religion, it is to be expected (though it is perhaps not inevitable) that certain laws will significantly reflect the outlook on life associated with that religion. These are among the reasons why a free and democratic society should adopt the equalitarian principle. Even when the libertarian principle is respected, the equalitarian principle is needed for protection against governmental *discrimination*.

What is the rationale for the neutrality principle? Recall that religious liberty, broadly conceived, includes the freedom to reject religious views. If the state shows preference for religious institutions as such (or for religion in general), there may well be pressure to adopt a religion, and quite possibly discrimination against those who do not. On the other hand, there are kinds of governmental preference that are consistent

267 *The Separation*
of Church and State

with religious liberty; hence, the neutrality principle cannot be simply derived from the libertarian principle. There are many domains of possible preference for the religious: prayer sessions in public schools, exemptions from combat duty, and eligibility to adopt children are examples. Such preference may also tend toward political domination by the religious. Thus, even if there is protection both from religious tyranny and from discriminatory exclusions on religious grounds, governmental preference of the religious as such is likely to give them political, economic, and other advantages that threaten a proper democratic distribution of political power. It can also reduce the level of free *exercise* of liberty, as opposed to its mere legal *scope*. What is legally permitted, or even solicitously protected by law, may still seem to many people too troublesome to be worthwhile in day-to-day life. If, for example, exercising a freedom goes against governmental policy or even social tradition, it may be costly. Consider someone who declines to participate in state-sponsored patriotic activities; here, and surely even in absenting oneself from state- or community-sponsored voluntary prayer sessions, one might conspicuously separate oneself from most others.

It might be argued that the only reason to avoid reducing the exercise, as opposed to the scope, of freedom is a commitment to fostering pluralism. But the distinction is not sharp: apart from a courageous few, making the exercise of a freedom costly shades into narrowing its scope. Moreover, quite independently of a commitment to fostering pluralism, a free and democratic society should avoid reducing the exercise of freedom, if only because that tends to lessen creativity both in the lives of individuals and in the solution of social problems.

A second ground for the neutrality principle is the ideal of equal treatment, an ideal that, like liberty, is an important element in a free and democratic society. Governmental preference for the religious as such is intrinsically unequal treatment of the religious and nonreligious, however minor the material differences involved. On balance, then, the neutrality principle seems required to guarantee protection from governmental *favoritism*, in the sense of preferential treatment of the religious over the nonreligious. Even if this does not involve discrimination in favor of one religious group, nonreligious citizens will tend to *feel* the preferential treatment as discrimination and not as a legitimate expression of the will of a democratic majority.

There may, however, be further reason for a free and democratic society to adopt the neutrality principle even if such a society need not be committed to protecting the freedom not to be religious. For once the state favors the religious over the nonreligious, at least three problems arise. (i) Where there is a majority affiliation, the views and even the interests of this group are likely to dominate legislation and policy affecting religion, sometimes to the detriment of religious minorities, for instance in the treatment of religious holidays and the celebration of major events, such as inaugurations. (ii) Religious disagreements are likely to polarize government, especially regarding law and policy concerning religion, say requirements for conscientious objector status or, at the institutional level, for tax exemption. (iii) If a government prefers the religious over the nonreligious, then, through the pronouncements and social policies that express the preference, that government will tend to influence churches, and, in deciding what to promote, to begin to set criteria for what counts as being religious in the sense in which that entitles institutions to preferential treatment. Once there are benefits to be had, there will be stretching to meet the criteria for getting them. This is a likely way to "entanglement" of the government in religious affairs. On balance, then, freedom and democracy seem best served by principles that keep the state from restricting *or* influencing the churches any more than is required for enacting laws and policies that are justified on nonreligious grounds.

III. Some Applications of the Institutional Doctrine

Even apart from the inevitable vagueness of the libertarian, equalitarian, and neutrality principles, their application to social issues is often difficult. One major problem is how to weight competing values. To see how this affects the principles in practice, let us explore some important cases.

Consider prayer in the public schools. Clearly, mandatory periods of prayer, such as daily assemblies addressed by clergy or others offering prayers, would violate the libertarian principle if that is understood, as it should be, to protect freedom *not* to practice a religion. Moreover, if, as may well be so, it is impossible to frame prayers equally acceptable to all faiths, then mandatory oral or written prayers in public schools would likely violate the neutrality principle. One natural course would be to displease as few as possible by reflecting those majority preferences least

269   *The Separation*
                         of Church and State

offensive to any significant minority attending. Majority preferences
would tend to be felt.

What, then, of *voluntary* periods for silent prayer? This is a difficult
case.[10] Here the nonreligious are left free to absent themselves. Moreover, since there is no oral prayer, presumably none of the religious need
be offended—though someone might object to being asked to pray without the chance to hear or speak certain crucial words. On the other hand,
given the conformism of many school children, might there not be pressure on many of the nonreligious to join, or pressure on some of the
religious to boycott as a gesture of support for nonreligious friends? People being as they are, even voluntary silent prayer periods might diminish religious toleration and, ultimately, religious liberty.

A quite different point is that even if no particular religious outlook
colors a prayer, in requiring or even sponsoring the offering of that
prayer, the state is still, at least by proxy, establishing a religious practice.[11] The voluntariness of a practice must not be thought to imply that
it is not officially established; nor would its nondenominational character
show that it does not implicitly endorse a religion. The institutional and
content requirements for a religion can be met by agents of government
even without their preferring any standing church. A religion need not
be inaugurated by a prophet, and it can be constructed by eclectic com-
pilation, as well as by scriptural sanctification. Thus, the neutrality principle is favored by the antiestablishment premises of the separation doctrine, and not only by libertarian or pluralistic considerations, or by the

10. For discussion of the Burger Court's treatment of the prayer issue up to 1984, see
Leo Pfeffer, *Religion, State, and the Burger Court* (Buffalo: Prometheus Books, 1984), esp.
chap. 3. For a useful recent survey, see David M. Ackerman, "Church and State in the
Supreme Court: The Non-Revolution of the '80s," *Federal Bar News and Journal* 33, no. 7
(1986).

11. That the establishment clause can be violated by state sponsorship of noncompulsory
activity seems to have been recognized in a number of Supreme Court decisions. In *Illinois
ex rel. McCollum* (333 U.S. 203, 1948), for example, Justice Black, writing for the majority,
said of a program of (voluntary) released time for religious education: "This is beyond all
question a utilization of the tax-established and tax-supported public school system to aid
religious groups to spread their faith. And it falls squarely under the ban of the First
Amendment (made applicable to the states by the Fourteenth) as we interpreted it in Everson v. Board of Education [330 U.S. 1, 1937]. There we said: 'Neither a state nor the
Federal Government can set up a church. Neither can pass laws which aid one religion,
aid all religions, or prefer one religion over another. . . . No person can be punished for
entertaining or professing religious beliefs *or disbeliefs,* for church attendance or nonat-
tendance" (emphasis added).

ideal of equal treatment of churches. A government could establish a religion even without preference toward any existing church and hence without violating the equalitarian principle. Establishing a religion requires neither coercion nor an antecedently existing institution as a candidate for establishment.

In a different vein, voluntary periods of prayer in public schools are by no means clearly in the interest of the religious. By confronting religious children with nonbelievers, the practice may easily give those children the impression—alien to most faiths—that religious conviction is only a matter of personal preference. Moreover, the division between those who go to prayer and those who do not may be dangerously polarizing. A period of each day or week described as devoted to prayer *or* meditation might seem to solve the problem, since everyone should appreciate the secular values of meditation. But this would at best reduce the polarization, particularly if, as is likely, students generally recognize that it is mainly for encouraging or facilitating prayer that the relevant periods are set aside. A time reserved simply for mediation might avoid these difficulties; but if it were described in a way that makes that likely, it might also have less appeal to those who hope that it will promote religious practice.

The singing of Christmas carols and perhaps certain hymns in public schools should not be assimilated to the case of prayer in those schools. For one thing, what is said in prayer is affirmed, and it tends to express, and to be taken to express, one's beliefs. It is at least in some sense *confessional*. But what one sings in carols, and even hymns, one need not be affirming; nor need it be taken to express what one believes, any more than a student asked to recite a poem celebrating spring must be thought to accept its sentiments. These performances may be simply *aesthetic*. Nonetheless, singing carols or hymns is difficult to blend into mere musical training or simple celebration of the Christmas season conceived as a time of merriment and gift-giving. There is a continuum from presenting songs and other works as simply of aesthetic or academic interest, to treating them as sacred. Some students, however, might feel alienated from the activity if it is even religiously tinged. Hence, despite the importance of the distinction between confessional and aesthetic self-expression, care must be taken by public schools having Christmas carols and hymns during school hours; doing so can easily infringe the equalitarian principle. To add non-Christian songs would help, though

271   *The Separation*
                                of Church and State

the problem of finding a balanced mix remains. Suppose one finds such a mix. Does one still violate the neutrality principle? This depends on the details; for instance, at least some of the carols, like "Rudolph the Red-Nosed Reindeer" and "White Christmas," seem to blend into the cultural meaning of the holiday season. It matters greatly, of course, not only what songs are selected, but in what context they are sung.

Another major problem area is that of state aid to sectarian schools. Again, my concern is to clarify the three principles, not to settle specific issues about their scope. Conceptually, one can distinguish aid that furthers a school's sectarian purposes from aid which serves its secular educational ends. The latter kind of aid need not violate separation of church and state, provided nonreligious private schools receive comparable support. But in practice it may be impossible to prevent aid to a sectarian school from furthering its overall aims and thereby its religious purposes. It might help to give aid directly to students, perhaps approximately what they would receive if attending a public school. But since this aid might relieve the school's general budgets, it might again help to further sectarian purposes. There is, however, a wider issue: *any* aid to religiously affiliated schools helps them compete with secular institutions—private as well as public—and thereby arguably favors the religious as such; yet providing *no* aid for such education makes the exercise of religious liberty more expensive for citizens committed to sectarian schools than for citizens willing to use public schools. It is hardly surprising that aid to private schools continues to be hotly contested, and that the principles I propose yield no simple resolution.[12]

The question of support for sectarian schools raises the issue of how the tax-exempt status of churches squares with the separation doctrine. Prima facie, it is preferential treatment of religious institutions. But churches are nonprofit, charitable institutions, and these points may justify their exemption. To be sure, if there are criteria for nonreligious nonprofit organizations which churches do not have to meet, then there is prima facie preference. I cannot pursue any specific criteria for exemption; my point is just that as long as churches have significant charitable

12. I am assuming that a condition of aid would be educational adequacy. For an interesting recent discussion of the related question of teacher competence in religious schools, see *State of Nebraska ex rel. Paul L. Douglas et al., Appellees, v. Faith Baptist Church of Louisville, Nebraska, A Corporation, et al., Appellants, Nebraska Reports* 207 (January 1981).

and philanthropic functions, their tax-exempt status does not by itself entail preferential treatment of religious institutions as such.

It may be, however, that the libertarian principle should also come in here; it might warrant tax exemption for churches even if charity and philanthropy are not a major part of their function. Consider the power to tax, with all its regulative and investigatory tentacles. It is the power to restrict, pressure, sometimes control, and sometimes choke to death. If we are to preserve religious liberty, and particularly to prevent the government from treating some religions better than others, it may be best not to give the state this power over churches, at least over their nonprofit functions (any activities they may conduct for profit presumably should be taxable). If this is so, however, what justifies taxing businesses? The short answer is that they are run for profit. A long answer would begin by pointing out that, even if they were not, one's relation to one's business is quite different from one's relation to one's religion. One can go from one business to another and retain one's basic ideals, capacities, and identity as a person. But losing one's religion is (or certainly can be) far more profound. Even the capitalistic right to own a business at all is of lesser status in a free and democratic society than the right to practice one's religion. Moreover, a failed business can often be revived or its proprietors equally well sustained in some other venture. Whole sectors of an economy can become moribund and be resuscitated. But a religion's being choked out is quite different. Unlike viable commercial enterprises, a religion may not be supported by such ever-present incentives as the profit motive, and the state is certainly not entitled to assume that there would inevitably be a second coming.

So far, I have largely neglected the problem of how to tell what constitutes a religious institution or a religion. The situation is doubly difficult because decisions as to what counts as a religion may be religiously biased in a way that violates a proper separation of church and state. Must a religion be theistic, as many adherents of the main religions of the Western world tend to think? We are unlikely to find any simple, uncontroversial definition of 'religion'.[13] But this need not be crippling,

13. For a valuable definitional discussion, see Philip E. Devine, "On the Definition of Religion." *Faith and Philosophy* 3, no. 3 (1986). While he holds that "A value-free definition of 'religion' is . . . impossible" (p. 271), he also offers two central criteria, which (he maintains) together yield a sufficient condition, and singly yield such a condition when supplemented by certain noncentral factors. One criterion is "doctrinal: a religion affirms the existence of one or more superhuman agents, on whose favor the welfare of human agents depends. . . . The second is psychosocial or functional. A religion by the second

The Separation
                                        of Church and State

either conceptually or legally. For there is a long list of uncontroversial cases, including most of those that raise the gravest cultural and legal issues; and there are some clearly significant features that guide our use of the term, including devotion to a deity, rites and practices related to a deity, a conception of the meaning or value of human life, attitudes of reverence, and a central place in the life of the people in question. Possession of a great majority of these features is *normally* both necessary and sufficient for the presence of a religion.

As these points suggest, while a good detailed definition of 'religion' is an immense task, it is not needed for case-by-case application of the three principles of separation. For that, a broad conception should be one's guide: it is generally better to extend a liberty to someone using 'religion' loosely than to deny it because of a too restrictive definition. Error on the inclusive side is at least limited by the point that separation of church and state does not protect violations of basic human rights, even if, like other doctrines meant mainly to preserve liberty, it does protect speech and ritual in which those violations are advocated. Suppose, indeed, that no precise, sound definition of 'religion' can be framed. It remains true that on the basis of the three proposed principles of separation, resolving specific church-state issues is usually possible given the intuitions we have about what constitutes a religion, provided these intuitions are tempered by an understanding of the uncontroversial cases, both of religion and of its separation from the state. Two negative points can also help. First, a moral outlook on life, even reverently held, is not sufficient for its possessor's being religious in the sense relevant to separation of church and state. Second, one does not have a religion simply because *some* coherent set of ideals is central in one's life. Even holding a world view *religiously* does not imply that that view is itself a *religion*, or that one is a religious person. (The moral and existential-centrality notions of religion I am rejecting here, which are often uncritically accepted, also seem defective in other ways, but there is no need to discuss them further now.)

I believe, then, that we need not violate the separation doctrine in the very act of interpreting it, particularly if we observe certain distinctions. The most important cases in practice, moreover, are those involving

---

criterion unifies . . . the framework by which an individual or group regulates its thought and its life" (p. 272). For a different approach, consistent with definitions of 'religion' being value free, see William P. Alston, *Philosophy of Language* (Englewood Cliffs, N.J.: Prentice-Hall, 1964), esp. pp. 87–90.

churches whose religious character is not in question. There have, however, been both debatable cases and arrant pretensions, as when, some time ago, year-round residents of a New York resort town, tired of paying property taxes to compensate for churches' having bought up the old hotels, became "ordained," with a parsonage cropping up for every household. Though a legal failure, the venture did illustrate the important point that an elastic doctrine can be stretched from both ends.

IV. Separation of Church and State in the Political Arena

My concern so far has been governmental activities as they affect religion. But the institutional separation doctrine has another component, also based on ideals underlying a free and democratic society. For many of the same reasons why the state should not interfere in religion, churches should not interfere in government. The point is not legal or even constitutional. I am not suggesting, for example, that church donations to political candidates must be illegal in a free and democratic society—though a good case can be made that they should be *if* churches have tax-exempt status. My point is that protection of religious liberty, and certainly of governmental neutrality toward religious institutions, is better served if churches as institutions do not take political action. I suggest, then, *an institutional principle of political neutrality*: churches have a prima facie, obligation to abstain from supporting candidates for office or pressing for specific public policies, especially the kind typically included in the platform of a particular party.

I am construing 'political' not in the broad sense of 'contested in the arena of politics' but rather narrowly, so that moral issues are not included, even if they enter into political debates. The separation of church and state does not require, nor do any sound principles demand, that churches should not take moral positions, even if there is political controversy about them. There are, to be sure, different ways of supporting moral positions; and some are closer than others to political statements, as when government officials of only one party are cited as offenders despite the prominence of offenders among their counterparts in another party. These matters call for discretion and do not admit of codification. But there is still much conduct that is clearly ruled out by the separationist standard in question.

The principle of political neutrality would not, however, prevent churches' encouraging their members' *participation* in politics; and it

275   *The Separation*
                       of Church and State

certainly does not restrict political participation by religious citizens, or
imply that they should not consider such participation an aspect of their
religious commitments. The clergy could, under this principle, both oppose the arms race in public meetings and preach against political apa-
thy from the pulpit. It is only taking political positions from the pulpit
(and in other institutional ways) that the principle implies would be
(prima facie) unjustified. To be sure, there are moral statements which,
combined with certain obvious facts about politicians, government officials, or foreign powers, imply condemnation or approval of them. But
there is a crucial difference between affirming moral truths which, *with*
certain facts, imply political judgments, and, on the other hand, making
political judgments themselves. Matters of fact may be controversial; and
in any case, when the suggested distinction between the moral and the
political is observed, the assessment of factual issues is left to the individual judgment of those in the congregation. That judgment constitutes
an important filter between ministerial deliverances and political action.

I do *not* believe that the principle of political neutrality should be written into law; but if it is not conscientiously observed, then candidates for
public office may be unduly influenced to serve the special, even the
distinctively religious, interests of certain churches, particularly if there
is a majority church.[14] Furthermore, the polarities afflicting relations between certain religious groups are more likely to surface in government
decision making, where the public interest should be the overriding concern. Admittedly, some polarization may arise from any public political
disagreement, particularly when institutions themselves square off. But
whereas, in a free and democratic society, political controversy is inevitable, religious polarization is not. Moreover, some clergy represent
themselves as having, or in any case are generally taken to have, special
insight into matters of human conduct; this (among other factors) increases the chance of polarization if corporate religion enters into politics

14. Cf. the quite different view of Leo Pfeffer: "I do not . . . think it improper or undesirable for the [Catholic] Church to take political action. . . . I think it was entirely proper for
the Catholic bishops in Connecticut to warn legislators that how they vote on the parochial
school bus bill would be remembered on Election Day. It would, of course, have been
equally proper for Protestant ministers to issue the same warning. It has long been the
policy of labor unions to reward their friends and punish their enemies on Election Day"
(*Creeds in Competition* [New York: Harper Brothers, 1958]). There are better grounds for
Pfeffer's view than the analogy between churches and unions; but on my account of separation of church and state the reasons for rejecting the view are far better than those for
accepting it.

and public policy debate. Locke commented vividly on dangers of the sort I have in mind:

> Immediate revelation being a much easier way for men to establish their opinions and regulate their conduct, than the tedious and not always successful labor of strict reasoning, it is no wonder that some have been very apt to pretend to revelation, and to persuade themselves that they are under the peculiar guidance of heaven in their actions and opinions, especially in those of them which they cannot account for by the ordinary methods of knowledge and principles of reason.[15]

To be sure, however hard we try to avoid basing political positions on religious considerations, there is no sharp distinction between moral and political issues, and certainly an admirable moral sermon on, for example, the duties of charity, could have obvious implications for legislative decisions on welfare policy. But if, in borderline cases, the moral and political intermingle, there is still a generally plain difference between, say, giving a moral sermon and endorsing candidates, political parties, or politically contested public policy positions.[16]

The principle of political neutrality is institutional; it does not imply that clergy may not take personal and even public positions on topics connected with politics or public policy, or even concerning personalities in government. Granted, in some churches what the clergy say even privately might often be taken for church doctrine; but there is still a great difference between what is so interpreted and what is publicly announced as church doctrine or policy, or paid out from church coffers.

15. Locke, *Essay concerning Human Understanding*, chap. XIX, sec. 5.

16. Three qualifications are in order. First, the matter becomes complicated if the *content* of a religion dictates political action. There one would hope votaries are as restrained as possible; in any case, a proper separation does not warrant unlimited freedom of religious practice, and reasonable limitations on the relevant church, for instance on its use of coercion in political matters, would remain warranted. Second, in tyrannical states things are different; my concern is free and democratic societies. In any case, preaching against a Hitler is not on a par with preaching for or against a candidate in a democracy. Third, here as elsewhere in this article I am talking not about the scope of the *right* of free expression but only about what principles *ought* (ideally) to govern behavior *given* a proper separation of church and state. On rights of free expression I agree with much of Mill's *On Liberty*. For pertinent discussion of free expression, including Mill's account of it, see Thomas Scanlon, "A Theory of Freedom of Expression," *Philosophy & Public Affairs* 1, no. 2 (Winter 1972).

277   *The Separation*
                              of Church and State

Even in making avowedly personal statements or in giving private counsel, however, clergy who believe in freedom and democracy should follow
an individual principle of political neutrality to the effect that clergy
should (i) observe a distinction between their personal political views
and those of their office, especially in making public statements, and (ii)
prevent any political aims they may have from dominating their professional conduct. Such domination is possible even where one specifies
that one is not speaking for one's church institutionally; but disclaimers
of that kind can help in keeping official pronouncements distinct from
personal conviction.

This principle does not imply that clergy should not *connect* their religious views and their political position; any citizen may put political
stances in that wider context. Indeed, applying religious principles and
insights to issues of law and public policy can be highly beneficial: it may
have heuristic value in leading to discovery of new points; it may serve
as a moral corrective, for instance in bringing out injustices; it may
strengthen moral motivation; it may reduce strife and recrimination
among disparate social groups, as when tolerance and forgiveness are
stressed as part of a religious commitment; it may enhance the aesthetic
and cultural aspects of civil life; and it may encourage a vivid and salu-
tary modeling of the forms of life people cherish as part of their religious
faith. Nonetheless, it is appropriate that clergy exercise restraint in
touching on political issues, particularly in broaching them from the vantage point of the pulpit. If they do not, they invite peers who disagree to
use religious leverage for opposite ends; and the public, possibly including their own congregations, may suffer. In such individual conduct,
there are some specific principles that should be observed, especially by
those who, by virtue of office or public visibility, may sometimes exercise
an influence on others that goes beyond the credibility of their views.
Principles of this sort are the main topic of the next section.

V. Separation of Church and State as a Doctrine
of Conscience

The threefold institutional doctrine of separation of church and state I
have set out rests mainly on ideals of freedom and democracy, including
ideals that I take to be among those informing the United States Constitution. These are above all moral ideals, in the widest sense of the

phrase. Thus, it should not be surprising that the ideals of freedom and democracy underlying the proposed principles of separation imply certain principles of *individual* conduct. These further principles are applicable to church-state issues and indeed to the interaction between people's religious commitments and their duties as citizens. The principles apply whether one is acting for the public, for a religious institution, or as an individual considering what laws or social policies to support.

This section is devoted to articulating and defending such principles of conscience, as we might call them. One underlying idea is this: in a free and democratic society, people who want to preserve religious and other liberties should not argue for or advocate laws or policies that restrict human conduct unless they offer (or at least have) adequate secular (nonreligious) reasons to support the law or policy in question (where an adequate reason for a law or policy is a proposition whose truth is sufficient to justify it). By 'secular reason' I do not mean one that is consciously held in contrast to a religious one, nor is there anything antireligious implicit in a proper use of the term. Indeed, a secular reason may be fully *aligned* with a religiously sanctioned view, say in affirming a universal right to liberty; any notion of secularity that would preclude such alignment would prevent many *moral* reasons, such as those grounding the prohibitions of murder, rape, and theft, from counting as secular. Rather, a secular reason is, roughly, one whose normative force, that is, its status as a prima facie justificatory element, does not (evidentially) depend on the existence of God (for example, through appeals to divine command), or on theological considerations (such as interpretations of a sacred text), or on the pronouncements of a person or institution qua religious authority. This notion of a secular reason has some of the vagueness of 'religion'; nor can I precisely define 'theological considerations'. But much can be accomplished here without definitions.

The suggested idea does not apply to the same extent to nonrestrictive laws and policies, for example to excusing absences for religious observances. It also applies to a lesser degree to exempting children from public education beyond a certain point, as with the Amish,[17] and to providing for the public's enjoyment, say in commissioning sculptures as opposed to gardens. To be sure, as draft exemptions illustrate, one per-

17. A crucial case here is *Wisconsin v. Yoder* (1972), decided by the Burger Court. For discussion of the case, see Pfeffer, *Religion, State, and the Burger Court*, chap. 3.

The Separation
of Church and State

son's right or privilege may be another's restriction. But there is a vast difference between, for instance, allowing one's religious views to lead one to support religious tests for certain public offices and letting one's sense of what best does homage to God determine one's voting to use public funds for a garden rather than abstract sculpture. The central idea is that citizens in a free and democratic society are obligated, by their commitment to freedom and democracy and (I believe) morally as well, not to make decisions, as citizens, in support of laws or policies that restrict the scope, or even the de facto exercise, of liberty, unless they have a sufficient secular basis for so deciding. It might seem that stressing this is unnecessary if there is institutional separation of church and state; but that is not so. We have already seen that the institutional doctrine is unavoidably vague and that its application is itself subject to religiously grounded biases. Other reasons for a further principle will emerge shortly.

The points just made suggest the plausibility of what I shall call *the principle of secular rationale*: one should not advocate or support any law or public policy that restricts human conduct unless one has, and is willing to offer, adequate secular reason for this advocacy or support. This principle is normative, not genetic; thus, it allows advocacy that is religiously *inspired*, for example by one's reading of the Bible, and, in addition, allows one to be *more* impressed by the religious arguments for one's position than by the secular grounds for it. The principle also permits expressing religious as well as secular reasons in the course of advocacy, though this has its dangers. It might, for instance, invite impassioned religious opponents to respond with their own theological fire, and a resolvable matter, such as aid to a third-world nation, could go unsettled, or be less adequately concluded, because the parties are divided by unnecessary disputes about the religious status of the nation in question. A similar principle may well hold for laws or policies that create inequalities, even if that need not reduce freedom, and perhaps even for laws or public policies in general; but here and in what follows I concentrate on principles that concern laws or policies that would restrict conduct.[18]

18. Similar principles might also apply to nonreligious considerations, for example of social privilege. But (a) people may be presumed more nearly alike in some matters, such as self-preservation, than in religious ones; (b) the potential for irreconcilable conflict is less in most other matters; and (c) I am simply not concerned with the principle as a model

For the same reasons supporting the principle of secular rationale, one might hold a *principle of secular advocacy* to the effect that, in addition to adhering to the principle of secular rationale, we should keep religious considerations out of the relevant public debates, except where they are necessary to clarify positions or prevent misunderstanding of motives. I am not here arguing for this stronger principle, but only for the rationale principle, which simply demands that, whatever other considerations one brings to the relevant contexts of advocacy or support, one put forward such advocacy or support only if one *also* has and is willing to offer adequate secular reason for the view in question. Thus, while one may be *led* to consider polygamy wrong because of religious scruples against adultery, one could support its legal prohibition only if one had adequate secular ground, say its danger to children.

In practice, commitment to the principle of secular rationale will tend to lead conscientious citizens to follow a related one, *the principle of secular resolution*, which requires that, particularly in discussing laws or policies that would restrict human conduct, final resolution should be made along secular lines; more specifically, that while any kind of factor may enter into the discussion of such issues, a final decision to adopt a policy should be fully warranted by secular considerations and promulgated in that light.

One might object that so long as one brings adequate secular reasons for one's position to the debate, one should be free to give priority to other sorts of reasons, including religious ones, and the basis of decision may thus be a democratic balance of pluralistic considerations. The underlying model here might be called a *compromise model*. It contrasts with the kind of *secular decision model* favored (though not entailed) by the principle of secular rationale. The former endorses the results of compromises freely reached on the basis of unrestrictedly diverse considerations; the latter requires that secular considerations be the basis of policy discussions and provide the main warrant for decisions that issue from them. Given the reasons for institutional separation of church and state, and for the principle of secular rationale as a separationist counterpart for individual conduct, I believe that the principle of secular resolution is reasonable and that the compromise model yields too weak a basis of

---

for the nonreligious domain: if it is in some respects a good model, as is arguable, all the better.

The Separation
of Church and State

public civility. Compromise cannot be expected to yield optimal results unless the debate is appropriately constrained in the first place. But defending the secular decision model requires far more than arguing for the principle of secular rationale, and it is only that principle, together with a strengthened version of it to be introduced shortly, that I am endorsing here.

There are of course practical difficulties in trying to follow the principle of secular rationale. Consider people who think that moral considerations are *not* secular—or hold the panreligious view that everything is religiously significant in some way. They would feel too restricted by the rationale principle, even though, within their category of religious considerations, they could make distinctions among degrees of closeness to the religious center and might allow some moral reasons to be a good distance from that center. By contrast, anyone attracted to the principle of secular rationale would tend to acknowledge quite readily a distinction between moral and religious considerations. In any case, here practice can be superior to theory: *using* moral reasons thinking them to be religious would not violate the principle, any more than using religious reasons thinking them to be secular would conform to it. It is true that adopting the principle would force one to think hard about what kinds of reasons one is using, and it would sometimes produce challenges of the admissibility of certain purported reasons; but that should be beneficial.

When we reflect on what the principle of secular rationale actually requires of us, however, it should become apparent that one can act with a secular rationale that functions in one's mind only as a *rationalization*—as a purported justification (or purported explanation) that does not explanatorily underlie the action or belief to which one applies it. My rationale for prohibiting polygamous marriages might be that they are dangerous to children, while my real reason for prohibiting them—what really motivates me in my opposition—is my belief that they violate God's law. Thus, my moral point might be just a secular rationalization that would not move me to oppose polygamy apart from my religious reason for condemning it. Surely I would be criticizable here, and the reasons why this is so suggest that the principle of secular rationale is not strong enough to express my obligation (even granting, as we should, that the obligation is prima facie as opposed to absolute). This is a subtle matter, and several aspects of it must be considered.

First, notice that I would be offering to others a consideration that does not move me. Even if, in the abstract, it is a sound basis for my action, I do a wrong when, in this way, I give others a reason that does not move me, and invite them to be convinced by it. Does it not smack of manipulation to give reasons that do not move me, in order to get others to do what I want? I use the reasons as psychological levers to produce belief on a basis that does not carry my own conviction. It is as if I invited you to join me on a journey, but by a route I do not sufficiently trust to take it myself. You are entitled to wonder why, if the route is not good enough, or appealing enough, for me to take, I think it good enough for you.

It may be objected that there is no manipulation *if* I think the route is trust*worthy*, but simply do not trust it myself. This is parallel to the case of offering what one believes is a good secular reason, though one is not motivated by it. But if I think the route trustworthy, yet do not trust it, my rationality is suspect, and I should thus be quite uncomfortable with offering you my assurance about the route. For your part, you may reasonably think my (cognitive) actions speak louder than my words, and you might be hard pressed to believe that I really do think the route safe in the first place. Surely, then, the kind of argumentation and persuasion I would be using exhibits at best surface cooperation; it does not achieve the shared decision so characteristic of a successful democracy. I want to get you to my destination; but I will not journey there by your route, nor is there any route we are willing to take *together*. If I should candidly admit that I am not moved by the secular reasons I offer, I would at best extenuate my offense; indeed, the candid admission of regretted behavior often serves to reduce suspicion and thereby enhance its influence.

If we consider the long run, a second point emerges. If I persuade someone only by adducing secular reasons that do not move me, I tend to produce only a fortuitous and unstable agreement. For if I had not found the secular rationale, then (other things being equal) I would have been either intransigent in maintaining my position, or at least tempted to compromise my commitment to the principle of secular rationale by arguing for my view on religious grounds alone. Furthermore, suppose I later decide that the secular reasons I offered were not good after all—as I may well tend to conclude if they did not move me in the first place. Then I might no longer share, with the nonreligious or those of differing religious views, *any* reason for the position I advocated, and would thereby be more likely to disagree on its interpretation in practice. Again, it appears that if one should give adequate secular reasons at all, they should be reasons that move one, not simply rationalizations designed (or at least expected) to move or satisfy others. Arguments that do not move both parties to a dispute are, at least on one side, a poor basis for agreement even if both believe them to be acceptable. They are also a weak social glue.

There is a third, still more important reason why it would be wrong to act on a religious ground while offering a secular rationalization to conform to (individual) requirements of separation of church and state. If what actually moves me to hold my position is religious considerations, are not my religious commitments the main determinants of my views and actions concerning how *others* should behave in civil society, including others who lack those commitments? It seems so, and my allowing this clearly violates the spirit of separation of church and state, understood to rest on the ideals of freedom and democracy presupposed in our discussion. The point is especially clear if the shoe is on the other foot: I would not want others to argue for laws to restrict my conduct, when their motivation is religious, so long as they could offer me an adequate secular reason. For one thing, if this is their motivation, I will mistrust their secular argument, however compelling it sounds. I will also feel that I am being pacified by such argument rather than respected as a partner in a shared civil life. What they are really *doing*—as judged, naturally enough, by the motivation underlying it—is pursuing a religious aim or commitment, or even agenda; but I am to be at ease because they can provide, and—in the abstract—they apparently respect, a secular reason that legitimates the laws in question.

A fourth, closely related consideration concerns the basis of mutual respect that should underlie public policy discussions in a free and democratic society. Even if the criteria for an *adequate* reason were clear enough to enable us to recognize an adequate secular argument regardless of its motivation, I would tend to resent being given such an argument when the underlying motivation for accepting its conclusion is religious. There is a certain lack of respect implied in seeking my agreement to a policy by offering reasons by which one is not oneself moved. I can see that I might get justice, since there would *be* a reason for the policy; but it would be like having a debt paid by someone who would not have paid it had that not been convenient. One feels neither treated with respect nor secure regarding future relations with the persons in question.

I believe, then, that if the spirit of separation of church and state is to be adequately reflected in individual conduct, we need something stronger than the principle of secular rationale. That principle is powerful and important; and it can stand as a far-reaching separationist principle of conscience. But a stronger principle seems warranted, which I shall call *the principle of secular motivation*: it says that one should not advocate or promote any legal or public policy restrictions on human conduct unless one not only has and is willing to offer, but is also *motivated by*, adequate secular reason, where this reason (or set of reasons) is motivationally sufficient for the conduct in question. This principle solves the problems I have just raised, yet is by no means extreme. It not only countenances inspiration by religious considerations; it also permits one to be motivated by them *as well as* by secular ones. Its intent is simply to require that one either not perform the relevant acts or see to it that one's secular, for instance purely moral, motivation is strong enough so that (other things being equal) one would do the thing in question even if one had no further motive. I leave open whether, as I am inclined to grant, there is a moral *right* to act otherwise; but I assume that rights do not exhaust oughts—that there are things one ought not to do even if one has a right to do them.

There is a general reason, independent of church-state issues, for preferring the motivational principle over the rationale principle. Surely an action is *justified by* a reason one has for doing it only if one does it *for* that reason, and hence would not be merely rationalizing in citing that reason to explain one's doing it.[19] Suppose, for instance, that Tom avoids a storm out of sheer superstitious fear that the lightning will turn him into a devil until sunrise. He then does not do so rationally; and this holds even if the rain is so heavy that he can offer, to someone who wonders why he gave up his movie tickets, the rationalization that the drive was risky in a low-slung car. Granted, given the risk of stalling out, staying home was, for Tom, *the rational thing to do*; but, since he was motivated by superstitious fear and not at all by fear of stalling, he did not *rationally do it*.

To illustrate the distinction in the domain of separation of church and state, if a religious reason is not an adequate ground for supporting laws

19. I develop and defend this point in detail in "Rationalization and Rationality," *Synthese* 64 (1985).

The Separation
                               of Church and State

that prohibit polygamy—as it will not be for those who accept even the
secular rationale principle—then opposing legalized polygamy *for* that
reason is not acting *justifiedly* even though one may *have* a sufficient
secular reason which one can present as a rationalization. This point
helps to explain why we should go beyond the principle of secular rationale to that of secular motivation. If we do not, we condone actions that,
from the overall point of view of separation of church and state, have the
wrong kind of basis and hence are unjustifiedly performed. It is not that
there cannot *be* religious justification; the point is that actions permissible under separation of church and state should not *depend* on such justification. On the rationale principle, however, we would condone actions
whose only justification in terms of the motivating reasons of the agent
is religious, so long as they admit of a secular rationalization, whether
anyone is moved by it or not; and these actions are of a kind that would
not, from a secular point of view, be justifiedly performed.

A Kantian perspective may be useful here, though the case does not
depend on it. Suppose the secular reason that merely rationalizes a public policy decision is moral. Then the decision would be the very kind of
action of which Kant said that, though it conforms with duty and is thus
not wrong, it is not done *from* duty and therefore has no moral worth.[20]
For it exhibits mere conformity with the moral rationale; it is not
grounded in it: it is grounded in a religious reason and hence can be
justifiedly performed only by virtue of being done from that ground.
Hence, from a secular—in this case moral—point of view, the action is
not justifiedly performed and, by Kantian lights, has no secular worth.
This does not imply that the religious, motivating reasons *cannot* justify;
but even where they may, the nonreligious cannot be expected to accept
their doing so.

We might weaken the principle of secular motivation, for example requiring only that one's secular reason be *necessary* for one's action,
rather than sufficient. This would yield a *principle of essential secular*

20. Kant is well known for this view; but it is noteworthy that his great opponent, David
Hume, held a similar one: " 'Tis evident, that when we praise any actions, we regard only
the motives that produced them, and consider the actions as signs or indications of certain
principles in the mind. . . . After the same manner, when we require any action, or blame
a person for not performing it, we always suppose, that one in that situation shou'd be
influenc'd by the proper motive of that action, and we esteem it vicious in him to be regardless of it" (*A Treatise of Human Nature*, ed. L. A. Selby-Bigge [Oxford: Oxford University Press, 1888], pt. II, sec. I, p. 477).

motivation. The original principle can be weakened further, by degrees, until we come to the minimal requirement that an adequate secular reason be *some* part of what actually motivates one to act. We would then have merely a *principle of partial secular motivation.* The weaker principles seem less plausible. Consider the most reasonable of them, which says that secular motivation need only be necessary for one's action. Even if I would not have opposed legalized polygamy without a secular reason, my religious reasons can be *far* more influential in my thinking. Thus, if my acting solely for those reasons is unjustified from the point of view of separation of church and state, the much weaker influence of my secular reason seems only to extenuate my unwarranted behavior. It is significant that I would not have opposed polygamy without, say, believing that it is exploitive; but if I also would not have opposed it on this basis alone, without religious scruples, my opposition is strongly religious and may be predominantly so. My conduct toward others can thus be mainly colored by my religious preferences, so long as I find a secular rationale strong enough in my own thinking so that I would not press my religious views without it.

Certainly weaker versions of the principle of secular motivation would be better than none. But a conscientious citizen strongly committed to preserving religious and other liberties should probably strive to follow the stronger principle, which requires that one do one's best to have sufficient secular motivation, particularly for actions in support of laws or policies that would restrict human conduct. What follows will help to show why.

VI. The Application of the Principles of Conscience

We can clarify the two proposed individual principles of separation—the rationale and motivation principles—by applying them to a major issue of our time: abortion. Suppose I believe that the fetus is, from conception onwards, a human person. I might then argue that abortions are permissible at best as self-defense, say where a pregnancy due to rape threatens to kill the pregnant woman. Now, prima facie, the view that the fetus from conception is a person is not religious but moral or, in a broad sense, philosophical. Yet if I am conscientious, then, realizing that this view itself is controversial, I will ask myself why I hold it. It may occur to me that all the genetic information is encoded in the zygote and that this implies that the fetus is a person from conception on. This is a sec-

ular consideration; and if it provides an adequate reason for my conclusion and is the reason *for* which I believe the fetus is a person, my opposing abortion on that basis (and opposing laws permitting it) does not
violate the principle of secular motivation.

Imagine, on the other hand, that I am like many people for whom,
whatever the plausibility of such arguments as the genetic one, what
really underlies their belief that the fetus is a person from conception is
the religious conviction that at conception the zygote is ensouled by God,
or at least has a divine blessing. It is not that they do not accept the
secular arguments. The point is that if they were not disposed to embrace them by this deeper commitment, they would not; they would, for
example, consider the fetus a potential person (rather as the implanted
acorn might be thought a potential oak), but, at least in the first trimes-
ter, not yet a person. This is where it makes an immense difference
whether I adhere to the rationale or the motivation principle. For if I live
up to the latter, I will not support restrictive laws on abortion unless I
find myself really convinced by secular argument taken on its own merits. I will hold that if the genetic argument, say, would not convince me
except through nonevidential factors deriving from my independent religious commitments, then I should not try to restrict the conduct of
others using that argument as a rationale. For I will likely suppose that
if they do not share my religious convictions, they may reject it, which
would leave me opposing their freedom on a religious basis they do not
accept. Even if they do accept the argument, I would tend to feel that
my action causing them to accede to the restrictions is *based* on religious
convictions which they need not accept. Moreover, I would not want
such action taken toward me if the roles were reversed.

This example can be better understood if we distinguish two importantly different ways in which an action may depend on religious considerations. First, it may depend on a belief, such as that the fetus is a person, which one holds for a reason that expresses a kind of religious
premise, say that the fetus is ensouled by God. Here one's belief that the
fetus is a person, and, derivatively, one's actions based on that belief,
exhibit *evidential dependence* on a religious consideration. Second, one
may simply be caused to believe that the fetus is a person by religious
influences that do not produce this belief through any premises they may
provide one; rather, the belief may be produced, either as a kind of axiom
or as a sort of article of faith, through repeated statements by those
whose religious authority one respects, or through rituals, repetitions of

texts, or the social influence of parents or peers. Here the belief and, indirectly, one's actions based on it exhibit *nonevidential, causal dependence* on religious considerations. This is not to say that one could not find, or think up, various kinds of evidence for it; the point is that there are (at least) two importantly different ways that beliefs, and thereby actions, can depend on religious considerations, and the secular motivation principle requires that one try to prevent one's conduct in matters regarding church and state from depending on them in either way. For on this principle, a secular reason should be motivationally as well as evidentially sufficient for the conduct in question.

With this distinction in mind, recall the example. Suppose I am so anxious to conform to the motivation principle that (perhaps nondeliberately) I manipulate myself, exposing myself to people and other sources of information likely to convince me of the cogency of secular arguments for the personhood of the fetus. Compare people who want mandatory periods of school prayer in order to promote religion, but come, through repetition and self-manipulation, to be moved by their own rationalization in terms of giving students a time for reflection and a peace that reduces anxiety. If one really thinks this *is* a reason for the practice, one will surely *tend* to be moved by it in any case: such, fortunately, is our normal psychological makeup. Thus, successfully cultivating that tendency is by no means a psychological feat.

Where nonevidential factors, in this way, transform a reason one merely *has* to believe something into a reason *for which* one does—a cognitively motivating reason—I shall speak of *artificial sustenance*. One has, as it were, upgraded a plausible rationalization for a belief into a real reason underlying that belief. This is not a change *in* beliefs, but a change of relations *between* beliefs. It need not alter what one believes; one belief may simply become a sustaining basis of another. Cases like this may in fact be fairly common. Nevertheless, there is an insidious immorality in trying to make oneself fall for one's own rationalizations so that one can argue for one's deep-seated views—or prejudices—with a good conscience. As Christianity and other religions teach, morality is not wholly a matter of external conduct; and the principle of secular motivation is intended to proscribe one's producing appropriate cognitive motivation by an artificial, nonevidential route. It is a principle of conscience; it speaks to both inner and outer conduct, and to the heart as well as the head.

Once we notice the possibility of self-manipulation and self-deception, it becomes plain that others can similarly manipulate a person, for instance offering secular arguments in a context of authority, or of religious sanction, that makes them seem cogent even if, on their evidential merits, they would not carry conviction. Thus, we should also take the principle of secular motivation to rule out *artificial conviction* as a main factor in the relevant action. (I take a *main* factor to be a condition at least necessary for the performance of the relevant action.) To illustrate a common objectionable ground of conviction, the motivation for the action must not be based on manipulation, including one's own, which causes acceptance of secular arguments that, on their evidential merits, would not convince one. The restriction applies both to artificial belief of a proposition expressing a purported reason (for example, that polygamy is exploitive) and to artificially taking a proposition to support another (for instance, the conclusion that polygamy should be illegal).

More broadly, if one's action, say in pressing to outlaw certain conduct, rests on considerations that, evidentially or just causally, depend themselves on religious considerations, then it violates the principle of secular motivation as I am construing it, and is inappropriate for a conscientious citizen committed to separation of church and state. (There may be wayward or other kinds of causal chains to be ruled out, but such cases would be rare and need not be considered here.) Granted, *non*religious influences can also produce artificial conviction or artificial sustenance; and an action based wholly on either of them, whatever it is, may be no better justified than in the cases we have considered. But the generalizability of the proposed principle of secular motivation does not imply that it is inappropriate to a sound theory of separation of church and state. If some of the arguments that support the secular motivation principle show that a commitment to freedom and democracy makes it objectionable to vote one's pocketbook as well as to vote one's religion, so be it.

There are countless kinds of conduct to which both the secular rationale and the secular motivation principles apply. They apply to legislators making law, to judges and lawyers interpreting it, and to citizens proposing it; they apply to government officials carrying out laws and policies, including foreign policy,[21] to educators, particularly in public

21. Regarding foreign policy, in addition to controversy over appropriate U.S. relations to the Vatican, there are questions about how the U.S. government should coordinate foreign aid with religious institutions. Writing for the *Los Angeles Times*, Bernard Cooke criticized the view that U.S. aid to the Philippines should go through the Catholic Church: "one can see a certain logic in wanting to distribute such aid through the church. . . . But given the

institutions, and to clergy and laity alike in their activities that affect society as a whole. The application of the principles is not always straightforward, for instance because it may be difficult to discern why one believes what one does, or to see just what *is* the evidential force of certain reasons. But often it is obvious what the principles imply for a given issue, and a society whose citizens do their best to observe them is more likely to be free than one whose citizens do not.

Surely in a free society, questions of the scope of freedom should be settled mainly by secular arguments. Adherence to the principle of secular rationale helps to ensure that, in determining the scope of freedom in a society, the decisive principles and considerations can be shared by people of differing religious views. or even no religious convictions at all. If, beyond this, people follow the principle of secular motivation to the best of their ability, the issues are much less likely to be decided along religious lines. For if one adheres to that principle, one's drive is for reasonable solutions that observe general moral and social-political principles. If we obey only the weaker principle of secular rationale, we too easily seek to build our religious preferences into law wherever we can find what we take to be good secular arguments for their legitimation.

VII. RELIGION AND MORALITY IN A FREE AND DEMOCRATIC SOCIETY

It is appropriate to conclude with some general observations on religion and morality.[22] If one thinks, as many seem to, that a person cannot be solidly moral without being religious, then one will view separation of church and state differently than I do. Referring to "four decades of misguided [Supreme] Court decisions," William Bennett has maintained

---

open alliance of the Philippine bishops with Corazon Aquino's candidacy and the post-election resistance, any aid sent through the bishops would have been seen as subtle assistance to one side of the struggle" (*Lincoln Journal*, 1 March, 1986). Arguably, if the church were completely nonpolitical, separation of church and state would not be needed in such instances; but there is in any case the issue of preference of one church over another (as when one is dominant in a foreign country needing aid) or at least of religious institutions over nonreligious ones.

22. For a lucid short discussion of the relation between religion and morality, see William K. Frankena's article on the subject in the *Dictionary of Christian Ethics*, ed. James F. Childress and John Maquarrie (Philadelphia: Westminster Press, 1986). Another valuable treatment of the topic is Jude P. Dougherty. "Assessing the Value of Religion," *Homiletic and Pastoral Review*, July 1984; it stresses both the ways in which religion may be foundational to civilization and the point that "morality does not depend on religion. Moral norms have a life of their own" (p. 24).

291   *The Separation*
                          of Church and State

that "neutrality to religion turned out to bring with it a neutrality to those
values that *issue from* religion. 'Values clarification' flourished in our
schools." In the same speech he said—citing the Declaration of Independence—that our "unalienable rights" come from our Creator, and that
"our values as a free people and the central values of the Judeo-Christian
tradition are flesh of the flesh, blood of the blood."[23] Proponents of these
views may wonder why the liberty of the nonreligious should be fully
protected, and may think it reasonable for the state to treat religious institutions preferentially. I suspect that some of the impetus behind the
move to have periods of prayer in the public schools stems from this sort
of view: many apparently hope to make students moral by making them
religious, or more religious.

My view is that a person can be moral without being religious and that
there could be moral truths even if there should be no religious truths
that support them. This is not to deny that religious commitments often
motivate people to be moral; indeed, it is not to deny that there might be
religious truths sufficient to *guarantee* moral ones or that, other things
being equal, people who are religious—in some traditions—have a
stronger tendency to be moral than those who are not. My point is simply
that moral truths need not derive from religious ones, or, even if they
should so derive, need not be knowable only through the latter; and
whatever causal connections there may be between commitment to one
or another religion and being moral, a moral agent need not necessarily
be religious.[24]

23. William J. Bennett, address to the Knights of Columbus (Washington, D.C.: U.S.
Department of Education, 7 August, 1985), italics added. Bennett does not distinguish
values in the *psychological* sense of (roughly) 'positive attitudes' from values in the objective sense of 'items of real intrinsic worth'. That religion is historically the, or a, basis of
values in the former sense is a highly plausible thesis; but Bennett appears to hold—
though I do not find him explicitly stating—the controversial and very different view that
religion is the (normative) basis of values, including moral ones, in the latter sense. Cf.
James Hitchcock, "Church, State, and Moral Values: The Limits of American Pluralism."
Law and Contemporary Problems 44, no. 2 (1981): "The classical doctrine of strict separationism rests on an assumption that the state can and must be neutral. But in practice
this is impossible. Values are necessary for the functioning of any society" (p. 21). I reject
the implicit suggestion here that the state cannot achieve *religious* neutrality, which is the
kind I am concerned with; but even if such neutrality can only be approached, my theory
would still warrant a directive that the state should come as close as possible to it.

24. Ernest van den Haag makes a case for a stronger view: "I am not arguing that there
can be no morality without religion. I am arguing, however, that historically religion has
been the source of morality, and it remains the source of meaning and morality for most
people who cling to either" ("Religion in the 1980s," *National Forum* 68, no. 1 [1988]).

The relation between morality and religion is an important matter. If moral truths do not depend on religious ones, then not only can the religious and the nonreligious presumably agree on a set of moral principles basic to civilized life, but when different religions hold certain *incompatible* moral principles (say, regarding capital punishment) their adherents can perhaps settle their moral disputes by secular argument— or can at least agree to structure the coercive machinery of the law by such arguments. Moreover, it is also possible to concur on certain general moral principles as a basis for moral education; and that, in *some* form, seems desirable in a free and democratic society, particularly one that follows the principles suggested here. Thus, far from the (at least partial) independence of morality and religion hindering moral education, it increases the chance that, in a religiously pluralistic community, agreement can be reached on the core of a program of moral instruction—one which emphasizes moral values that are almost universally recognized, for instance liberty, justice, equality of opportunity, and respect for persons.

It is difficult to overemphasize the need for an approach to moral, legal, and social-political issues which, however much scope it allows for religious expression and religious inspiration in the invention and execution of policy, does not *depend* on religious convictions. Such an approach is crucial both for religious liberty and, as the issue of abortion shows, for determining the scope of other liberties. The theory of separation of church and state proposed here is meant to help in protecting those various liberties and to strengthen rational discussion in democratic societies. The theory stresses three principles concerning governmental and other institutions: the libertarian principle, prohibiting unwarranted governmental restrictions of religious freedom; the equalitarian principle, prohibiting governmental preference of one or more religions; and the neutrality principle, proscribing governmental preference toward the religious as such. These principles protect us, in religious matters, against governmental coercion, discrimination, and favoritism. For similar reasons, I have suggested a principle of political neutrality applicable to the converse relation, the church's behavior toward the state. It says that churches should not take political positions, whether toward candidates, legislation, or public policy issues, particularly but not exclusively where restrictions of liberty are at stake.

On the basis of the moral and social-political ideals underlying the in-

293   *The Separation*
                             of Church and State

stitutional separation doctrine, I have extended the theory to include
principles of conscience. If those ideals constrain the state, they may be
expected to require similar conduct of individuals. The state is not just
an abstraction, after all; its actions are a matter of certain individuals'
doing specific things that affect actual people. I have argued for two principles of conscience in particular, applicable especially to cases in which
the restriction of human conduct is at stake: the principle of secular rationale, which requires that, for any such restrictive action we take,
whether as legislators or as lawyers or as private citizens, we have, and
be willing to offer, adequate secular reason; and the stronger principle of
secular motivation, which, for the same range of conduct, rules out using
adequate secular reasons merely as rationalizations, and requires that, in
addition to having and being willing to give such reasons, we be (sufficiently) motivated by at least one such reason for the action in question.

I want to stress again that the two principles of conscience allow one
to draw *both* inspiration and motivation from religion in framing or supporting laws and public policies. Religious factors are altogether legitimate in the order of discovery, in the attempt to find new truths and to
construct one's position. They are also appropriate in choosing *what* public issues to concentrate on, for instance disarmament versus education,
just as moral commitments may properly influence one's choice of what
scientific research to undertake. But in the order of justification, in the
attempt to justify actions or beliefs—particularly action that would restrict human conduct—a commitment to a free and democratic society
requires that one have, and be sufficiently motivated by, adequate secular reasons.

It might be objected that the principle of secular motivation is too
strong, at least where secular considerations are not decisive, and particularly if they leave conscientious citizens in disagreement even after extensive discussion.[25] For surely some principle of resolution is required

25. This objection is suggested by Greenawalt, *Religious Convictions and Political
Choice*. He plausibly argues that "legislation must be justified in terms of secular objectives, but when people reasonably think that shared premises of justice and criteria for
determining truth cannot determine critical questions of fact, fundamental questions of
value, or the weighing of competing benefits and harms, they do appropriately rely on religious convictions that help them answer these questions" (p. 12). He takes the abortion
issue to be a case in point (chap. 7). Much of what he says is consistent with my views;
but most of the time he does not distinguish degrees of influence of religious considerations, and even apart from that he allows them considerably more influence than my view

here, and there is no more warrant to make it wholly secular than to
allow religious considerations to determine the balance: reason has done
its work and need not be pressed into deciding how we are to go beyond
it. This view is initially plausible, but it overlooks a *second-order principle of liberty* implicit in a full commitment to a free and democratic society: where extensive, conscientious use of secular reasoning cannot
decide whether a kind of conduct is morally permissible, that conduct
should not be prohibited by law. This principle would provide no reason
not to use religious considerations to oppose such conduct by the force
of one's example and in arguments aimed at producing voluntary compliance with one's ideals; but to allow those considerations to tip the balance in determining restrictive legislation would give them a role not
appropriate under a proper separation of church and state. It also might
encourage an unwarrantedly strong tendency to judge public policy issues to be irresoluble on secular grounds; for those who take religious
reasons as an appropriate basis for settling such issues may well be prone
to conclude prematurely that secular considerations cannot yield a solution. Whatever our personal beliefs may be, when it comes to imposing
legal sanctions, conduct, like persons, should be presumed innocent.
This seems particularly so where there is no decisive secular objection
to it; and such a presumption protects religious freedom at least as much
as it restricts the role of religious reasons.

One might also object that the proposed principles would preclude religious elements from coloring the life and institutions of a society in a
way perfectly appropriate to a free and democratic nation in which religion is a major cultural force. Why should our cultural existence be a
pale still life, instead of a multicolored *tableau vivant* that displays the
people's character—their religious views as well as their moral and aesthetic preferences? This objection is poignant, but misplaced. If one's
religion commands loving one's neighbors, nothing said here would prevent one's so conducting oneself and indeed publicly proclaiming one's
motivating faith. One can live one's faith—acting, arguing, and even
preaching it—even while constraining one's efforts in supporting restrictive laws and policies, or indeed other sorts of legislation or social programs, in accord with the principle of secular motivation. The same

would countenance. I discuss his position in detail in "Religion and the Ethics of Political
Participation," *Ethics*, in press.

295   *The Separation*
                          of Church and State

holds for religiously motivated ideals of conduct that stress justice, reverence, prophecy, or any other peaceful behavior and attitudes.

Religious expression, like individual diversity, is protected by the framework I have laid out. Nor need the framework prevent a society from being, by virtue of the voluntary conduct of enough people, in a significant sense Christian or Jewish or Moslem or Buddhist. It is only in certain ways, however, that this can be warranted in a free and democratic society. The institutional principles of separation of church and state are essential here, but not sufficient. The principle of secular motivation is needed to ensure *both* that religious liberty will be protected and that the nonreligious will not feel alienated or be denied adequate respect. To count on the institutional principles alone to secure separation of church and state, and to consider oneself otherwise free to act wholly for religious reasons, is a special case of the tendency to leave to government too much of the work of the world.

There is something more to be said about the relation between religious commitment and the principles of conscience I have proposed. Even if one believes that the truth of moral principles depends on God, one need not doubt that there should be adequate and generally convincing secular reasons for holding them. Indeed, it is difficult to understand how an omnibenevolent God could allow that the only possible way for a rational agent to discern correct moral principles is through scripture or revelation; and many of the greatest religious thinkers have not held or implied that it is impossible. If, on the basis of my religious experience or my interpretation of scriptures, I hold a moral view for which I *have* no adequate and convincing secular justification, then I should reconsider my interpretation, or the authenticity of my experience. Religiously grounded moral and political views that have no adequate and convincing basis in secular considerations are suspect. This claim should not offend the religious; it is quite consistent with the counterpart view that moral and political views with no adequate and convincing basis in some appropriate range of religious considerations are suspect. If, however, a moral or political view *is* grounded in God's will, God's goodness may plausibly be taken to imply that some secular basis is accessible to rational inquiry. On the other hand, if such a view does not depend on God's will, it is even more plain that it should be accepted only if an adequate, convincing secular basis is found.

It is to be hoped, of course, that a desirable separation of church and state can be maintained without civil strife or frequent litigation. In this effort, the religious who want to pass laws linking religion and government have the primary responsibility; but the nonreligious also have obligations to help in reducing conflict, and one step toward this end is to avoid gratuitous or captious complaints. Prayer in the public schools is clearly a major and perhaps unavoidable issue; but the inscription 'In God we trust' on money is arguably of more historical than religious significance, and it often goes unnoticed. A challenge of it under separation of church and state, while theoretically plausible, might produce rulings or reactions detrimental to the overall cause of liberty. Debate and, especially, litigation can harden or even exaggerate positions which, in an atmosphere of pluralistic good will, need never clash. There is no substitute for good judgment in the application of social-political principles, and wisdom may dictate waiving their application in some cases or at some time.[26] But a free society must still constantly respect, and, in some cases, legally guarantee, principles of separation of church and state. We are prone to extremes in the service of our holy causes. Conflicting secular ideas, even when firmly held, can often be blended and harmonized in the crucible of free discussion; but a clash of gods is like a meeting of an irresistible force with an immovable object.[27] The separation of church and state, both as a body of principles addressed chiefly to the state and as a set of principles of individual conscience, should be steadfastly preserved.

26. The point applies not only to challenging governmental practices, but to challenging individual ones as well. The case of S. Simcha Goldman, a nonpracticing rabbi in the Air Force, seems to illustrate this. Until he had to testify in court, no one challenged his wearing his yarmulke indoors. While it is not clear that the Supreme Court erred in deciding (five to four) in favor of the regulation (in *Goldman* v. *Weinberg*, 106 U.S. 1310, 1986), in this case it is doubtful that the religious practice should ever have been questioned. For discussion, see Ackerman, "Church and State in the Supreme Court," and former Supreme Court Justice Arthur Goldberg's article on the First Amendment in the *Christian Science Monitor*, 12 May 1986.

27. Strictly speaking, an irresistible force and an immovable object are incompossible: they cannot simultaneously exist. But that may just enhance the aptness of the simile, since, for the same kind of reason, the existence of one omnipotent being apparently precludes that of another, and this may in part explain why those confident that they worship the true God, conceived as omnipotent—or that they have the best access to interpreting God—tend also to be confident that proponents of different interpretations of God's will are in error, and that worshipers of another god are at best misplacing their devotion.

[3]

PRIVILEGE, POSTURE AND PROTECTION "RELIGION" IN THE LAW

JONATHAN WEISS†

"It was a . . . part of the said scheme and artifice to defraud that the defendants . . . did create, organize and operate a . . . movement known as the 'I Am' movement and by means of false and fraudulent representations, pretenses and promises hereinafter more particularly set forth, solicit, induce, encourage, persuade and entice the persons to be defrauded to become members and followers of the said 'I Am' movement."[1] To this indictment, the defendants, the leaders of the movement, demurred, saying that the indictment and prosecution sought "to attack the establishment of said religion or religious beliefs, or to prohibit or restrict the free exercise thereof, contrary to the Constitution of the United States and the law of the land."[2] The issue thus was joined in *United States v. Ballard*,[3] a case of conflict between religious expression and criminal law. The problems, issues and theories raised by the two conflicting positions—the one regarding the movement as a scheme to defraud; the other, as a religion protected from prosecution—will be the starting point for this article's exploration of the meaning and implications of a legal conception of privacy in the realm of religious expression. From this basis we will seek to arrive at tools for adjudication and analysis in all cases where religious rights are claimed by one of the parties.

The "I Am" movement embraced many doctrines. The Ballards professed to be divine messengers. Some of the leaders claimed to have met Saint Germain and Jesus Christ. In particular, they claimed to have attained a supernatural state of "self-immortality" which enabled them to heal persons of injuries and diseases, including some that were classified by medicine as incurable. Members were told to abstain from meat and stimulants, and to study books published and sold by the Ballards.[4] The Ballards kept their organization functioning by using the mails: members wrote letters to each other, sent and received records, books, magazines and contributions through the post office. All the judges dealing with the litigation assumed that "I Am" was a religion. We will not make that assumption, but instead will analyze the

†Legal Staff of U.S. Department of Labor. I owe an infinite debt of gratitude to Professor Joseph Goldstein, who has been a continuing source of guidance and inspiration.

1. Indictment, Count 1(a), set forth in Record, vol. 1, pp. 4-5, United States v. Ballard, 322 U.S. 78 (1944) [hereinafter called Record].

2. Demurrer to Indictment, Paragraph II, Record; *id.* at 64.

3. 138 F.2d 540 (9th Cir. 1943), *rev'd*, 322 U.S. 78 (1944), *on remand*, 152 F.2d 941 (9th Cir. 1946), *rev'd*, 329 U.S. 187 (1946). *Cf.* 35 F. Supp. 105 (S.D. Cal. 1940).

4. All these facts were asserted in the Indictment, Record, *supra* note 1, at 8-20; see also *id.*, vol. 2, pp. 814-21, vol. 3, pp. 123-65, 953-1178. At the trial, the meaning of some of the claims was disputed. An appendix to Respondent's Brief in the Supreme Court reproduces the text of a 1937 radio broadcast revealing some of the group's claims.

definitional problem in such a way that we can determine precisely how and when religion enters the case.

Federal law makes it criminal to obtain money through the mails by false pretenses.[5] It was this statute which the Ballards were charged with violating. The elements of the crime—the fraudulent scheme, an intent to defraud, and a use of the mails [6]—seem to have been interpreted broadly. It has been held that the fraudulent scheme must dominantly characterize some part of the business.[7] Although the victims need not have suffered pecuniary loss,[8] fraud must be predicated on more than disagreement of some with the accused. As for intent, Learned Hand dealt with the matter as follows: "It was only necessary in the case at bar that the defendants had no belief that they would perform the promises held out to prospective members."[9] He concluded that the jury could reasonably infer intent from the nature of the promises and the difficulty of fulfilling them. Finally, the statute is violated if the mail is in fact used, even if the use be incidental and unpremeditated.[10] Only the third element is indisputably present in *Ballard*.

Prior to *Ballard*, *Crane v. United States* [11] showed how easy it is to intertwine the two elements of misrepresentation and intent in a "religious" prosecution. The *Crane* court upheld a conviction of a man who advocated "mental healing" and wrote tracts in which he said, "I am God." The issue tendered was whether he had made his representations in "good faith."[12] Such a view-

5. 18 U.S.C. § 1341 (1958).

6. Stunz v. United States, 27 F.2d 575 (8th Cir. 1928), stated the three necessary elements. See West v. United States, 68 F.2d 96 (10th Cir. 1933) (knowledge that representations are false); United States v. Zalewski, 29 F. Supp. 755 (W.D. Kan. 1939) (intent). Throughout the analysis of the Ballard case, it is assumed that there must be a specific misrepresentation included in the fraudulent scheme. This assumption could be questioned by reference to considerable authority such as Linden v. United States, 254 F.2d 500 (1958), which holds that a specific misstatement is not necessary. But it would seem that a particular item of deceit is a necessary element of fraud, for otherwise there is no falsity but merely, for example, betrayal of confidence. Whether betrayal of confidence is a basis for fraud, absent a representation of trustworthiness, is ambiguous in the cases. See Parr v. United States, 363 U.S. 370 (1959). In any event, it would seem hard to predicate fraud for religion as a whole under the Constitution, so we are driven to find specific misrepresentations, and in this case the indictment alleges them. If a particular item of deceit is not a requisite element, some of the conceptual analysis would lose its neatness but not its logic; the subsidiary attacks on fusing of the requisite elements would lose some of their justice with respect to the deceitful defendant's position. See *infra* note 17.

7. McLendon v. United States, 2 F.2d 660 (6th Cir. 1924); Graham v. United States, 102 F.2d 436 (2d Cir.), *cert. denied*, 307 U.S. 643 (1939).

8. Wine v. United States, 260 Fed. 911 (8th Cir. 1919).

9. Knickerbocker Merchandising Co. v. United States, 13 F.2d 544, 546 (2d Cir. 1926). *But see* Norton v. United States, 92 F.2d 753 (9th Cir. 1937).

10. Henderson v. United States, 202 F.2d 400, 405 (6th Cir. 1953).

11. 259 Fed. 480 (9th Cir. 1919). A similar result was reached in New v. United States, 245 Fed. 710 (9th Cir. 1917), which upheld the conviction of Bishop New since he was not "the immaculate personage he pretended to be." *Id.* at 721.

12. 259 Fed. at 482.

point intertwines misrepresentation and intent because it makes a finding of misrepresentation rest on an analysis of intent. We may suggest that this fastening on "good faith" is a consequence of the absence, in this area of the law, of common criteria for evaluating the truth or falsity of representations.[13]

The government's theory in *Ballard* as to which particular representations were false was not constant throughout the litigation, but the veracity of the claims concerning healing and other powers (*e.g.*, immortality and ascension), the honesty of belief of the leaders in their representations and religion, and the truth of the religion as a whole, were each questioned at various times. The case suggests the following issues. (1) What is the domain of religion and how do we proceed to define and apply it to legal problems? (2) What comprises a fraudulent representation? (3) What comprises a religious expression? (4) What is religious expression in its different manifestations: belief, ritual, action? How do we classify claims labeled as religion in domains where other authorities traditionally hold sway? In *Ballard*, for example, certain claims conflict with medical theory. (5) Is there a distinction between religious belief and action?

These five issues can be approached from two directions. First, *Ballard* presents the problem of fraud in religious representation. An understanding of the concepts "representation," "religion" or "fraud" may solve this case. The inquiry into representations and religion can focus on the first element of the crime of mail fraud—what constituted a fraudulent scheme? Second, there is the problem of at what point the first amendment enters discussion of a situation which may affect freedom of religion, and what it commands. Our inquiry will seek to understand how religion is related to representations, with an eye to when the first amendment should be invoked. We will have to confront the problem of whether a representation can be religious, whether it can be fraudulent, or whether it can be both. The gravamen of this search will be the effect of the claim of religious characteristic on the application of the mail fraud statute. In the search we will attempt to define for ourselves the nature of religion for the purpose of the law and the first amendment and try to decide its applicability as a defense to the application of this statute.

The *Ballard* defendants fought their way up to the Supreme Court. During the course of the litigation, the judges involved produced five responses to the apparent clash between the statute and the defense based on the first amendment. The first of these was articulated in the trial judge's charge to the jury, which formed one of the bases for appeal. A statement in conference, which formed the substance of the disputed charge, is as follows:

> . . . Some of the teachings of the defendants, representations, might seem extremely improbable to a great many people. . . . As far as this court sees the issue, it is immaterial what these defendants preached or wrote or taught in their classes. They [the jury] are not going to be permitted to speculate on the actuality of the happening of those incidents. . . . The issue is: Did these defendants honestly and in good faith believe these

13. Compare Dolan v. Hurley, 283 Fed. 695 (D. Mass. 1922) on the permissibility of selling lucky stones.

596   *THE YALE LAW JOURNAL*   [Vol. 73:593]

> things? If they did, they should be acquitted. . . . If these defendants did not believe these things, [if] they did not believe Jesus came down and dictated, or that Saint Germain came down and dictated, and did not believe the things that they wrote, the things that they preached, but used the mails for the purpose of getting money, the jury should find them guilty.[14]

This view of the problem, which can be labeled the *deceitful defendant* position, identifies as a jury issue the question whether the defendants lied about their beliefs in order to obtain money. The nature of religion is an irrelevant consideration, since the court conceives of the statute as punishing those who use the mails for personal deceitful aggrandizement. Once the mails have been used, the inquiry for fraud requires an examination, not of the representations of the religion itself, but of the degree of belief the leaders have in them, even in the absence of explicit criteria for a determination of amount of belief.

Speaking for a majority of the Ninth Circuit on appeal from conviction, Judge Mathews offered a second judicial response.

> The issues were (1) whether defendants and Guy W. Ballard devised the scheme described . . . ; (2) whether, for the purpose of executing the scheme, they used the mails . . . ; (3) whether they conspired to commit any of the offenses charged . . . ; (4) whether . . . any party . . . committed any . . . overt acts.[15]

Because the question "whether such representations were false or true" was not submitted to the jury, the Ninth Circuit granted a new trial.[16]

Such a view of the problem, which may be called the *factual fraud* position, seems to look to the effects that the judges feel the statute was designed to prevent. Unlike the *deceitful defendant* approach the *factual fraud* position does not examine motive but rather requires an inquiry into the truth or falsity of the representations claimed to be religious. It explicitly rejects the fusing of misrepresentation and intent, and considers the manner of reaching a finding of fraud in this area indistinguishable from the inquiry to be made about any other deceitful commercial scheme.

These judicial positions present two sets of analytic difficulties: The first is the conjunction of religion and truth. What type of representations are capable of being fraudulent? What do we look for in finding fraud? When a belief is offered as "religious," what is being represented? Or, is there no such thing as a "religious" statement for the purposes of the law? Granted that there are statements which may be classified as religious statements, can they be deceitful? The second set questions the factual basis for a finding of fraud. What type of claims and representations are factual in such a manner that they are for the jury? If the evaluation of a religion is involved, is this not a matter involving the First Amendment? In the realm of beliefs not

---

14. Record, *supra* note 1, at vol. 1, pp. 402-03, vol. 3, pp. 1475-76, 1545.

15. Ballard v. United States, 138 F.2d 540, 545 (9th Cir. 1943).

16. *Ibid.*

claimed to be supported by science or other "objective" disciplines, what is the nature of misrepresentation?[17]

Judge Denman, in denying a motion for rehearing, seemed to try to bridge the gap between the *deceitful defendant* and *factual fraud* positions.

> It would be strong evidence in support of this issue of mental condition of belief, that these transactions with Jesus actually occurred in their presence. The right to produce such evidence was denied appellants [by the ruling that] . . . they [the jury] are not going to be permitted to speculate on the actuality of the happenings of these incidents. . . . Here we have not only the exclusion of proof and instruction to disregard facts which would strongly tend to support an honest belief that they happened, but a suggestion of their improbability. The error is as prejudicial to the issue of honest belief as to the issue of purposeful misrepresentation.[18]

In brief, Denman suggested that the examination of the accuracy of the representations could have been utilized not only for completing the first element of the crime, the misrepresentation of fact, but also the second element of the crime, the intent to defraud. Such an analysis suggests that the improbability of truth should have an effect upon a decision as to the honesty of belief.[19] Judge Denman argues that exclusion of factual examination of the religious representations is prejudicial rather than lenient, and that rather than shifting a burden of proof, it offers them an opportunity guaranteed as a right. In Judge Denman's view, then, to deny that religion can be an objective part of every day life is to deny freedom of religion. The implication of his opinion is that religious beliefs are susceptible to ordinary discriminations, so that a factual examination can lead to a finding of fraud in matters of religion. But such a view may dictate a particular meaning for "religion," and seems to rest on the assumption that there are ways of clearly showing that a belief is not religious, or that if it is religious, it is "false."

At the Supreme Court, where the decision was reversed and remanded to the Ninth Circuit for reconsideration, three more responses emerged. Mr. Justice Douglas, writing for the majority, focused on the first amendment and solved the case on narrow grounds, fashioning a view that might be called *religious reservation*.[20] Mr. Chief Justice Stone, joined by Justices Roberts

---

17. In a different approach, Judge Stephens dissented from the Ninth Circuit's decision, merely saying that he was "not convinced that the judge's comments and instructions upon the decisive point of the majority opinion were not more favorable to the defendants than the law required." 138 F.2d at 545. He thus suggested that such an instruction could avoid issues of religious freedom while presenting enough support for a conviction. His reasoning must have been that the defendants weren't put to the proof or defense of their representations—just their honesty. But to say that the question of what is believed can be separated from the question of what is believable seems to carry three implications. (1) That it is impossible to believe that what one is saying is false, and still to tell the truth. (2) That, in fact, the jury could conclude that the defendants were lying both in intention and reality. (3) That, in this case, the idea that the Ballards could believe what they were claiming was a generous notion.

18. *Id.* at 546.

19. See dissenting opinion by Jackson, J., in *Ballard*, 322 U.S. 78, 92-93 (1944).

20. 322 U.S. 78 (1944).

and Frankfurter in dissent,[21] combined elements of the deceitful defendant and factual fraud positions into what might be called the *clearly culpable* theory. Mr. Justice Jackson, in a separate dissent,[22] took a *hands-off* approach.[23]

The Chief Justice stated his basic position in the first sentence of his dissent. "I am not prepared to say the constitutional guaranty of freedom of religion affords immunity from criminal prosecution for the fraudulent procurement of money by false statement as to one's religious experience, more than it renders polygamy or libel immune from criminal prosecutions."[24] He gave as an example a statement about Ballard meeting Saint Germain at a particular place and time when it could be clearly proved that Ballard was elsewhere. This is a kind of *factual fraud*. But he also said that "certainly none of respondents' constitutional rights are violated if they are prosecuted for the fraudulent procurement of money by false representations as to their beliefs, religious or otherwise."[25] This argument recasts the prosecution, by conceiving of the fraud as depending upon whether the defendants actually believed their own representations. If the jury finds that the defendants did not believe their representations to be true, then they have misrepresented a fact. Their intent becomes a representation.

The *clearly culpable* position thus holds that if it is clear to the jury beyond a reasonable doubt that an item is false as represented, be it belief or what is believed, then the jury has a sufficient factual basis on which to find fraud. Such a theory implies that representations can be divorced from their religious context and that such separated representations can be objectively judged by a jury. That theory perhaps rests primarily on a concern for those who join the religion in the hope of receiving the benefits which have been represented as flowing from it. Given misrepresentations that enticed these people to join, the Chief Justice found that religion did not comprise a defense to the presentation of evidence any more than it would for bigamy. He saw religion as in no way altering an investigation for fraudulent representation.

---

21. *Id.* at 88. Interestingly enough, Chief Justice Stone's position was followed by the *majority* on remand from the Supreme Court in the decision below. 152 F.2d 941 (9th Cir. 1945). Further, a Lawyer's Edition annotation cites *Ballard* for what appears to be his view. 96 L. Ed. 968, 974 (1952). The opinion of the lower court on remand was later reversed on totally different grounds, the exclusion of women from the jury. 329 U.S. 187 (1946). See also 35 F. Supp. 105 (S.D. Cal. 1940).

22. 322 U.S. at 92.

23. In about the only comment on these responses, Justice Brennan stated, "The dilemma presented by the case was severe . . . [vis-a-vis] close adherence to the neutrality principle." School District v. Schempp, 374 U.S. 203, 245 (1963). But, accompanying this comment on the case are two mistaken descriptions as to the requested instructions and affirmance of conviction. Thus, his characterization should not be read as exhaustive of the issues and factors in the litigation. See his comment in Braunfeld v. Brown, 366 U.S. 599, 615 (1961).

24. 322 U.S. at 88-89.

25. *Id.* at 90.

Mr. Justice Douglas took another tack. He was concerned with the demands of the first amendment, and did not consider whether the fact that challenged representations occurred in the context of a claimed religious movement would affect an examination for fraud. With Justices Black, Reed, Murphy, and Rutledge, the liberal wing of the court, he held that the first amendment commanded exclusion of evidence as to the truth or falsity of the Ballards' religious credos.

> Heresy trials are foreign to our Constitution. Man may believe what they cannot prove. . . . Religious experiences which are as real as life to some may be incomprehensible to others. . . . So we conclude that the District Court ruled properly when it withheld from the jury all questions concerning the truth or falsity of the religious beliefs or doctrines of the respondents.[26]

For Mr. Justice Douglas, the first amendment compels *religious reservation*—any examination of a religion's "truth" for whatever purposes is forbidden by the Constitution.

But although he repudiated the circuit court's *factual fraud* approach, Mr. Justice Douglas did not reach the trial court's *deceitful defendant* view.[27] Offering no criteria for determining either what is "religious" or what comprises an actual "submission" to the jury, he rejected explicitly the proposition that religious propositions are susceptible to normal factual examination. Such a rejection makes a curious contrast with the position taken by the Chief Justice. Whereas the Chief Justice said that religion *should* not serve to shield a defendant from a conviction for a criminal offense, Mr. Justice Douglas said that religion can not so serve, because the Constitution forbids analysis of the issues by a jury. Thus, while the Chief Justice regards religion merely as a factor to consider in a scheme of representations, Mr. Justice Douglas would exclude it from the trial altogether. Whereas Mr. Justice Douglas does not consider whether leaders' beliefs are part of the religion, the Chief Justice considers them only as representations connected with a fraud.

The motif of Mr. Justice Jackson's *hands-off* attack can be found in his last sentence: "I would dismiss the indictment and have done with this business of judicially examining other people's faith."[28] His epigrammatic attacks can be used as a basis for rejecting the alternative positions and for beginning the elaboration of an answer to the issues posed by *Ballard* and suggested in general by the first amendment's religious commands. Mr. Justice Jackson viewed the problem from the vantage of the movement itself. He argued implicitly against the separation of particular representations from the religion as a whole, and explicitly against the view that religion did not cut across the grain of all the legal issues in the case. His main attack was levelled at the *deceitful defendant* position. First, he pointed out the difficulty of establishing the amount of sincerity in a religious belief. "I do not know what degree of

26. *Id.* at 86-88.
27. *Id.* at 88.
28. 322 U.S. at 95.

skepticism or disbelief in a religious representation amounts to actionable fraud. . . . When does less than full belief in a professed credo become actionable fraud"?[29] Second, Mr. Justice Jackson pointed out that "any inquiry into intellectual honesty in religion raises profound psychological problems . . . [Religion's] vitality is in the religious experiences of many people."[30] Third, he emphasized that really religious people may not be sincere in the normal use of the word. "Even the most regular of them (unconventional religious teachers) are sometimes accused of taking their orthodoxy with a grain of salt."[31]

Historically, many have not considered belief necessary either to the honesty of a position taken or its truth. Freud, on one occasion, confessed that he lacked certainty concerning the truth of what he affirmed, stating only that his methodology dictated the answers he gave. In Poland, a "Messiah" recanted under Catholic pressure, and some of his followers still kept faith. The "dark night of the soul" is well known to many who are commonly accepted as religious. Further, the *deceitful defendant* position mistakes what religion is and the claim it makes on people. Religion is a body of beliefs and affirmations rather than a description of a leader or his opinions. To ask a man to believe your religion does not mean that you ask him to believe you or to believe that you believe, but to assent to propositions represented as being that religion. The quality of the leader's beliefs and motives are not a necessary part of a religious system, except perhaps as an example or inspiration.

It is possible to talk of a *deceitful defendant* in a way which minimizes inquiry into degree of belief or sincerity, as ordinarily understood. One may contrast Freud, the Polish messiah, and the agnostic or even atheistic priest —each of whom seems to be caught up in the existential involvements of religion or truth-seeking—to a venal businessman, whose only apparent concern is making money, not religious truth. The latter creates a system which will earn him the largest amount of income, and is neither involved in an evaluation of the truth or falsity of religious experience nor concerned with offering his religion for people to evaluate its truth. We could not ask about his "degree of belief" because, for him, such a question is irrelevant. Would his prosecution transgress the values which support Jackson's refutation of the *deceitful defendant* position?

To find fraud when a leader states "I believe," it is necessary to show two things: first, that the "I believe" is one of the foundations of the religion on which the people are asked to base their assent; second, that a non-religious standard by which the leader invites proof of his belief demonstrates his disbelief when applied to him. Only infrequently is the belief of the leaders offered as a basis for popular assent. Moreover, the first amendment precludes us from establishing religious standards to evaluate religions or the degree of belief involved. So, even in the extreme case in which evidence is presented

---

29. *Id.* at 93, 95.

30. *Id.* at 93.

31. *Id.* at 95. See also *id.* at 94.

as to the leader's disclaimed or disengaged belief, in the absence of a showing
that the leader represented his belief as verifiable by some non-religious perspective, and that that perspective proves his non-belief, we cannot convict
him for fraud.[32]

The *factual fraud* position is refuted summarily in Mr. Justice Jackson's
opinion.

> Belief in what one may demonstrate to the senses is not faith. All
> schools of religious thought make enormous assumptions, generally on
> the basis of revelations. . . . The appeal in such matters is to a very dif-
> ferent plane of credulity than is invoked by representations of a secular
> fact in commerce.[33]

In short, religious representations are not like other representations and fraud
cannot be predicated on them.

From the *factual fraud* refutation comes the destruction of the *clearly
culpable* position. Since, in fact, religious representations are not like others
it is not at all clear that preachers such as the Ballards can defraud their
followers in the ordinary sense of that term or that there can be a particular
item of deceit to locate. Mr. Justice Jackson rejected looking at those who
joined the religion as people who entered searching for particular benefits
which were misrepresented. "If the members of the sect get comfort from the
celestial guidance of their 'Saint Germain' . . . it is hard to say that they do
not get what they pay for. . . . The chief wrong which false prophets do to
their following is not financial."[34] The Ballards offered a system or at least
an accumulation of beliefs. As a religion, its "selling point" was its effect
taken as a whole. Isolating individual items is a method which ignores the
nature of religious participation. The dissection or examination of a religion
to discover what advantages were claimed is precisely what the Constitution
forbids.[35]

Finally, standing alone, the *religious reservation* position enunciated by Mr.
Justice Douglas falls as well. The religious issue permeates the whole prosecution. To follow the first amendment's command forbidding an examination of religion only by proscribing a jury charge relating to religion does
not meet the problem.

> In the first place, as a matter of either practice or philosophy I do not
> see how we can separate an issue as to what is believed from considera-
> tions as to what is believable. The most convincing proof that one be-
> lieves his statements is to show that they have been true in his experience.
> Likewise, that one knowingly falsified is best proved by showing that
> what he said happened never did happen. . . . If we try religious sincerity

---

32. Mr. Justice Jackson in this connection raised many problems. First, he pointed
out that an examination of sincerity raises serious difficulties in psychological fact finding. Second, he suggested that leader's belief in a religion is rarely a tenet of the religion.
Finally, he stated that any examination of sincerity necessarily requires an examination
of the religion itself.

33. 322 U.S. at 94.

34. *Ibid.*

35. *Id.* at 95.

severed from religious verity, we isolate the dispute from the very considerations which in common experience provide its most reliable answer.[36]

This position suggests that keeping the issue of the truth of the doctrine from the jury is prejudicial on the issue of the sincerity of belief. Reservation of the matter will not work since the heresy trial continues, Mr. Justice Jackson implies, if we question their sincerity. Since religion cannot help but be involved in an examination of sincerity of belief, the Douglas position cannot save the prosecution from first amendment objections.

Mr. Justice Jackson's positive position can be inferred from his attacks. He recognizes and deals with the problem that poor people appear to have been bilked by the Ballards' activity.

> I doubt if the vigilance of the law is equal to making money stick by over-credulous people. . . .
> The wrong of these things, as I see it, is not in the money the victims part with half so much as in the mental and spiritual poison they get. But that is precisely the thing the Constitution put beyond the reach of the prosecutor.[37]

This argument suggests that religion is a domain wholly separate from others, in which traditional standards of fraud do not apply. "Belief in what one may demonstrate to the sense is not faith."[38] Transactions which involve money for religious beliefs—matters of faith—are not in any way reducible to normal transactions, and so the whole inquiry into that realm must be excluded.

The trouble with this inferred position is that it provides no standards for defining faith or religion, and does not focus sharply enough on the issue of what constitute religious and/or fraudulent representations. The fraud originally alleged in the case concerned various representations; the representations, not necessarily the religion as a whole, may have induced people to part with their money. Stone maintained that those representations can be treated separately from the religion. The prosecutor based his argument, in part, on the view that the religion was a cloak for specific misrepresentations dealing with medicine, politics, and certain catastrophic happenings, as well as a tissue of implausible stories about Christian figures. Is it possible to separate these representations? Can a representation be both religious and fraudulent?

More generally, what is "religious"? Can a man legally sell drugs, claiming on the front of the label that they cure cancer, and on the back that God told him this? Can religion be used as a defense to a substantive crime? A man may defend by saying that God told him to murder, but is it sufficient if he

---

36. *Id.* at 92-93. As an example of this point, the actual trial is ideal. In proving the lack of sincerity, the prosecutor compared the "ascended masters" of the movement to Charlie McCarthy, the puppet, Superman and Flash Gordon, while suggesting that their method of ascension was stolen by Donald Ballard from Popular Mechanics. Record, *supra* note 1, at 1211, 1237, 1503.

37. *Id.* at 94, 95.

38. *Id.* at 94.

announces the basis for his action only after the act?[39] Was the Catholic Church not pronouncing religious dogma when it told Galileo to recant? Aren't things demonstrated to the senses often a matter of faith? How do I discover the motives of a man buying? If I buy rotten meat on a type of faith in the advertisement am I still not gypped? Could a butcher defend the sale if he could prove that I thought God ordered me to buy the particular rotten piece of meat, so I got what I wanted? Suppose I solicit funds and ask you to join my religion saying I will meet St. Jerome or the books I sell you tell about St. Jerome and when I am supposed to meet him I am elsewhere or the book has nothing but blank pages? These questions exemplify the difficulty in separating demonstrations to the senses from appeals to faith, in using motives of buyer or seller as relevant to fraud, and in denying that some followers do rely on the existence of concrete benefits from the religion, and believe that concrete events claimed by the religious leaders to have occurred did occur.

The beginning of an answer to the conflict between constitutional mandate and statutory proscription lies in the realization that propositions bring with them implicit presuppositions. Concepts arrive in contexts. To describe or discuss anything implies some type of meeting ground, some commonality of experience and vocabulary. Religious belief provides one such experience and vocabulary; science, another; philosophy, yet another and so on. Intellectual disciplines provide a perspective and system from which we derive the meaning of particular entities. A particular object, or even a particular idea has a different nature depending on the context or the perspective of the discipline or disciplines from which we approach it. A cup of wine may be religious or profane depending on what one does in relation to it.

Given this understanding, we can describe a fraudulent representation. For our immediate purposes, such a misrepresentation may occur in two ways: (a) I can misrepresent the results that a given discipline achieves. I can say that water tests out chemically as H_2SO_4 in my laboratory. (b) I can misrepresent what discipline or world perspective I work in. As a layman I can say, "Speaking medically, I will cure you of cancer." Thus fraud may be perpetrated either by misrepresenting what perspective is brought to a problem, or what results obtain therein.

Religion is one type of perspective. Religious expression involves assent to propositions that define the world we live in. A cross, a cup of wine, a candle, a baby's cry, sex,—all have different meanings in different religions for different people. To recognize the plurality of faiths is to recognize the plurality of possible descriptions of these things. What may be a scientific

---

39. The recent case approving a judicial act which forced a transfusion on a Jehovah's Witness is worth considering here. Application of the President and Directors of Georgetown College Inc., A Body Corporate, ——— F.2d ——— (D.C. Cir., Feb. 3, 1963) (Misc. No. 2189). Though solved on different grounds, this case seemingly pitted a person's own notion of his meaning in life and what death was to him against the state's interest in his life. The opinion explicitly acknowledges that religious people have no license to commit suicide when non-religious people have no such right.

aberration to some is a miracle to others. Bad history may be divine scriptures.

Yet to define the limits of religious expression may be impossible if philosophically desirable. Moreover, any definition of religion would seem to violate religious freedom in that it would dictate to religions, present and future, what they must be: inability to give an authoritative definition is justified by the conjunction of the first amendment's two religious clauses. Read together, they define religious freedom but do not establish religion as a defined domain. That is, religious freedom is served by allowing a completely open realm for defining religion rather than by establishing a domain or definition in which religions can freely operate. Furthermore, an attempt to define religion, even for purposes of increasing freedom for religions, would run afoul of the "establishment" clause, as excluding some religions, or even as establishing a notion respecting religion. How then can we handle the problem of claims labeled "religious" in domains where other authorities are generally accepted, where people do not normally assent to perceive an experience in a religious way?

Since we are prevented from prescribing what claims are "religious" by delimiting the bounds of religion, we can only say that those claims are "religious" that are clearly so, either by virtue of their characteristics or explicit labels that lead to recognition of them as such. Since religion is traditionally an area of faith and assent, we may say that a religious claim is one which asks for adherence on the grounds of religious truth, or one which is defined or spoken by its author as religious. Because religion can be in conflict with other disciplines, because it cuts across everyday life, we can only know that a claim is based on religion when we are told that it is. The legal basis for stating that a claim is in the religious domain can be that it is held out as being religious in nature. Such a conception enables us to avoid judicial prescription of the range of religion as well as jury decisions on the question of whether a claim is an issue of "fact" or of "religious belief."

If we combine our notion of fraudulent representations with our conception of religious expression within a legal system predicated upon toleration of all forms of that expression, we obtain the result that there can be no fraud in matters of religious belief. For we grant men the right to choose their religious perspective—a perspective which tells them what the nature of things is. Further, this perspective provides its own standard of application—to say that some water is "holy" is to say that using the standards of that religion the water is "holy." Since all standards are possible, no description using such a standard can be fraudulent. These conclusions follow from two guidelines: first, religion comes to a believer from the act of commitment by faith, a type of assumption and assent, not a persuasion by a series of demonstrations to reason; second, religion defines for itself the meaning of the commonplace. Its definitions are not representations but rather an integral part of the perceived reality of experience generated by the perspective that religion brings with it. Just as water is molecules for a physicist, so is trembling wine, a cup for Elijah.

Of course not every claim *touching upon* religion would be protected. A man can misrepresent his authoritative basis—he can fail to make it clear that his claim is based on "religion." If a man simply sells bad drugs and defends on religious grounds, we can find his defense insufficient. For we say : first, you failed to define your claims as religious and they were claims of a nature that would not ordinarily be understood as religious; second, holding yourself out as a drug salesman implied that you spoke with medical authority. To defend now that the drugs you sold were good on religious grounds requires that you must have affirmatively and clearly shown to people at the time of sale that the value of the drugs was rooted in a religious system which they had to affirm in order to perceive that value. If a man pretends to speak with authority he does not have, or acts in such a way as to imply that he speaks with that authority, he is guilty of misrepresentation and fraud. When a man acts publicly in a domain where the normal expectations are of secular contentions, he must make it clear that his claims are made as elements of a faith which describes the nature of things about which he is making the claims. Since the Constitution prohibits defining an area of belief as "religious," a man must make it clear that the beliefs he represents are "religious" if he wants to be free to express them under the constitutional warrant of freedom of religious belief. He has the burden of communicating that he speaks only from the authority of religion. But, once such a burden has been met, then we cannot attack the particular aspects of his faith as fraudulent. We examine the representation in terms of its authoritative referent and predicate fraud accordingly.

What a man presents as a religious claim, then, cannot be attacked. It is only when he makes a representation beyond religious authority that we can apply laws of fraud. For these purposes we employ only the minimal understanding of religious activity for the law that it involve an assent of faith to dogmas and propositions that offer some orientation as to the nature of things. This minimal understanding of principles of claiming religious protection together with the concepts that ideas imply contexts and that man is legally responsible for what he presents himself to be, enables us to hold Mr. Justice Jackson's *hands-off* position, using Mr. Justice Douglas' argument prohibiting "heresy" trials, while avoiding the realization of Mr. Chief Justice Stone's fear that religion might be used as a cloak for fraud.

We can restate the whole position as follows : A misrepresentation comes about when false characterizations of the objects discussed are made. Characterizations are made as the result of applying a discipline's perspectives or standards to perceived objects. The Constitution removes from condemnation those beliefs that are put forth as religious. If a man clearly presents that which he wishes others to believe or act upon as religious, the Constitution prevents a prosecution for misrepresentation.

For the purposes of this analysis, the representations made by the Ballards can be divided into two major classes. These were those representations which were clearly a part of the religion—the movement being a religion in that it called for an assent of faith to its propositions—without specific labeling as such. Its representations as to supernatural characteristics and effects upon the soul require an assent of faith; they are the sort traditionally said to be in the religious domain. The tenor of the presentation by the Ballards would indicate these are a matter of faith. No proof that these representations were "religious" can be made rigorously—each statement was not preceded by a formal call to faith or a formal labeling of religion. That they called for an assent can be seen by using traditional conceptions of faith or by examining the presentation. To make a common sense decision whether a movement is a religion and a claim clearly religious, we look in general to: (a) whether the movement claims through an asking for assent (a rigorous proof of religion would probably refer to grounds of assent); (b) "supernatural" claims traditionally connected with religion; (c) whether the traditional customary activities and trappings of "religion" are present. These forms of representation may be classed as "religious," even if not explicitly held out as related to faith, because they are early recognizable by the person represented to as associated with such a form of assent.

The second broad class of representations were not clearly part of the religion. This class itself breaks down into two categories: those representations which might be said to have induced people to join the religion by forming a "factual" basis for belief in the religion and those representations that were of a sort usually strongly associated with non-religious perspectives. The first variety included allegations of the type that worried the Chief Justice—for example, that Guy Ballard had met St. Germain on Mt. Shasta. This historical event seems like an item which if true would be a reason to believe in Guy Ballard's connection with the divine and a reason to join his faith. Such a "fact" might be undermined by proof that Guy Ballard was in St. Louis at the time. I might say "Chemists agree that I can transform water into sulphuric acid. I am a miracle worker. Worship me." Such a scientific claim would then be the offered basis for assuming the religious belief. The second sub-class is comprised of propositions that most people in a common sense way, or in a way informed by various disciplines, find factually absurd. Moreover, they are propositions that one normally finds discussed in particular contexts of other disciplines. Throughout the case scoffing remarks were made about the Ballards' preference for blue, about the claim that they prevented a San Francisco earthquake, sunk a submarine, could help heal and other achievements.

Should any of these representations be found fraudulent? The first broad class, which would be understood even without explicit labeling as religious, clearly must be immune from the application of the statute. In the second broad class, the second sub-class of claims gives no trouble, for these were consistently identified with the religious perspective. Granting freedom of religion to include religious beliefs in all realms, beliefs are not susceptible to being called fraud when they are clearly identified as part of a religion, however unusual such an identification. The most "preposterous" remarks are safe precisely because faith is free. But the first sub-class of claims raises difficulties. These representations sound like facts which, if proved true by specified non-religious perspectives, comprise reasons to make a general assent of faith. The examination for fraud of representations founding a creed is an examination whether acceptance of them can be totally predicated on other standards and whether they are so held out. Under the preceding analysis such a representation totally based and justified on a false application of non-religious standards would appear to be fraudulent. If in this first subclass we can show that the statement was held out as a factual, not a religious, foundation for assent and that the asserted factual basis has been intentionally misrepresented, *then* we have isolated a representation upon which a prosecution may be based.

The reasons for excluding statements identified by their characteristics or presentation as "religious" from "fraud" is a general fear of "heresy trials." If we allow juries to categorize what representations are really not part of the religion, but were claimed to be facts, then we give license to prosecutions against religious freedom. Rather, it is safer to say that once a movement has clearly been identified with religious overtones to those who hear the representations, we will accept the fact that all the movements' representations come warranted as religious, and entice only as they evoke response and recognition. Though such an account may do violence to the way people actually judge religions for themselves and even to what religion "is," it preserves religious freedom. We cannot allow discriminations in a religion between representations justified by recourse to that religion and representations justified by the application of objective standards, so long as assent and affirmation is sought overall. As the historical claim that Christ arose from the dead is clearly religious, so is any claim which founds a religion so long as it is ultimately connected with assent and other religious concomitants. Only if a claim is clearly taken out of the religious domain by specifically and explicitly representing it as objectively verifiable by others without faith, applying standards drawn from other domains, can we have a fraudulent representation. Even then, prosecution must be couched in terms of the man who makes the fraudulent claim and then seeks the shelter of religion, and not in terms of the religion whose shelter he seeks. Religious freedom dictates that we may not divorce particular representations from a religion taken as a whole, nor may we call them fraudulent when they carry with them a religious warrant. We look to the presentation of the representation to see if its context suggests "religious" connections.

The principle discovered — that the law must not entertain descriptions and accounts of religion — not only solves the problems of the prosecution for religious fraud raised by *Ballard*, but also serves as the foundation for a realistic approach to a more general application of the first amendment freedoms of religion. A constitutional prohibition against assessing or regulating belief clearly labeled as religious exempts religious belief from prosecution. But what manifestations of this religious belief are protected? The exemption has its application in the public world, where action takes place and is regulated. A crucial problem is that of the distinction between religious belief and public action. A traditional feeling about the world of law and the world of religion is that the state may not interfere in the world of religion but that when a man participates in the world of public life he must meet its secular and legal standards. How is one to tell which world one is in and when one crosses over?

Law we can say is yet another perspective, but an unusual one. Rather than a descriptive framework, it is, loosely speaking, a prescriptive system for action. It demands and proscribes particular activities—establishes norms of action. Lawyers apply the demands and proscriptions. There is no *defense* to the application of law. But, under the Constitution there is an *exemption* which applies when the act in question takes place in the realm of belief or religious perspective.

There is an aspect of our solution to the *Ballard* case that we need to focus on in connection with this discussion. Throughout the discussion we talked of the privacy of an act of affirmation. We did not precisely define what we meant by privacy nor will we entirely. Rather we have to distinguish three realms of behavior: (1) the realm of pure belief that everybody would grant is private; (2) the realm of religious action which may have public manifestations; (3) the realm of action clearly public. It is usually agreed that the law cannot trifle with the first—no legislature may pass a law commanding people to believe in God. The issue is either to distinguish the latter two, or to provide principles to justify legal regulation of the second. We will do the former.

The distinction in tentative form is: religious action is action the function of which is *only* to establish and perpetuate a private meaning for individuals — a meaning given to it by a religion. Religious actions create results whose effects are private, felt only by those who believe or are concerned with belief. Some actions will occur which have real meaning or effect only in the world of ideas. Thus, purely symbolic actions may be distinguished from actions, such as polygamous cohabitation, which have tangible, worldly consequences. And among those actions which effect only the world of ideas are religious actions, defined as such by the religion which adopts them. That is, religious action takes place in but does not exhaust the realm where actions induce, signify, or reject beliefs. Public action, on the other hand, is that which affects others in ways not limited to their belief. Further, these effects, for the purpose of the law, must already have been described, prescribed, or proscribed by an authoritative decision of the governing political powers. This distinction should grow in meaning in the following discussion.

Religion serves as no defense to a law regulating what we have defined as public actions. Only if action can be seen to be exhausted in an individual's private affirmation, and relates to his assumption of a perspective, is it religious action and thereby sacrosanct. For example, buying a drug clearly warranted as "good" by religion and whose contents are not condemned by law concerns only the private individual in his belief. Erecting a building which does not meet public legal requirements is not defensible since that forbidden act affects people in a very tangible way if the building falls. In the first case, absent negative proscriptions, there is only an individual in the religious world. In the second case, by virtue of the existence of public demands regarding tangible conduct beyond the world of belief, we have activity in the public world.

West Virginia State Bd. of Ed. v. Barnette [40] would seem to militate against this distinction. In that case, children of Jehovah's Witnesses had been dismissed from school for refusing to salute the American flag although an order had been passed defining this as a public duty. Some would say that in this case justice demands that religion not be allowed to function as a defense to a charge of not complying with a public standard. Mr. Justice Frankfurter's dissent put this point forcefully.

> Much that is the concern of temporal authority affects the spiritual interest of men. But it is not enough to strike down a non-discriminatory law that it may hurt or offend some dissident view. It would be too easy to cite numerous prohibitions and injunctions to which laws run counter if the variant interpretations of the Bible were made the tests of obedience to law. *The validity of secular laws cannot be measured by their conformity to religious doctrines.* It is only in a theocratic state that ecclesiastical doctrines measure legal right or wrong. [41]

Mr. Justice Frankfurter distinguishes only between the realm of pure belief and the realm of action clearly public to use this distinction forcefully to reach his result. His opinion thus serves as a hard testing ground for the viability of the suggested third realm—that of religious action. The Jehovah's Witnesses are taught that saluting a flag is sacrilegious idolatry—the flag being a forbidden "image." The State Board of Education ordered the flag salute to be "a regular part of the program of activities in the public schools" with penalties attached for non-performance. Mr. Justice Jackson, for the majority, seemed to balance the public interest against private interests in the realm of belief, in the fashion of recent applications of a "balancing test" to free speech problems. [42] His opinion can be read then, as teaching that the Frankfurter position might be right but that this regulation of opinions is unconstitutional because unjustified. Yet if this is the case, Mr. Justice Frankfurter's argument that religious rights are irrelevant once one is securely in the realm of public action is cogent. [43]

One could, however, find a broader base for decision in this opinion—a base commensurate with our tripartite distinction. At one point Jackson discussed the fact that the involvement of creeds is an essential matter in the case. "If official power exists to coerce acceptance of any patriotic creed,

---

40. 319 U.S. 624 (1943).

41. *Id.* at 654 (emphasis supplied).

42. *Id.* at 638, 640, 641.

43. This is particularly true for purposes of a "religious" objection to a regulation if we refuse to define religion.

what it shall contain cannot be decided by courts, but must be largely discretionary with the ordaining authority, whose power to prescribe would no doubt include the power to amend."[44] He pointed out, at another place in the opinion, a focal fact of the case which would help to put the matter in the realm of privacy in accord with our distinction. "The freedom asserted by these appellees does not bring them into collision with rights asserted by any other individual. . . . Nor is there any question in this case that their behavior is peaceable and orderly."[45] In terms of the suggested distinction, we might say that their action of refusal could affect only the beliefs of others. Given the absence of tangible negative effects upon others, Mr. Justice Jackson concluded in the now familiar words that

> If there is any fixed star in our constitutional constellation, it is that no official, high or petty can prescribe what shall be orthodox in politics, nationalism, religion, or other matters of opinion or force citizens to confess by word or act their faith therein. If there are any circumstances which permit an exception they do not now occur to us.[46]

The dispute in *Barnette* narrows sharply to one issue: in the realm of public life are there some regulations we will prohibit because of their effect on religious people? Mr. Justice Jackson found the answer in his opposition to belief coerced without justification. Mr. Justice Frankfurter found no exception on the grounds that such a determination interferes with the government's proper domain of regulation. Our tentative distinction provides an answer when we discriminate carefully among Mr. Justice Jackson's attacks on the regulation. We can agree with the Frankfurter position that religion should be no defense to a charge of disobeying public regulations. Yet when we examine the nature of the public demand in *Barnette*, we arrive at Mr. Justice Jackson's conclusions.

The argument is as follows: these people were neither doing something that is ordinarily regulated, nor doing something which detracts from the effectiveness of other regulations, nor avoiding doing something which is required as a duty to protect others. The first of these observations is reinforced by noting that the regulation is aimed at the realm of beliefs. The latter two are strengthened by recognizing Mr. Justice Jackson's point that a refusal to salute does not interfere with the rights of others. It therefore lacks the characteristics of public action in that it has no effect on people beyond the

---

44. 319 U.S. at 634.

45. *Id.* at 630.

46. *Id.* at 642. To Mr. Justice Jackson's famous rhetoric Mr. Justice Frankfurter answered with his notion of religious freedom guaranteed by the Constitution. "[N]o religion shall either receive the state's support or incur its hostility. Religion is outside the sphere of political government. This does not mean that all matters on which religious organizations or beliefs may pronounce are outside the sphere of government." *Id.* at 654. He further replies: "Of course patriotism cannot be enforced by the flag salute. But neither can the liberal spirit be enforced by judicial invalidation of illiberal legislation." *Id.* at 670. Mr. Justice Jackson was challenged to find something beyond notions of free expression on which to base invalidation of this regulation. It is, in part, this challenge that is answered by discrimination among beliefs for a religious defense.

realm of their beliefs. Rather, the Board was calling on the Witnesses to affirm something against their will. They presented the children with a symbol and told them to act towards it in a certain way and invest it with a meaning of particular sort. A religion forbade such affirmations.

It is important to note exactly what type of action was called for. Its nature might have been more apparent if the required posture were more traditional. Suppose the regulation had required the children to kneel, fold their hands, close their eyes, and recite the pledge. A different position of hand than most people use to pray by does not make a ritual less a prayer. The action called for was one of private dedication rather than public participation. It defined a posture, a creed towards objects, symbols and beliefs. In short, this pledge had manifestations which are only cognizable by those who believe or those who are concerned with the beliefs of others. Such action was proscribed by the Jehovah's Witnesses.

Once it is granted that the Jehovah's Witnesses are a religion (since they both hold themselves out to be one and are easily recognizable as such) we can say that their refusal to salute is justifiable, not as a defense to a public demand on the ground of religion, but rather on the ground that the public standard invades that particular religion's particularly religious characteristics. Since the regulation achieves that impact with no justification other than encouraging the attitude of patriotism, it is invalid under the first amendment. We are not presented with a clash of perspective resulting from a legal definition of public results, but rather a clash which owes its origin to a regulation which defines actions designed to perpetuate a private meaning in conflict with a religion's private meaning.

This analysis does not use religion as a defense, but uses these religious objectors as an example to show that this regulation does invade the religious domain and involves no compensating public aspect. Law-makers may not themselves define what is a religion, nor can courts define what is an invasion of religious freedom in the abstract. But the religious objectors allow us to assess the public nature of this regulation. An affirmation is private, this regulation of affirmation is not a regulation of public action but an entrance into the religious sphere. Having no warrant in regard to public action the regulation must fall as prohibited once it can be shown that it invades a private realm, and seeks to order that realm in a manner contrary to an order imposed by a religion. In short, in the absence of a public justification, what condemns this regulation is its calling for affirmations. This the Justices condemn on free speech grounds. But we can go farther and suggest that it also may be condemnable under the "establishment" clause of the first amendment. The regulation's invasion of free speech suggests the establishing of a system of perspectives and affirmations. The Jehovah's Witnesses, by their objections, demonstrate that this system can have religious connotations and suggest an establishment question.[47] Yet we need not go that far. What this

_____

47. It is not clear whether the establishment question was at issue. An injunction was issued "restraining the State Board of Education from enforcing against them a

case shows is that the first amendment's guarantee of religious freedom prevents the establishing of purely ritualistic actions or affirmations which can be shown to clash with a particular religion. In other words, religion can serve as a ground for attack or defense against public regulations when those regulations are formulated purely in the realm of affirmation and ritualistic posture.[48]

In defining the relation of religion and law under the aegis of the Constitution we have examined and defined what types of assaults religion is protected against, what comprises its defensible integrity and exemptions. To arrive at a fuller understanding of the functioning of religion in the context of legality it is necessary to explore the way in which religion may infect a legal situation, or a religious institution participate in a public process. We have focused on the individual's freedom to ask for any affirmation of belief commensurate with standards of public action. The question that arises naturally is the converse: What benefits may a religion claim, if it meets public standards for the granting of benefits? The famous "School Bus" case, *Everson v. Board of Educ.*,[49] offers an answer. Written by Justice Black, it is perhaps the most difficult decision in this area, and perhaps the most brilliant.

Before we approach that case, one preliminary case must be understood. *Pierce v. Society of Sisters* [50] involved section 5259 of the Oregon statutes,

---

regulation of the Board requiring children . . . to salute the American flag." Barnette v. West Virginia State Bd. of Educ., 47 F. Supp. 251, 252 (1942). The judge's summary, however, reads without the phrase "against them" although he states the question of the case as whether or not the Jehovah's Witnesses can "lawfully be required to salute it." *Ibid.* The question is whether the ritual was attacked or the compulsion of the children to participate was held unconstitutional.

48. There is a sense in which any government establishment of ritual raises problems in the area of establishment of religion—although without a finding that religion is involved, the ritual is perhaps not assailable as such. Two separate concurrences suggest a concern with the meaning of establishing rituals relevant to belief. Mr. Justice Black, for himself and Mr. Justice Douglas, stated: "Religious faiths, honestly held, do not free individuals from responsibility to conduct themselves obediently to laws which are either imperatively necessary to protect society as a whole from grave and pressingly imminent dangers or which, without any general prohibition merely regulate time, place or manner of religious activity." 319 U.S. 624, 643 (1942). That pledge Mr. Justice Black regarded as a "test oath" and found "abhorrent," forbidden by the first amendment. His opinion notes that private rights underlie religious freedom. Mr. Justice Murphy puts the stress elsewhere. In a phrase suggesting Mr. Justice Black's general theory of amendments as commands he stated, "I have no loftier duty or responsibility than to uphold that spiritual freedom in its farthest reaches." *Id.* at 645. To this end he suggested a test. "I am impelled to conclude that such a requirement is not essential to the maintenance of effective government and orderly society." *Ibid.* Mr. Justice Murphy also mentioned private rights. "To many it is deeply distasteful to join in a public chorus of affirmation of private belief. . . . I am unable to agree that the benefits that may accrue to society from the compulsory flag salute are sufficiently definite and tangible to justify the invasion of freedom and privacy that is entailed." *Id.* at 645-46.

49. 330 U.S. 1 (1946).

50. 268 U.S. 510 (1925).

which compelled all children between eight and sixteen to attend public schools. Two schools, one parochial, the other private, contested the constitutionality of this statute before the Supreme Court. Mr. Justice McReynolds, for a unanimous court, affirmed a decree which had declared the statute unconstitutional; to reach this result he used the first amendment, applying it to the state law through the due process clause of the fourteenth amendment.

> No question is raised concerning the power of the State reasonably to regulate all schools, to inspect, supervise and examine them, their teachers and pupils; to require that all children of proper age attend some school . . . and [to require] that nothing be taught which is manifestly inimical to the public welfare.[51]

Having thus defined the state's permissible sphere of supervision of education in abstract terms, Mr. Justice McReynolds went on to say "that the child is not merely a creature of the state. Those who rear him have the right and the duty to recognize and prepare him for additional obligations."[52] If a school fulfills certain public standards, the state has exhausted its legal interest in those who attend them. The state has a right to set educational standards, but not to dictate where they are to be fulfilled or what accompanying characteristics must be. More specifically, the case limited the state's power to control what a student learns.

Mr. Justice McReynolds seems to have justified this conclusion by reference to a conception of parental right to choose the school to which they send their children. Perhaps the rationale is that because the rights involved are inherent in individuals, state regulations impinging them must be limited to what is required by the public purpose. Some Catholics have offered the additional argument in support of the case that religious freedom compels its holding.[53] To say that a school must have no religion, they argue, is to teach a theory of religion—that education and spiritual growth are separate. Such a theory runs counter to Catholic doctrine. It is thus a denial of Catholic religious freedom if parochial schools are outlawed. For then Catholics would be imprinted with a doctrine about religion which they do not accept. If, in fact, they fulfill the state's standards of education, shouldn't they be permitted to add on their own conditions? If everyone meets the state's standards and religious people meet them in their religious way, religion is served. If religious people are not so allowed, they are forced to practice what they preach against. Such an argument might call on our distinction of public actions from religious expression to say that to make Catholics go to a particular school only affects their beliefs. That conflict with an established religion's beliefs might be said to invade the domain of religious expression.

The difficulty with this argument is suggested by our earlier discussion of the conflict of perspectives. Religion is not always a clear or separable

---

51. *Id.* at 534.

52. See *id.* at 535. *Cf.* Meyer v. Nebraska, 262 U.S. 390 (1923).

53. Murray, *Law or Prepossession,* 14 LAW & CONTEMP. PROB. 23, 30-34, 36-37, 39 (1949).

domain. Many a public pronouncement may imply a position that a religion may reject. If the law requires drivers to stay on the right, and a religion urges the left on grounds that God speaks only to people on the left, the law forces one to practice what one does not preach. Further, the fact that Catholics meet some public standards does not in itself justify a conclusion that they do not have to meet all such standards. In order to justify such a conclusion, one must show that the religion's demand is separable from the other public requirements and that the state's demand affecting that religious demand only affects beliefs. But non-ideological reasons for putting all pupils in public schools can be found. The state can say that such a requirement is the most reasonable way to perpetuate public regulation. A regulation compelling parents to send children to particular public standard schools is not clearly separable from the aim of maintaining those public standards, nor is it clearly in a realm only affecting belief.

It is perhaps safer to say that once religious beliefs are involved, we should look carefully, as in the *Flag Salute Case,* to see that institutions of a religious nature are not established, and, that in general, we should try to permit maximum freedom for divergence. Under such a nebulous warrant, we find the *Pierce* case, as a matter of law, holding in favor of the freedom to educate up to standards in whatever place desired—a view bottomed on the parental right to freedom within the framework of public standards. Public standards dictate only certain educational requirements.

Given, then, that the state cannot dictate observance beyond its standards in education, the question arises as to what types of *benefits* the first amendment permits it to bestow on those agencies which both fulfill its standards and also partake of a religious nature. It is to this question that Black addressed himself in the "School Bus" case.[54] At stake in *Everson* was the constitutionality of a New Jersey Board of Education's decision, made under statutory authority, to reimburse parents for "money expended by them for the bus transportation of their children on regular buslines operated by the public transportation system"[55] to and from schools. The difficulty was that "part of this money was for the payment of transportation of some children in the community to Catholic parochial schools."[56] Everson, "in his capacity as a district taxpayer, filed suit in a state court challenging the right of the Board to reimburse parents of parochial school students."[57]

First, and most important, Mr. Justice Black established that he was examining the *statute*, not the particular practice in this town which happened to result in the giving of money only to Catholic school pupils. The Justice noted in a crucial footnote that the statute was not challenged under the equal protection clause for "excluding payment for the transportation of *any*

54. 330 U.S. 1 (1946).
55. *Id.* at 3.
56. *Ibid.*
57. *Ibid.*

pupil who attends a 'private school run for profit.' "[58] Given the limited nature of Mr. Justice Black's inquiry it is possible to reconstruct his argument from parts of the opinion.

The establishment of religion clause, he stated, means that

> Neither a state nor the Federal Government can set up a church. Neither can pass laws which aid one religion, aid all religions, or prefer one religion over another. Neither can force nor influence a person to go to or to remain away from church against his will or force him to profess a belief or disbelief in any religion. . . . No tax . . . can be levied to support any religious activities or institutions, whatever they may be called, or whatever form they may adopt to teach or practice religion.[59]

On the other hand, "That Amendment requires the state to be a neutral in its relations with groups of religious believers and non-believers; it does not require the state to be their adversary. State power is no more to be used so as to handicap religions than it is to favor them."[60] In a situation where the state acts towards an organization, the question to ask is whether the state's action is in any sense *determined* by the religious characteristic of the organization. If it is, the action or the statute authorizing it is unconstitutional. On the other hand, if there are public standards, not a function of religion or belief, religion should furnish no excuse or reason for deviation. Black argued further that this reasoning applies to the allocation of benefits as well as to the promulgation of restraints.

Then, Mr. Justice Black asked, is there anything wrong with providing transportation to children attending schools? He saw no defect. Moreover, the statute certainly does not fall because of any religious characteristics, as there are none relevant to the standards in the statute. Since there is nothing constitutionally objectionable in the standards or statute, there is nothing wrong with applying the statute to schools which happen to be Catholic. Indeed, it would be unconstitutional to preclude the giving of aid to Catholic schools if others received aid. This is the nub of the case. Mr. Justice Black stated it with a type of reverse English.

> While we do not mean to intimate that a state could not provide transportation only to children attending the public schools, we must be careful, in protecting the citizens of New Jersey against state-established churches, to be sure that we do not inadvertently prohibit New Jersey from extending its general state law benefits to all its citizens without regard to their religious belief.[61]

In effect, religion cannot be used to prevent extension of "general state law benefits." Once we find that a statute operates reasonably in dispensing benefits and is not defined by religion, freedom dictates that it be applied equally to those who mix religion in with the conditions of benefit. The constitutional mandate does not prevent all persons, religious and non-religious, from re-

---

58. *Id.* at n.2 (emphasis added). See also *id.* at 6.
59. *Id.* at 15-16.
60. *Id.* at 18.
61. *Id.* at 16.

ceiving those benefits. Indeed, since it is impossible to define a domain for
religion, and since religions may introduce prescriptions into other domains,
to decide the constitutionality of this kind of statute on the basis of "religion"
is to decide on something which is not necessarily or directly at work in the
secular choice itself.

Mr. Justice Black had yet another point to make.

> State-paid policemen, detailed to protect children going to and from
> church schools from the very real hazards of traffic, would serve much
> the same purpose and accomplish much the same result as state provisions
> intended to guarantee free transportation of a kind which the state deems
> to be best for the school children's welfare.[62]

One could object that the policemen direct the traffic for the sake of order
as well as for the sake of children, but this would not destroy the analogy
between police protection and public transportation. Both function to facilitate
choices of where to go, and both are justified if extended without predication
on religious preference. It provides a public freedom to choose means, not an
aid to the private practice of a state recognized religion.

Mr. Justice Black stated that there is a "difficulty in drawing the line between tax legislation which provides funds for the welfare of the general public and that which is designed to support institutions which teach religion."[63]
In *Everson*, he had no difficulty.

> It is much too late to argue that legislation intended to facilitate the
> opportunity of children to get a secular education serves no public pur-
> pose. . . . Nor does it follow that a law has a private rather than a public
> purpose because it provides that tax raised funds will be paid to reim-
> burse individuals on account of money spent by them in a way which
> furthers a public program. . . . Subsidies and loans to individuals such
> as farmers and home owners, and to privately owned transportation sys-
> tems, as well as many other kinds of businesses, have been common-
> place practices in our state and national history.[64]

Where aid is given directly to institutions for apparently non-religious purposes, the difficulty in "drawing the line" might be heightened by the possibility that the guide for disbursement, which appears not to distinguish on
a religious basis, cloaks a practical effect of so doing. But in *Everson*, the
money was given to individuals, not to a church organization. The fact that
it may be employed by individuals to help a church or to further a church
program should be considered irrelevant and in the area of free choice. Admittedly this is a tenuous, easily blurred, sometimes quantitative distinction;
it is true that aid to individuals could be in fact designed to be aid to a church.
At a minimum, the distinction operates to indicate that the aid allows choice
within a range not proscribed by public standards, rather than furnish aid to

---

62. *Id.* at 17.

63. *Id.* at 14.

64. *Id.* at 7. At this juncture Mr. Justice Black's citation of Cochran v. Louisiana
State Bd. of Educ., 281 U.S. 370 (1930) is very important. See note 65 *infra*.

religion. At a maximum, the distinction indicates that religion is not involved; the reimbursements are just aid to individuals.[65]

We can restate this part of the argument as follows: having justified the aid as allowing freedom of choice, there are two agencies of aiding to be examined. The agency of implementing the choice; the agency for distributing the benefit. The agency of implementing the choice is public transportation which is not defined by religion. It functions to serve all, in a way analogous to the way a policeman serves all. The agency for distributing benefits is the reimbursement of individuals. This is a traditional way of giving money for public programs, and as long as it is not predicated on religious discrimination it certainly does not fall afoul of the establishment clause. The statute is valid both in terms of the benefits distributed and the agencies chosen.

The soundness of *Everson* as a holding of law should be manifest, once the idea of parochial schools fulfilling public educational standards is accepted. If children can go to those schools they certainly can take buses there. *Pierce* suggested the focus on individuals that Black amplified into a distinction. Going to parochial schools is an acceptable way of fulfilling public standards. The conjunction of two propositions yields *Everson's* result: Law demands only that public standards be fulfilled, not that the perspectives of other domains be preempted. Public aid for private choice into which religion does not necessarily enter is acceptable.

We can reformulate the legal argument as follows: the Constitution prohibits aid to religion and support of any state religion. *Everson* presents a statute offering benefits to those who meet public standards and, only incidentally to statutory language or purpose, go to church schools. The statute does not breach the "wall of separation," since (a) the aid it authorized went to individuals as an expression of public policy towards private choice, (b) the statute was not defined in terms of religious goals, nor did it discriminate according to religious characteristics, (c) the benefactors fully met the requirements of the state in all relevant respects.

It is surprising that Mr. Justice Black's position found but a bare majority of the Court. Mr. Justice Jackson, whom one might have expected to follow, dissented. He saw the question as "Is it constitutional to tax this complainant to pay the cost of carrying pupils to Church schools of one specified denomination?"[66] The majority opinion stated that the particular usage was not an issue in this case.[67] Mr. Justice Rutledge was joined by Justices Frankfurter, Jackson and Burton in a thirty-six page dissent.[68] His argument was based on the analogy of "An appropriation from the public treasury to pay the cost

65. Cochran v. Louisiana State Bd. of Educ., 281 U.S. 370 (1930) declaring constitutional the provision of free public school books to children at private and parochial schools, also supports the correctness of the *Everson* holding as a matter of law. In that case, it was said that "schools . . . are not the beneficiaries"—the children and the state are. *Id.* at 375.

66. Everson v. Board of Educ., 330 U.S. 1, 21 (1947).

67. *Id.* at 4 n.2 and accompanying text.

68. *Id.* at 28.

of transportation to Sunday school . . . or to the meetings of various young
people's religious societies . . . [which] could not withstand the constitutional
attack."[69] But the analogy was false: this is not aid to exclusively religious
facilities, but aid intended to facilitate the fulfillment of state standards in
facilities recognized by the state as serving its public goals. That these facilities
happen to offer an option as to the mixture of religion in education is irrelevant to the public purpose.[70]

In our framework, the sense of Mr. Justice Black's legal position emerges.
To prevent aid when there is a possibility of encouraging religion would
destroy our conceptual dichotomy of the domains and vitiate the idea that
legal reasoning should proceed on the basis of their separateness even when
both religion and other perspectives apply, in fact, to the same fact situation.
Our position recognizes that, since the state and religions have different perspectives and different goals to be achieved by implementing certain regulations, to judge one by the other is to violate the mandate of the first amendment. If, after we have defined our public standards and our public aid exclusive of religious considerations, we then destroy them as a judicial matter
because of some participant's religious characteristics, we once again enter
into a judicial determination of a religious sphere. The fact that aid may foster
the manifestations of belief does not make it aid to private *religious* expression. Such aid functions to affect people in a realm apart from belief. Easing
the way to education makes it public action aid. The question is whether the
public standards or public aid are dependent on an evaluation of private religious belief.[71] If not, then to apply judicial reckoning is to enter the domain
of religion forbidden under the first amendment.

The converse implications of this opinion can be suggested by a brief excursion into the Sunday Closing Law cases: *McGowan v. Maryland*,[72] *Two
Guys from Harrison-Allentown v. McGinley*,[73] and *Braunfield v. Brown*.[74]
These cases involved the constitutionality of statutes which made it mandatory
to close stores on Sunday. Since some Jews closed on Saturday in observance
of their religion, it was argued that such a regulation was unconstitutional,
because it penalized people for practicing their religion.

The Court did not find the laws unconstitutional—a result which may be
justified as the converse of *Everson*. Just as we cannot invalidate aid because
religious people may use it to benefit their religion, so we cannot invalidate
regulations solely because people may be affected adversely in their religion.
Since we cannot use the content of any particular religion to judge the

---

69. *Id.* at 47.

70. The appositeness of the analogy might also be questioned in light of Zorach v.
Clauson, 343 U.S. 306 (1952).

71. See text accompanying notes 86-93 *infra*.

72. 366 U.S. 420 (1961).

73. 366 U.S. 582 (1961).

74. 366 U.S. 599 (1961).

application of a public standard, we cannot strike down Sunday-closing legislation because it affects Jews.[75]

Two arguments can be made against this position. First, the statute is, in fact, designed to hurt Jews and as such infringes free religious practice; second, although the state has a right to declare that there should be a day of rest, it can show no non-religious reason to pick Sunday. This latter argument resembles those that Catholics have made about *Pierce*. A day of rest is justified, but not Sunday, if picking Sunday is but a manifestation of religious belief. The answer to the first argument is that malicious legislative intent has to be shown conclusively. If it is shown that the exclusive function and purpose of the law was to attack a particular religion then it is invalid—but such an allegation has no specific support, and secular reasons for having everybody closed the same day—for example, ease of enforcement—can be advanced to support choice of that day when most citizens will choose to rest. Again, it is impossible to separate this part of the regulation—the choice of day—from the whole public purpose, and the state has the right to define that one day which it thinks the stores should be closed. Many examples of difficulties in allowing religious criteria to affect closing regulations can be imagined.[76] If one were to judge the choice of a day by its religious effects, this would be to do what the *Ballard* analysis showed to be a mistake—to entertain descriptions and accounts of religion. Rather, since the statute defines public action by regulating people in the operation of commerce, it does not enter into the range of private religious expression and cannot be judged by the fact that the goals of religion may coincide or clash with the actuality of the legal regulations unless an attempt to create such a clash can be clearly shown.

These principles of interpretation of the first amendment's commands, derived from *Ballard*, manifest in *Everson* and *McGowan*, and amplified by a distinction evidenced in *Barnette*, can be summarized as follows: (1) The function of the Constitution is to exclude calculation of religious values, be they motives for deceit, or aid, or violation of statutes. (2) The Constitution also prevents the formulating or examining of the possible private ways of acting on religious beliefs.

That these simple commands can be applied in other cases is demonstrated by an excursion into the recent and controversial school prayer case, *Engel v. Vitale*.[77] Once again, Mr. Justice Black wrote the majority opinion. The prayer which the state prescribed for morning recitation was as follows: "Almighty God, we acknowledge our dependence upon Thee, and we beg Thy blessings upon us, our parents, our teachers, and our Country."[78] The schools,

---

75. The strength of this statement has been considerably weakened as law by Sherbert v. Verner, 83 Sup. Ct. 1790 (1963). See text accompanying notes 86-93 *infra*.

76. *Cf.* Mr. Justice Black's opinion in *Barnette*, 319 U.S. 624, 643 (1943).

77. 370 U.S. 421 (1962).

78. *Id.* at 422.

unlike those in *Barnette*, did not compel any pupil to join in this affirmation over his or his parents' objections.

Mr. Justice Black based his argument on two points. "There can be no doubt that New York's state prayer program officially establishes the religious beliefs embodied in the Regents' prayer."[79] The particular defect was that the *state* promulgated religious doctrines in the schools. Clearly that falls under the ban of state-established religions. Secondly; "When the power, prestige and financial support of government is placed behind a particular religious belief, the indirect coercive pressure upon religious minorities to conform to the prevailing officially approved religion is plain."[80] Given the existence of such compulsion towards belief, the case's similarity to *Barnette* becomes evident. The state uses its machinery to make people act in such a way as to affect their beliefs. To utilize schools for religious activities is to foster religion unconstitutionally.[81]

In short, the prayer is a religious formulation. Even to say that it is common to all religions is to prescribe for future religions. The prayer utilizes state machinery to foster a religion. Both are banned under the Constitution. The prayer functions to permit the state to define religious affirmations. That breaches the separation of the domains.[82]

Two recent Supreme Court actions, however, cannot be reconciled with the suggested approach to the problems of religion under the first amendment; they illustrate the confusion sometimes resulting from tenderness towards religious defenses. In *Sherbert v. Verner*,[83] Mr. Justice Brennan,

79. *Id.* at 430. See also *id.* at 435.

80. *Id.* at 431.

81. Not only is the prayer religious, but it is clearly so. Imagine the furor if parochial schools were compelled to start with that prayer; or Jewish Orthodox Sabbath Schools, to use it before starting to teach Hebrew. The religious character of the ceremony was implicitly conceded by the state when it permitted religious objectors to abstain. In discussing other school prayers, Justice Goldberg, referring to this case, asked whether "the state cannot compose but can select?" 31 U.S.L. WEEK 3276 (March 5, 1963).

82. Mr. Justice Douglas, in concurring, took off from the constitutional financing of religious exercise to worry about all the uses of money involving state and religion. But the question is whether the money and the statute related to its expenditure function to give state aid to particular religious formulations of belief. Mr. Justice Stewart, on the other hand, noted that "God Save the United States and this Honorable Court" precedes the Court's session. If a similarity in nature of the ritual exists, we should strike down the Court's ritual. But that issue has not arisen, and may be distinguishable on grounds of vacuity. Mr. Justice Black's footnote 21 is relevant here. Engel v. Vitale, 370 U.S. 421, 435 (1962). Mr. Justice Stewart also states that we, as a people, presuppose a Supreme Being though the Constitution does not say so. As legal argument such an invocation is very weak. It is a dictum from Zorach v. Clauson, *supra* note 70, which in allowing for released time from schools for religious services, affirmed as most important in McCollum v. Illinois, 333 U.S. 203 (1947), the fact that the classrooms were used for religious instruction and the force of the public school was used to promote that instruction. To use a dictum from a case which explicitly held that the use of classrooms for fostering religious exercises was a crucial constitutional defect to try to uphold the school prayer is almost weaker in law than constitutional analysis.

83. 374 U.S. 398 (1963).

Law and Religion   95

1964]   *RELIGIOUS FREEDOM*   621

speaking for a majority which included Mr. Justice Black, concluded that
the "benefits" of state unemployment compensation could not be kept from
a Seventh Day Adventist, who could not get a job because she refused to
work on Saturday. He reasoned that the opposite decision would condition
the "availability of benefits upon . . . willingness to violate a cardinal principle of her religious faith."[84] In *Re Jennison*,[85] the Court hinted a willingness to extend this reasoning by remanding, for reconsideration in the light
of *Sherbert*, the Minnesota Supreme Court's affirmance of a decision holding
a woman in contempt of court for refusing jury duty on claimed religious
grounds.[86] The woman claimed the refuge of biblical command—"Judge not
that ye shall not be judged"—in refusing her civic duty.[87]

To permit a *religious* defense in either of these cases is to adopt a view of
the first amendment very different from that presented here.[88] This different
view finds in the Constitution and its amendments the suggestion of an ideal
society, and supports that finding with a conception of constitutional interpretation designed to implement the discovered ideal in each fact situation.
This view interprets the first amendment command of religious freedom as an
instruction to decide each case so as to choose freedom for religious activities
to the maximum degree consistent with social order. The establishment clause
is interpreted as a complement to the command for freedom in that it prevents any one religion from gaining ascendance to the detriment of others.
Religion is then an allowable defense to the operation of those rules which,
although neutral in the abstract, in practice infringe particular religious practices—Sunday closing laws, laws outlawing polygamy,[89] rules enforcing jury
service, etc. And to foster the free exercise of religion, exemptions and benefits may be bestowed—tax exemptions for religions, draft exemptions for
pious conscientious objectors, chaplains for the armed services. The role of
the decision maker is the practical one of examining factual situations with
the goal of structuring the legal order so as to reduce to the minimum its
conflict with particular religions.[90]

---

84. *Id.* at 406.

85. 84 Sup. Ct. 63 (1963).

86. — Minn. —, 120 N.W.2d 515 (1963).

87. *Id.* at 516.

88. This view was most ably suggested to me by Professor Alexander M. Bickel,
whose friendly criticism has been an aid in many respects.

89. *Cf.* Davis v. Beason, 133 U.S. 333 (1890).

90. The scope of the balancing process involved, and the inherent slipperiness of the
approach as a tool for sensitive inquiry, are suggested by Mr. Justice Frankfurter's dissent in West Virginia State Bd. of Educ. v. Barnette, 319 U.S. 624, 646 (1942). See
also Prince v. Massachusetts, 321 U.S. 158 (1944) where a young Jehovah's Witness was
held validly convicted for sale of magazines on Boston streets, in violation of a city ordinance. Rather than *balancing* religious interests with community interests, courts should
treat all citizens before them equally, once it is shown that the community interests involved (here, protecting the health of minors) exist in the realm of public action. Of
course, any argument that the statute was, in fact, directed at these particular religious
distributions would also be treated independently of any considerations of balancing.

622   THE YALE LAW JOURNAL   [Vol. 73:593

As a principle of constitutional interpretation, this practical approach is neither exclusive nor—at least to the author[91]—persuasive. In its particular application to the problem of religions operating in society, it presents many difficulties. Assessing or assisting particular religions—defining the concept "religion"—not only tends to establish those religions but also seems to limit the domain of future religions by requiring them to be similar to present ones if they wish to claim similar defenses or benefits. The state should not define religion and, therefore, cannot pass laws or entertain defenses that are directed to the aid of particular religious establishments. The activities of religions have their meaning in their effects on religious peoples' assents—we do not want the state performing assessments in that domain. Further, the "practical results" of this alternative approach are not uniformly beneficial. How does the woman in *Jennison* differ from those pacifists who refuse to pay taxes to support war? Or Vivian Kellems, whose tax reprisals are based on anti-welfare sentiments? Are Jehovah's Witnesses or Catholics pleased that their religions are thought by Draft Boards not to justify pacifism or conscientious objection? In the implementation of standards of exemption designed to aid the practice of religions, many religious groups and many positions labeled as religious may be excluded, to the detriment of their freedom of religion.

I find no constitutional compulsion to give conscientious objectors exemptions, Mormons many wives, or churches freedom from taxes. More important, these goals can and must be achieved in a way that removes the state from the business of defining and enshrining religions. As the Second Circuit has very recently recognized,[92] the exemption for conscientious objectors cannot be made dependent upon belief in a Supreme Being. Unfortunately, the Second Circuit failed to follow the logic of its position through, and implied that the state could establish a definition of religion—so long as it included non-deistic religions — and condition grant of the exemption upon belief in a "religion." The exemption should be made available on grounds of moral belief in the wrongness of war, because we tolerate dissent on a model of free society; but we are not compelled to make the exemption available because that dissent is labeled "religious." Activities in a religious group might be one of the factors considered in granting such an exemption, but only in the process of determining sincerity.[93] On similar grounds of tolerance,

---

91. Weiss, Book Review, 72 YALE L.J. 1665 (1963).

92. United States v. Seeger, 326 F.2d 846 (2d Cir. 1964). See also United States v. Jakobson, 325 F.2d 409 (2d Cir. 1963), which found as religious a particular notion of "horizontal" relation to God. *Seeger* explicitly recognizes the conceptual difficulty of insisting upon a distinction between Jakobson's devotion to a mystical force of "Godness" and Daniel Seeger's compulsion to follow the paths of "goodness," suggesting further the efficacy of avoiding judicial analysis of religious content as a requirement for exemption.

93. A difficult problem for those who adopt the view that religious freedom just commands toleration of religious practices is found in H.R. REP. No. 7152, 88th Cong., 2d Sess., tit. 7, § 704(b) (1964) (on unfair employment practices). It states: "It shall not be unlawful employment for an employer to refuse to hire . . . because of said person's atheistic practices and beliefs." The couching of a refusal in apparently non-religious terms might raise no difficulties for their views. I find five insurmountable constitutional objections. (1) In general, there is a violation of equal protection. (2) To define

it would be advisable to permit polygamy for those who recognize its moral rectitude; yet there is no constitutional compulsion to do so. Persons who do not wish to judge on juries, for whatever moral grounds, are probably unfit for jury duty, and perhaps should be excused on that basis; but there is no constitutional compulsion to accept an excuse based on a personal reading of a religious document for failing to fulfill public duties in the realm of public action. Religions with charitable aspects might be granted tax exemptions as charities; but to discriminate between what is and is not "religious" as a basis for denial or grant of government benefits should be forbidden. In short, if it is true that freedom is benefited by giving exemptions to extreme groups when they do nothing of serious harm to the commonwealth, the religious nature of some of these groups should neither include or exclude them from the total class. When we run across results of apparent injustices, we can correct them, should we choose to, using notions of freedom for dissent, rather than definitions, confusions, and establishments of religions.

In sum, religion calls for affirmations and is expressed in actions manifesting those beliefs. It is protected by the first amendment when clearly represented as religious, but only in the realm of belief or pure manifestations affecting belief. The state operates in many perspectives and can regulate the public domain. Both the law's perspective and a particular religion's perspective may overlap in a particular fact situation. But the Constitution prevents law from entering the purely private domain of religious expression and belief. This implies that the state can neither tamper with nor examine religious affirmations nor prescribe religious perspectives. Moreover, the state cannot predicate its statutes or their application on the nature of an affirmation or its conjunction with a statute. Beyond the realm where the two are conjointly prescriptive, the lawyers' and judges' job is to apply the public standard and only that, once it is found that the statute's operation is not predicated upon a distinction in affirmation or belief. These categories allow us to develop a rationale for the most important of the Supreme Court's decisions involving religion, and to discriminate the range of permissible activities for purposes of future decisions. The task is to discern whether religion forms a variable in the statute's formulation or application by seeing whether an assumption or decision on a perspective of belief is called for. If so, then the statute is unconstitutional. If not, then religion can form neither a defense to its application nor a justification after application for calling the statute unconstitutional.

atheism as something special denies any atheist the status of a participant in religion. Confucianism causes trouble, as such a doctrine of interpretation would attempt a mistaken definition of religion. *Cf. Seeger, supra* note 92. (3) To enact a statute about atheism on practice and belief and give it to someone to administer would lead to serious troubles. For one thing, it is probably unconstitutionally vague. For another, to allow government agents to decide about religion for qualification is to allow the state into religious decisions unconstitutionally. Torcaso v. Watkins, 367 U.S. 488 (1960). (4) There is an unconstitutional test oath implicit here. (5) To reject atheism as encouraging religion seems to be a law in its very terms "respecting the establishment of religion."

[4]

THE IRRELEVANCE OF THE CONSTITUTION: THE RELIGION CLAUSES OF THE FIRST AMENDMENT AND THE SUPREME COURT*

PHILIP B. KURLAND†

MEMORIAL LECTURES USUALLY BEGIN WITH amenities that deprive sincerity of its due. Yet, I must say because I know it to be true, that it is a privilege to be invited to deliver the Donald A. Giannella Lecture at the University that was his intellectual home. The invitation of Villanova University would be honor enough, especially on the occasion of the law school's silver anniversary. But the fact that the lectureship memorializes a distinguished faculty member, rather than a gracious donor or a famed jurist, doubles the honor, for implicit in the invitation is the suggestion that the speaker is expected to fill a part of the void that was left by the departure of a faculty member who was a vital part of this academy. Of course, in this case, there must be more to the wish than the fulfillment. Don Giannella spoke learnedly and cogently to the subject I am about to address, *inter alia,* in his two articles in the *Harvard Law Review*[1] and one in *The Supreme Court Review.*[2] Although I can only offer a footnote to his work, I hope that I can speak to the subject in the same spirit that he did: with concern, with honesty, and with a bias only in favor of the Constitution. At least, that is my aspiration, despite my shared recognition with T.S. Eliot of the cruelty implicit in a mixture of memory and desire.

The thesis of my lecture is that the Constitution has been essentially irrelevant to the judgments of the United States Supreme Court in the areas designated freedom of religion and separation of church and state. I would quickly add, moreover, that my allegation regarding the irrelevance of the Constitution is not limited to the interpre-

---

* This article was prepared from the second Donald A. Giannella Memorial Lecture of the Villanova University School of Law, April 6, 1978. The lecture has been supplemented by documentation and edited where necessary to accommodate the written form.

† William R. Kenan, Jr., Distinguished Service Professor, University of Chicago. A.B., University of Pennsylvania, 1942; LL.B., Harvard University, 1944.

1. Giannella, *Religious Liberty, Nonestablishment, and Doctrinal Development. Part I. The Religious Liberty Guarantee,* 80 HARV. L. REV. 1381 (1967) [hereinafter cited as *Religious Liberty Guarantee*]; Giannella, *Religious Liberty, Nonestablishment, and Doctrinal Development. Part II. The Nonestablishment Principle,* 81 HARV. L. REV. 513 (1968) [hereinafter cited as *Nonestablishment Principle*].

2. Giannella, *Lemon and Tilton: The Bitter and the Sweet of Church-State Entanglement.* 1971 SUP. CT. REV. 147.

tation of the so-called religion clauses of the first amendment.[3] The cases decided under that rubric are but examples, and not the most egregious examples at that, of the Court's substitution of its judgment for those of the founding fathers. Perhaps my tale is no more than still another version of *The Emperor's New Clothes*, but I have never been sure of the proper moral to be derived from that story. Was it that the child pierced the propaganda that had brainwashed the populace? Or was it that the adult population demonstrated more civility than could be expected from a child by indulging the Emperor in his peculiar form of exhibitionism?

To say that the Constitution is essentially irrelevant to Supreme Court decisionmaking, however, purports to be a statement of fact. To explain why that has come about is an exercise in speculation. To determine whether, if this proposition is true, the court's behavior should be approved or condemned is a question of judgment. I shall address, at least tangentially, each of these issues. But ultimately, it is for you to decide what case I have made.

The place to begin is at the beginning, or perhaps before that. As we all know, the Constitution was adopted without a Bill of Rights,[4] but with vehement demand for one. Proponents of such a device were seeking to secure hard-won freedoms against national government intrusions. For the most part, the Bill of Rights was aimed at preventing the repetition of evils recorded in English history. The opponents of the Bill of Rights were not in favor of denying these liberties, but rather were convinced that there was no need to provide negatives to powers that were never granted, lest the negative be pregnant with authorizations to act in fields of government which the Constitution did not specify in article I.[5]

Our nation's history begins with religious persecution. The emigrés from old England to New England's shores fled the home country in order to be free to worship as they pleased or as they believed they must. This was not, however, a principled adherence to a doctrine of freedom—or even tolerance—for religious beliefs not held by the majority. The origins of Rhode Island and Connecticut are evidence enough that the Massachusetts Bay Colony was no more willing to afford freedom of worship to nonadherents to the majority's faith than was the England of its day. One is reminded that Milton's plea for freedom of speech, in *Areopagitica*,[6] would not afford such

---

3. U.S. CONST. amend. I. The first amendment provides in pertinent part: "Congress shall make no law respecting an establishment of religion, or prohibiting the free exercise thereof . . . ." *Id.*

4. *Id.* amends. I-X.

5. *Id.* art. I.

6. J. MILTON, PROSE WRITINGS 145 (Everyman ed. 1974).

freedom for "Popery"[7] no less for infidels, Jews, or Turks. It would seem that freedom of religion then was only freedom for one's own religion and not that of others.

State churches were the rule rather than the exception in our colonial origin. Nonetheless, the example of the Church of England, with political and social privileges for members and political and social disabilities for nonmembers, afforded the background for the antagonism toward a national established church. Indeed, the body of the Constitution speaks to the abolition of some such privileges that pertained to the Church of England. Thus, the Constitution provides in clause 3 of article VI that "no religious Test shall ever be required as a Qualification to any Office or public Trust under the United States."[8]

This clause was derived from a proposed bill of rights offered at the 1787 Federal Convention by Charles Pinckney.[9] Luther Martin, at the Maryland ratifying convention, pointed out that the provision was adopted without difficulty, but not without dissent:

> The part of the system which provides, that *no religious test* shall ever be required as a qualification to any office or public trust under the United States, was adopted by a great majority of the convention, and without much debate; however, there were some members *so unfashionable* as to think, that a *belief of the existence of a Deity*, and of a *state of future rewards and punishments* would be some security for the good conduct of our rulers, and that, in a Christian country, it would be *at least decent* to hold out some distinction between the professors of Christianity and downright infidelity or paganism.[10]

James Madison refused to make much of this provision. In a letter to Edmund Randolph, he wrote: "As to the religious test, I should conceive that it can imply at most nothing more than that without that exception, a power would have been given to impose an oath involving a religious test as a qualification for office."[11] But Randolph, at the 1788 Virginia ratifying convention, made more of it, with an argument that was later to be adopted by the authors of *The Federalist*.[12] He said:

---

7. *Id.* at 182.
8. U.S. CONST. art. VI, cl. 3.
9. *See* 2 M. FARRAND, RECORDS OF THE FEDERAL CONVENTION OF 1787, 342, 468 (1st ed. 1911).
10. 3 *id.* at 227 (emphasis added).
11. *Id.* at 297.
12. *See* THE FEDERALIST No. 52 (J. Madison), at 358 (B. Wright ed. 1961) [hereinafter cited as FEDERALIST].

Although officers, &c. are to swear that they will support this constitution, yet they are not bound to support one mode of worship,
or to adhere to one particular sect. It puts all sects on the same
footing. A man of abilities and character, of any sect whatever, may
be admitted to any office or public trust under the United States. I
am a friend to a variety of sects, because they keep one another in
order. How many different sects are we composed of throughout
the United States? How many different sects will be in congress?
We cannot enumerate the sects that may be in congress. And there
are so many now in the United States, that they will prevent the
establishment of any one sect in prejudice to the rest, and will
forever oppose all attempts to infringe religious liberty . . . .[13]

This conception of a multiplicity of factions as a check against the
dominance of any of them, and the consequent protection of the
rights of all minorities, was a central theme of the supporters of the
proposed Constitution. Thus, Madison wrote in the *51st Federalist*:[14]

Whilst all authority in [the United States] will be derived from and
dependent on the society, the society itself will be broken into so
many parts, interests and classes of citizens, that the rights of individuals, or of the minority, will be in little danger from interested
combinations of the majority. In a free government the security for
civil rights must be the same as that for religious rights. It consists
in the one case in the multiplicity of interests, and in the other in
the multiplicity of sects. The degree of security in both cases will
depend on the number of interests and sects; and this may be presumed to depend on the extent of country and number of people
comprehended under the same government.[15]

The word "sects" is, of course, ambiguous. It could mean any
organized religious group, or it could mean only divisions within the
Christian religion. It has been assumed that the first is the proper
meaning, thus including Jews, humanists, infidels, and Mohamme-
dans. Joseph Story's reading of article VI asserts: "[T]he Catholic and
the Protestant, the Calvinist and the Arminian, the Jew and the Infidel, may sit down at the common table of the national councils,
without any inquisition into their faith, or mode of worship."[16] And
it may be instructive that a 1796 treaty with Tripoli[17] provided that

    13. DEBATES AND OTHER PROCEEDINGS OF THE CONVENTION OF VIRGINIA 151 (2d ed.
Richmond 1805).
    14. FEDERALIST, *supra* note 12, No. 51 (J. Madison).
    15. *Id.* at 358.
    16. J. STORY, 3 COMMENTARIES ON THE CONSTITUTION OF THE UNITED STATES § 1873, at
731 (Boston 1833) (footnote omitted).
    17. Treaty of Peace and Friendship, November 4, 1796, United States-Tripoli, art. XI, 8
Stat. 154.

"the government of the United States of America is not in any sense
founded on the Christian religion."[18]   But the fact remains that it
was close to the time of the Civil War before all religious qualifications for state office were abolished.[19]   Moreover, the requirement of
the Maryland Constitution that an office holder swear to his belief in
God was not held invalid until 1961.[20]   Indeed, in 1892, the Supreme Court had referred with approval to the Delaware Test Oath.[21]
And in the same case, the Court declared that "this is a Christian
nation."[22]   It is no wonder that at that time Lord Bryce could write:
"[T]he National government and the State governments do give to
Christianity a species of recognition inconsistent with the view that
civil government should be absolutely neutral in religious matters."[23]   But back to the beginning.

When the time came, the First Congress adopted a Bill of
Rights, which had been implicitly, if not explicitly, promised to secure the necessary ratification. The provisions that emerged as the first
of the Bill of Rights were devoted to the issues of religious freedom
and establishment: "Congress shall make no law respecting an establishment of religion, or prohibiting the free exercise thereof.
. . . "[24] Before discussing the conflicts of opinion on the desirability
and use for such provision, I should like to trace the genesis of the
words that were ultimately utilized.

Madison's original proposal for inclusion in the Bill of Rights declared: "The civil rights of none shall be abridged on account of religious belief or worship, nor shall any national religion be established, nor shall the full and equal rights of conscience be in any
manner, or on any pretext, infringed."[25] The proposal continued:
"No State shall violate the equal rights of conscience, or the freedom
of the press, or the trial by jury in criminal cases."[26]

---

18. *Id.*, *quoted in* I. CORNELISON, THE RELATION OF RELIGION TO CIVIL GOVERNMENT IN
THE UNITED STATES 163 (1895).

19. *See* Wright, *Introduction* to FEDERALIST, *supra* note 12, at 64.

20. Torcaso v. Watkins, 367 U.S. 488, 495-96 (1961).

21. DEL. CONST. of 1776, art. XXII, *reprinted in* Church of the Holy Trinity v. United
States, 143 U.S. 457, 469-70 (1892). The Delaware Test Oath required all officers to make and
subscribe to the following oath: "I, A.B., do profess faith in God the Father, and in Jesus Christ
His only Son, and in the Holy Ghost, one God, blessed for evermore; and I do acknowledge the
Holy Scriptures of the Old and New Testament to be given by divine inspiration." DEL.
CONST. of 1776, art. XXII, *reprinted in* Church of the Holy Trinity v. United States, 143 U.S.
457, 469-70 (1892).

22. Church of the Holy Trinity v. United States, 143 U.S. 457, 471 (1892).

23. 2 J. BRYCE, THE AMERICAN COMMONWEALTH 701 (3d ed. 1895).

24. U.S. CONST. amend. I.

25. 1 ANNALS OF CONGRESS 434 (Gales & Seaton eds. 1789).

26. *Id.* at 435.

8   Villanova Law Review   [Vol. 24: p. 3

This proposal came to naught, however, and when the issue was
mooted in House debate, the clause under consideration read: "[N]o
religion shall be established by law, nor shall the equal rights of conscience be infringed."[27] Madison stated that these words meant to
him "that Congress should not establish a religion, and enforce the
legal observation of it by law, nor compel men to worship God in any
manner contrary to their conscience."[28] Congressman Huntington, although agreeing with the Madisonian construction, feared that the
clause might be construed by some as antireligious.[29] In his view,
such a construction might lead to the infringement by the federal
government of the powers of the states to support religion, for example, by the refusal to allow the national courts the power to enforce
commitments "for a support of ministers or building of places of worship."[30]

Congressman Samuel Livermore wanted the provision to read:
"Congress shall make no laws touching religion, or infringing the
rights of conscience."[31] This motion was passed by the House by a
vote of thirty-one to twenty.[32] Livermore, one of the unsung contributors to the founding of this nation and the creation of its Bill of
Rights,[33] was a member of the Continental Congress. He was instrumental in bringing about New Hampshire's ratification as the
ninth state to do so, and served as chief justice of the state even
while he was both a Congressman and Senator.[34] As with Madison's
original proposal, Livermore again wished to place restraints on state
governments as well as the federal government. "[T]he equal rights of
conscience, the freedom of speech or of the press, and the right of
trial by jury in criminal cases, shall not be infringed by any State."[35]
The House committee approved this limitation on the states, but it
was not adopted by the full House.[36] A few days later, on August
20, 1789, Fisher Ames of Massachusetts amended the proposed provision to read: "Congress shall make no law establishing religion, or
to prevent the free exercise thereof, or to infringe the rights of conscience."[37]

---

27. *Id.* at 729.
28. *Id.* at 730.
29. *Id.*
30. *Id.*
31. *Id.* at 731.
32. *Id.*
33. *See* A. Stokes & L. Pfeffer, Church and State in the United States 46 (rev.
ed. 1964) [hereinafter cited as Stokes].
34. *Id.* at 46-48. Interestingly, Livermore was married to the daughter of the first minister
of the Church of England to establish a parish in New Hampshire.
35. 1 Annals of Congress, *supra* note 25, at 755.
36. *Id.* at xx.
37. *Id.* at 766.

In the Senate, motions to change the language to prohibit only preferences for one religion over another were rejected.[38] The Senate did approve a provision reading: "Congress shall make no law establishing articles of faith or a mode of worship, or prohibiting the free exercise of religion . . . ."[39] The result was the necessity for a joint conference committee,[40] in which Madison played a large part in bringing forth the language that was adopted as the religion clauses of the first amendment.[41]

From this legislative history of the religion clauses, a few propositions can be derived that should be beyond debate. First, the restraints, whatever they were, were to be restraints only on the United States.[42] The states had not forfeited, by the promulgation of the amendment, any of their rights to establish a state religion[43] or to afford preferences to one religious sect over others.[44] Second, the national government could not establish a state religion or afford privileges to any religious group or impose disabilities on any individual on the basis of religious preference or affiliation.[45] Or, in sum, religion was to be no business of the national government.

A third proposition emerges from the legislative history of the religion clauses, I think, and that is that they were not separate and distinct conceptions, but rather a unified one. The existence of an established church implied intolerance for the nonestablished religions. The ban on a national church monopoly would factionalize the churches and thereby assure religious freedom.

The most important change in the original meaning, a change with which none would seem any longer to quarrel, came when the Supreme Court decided that the fourteenth amendment's due process clause[46] made the provisions of the first amendment religion clauses applicable to the states.[47] Of course, nothing in the history of the fourteenth amendment suggests that this was among its purposes or

---

38. *See* 1 DOCUMENTARY HISTORY OF THE FIRST FEDERAL CONGRESS OF THE UNITED STATES OF AMERICA, MARCH 4, 1789-March 3, 1791, 151 (L. Grant De Pauw ed. 1972).

39. *Id.* at 166.

40. *Id.* at 181, 189, 192.

41. *Id.* at 181.

42. *See* Permoli v. Municipality No. 1 of New Orleans, 44 U.S. (3 How.) 671, 694 (1845).

43. *See* S. COBB, THE RISE OF RELIGIOUS LIBERTY IN AMERICA 510 (1970 reprint of 1902 ed.); W. SWEET, THE STORY OF RELIGION IN AMERICA 189-93 (rev. ed. 1950). In fact, the disestablishment of state churches was not complete until 1833, when Massachusetts succumbed. *See id.* at 190.

44. *See* S. COBB, *supra* note 43, at 519.

45. *See id.* at 510.

46. U.S. CONST. amend. XIV, § 1. The due process clause provides: "[N]or shall any State deprive any person of life, liberty, or property, without due process of law . . . ." *Id.*

47. *See* notes 50-54 and accompanying text *infra*.

10   VILLANOVA LAW REVIEW   [VOL. 24: p. 3

goals. The transmogrification occurred solely at the whim of the Court. An attempt to pass a constitutional amendment providing for the application of the religion clauses to the states, the Blaine Amendment, [48] failed in 1876, [49] eight years after the effectuation of the fourteenth amendment. Presumably, any infringement of religious freedom by a state now invokes the fourteenth amendment's ban on deprivation of liberty without due process of law. Any invalid contribution by a state toward the establishment of religion constitutes a deprivation of property without due process of law.

In any event, the Court without argument—certainly without cogent argument—held the free exercise clause of the first amendment [50] applicable to the states in 1940 in *Cantwell v. Connecticut*, [51] and the establishment clause [52] applicable to the states in *Everson v. Board of Education* [53] in 1947. [54] It has been said that Justice Brennan's concurring opinion in the second school prayer case [55] best spells out the justification for this belated recognition of what the framers of the fourteenth amendment had wrought. [56] I leave it to the reader to judge the forcefulness of his argument. [57] Neither the reader nor I can deny that the fourteenth amendment now makes the

---

48. H.R. Res. 1, 44th Cong., 1st Sess., 4 CONG. REC. 5190 (1876). The Blaine Amendment provided that

> [n]o State shall make any law respecting an establishment of religion or prohibiting the free exercise thereof; and no money raised by taxation in any State for the support of public schools or derived from any public fund therefor, nor any public lands devoted thereto, shall ever be under the control of any religious sect or denomination; nor shall any money so raised or lands so devoted be divided between religious sects or denominations.

Id.

49. 4 CONG. REC. 5595 (1876).
50. U.S. CONST. amend. I. For the text of the free exercise clause, *see* note 3 *supra*.
51. 310 U.S. 296, 303 (1940). This conclusion was foreshadowed by dictum in Meyer v. Nebraska, 262 U.S. 390, 399 (1923).
52. U.S. CONST. amend. I. For the text of the establishment clause, *see* note 3 *supra*.
53. 330 U.S. 1 (1947).
54. *Id.* at 8.
55. School Dist. of Abington Township v. Schempp, 374 U.S. 203, 253-58 (1963) (Brennan, J., concurring). In *Schempp*, Justice Brennan stated:

> [T]he Fourteenth Amendment's protection of the free exercise of religion can hardly be questioned .... Even if we assume that the draftsmen of the Fourteenth Amendment saw no immediate connection between its protections against state action infringing personal liberty and the guarantees of the First Amendment, it is certainly too late in the day to suggest that their assumed inattention to the question dilutes the force of these constitutional guarantees in their application to the States. *It is enough to conclude that the religious liberty embodied in the Fourteenth Amendment would not be viable if the Constitution were interpreted to forbid only establishments ordained by Congress.*

Id. at 257-58 (footnotes omitted) (emphasis added).

56. *See* P. KAUPER, RELIGION AND THE CONSTITUTION 53-57, 72-74 (1964).
57. For a discussion of several arguments suggesting that the fourteenth amendment does not absorb the establishment clause and Justice Brennan's responses, *see* School Dist. of Abington Township v. Schempp, 374 U.S. 203, 254-58 (1963) (Brennan, J., concurring).

religion clauses applicable to the states. That is a *fait accompli*; whether it was effected by *ipse dixit* or by reason no longer matters.

The incorporation by the fourteenth amendment of the religion clauses, however, does not help to explicate their meaning. Whatever difficulties there may be in applying the provisions to actions by the national government are equally present when applying the provisions to the states. To resort to the suggestion by some Justices of a "two-tier" theory of the first amendment,[58] that is, to assume that the religion clauses are more stringent restraints on the national government than on the states, only compounds the confusion rather than relieving it.

Three distinct historical bases on which to ground the meaning of the religion clauses have been articulated. The so-called Madisonian position was that government should abstain from interference with religious belief or behavior so that each religious faction could compete on its own for adherents.[59] For Madison, as is indicated by the earlier quotation from *The Federalist*,[60] the multiplication of religious factions would assure freedom to each and the dominance of none.[61] To Thomas Jefferson is attributed the "wall of separation theory,"[62] utilized in the several opinions in the *Everson* case,[63] which sees the establishment clause as requiring strict separation of church and state for the protection of the state.[64] The third theory, labeled with Roger Williams' name, calls for the separation of church and state, but only to protect the church against corruption by the state.[65]

So far as the Supreme Court has chosen to assert which of these three constructions best bottoms the provisions of the religion clauses, it is clear that the Court first opted for the Jeffersonian "wall of separation," with such holes in the wall as it may desire to imagine or create.[66] As Shakespeare put it: "Thou wall, O wall! O sweet and

58. *See, e.g.*, Jacobellis v. Ohio, 378 U.S. 184, 203 (1964) (Harlan, J., dissenting); Roth v. United States, 354 U.S. 476, 503-06 (1957) (Harlan, J., concurring in part and dissenting in part); Beauharnais v. Illinois, 343 U.S. 250, 288-95 (1952) (Jackson, J., dissenting); Gitlow v. New York, 268 U.S. 652, 672 (1925) (Holmes, J., dissenting).
59. *See* J. MADISON, *Memorial and Remonstrance Against Religious Assessments*, in 2 WRITINGS OF JAMES MADISON 183 (1900). Madison adopted this position in 1785 in an attempt to dissuade the Virginia legislature from renewing Virginia's tax levy for the support of the established church. *Id.* at 183-84.
60. *See* text accompanying note 15 *supra*.
61. *See id.*
62. *See* T. JEFFERSON, THE WRITINGS OF THOMAS JEFFERSON 113 (H.A. Washington ed. 1854).
63. 330 U.S. at 16; *id.* at 29-30 (Rutledge, J., dissenting).
64. *See* T. JEFFERSON, *supra* note 62, at 113. *See also* P. KURLAND, RELIGION AND THE LAW 17 (1962).
65. For a discussion of Roger Williams' position, *see* P. KURLAND, *supra* note 64, at 17.
66. *See* 330 U.S. at 16.

lovely wall! Show me thy chink to blink through with mine eyne." [67]
In 1970, however, the Court seemed to have veered to the Williams'
argument in *Walz v. Tax Commission* [68] and has wobbled ever since.

The choice of the Jeffersonian wall with its notion of an absolute
ban on any government practice that "aids or opposes" any religion, [69]
rather than the Williams wall with a one-way door that would allow
aid to religion but not infringement on religion, roused the ire of
modern churchmen, most notably that of the late Professor Mark
DeWolfe Howe and Professor Wilber G. Katz. I quote at length from
Katz quoting Howe, lest any paraphrase that I may offer should be
affected by my personal bias toward the Jeffersonian approach:

> Professor Howe's views were expressed in a series of lectures
> published under the title *The Garden and the Wilderness*. His
> criticism could scarcely have been more severe. He charged that
> "By superficial and purposive interpretations of the past, the Court
> has dishonored the arts of the historian and degraded the talents of
> the lawyer." His principal complaint was that the Court's Estab-
> lishment Clause doctrine was spun exclusively out of the
> Jeffersonian threads in American church-state tradition. The Court
> erroneously assumed that the framers of the First Amendment
> "spoke in a wholly Jeffersonian dialect." Howe's thesis was that the
> American tradition of church-state separation includes not only the
> Jeffersonian threads, but also those running back to Roger Wil-
> liams. Both Jefferson and Williams wrote metaphorically of a wall
> of separation, but they viewed the wall as serving quite different
> ends. Howe described the Jeffersonian principle of separation as
> rooted in deistic rationalism and anticlericalism, Church and state
> should be separated "as the safeguard of public and private inter-
> ests against ecclesiastical depradations and excursions." Following
> this view, the Court seemed to have assumed that "the First
> Amendment intended to keep alive the bias of the Enlightenment
> which asserted that government must not give its aid in any form
> to religion lest impious clerks tighten their grip upon the purses
> and the minds of men."
>
>   . . . Williams' wall protected churches not only against re-
> straints but also against the corrupting effects of the government
> support. Williams and his followers believed that "the spiritual
> freedom of churches is jeopardized when they forget the principle
> of separation."

---

67. W. SHAKESPEARE, A MIDSUMMER NIGHT'S DREAM, Act V, sc. 1, 1. 11.172-73 (Cambridge University Press 1949).
68. 397 U.S. 664, 668 (1970).
69. *See* Epperson v. Arkansas, 393 U.S. 97, 106 (1968).

In Howe's judgment, the First Amendment's prohibitions:
. . . at the time of their promulgation were generally understood to be more the expression of Roger Williams'
philosophy than of Jefferson's . . . . [T]he predominant
concern at the time when the First Amendment was
adopted was not the Jeffersonian fear that if it were not
enacted, the federal government would aid religion and
thus advance the interest of impious clerks but rather the
evangelical hope that private conscience and autonomous
churches, working together and in freedom, would extend the rule of truth.
The Williams principle of separation does not forbid all government aids to religion, but only those incompatible with full religious freedom.[70]

With all due respect, Howe and Katz are guilty of the same violations of "the arts of the historian" as they condemn in the Court.
But they are half right. Little basis exists for the claim that the Jeffersonian "wall of separation" was the guide to the formulation of the
first amendment's religion clauses, except that the theory was written
by Madison, the Virginian who clearly espoused the Jeffersonian
view, at least for Virginia.[71] Equally, support is absent for the argument that the clauses were framed in accordance with the doctrines
of Roger Williams. The primary purpose of the amendment was to
keep the national government out of religious matters. Madison, the
prime mover of the amendment, thought the amendment unnecessary, except to calm the fears of those who worried that without it the
national government would be capable of invading the realm of the
states, a realm encompassing laws relating to religion.[72] The states
were to be unaffected by the amendment.[73] States like Virginia were
free to endorse, as they did, what Professor Howe called the
Jeffersonian concern to "safeguard . . . public and private interests
against ecclesiastical depredations and excursions."[74] Those like

---

70. Katz, *Radiations From Church Tax Exemption,* 1970 SUP. CT. REV. 93, 96-97 (footnotes
omitted), *quoting* M. HOWE, THE GARDEN AND THE WILDERNESS 4, 10, 2, 7, 2, 19 (1965).
71. *See* J. MADISON, *supra* note 59, at 183. In this work, Madison, like Jefferson, argued
that separation of church and state is necessary for the preservation of a free society:
Because if religion be exempt from the authority of the Society at large, still less can it be
subject to that of the Legislative Body. The latter are but the creatures and vicegerants of
the former. . . . The preservation of a free government requires not merely, that the
metes and bounds which separate each department of power may be invariably maintained; but more especially, that neither of them be suffered to overleap the great Barrier
which defends the rights of the people.
Id. at 185.
72. M. HOWE, THE GARDEN AND THE WILDERNESS 20-21 (1965).
73. *See* W. KATZ, RELIGION AND AMERICAN CONSTITUTIONS 8-10 (1964).
74. M. HOWE, *supra* note 72, at 2..

Massachusetts were left free to follow the pietistic views of Williams'
"dread of the worldly competitions which might consume the
churches if sturdy fences against the wilderness were not maintained."[75]   No dominant single theory of church-state relations prevailed, except the notion that it was no business of the national government. As Professor Edmund S. Morgan has written:

> In 1776 most colonies collected taxes for support of the ministry,
> and one church generally got the bulk of the funds, if not all of
> them, regardless of its size. In the southern colonies it was the
> Anglican church, in New England the Congregational. During the
> Revolution, partly because of the new disposition toward equality,
> the Angelican church everywhere lost its special position, and most
> states left the churches of every denomination to support them-
> selves by voluntary donation of their members. But the New Eng-
> land states continued their support, still favoring the Congregation-
> alists, in New Hampshire until 1817, in Connecticut until 1818,
> and in Massachusetts until 1833.[76]

Today's problems regarding a choice between the views of Jefferson and Williams derive, not from the language or purpose of the first
amendment, but rather from the attempted application of the first
amendment's language to state action, even though the amendment
was clearly framed not to be applicable to the states at all. And, as I
have suggested, there is no part of the history of the fourteenth
amendment that provides any guidance whatsoever for the application
of the religion clauses to the states. Thus, the constitutional provisions are not reasons for the decisions in the Court's church and state
cases, but only an excuse for them. But Howe and Katz are right in
their assertion that the Court uses the grab bag of history to choose
arguments that support positions reached for reasons other than those
which it marshals. This, however, is not different from the Court's
general use of legal precedents, picking among them to support conclusions rather than being guided to conclusions by the precedents.
That, of course, is easy when there are conflicting precedents to
choose from, as there usually are in this area of constitutional law.[77]
Sometimes a precedent is thought to be binding, even though it is
conceded to be patently wrong, apparently because it dictates a result
desired by the Justice who cannot otherwise justify either that result
or the precedent.[78]

75. *Id.* at 6.
76. E. MORGAN, THE BIRTH OF THE REPUBLIC, 1763-89, 96-97 (rev. ed. 1977).
77. *See* Wolman v. Walter, 433 U.S. 229, 265 n.2 (1977) (Stevens, J., concurring in part and dissenting in part). As Justice Stevens cautioned, "the doctrine of *stare decisis* cannot foreclose an eventual choice between two inconsistent precedents." *Id.*
78. *See* Runyon v. McCrary, 427 U.S. 160, 189 (1976) (Stevens, J., concurring).

Having long since abandoned the search for the original meaning of the religion clauses, the Court has come up with a formula for use in measuring the validity of governmental acts claimed to be in conflict with the first amendment. Alas, like Hamlet's reading matter, it is best described as "words, words, words."[79] And as Pascal told us: "The world is content with words; few think of searching into the nature of things."[80]

Some anguish is avoided for the Court, if not for its critics, by treating the religion clauses as two distinct mandates rather than as a single injunction. The determination of which clause is involved is accomplished by stamping a label on the case before considering the issues as one invoking either the free exercise clause or the establishment clause. In most situations, of course, to afford a privilege of freedom claimed for adherents to one religion necessarily results in aiding the religion over others or over the nonreligious. The labeling frequently accomplishes what the modernists would write into the Constitution—a provision that where there is a conflict between the free exercise clause and the establishment clause, the free exercise clause should prevail.[81] That no basis exists for such a proposition either in the language, the history, or the avowed purposes of the first amendment is overcome by the argument that such a construction best comports with our contemporary libertarian ethos.[82]

Even with the ease of judgment that derives from the creation of the dichotomy that the Court now indulges, the Court's rulings have resulted in decisions that are hardly compatible with each other. Such inconsistencies as the Court has wrought hardly suggest a constitutional principle that controls the Court's judgments. Unless, of course, it be that constitutional dictum once privately uttered by a deceased Justice: "So long as the principle is clear, what difference does its application make?"

Thus, in the area labelled freedom of religion, sometimes the question that seems to be asked is whether the government action imposes restraints on the individual because of his religious affiliation or practice or whether the imposition derives from grounds distinct from the religious beliefs or affiliations of the persons regulated? Sometimes the question is whether the regulation in fact inhibits freedom of religious exercise, whatever the nonreligious basis for the promulgated regulation? And here, as elsewhere, the right answer depends on the right question.

---

79. W. SHAKESPEARE, HAMLET, Act II, sc. 2, 1. 1.193 (G. Kittredge ed. 1939).
80. B. PASCAL, PROVINCIAL LETTERS, Letter II 338 (1657) (Mod. Lib. ed. 1941).
81. See L. TRIBE, AMERICAN CONSTITUTIONAL LAW § 14-7 (1978).
82. See id.

16 VILLANOVA LAW REVIEW [VOL. 24: p. 3

The decisions reveal that Mormons may be prosecuted for polygamy although it is—or was—mandated by their religion.[83] And Jehovah's Witnesses may be punished for violation of the child labor law by permitting or requiring children to engage in the street sale of literature, as their faith requires.[84] On the other hand, the Amish—and apparently only the Amish—may be exempted from the compulsory education laws because of their religious beliefs.[85]

Adverse economic effects on seventh-day observers resulting from the state's requirement of abstention from business affairs on Sunday are not invasions of religious freedom.[86] But adverse economic effects on seventh-day observers from unemployment compensation laws requiring availability for employment are invasions of religious freedom.[87] And the payment of benefits to those who have done compulsory military service, which is denied to those who have performed compulsory civilian service because of religious conscientious objections to military service, is not an infringement of religious freedom.[88]

While government is precluded from determining the validity of religious beliefs, the courts may determine whether the beliefs are sufficiently religious to qualify for the benefits of the free exercise clause of the first amendment.[89] Some religious beliefs command exemption from military service, while others do not.[90]

The result of all this is not the application of constitutional principles, but the determination of license to violate the laws with impunity wherever the Court is satisfied that the violations are the consequence of sincere religious beliefs that warrant judicial protection. Thus, the Court's most recent decision is that Jehovah's Witnesses are entitled to be free of New Hampshire's command that license plates display the state motto: "Live Free or Die."[91] But it should be pointed out that the Court derived this freedom, not from the religion clauses alone, but from the undifferentiated application of the entire first amendment.[92]

---

83. Reynolds v. United States, 98 U.S. 145 (1878).
84. Prince v. Massachusetts, 321 U.S. 158 (1944).
85. Wisconsin v. Yoder, 406 U.S. 205 (1972). *See also* Kurland, *The Supreme Court, Compulsory Education, and the First Amendment's Religion Clauses*, 75 W. VA. L. REV. 213, 224-45 (1973).
86. Braunfeld v. Brown, 366 U.S. 599 (1961).
87. Sherbert v. Verner, 374 U.S. 398 (1963).
88. Johnson v. Robison, 415 U.S. 361 (1974).
89. *See* Welsh v. United States, 398 U.S. 333 (1970); United States v. Seeger, 380 U.S. 163 (1965); United States v. Ballard, 322 U.S. 78 (1944).
90. *See* Gillette v. United States, 401 U.S. 437 (1971). *See generally* Greenawalt, *All or Nothing at All: The Defeat of Selective Conscientious Objection*, 1971 SUP. CT. REV. 31.
91. Wooley v. Maynard, 430 U.S. 705 (1977).
92. *See id.* at 714-15.

The Court's behavior in what it labels freedom of religion cases might be compared with the ancient royal prerogative of dispensation, pursuant to which the Crown could exempt individuals from conforming to the laws of Parliament, particularly for reasons of religious affiliation.[93] That the English Bill of Rights[94] deprived the Crown of such authority is regarded only as testimony to the accepted proposition that courts may be entrusted with arbitrary powers that cannot be left to the discretion of executive or legislative branch action. We are never told why.

When we turn to the establishment cases, the Court purports to have a more clearly defined formula for their resolution. As the Court stated in a recent decision:

> The mode of analysis for Establishment Clause questions is defined by the three-part test that has emerged from the Court's decisions. In order to pass muster, a statute must have a secular legislative purpose, must have a principal or primary effect that neither advances nor inhibits religion, and must not foster an excessive government entanglement with religion.[95]

It becomes immediately apparent how the labeling of a case may be determinative of its outcome. There is no doubt, for example, that the exemption granted exclusively to the Amish in *Wisconsin v. Yoder*[96] would fall afoul of the establishment clause standards announced by the Court, unless the decision can be distinguished on the grounds that a state court judicial decree rather than a state legislative exemption was at issue.[97]   And once again, the connection between the Court's rule and the constitutional mandate is certainly difficult to ascertain, although the excessive entanglement proposition may be traced to the Roger Williams notion and the secular purpose and effect proposition might be derived from the Jeffersonian argument. It should be noted, however, that the three-prong test requires that the governmental action satisfy each requirement and not simply one of them.[98]

---

93. *See* F. MAITLAND, THE CONSTITUTIONAL HISTORY OF ENGLAND 302-06 (H.A.L. Fisher ed. 1961); 2 W. STUBBS, THE CONSTITUTIONAL HISTORY OF ENGLAND 583-84 (Clarendon Press 1880).

94. 1689, 1 W. & M., c.2.

95. Wolman v. Walter, 433 U.S. 229, 235-36 (1977), *citing* Roemer v. Board of Pub. Works, 426 U.S. 736, 748 (1976); Committee for Pub. Educ. v. Nyquist, 413 U.S. 756, 772-73 (1973); *and* Lemon v. Kurtzman, 403 U.S. 602, 612, 613 (1971).

96. 406 U.S. 205 (1972).

97. *See id.* at 207, 213. *cf.* Shelley v. Kraemer, 334 U.S. 1 (1948) (fourteenth amendment prohibits judicial enforcement of racially discriminatory covenants as unconstitutional state action).

98. *See* Wolman v. Walter, 433 U.S. 229, 235-36 (1977).

Nevertheless, the three-prong test has resulted in as much confusion and conflict under the establishment clause as the Court's decisions under the free exercise clause. How, for example, can a law which exempts churches from taxes that others must pay be justified as without the purpose or effect of advancing religious interests and without avoiding entanglement? Yet, that was the Court's conclusion in *Walz v. Tax Commission.*[99]　A more tortured opinion would be hard to find.

The bulk of the establishment clause cases have been concerned with aid to private schools. And within this narrow but important area there is again no sign of consistency. Seemingly, the supplying of bus transportation by the government exclusively to parochial school students is valid.[100]　So too, may a government make books available to parochial school students as well as public school students without violating the establishment clause.[101]　It may not afford reimbursement for testing in church sponsored schools if the tests are created and administered by parochial school teachers,[102] but it may do so if the tests are state created.[103] So too, may the state provide funds for "diagnostic speech and hearing services and diagnostic psychological services,"[104] as well as "physician, nursing, dental, and optometric services in non-public schools."[105]　Governmental supply of "therapeutic services" off the school premises does not violate the establishment clause, but the provision of such services on the school premises would.[106]　Although "released time" for catechism classes on school premises has been held invalid,[107] "released time" for catechism classes off school premises has been held valid.[108]

If government may supply textbooks to parochial school students, it may not supply other instructional materials[109] even when they are "incapable of diversion to religious use."[110]　Funding for school field

99. 397 U.S. 664 (1970).

100. Everson v. Board of Educ., 330 U.S. 1 (1947).

101. Board of Educ. v. Allen, 392 U.S. 236 (1968).

102. Levitt v. Committee for Pub. Educ., 413 U.S. 472 (1973).

103. Wolman v. Walter, 433 U.S. 229, 240 (1977), *citing* Lemon v. Kurtzman, 403 U.S. 602, 614 (1971); Board of Educ. v. Allen, 392 U.S. 236, 245-46, 246 n.7 (1968); *and* Pierce v. Society of Sisters, 268 U.S. 510, 534 (1925).

104. Wolman v. Walter, 433 U.S. 229, 242 (1977).

105. *Id.* (footnote omitted), *citing* Meek v. Pittenger, 421 U.S. 349, 364, 368 n.17 (1975); *and* Lemon v. Kurtzman, 403 U.S. 602, 616-17 (1971).

106. *See* Wolman v. Walter, 433 U.S. 229, 244-48 (1977).

107. McCollum v. Board of Educ., 333 U.S. 203 (1948).

108. Zorach v. Clauson, 343 U.S. 306 (1952).

109. Wolman v. Walter, 433 U.S. 229, 248-51 (1977), *citing* Meek v. Pittenger, 421 U.S. 349, 359-62, 366 (1975); Committee for Pub. Educ. v. Nyquist, 413 U.S. 756, 783 (1973); *and* Board of Educ. v. Allen, 392 U.S. 236, 248 (1968).

110. Wolman v. Walter, 433 U.S. 229, 248 & n.15 (1977), *quoting* OHIO REV. CODE ANN. §§ 3317.06(B)-.06(C) (Page Supp. 1977) (repealed).

trips is invalid, although it provides no more than transportation, because field trips involve an educational function and not, as in *Everson*, merely transportation to school.[111]   Providing funds to a religious school, or its students or their parents violates the establishment clause,[112] even if the funds are usable only for maintenance and repairs of buildings.[113]   All of this because "[i]n view of the impossibility of separating the secular education function from the sectarian, the state aid inevitably flows in part in support of the religious role of the schools."[114]

It may equally be said of church related colleges and universities that "[i]n view of the impossibility of separating the secular education function from the sectarian, the state aid inevitably flows in part in support of the religious role of the schools."[115]   Yet, the Court has made it quite clear that both the national and state governments are free to dispense large sums of money to these colleges and universities, so long as the moneys are not directly used for sectarian purposes.[116]

The entanglement part of the Court's triad is either empty or nonsensical. If entanglement means intercourse between government and religious institutions, then no law is more entangling than that which imposes governmental regulation on private schools as all compulsory education laws do. *Pierce v. Society of Sisters*[117] forbade state monopoly of lower school education but implicitly commanded that the state set and enforce proper standards of secular education for parochial schools.[118]   The oversight demanded by these laws is certainly far greater than in the public aid to private school statutes that the Court has struck down.

If entanglement means the avoidance of conflict between religious factions over public issues, it says only that state regulation of, or contribution to, religious institutions will be limited to that which the public will placidly tolerate. By this test, the Supreme Court's own opinions in the school prayer cases[119] and in the abortion cases[120] would themselves be violations of the first amendment.

---

111. Wolman v. Walter, 433 U.S. 229, 252-55 (1977).
112. Sloan v. Lemon, 413 U.S. 825 (1973); Lemon v. Kurtzman, 403 U.S. 602 (1971).
113. Committee for Pub. Educ. v. Nyquist, 413 U.S. 756 (1973).
114. Wolman v. Walter, 433 U.S. 229, 250 (1977).
115. *Id.*
116. *See* Roemer v. Board of Pub. Works, 426 U.S. 736 (1976); Hunt v. McNair, 413 U.S. 734 (1973); Tilton v. Richardson, 403 U.S. 672 (1971).
117. 268 U.S. 510 (1925).
118. *See id.* at 535.
119. School Dist. of Abington Township v. Schempp, 374 U.S. 203 (1963); Engel v. Vitale, 370 U.S. 421 (1962).
120. Doe v. Bolton, 410 U.S. 179 (1973); Roe v. Wade, 410 U.S. 113 (1973).

The word entanglement is only an antonym for separation. The former assures no more guidance than the latter. The Court is left to decide how much separation is required or how much entanglement is too much entanglement. Once again, we are reminded of Professor Thomas Reed Powell's comments on the creation of a Restatement of the Commerce Clause: "In the usual form, the black-letter text would read: 'Congress may regulate interstate commerce.' A comment would add: 'The states may also regulate interstate commerce, but not too much.' And then, there would follow a caveat: 'How much is too much is beyond the scope of this Restatement.'"[121] We may also be reminded of Powell's remark when, in introducing Harlan Fiske Stone at a *Columbia Law Review* dinner, he said that Justice Stone was "neither partial, on the one hand, nor impartial, on the other." When we learn to parse that, we may also find the key to the Court's entanglement language.

The primary purpose and primary effect language lead us little way toward any fixed rule. Clearly the primary purpose and the primary effect of the New York tax exemption for church property in *Walz* was to aid the churches or their adherents. That was not only its primary purpose and effect, it was its sole purpose and effect. But it was held to have passed the test.[122]

It is clear that the Court expects that both the purpose and effect requirements be met before a state law can pass muster under the establishment clause. Should a law passed with the purpose of helping religious institutions, but which in fact did not do so, be considered a violation of the first amendment? True, we have seen the Court, for better or worse, pick up the notions of intent—which may be different from purpose—as the essence of a constitutional violation, as in recent racial segregation cases, for example.[123] But it is even less clear why we should be concerned in the church-state cases with unlawful motives rather than unlawful acts. Perhaps, if the road to hell is paved with good intentions, the road to constitutional violations is paved with bad ones.

In any event, the three-prong test hardly elucidates the Court's judgments. Nor does it cover the plastic nature of the judgments in this area. Judicial discretion, rather than constitutional mandate, controls the results.

---

121. Freund, *Foreword*, in T. POWELL, VAGARIES AND VARIETIES IN CONSTITUTIONAL INTERPRETATION IX (1956).
122. *See* 397 U.S. at 680.
123. Village of Arlington Heights v. Metropolitan Hous. Dev. Corp., 429 U.S. 252 (1977); Washington v. Davis, 426 U.S. 229 (1976).

The lack of principles, no less constitutional principles, in these cases was plainly acknowledged by both Justice Powell and Justice Stevens in the recent case of *Wolman v. Walter*.[124]   Justice Stevens would eliminate the chaos by returning to the absolutism of the Jeffersonian wall, but not without acknowledging the Roger Williams argument, because for him the two result in the same end.[125]   Although one may wish that Stevens had relied on better authority than the argument of Clarence Darrow in *Scopes v. State*,[126] his position is a demand for consistency:

> The line drawn by the Establishment Clause of the First Amendment must also have a fundamental character. It should not differentiate between direct and indirect subsidies, or between instructional materials like globes and maps on the one hand and instructional materials like textbooks on the other.[127]

He would return to the statement, but not the ruling, of Justice Black in *Everson*:[128]   "Under that test, a state subsidy of sectarian schools is invalid regardless of the form it takes."[129]   Nevertheless, he, too, would draw lines that would permit public health services and, perhaps, even public diagnostic and therapeutic services, although he had "some misgivings on this [latter] point."[130]   But for him, the "Court's efforts to improve on the *Everson* test have not proved successful. 'Corrosive precedents' have left us without firm principles on which to decide these cases."[131]   Justice Stevens' resort to Roger Williams' theory may be found in a footnote, where he said:

> In *Roemer v. Maryland Public Works Bd.*, . . . I spoke of 'the pernicious tendency of a state subsidy to tempt religious schools to compromise their religious mission without wholly abandoning it.' This case presents an apt illustration. To qualify for aid, sectarian schools must relinquish their religious exclusivity. As the District

124. 433 U.S. 229, 262 (Powell, J., concurring in part and dissenting in part) (1977); *Id.* at 264 n.1 (Stevens, J., concurring in part and dissenting in part).
125. *Id.* at 265-66 (Stevens, J., concurring in part and dissenting in part).
126. Transcript of Oral Argument, Scopes v. State, 154 Tenn. 105, 289 S.W. 363 (1927). In *Scopes*, Darrow argued that "[t]he realm of religion . . . is where knowledge leaves off and where faith begins, and it never has needed the arm of the State for support, and wherever it has received it, it has harmed both the public and the religion that it would pretend to serve." *Id.* at 7, *reprinted in* 433 U.S. at 264 (Stevens, J., concurring in part and dissenting in part) (footnote omitted).
127. 433 U.S. at 265 (Stevens, J., concurring in part and dissenting in part).
128. *See* text accompanying notes 53-54 & 64 *supra*.
129. 433 U.S. at 265 (Stevens, J., concurring in part and dissenting in part).
130. *Id.* at 266 (Stevens, J., concurring in part and dissenting in part).
131. *Id.* (footnote omitted), *quoting* Everson v. Board of Educ., 330 U.S. 1, 63 (1947) (Rutledge, J., dissenting).

Court noted, the statute provides aid 'to pupils attending only those nonpublic schools whose admission policies make no distinction as to . . . creed . . . of either its pupils or of its teachers . . . .' Similarly, sectarian schools will be under pressure to avoid textbooks which present a religious perspective on secular subjects, so as to obtain the free textbooks provided by the State.[132]

Because parochial schools do not have a single function, a religious mission only, the problem of aid to private schools exists. A parochial school is not a church. It is, indeed, required to provide an adequate education in secular subjects as measured by state law. It must be accredited as a grammar school in order for its pupils to attend without violating the compulsory education laws. It is performing a state function as well as a religious function. It is not a place of worship; it is a school. And this is the reason that Justice Powell would abide by the implicit inconsistencies in the rules that his brethren have established as the law of the establishment clause.[133] Justice Powell wrote in *Wolman*:

> Our decisions in this troubling area draw lines that often must seem arbitrary. No doubt we could achieve greater analytical tidiness if we were to accept the broadest implications of the observation in *Meek v. Pittenger* . . . that "(s)ubstantial aid to the educational function of (sectarian) schools . . . necessarily results in aid rather than the institutions. . . . The persistent desire of a number would become impossible to sustain state aid of any kind—even if the aid is wholly secular in character and is supplied to the pupils rather than the institutions . . . . The persistent desire of a number of States to find proper means of helping sectarian education to survive would be doomed. This Court has not yet thought that such a harsh result is required by the Establishment Clause. Certainly few would consider it in the public interest. Parochial

---

132. 433 U.S. at 266 n.7 (Stevens, J., concurring in part and dissenting in part) (citations omitted), *quoting* Roemer v. Board of Pub. Works, 426 U.S. 736, 775 (1976) (Stevens, J., dissenting); *and* Wolman v. Essex, 417 F. Supp. 1113, 1116 (S.D. Ohio 1976), *aff'd in part and rev'd in part sub nom.* Wolman v. Walter, 433 U.S. 229 (1977). It is interesting to note that Justice Stevens was a law clerk to Justice Rutledge when the latter wrote the strong separationist opinion in *Everson*. Justice Rutledge stated:

> Two great drives are constantly in motion to abridge, in the name of education, the complete division of religion and civil authority which our forefathers made. One is to introduce religious education and observances into the public schools. The other, to obtain public funds for the aid and support of various private religious schools . . . In my opinion both avenues were closed by the Constitution. Neither should be opened by this Court. . . . Now as in Madison's day it is one of principle, to keep separate the separate spheres as the First Amendment drew them, to prevent the first experiment upon our liberties; and to keep the question from being entangled in corrosive precedents.

330 U.S. at 63 (Rutledge, J., dissenting) (citations omitted).

133. *See* text accompanying note 134 *infra*.

schools, quite apart from their sectarian purpose, have provided an educational alternative for millions of young Americans; they often afford wholesome competition with our public schools; and in some States they relieve substantially the tax burden incident to the operation of public schools. The State has, moreover, a legitimate interest in facilitating education of the highest quality for all children within its boundaries, whatever school their parents have chosen for them.[134]

Although accepting the reason behind the first amendment's religion clauses supplied by his fellow Virginians, Jefferson and Madison, Justice Powell further suggests that the wall should nevertheless be torn down, at least a little way:

> It is important to keep these issues in perspective. At this point in the 20th century we are quite far removed from the dangers that prompted the Framers to include the Establishment Clause in the Bill of Rights. . . . The risk of significant religious or denominational control over our democratic processes—or even of deep political division along religious lines—is remote, and when viewed against the positive contributions of sectarian schools, any such risk seems entirely tolerable in light of the continuing oversight of this Court. Our decisions have sought to establish principles that preserve the cherished safeguard of the Establishment Clause without resort to blind absolutism. If this endeavor means a loss of some analytical tidiness, then that too is entirely tolerable.[135]

These are strange words to be heard from Justice Powell, for they tell us two different things. First, that the religion clauses were meant to prevent evils that no longer threaten. Second, that the principles of the first amendment's religion clauses can be dispensed with so long as whatever violations which may occur are subject "to the continuing oversight of" the Supreme Court. What is in the "public interest" is to be measured, not by constitutional rules, but by judicial "oversight."

It would seem to me, however, that if the Constitution is to be rewritten by the judiciary, it should be written in terms of principles and not by way of ad hoc judgments to which no principle seems applicable. Many years ago, when I was young and naive, I wrote a piece describing what I thought was a principled constitutional

---

134. 433 U.S. at 262 (Powell, J., concurring in part, concurring in the judgment in part, and dissenting in part) (citation omitted), *quoting* Meek v. Pittenger, 421 U.S. 349, 366 (1975).
135. 433 U.S. at 263 (Powell, J., concurring in part, concurring in the judgment in part, and dissenting in part) (citation omitted).

ground for application of the religion clauses.[136] Strangely enough, now that I am old and cynical, I still think there is merit in what I said then.

My suggestion was based on the proposition that the religion clauses were not separate mandates but a single one and that the underlying proposition was assurance of equality of treatment.[137] I said then:

> The freedom and separation clauses should be read as stating a single precept: that government cannot utilize religion as a standard for action or inaction because these clauses, read together as they should be, prohibit classification in terms of religion either to confer a benefit or to impose a burden.[138]

That proposition met with almost uniform rejection. The strong adherents to religious faith damned it[139] or ignored it. The freedom riders ridiculed it.[140] Even so tolerant a critic as Professor Giannella would amend it beyond recognition.[141] And certainly the Supreme Court refused to have anything to do with it. Forgive me then if I sin by continuing to take pride in it. But it is not mere pride of authorship or stubbornness that leads me to this adherence—not that I lack either quality. I still think it best represents the meaning of the words and the intention of the authors of the amendment, certainly those of James Madison[142] and Samuel Livermore.[143] It still offers a proper rationalization for most of the cases that the Court has decided. It still offers a basis for the principled application that the Constitution would seem to demand. It would not resolve all questions, for there would necessarily remain, for example, the issue of what is religion? But that question is present whatever construction is given to the religion clauses.

I am so old-fashioned as to think that the provisions of the Constitution are only the mere "parchment barriers" that Madison feared they would become,[144] if they are no more than the current reflection of the predilections of the sitting Justices. Justice Story once told us: "The great mass of human calamities, in all ages, has been the

---

136. P. KURLAND, *supra* note 64.
137. *Id passim.*
138. *Id.* at 112.
139. *See* Katz, *supra* note 70, at 108.
140. *See* Pfeffer, Book Review, 15 STAN. L. REV. 389 (1963).
141. *See Religious Liberty Guarantee, supra* note 1; *Nonestablishment Principle, supra* note 1; Giannella, *supra* note 2.
142. *See* text accompanying notes 25-30 *supra. See also* STOKES, *supra* note 33, at 45-48.
143. *See* text accompanying notes 30-36 *supra. See also* STOKES, *supra* note 33, at 49-61.
144. *Federalist, supra* note 12, No. 48 (J. Madison), at 343.

result of bad government, or ill adjusted government; of a capricious exercise of power, a fluctuating public policy, a degrading tyranny, or a desolating ambition." [145]   These were the evils that a Constitution was framed to prevent. The Constitution cannot serve its function so long as it is regarded by the Court and the nation as a *tabula rasa* on which the Court is free to scribble at will.

Justice Powell's proposition that the evils at which the religion clauses were directed no longer threaten us states the primary problem that I raise—and leave with you. How should the Court undertake to decide cases for which there is no basis for resolution in the constitutional text? For, if one puts aside cases of clear constitutional violations—assuming the fourteenth amendment's incorporation of the first—as where the state requires a religious loyalty oath, [146] or where the state undertakes to prescribe compulsory religious ceremonies, [147] the modern day cases fall within neither the language of the first amendment nor the intent of its authors.

The Court has made clear its answer. When the Constitution affords no mandate, it will fill the hiatus with ersatz constitutional rules of its own making. This is neither a novel approach nor one limited to the construction of the religion clauses. One need look only. to *Lochner v. New York* [148] and *Adkins v. Children's Hospital* [149] for earlier examples, or to *Griswold v. Connecticut* [150] and to *Roe v. Wade* [151] and *Doe v. Bolton*, [152] for more recent ones, all more blatant usurpation of the constitution making function than the cases that I have canvassed here.

Of course, the Court might have said that in the absence of clear constitutional interdiction, the legislative judgment will control. That is what Chief Justice Marshall held when he started the Court on its road to judicial review in *Marbury v. Madison*. [153]   He said there, it will be recalled, that "the framers of the constitution contemplated that instrument as a rule for the government of *courts* as well as of the legislature." [154]   But that is not the road that the Court has cho-

---

145. J. STORY, *Lecture on the Science of Government*, in MISCELLANEOUS WRITINGS 147, 150 (Boston 1835).
146. *See* Torcaso v. Watkins, 367 U.S. 488 (1961).
147. *See* Engel v. Vitale, 370 U.S. 421 (1962). *See also* Kurland, *The Regents' Prayer Case: "Full of Sound and Fury, Signifying . . . ",* 1962 SUP. CT. REV. 1.
148. 198 U.S. 45 (1905).
149. 261 U.S. 525 (1923).
150. 381 U.S. 479 (1965).
151. 410 U.S. 113 (1973).
152. 410 U.S. 179 (1973).
153. 5 U.S. (1 Cranch) 137 (1803).
154. *Id.* at 179-80 (emphasis in original).

sen and it is probably not going to turn back on the powers it has
assumed. The corruption of power affects the judiciary no less than
the executive.[155]

Surely, in a would-be democracy, the people are entitled to
know who their masters are. When the Court pretends to gather its
judgments from the mandates of the Constitution it is engaging in
flagrant mis representation. Even when it attempts to extrapolate
from the limited commands that the basic document affords, it is usually engaged in a fraud that would get lesser men penal servitude for
violation of the federal mail fraud statute[156] or the Federal Trade
Commission Act.[157]

I would conclude, then, by quoting Judge Learned Hand. The
Court's use of the language and history of the religion clauses operates

> to disguise what they are doing and impute to [its rulings] a deriva-
> tion far more impressive than their personal preferences, which are
> all that in fact lie behind the decision. If we do need a third
> chamber, it should appear for what it is, and not as the interpreter
> of inscrutable principles.[158]

The point, here, then is not that the Court has reached the
wrong results in many or any of its church-state decisions. As declarations of what the Constitution should have said if it had spoken to the
question, they may well be better than their alternatives. The question remains whether in the absence of clear constitutional mandate,
the Court should have spoken at all in many of these cases. That
concern is shared even by one who as academic has applauded and,
as advocate, has urged the results that the Court has declared in the
name of the Constitution. As Archibald Cox said in his 1975 Chichele
Lectures at Oxford, delivered under the auspices of All Souls College:

> The rules of constitutional law written by the Warren
> Court . . . impress me as wiser and fairer than the rules they re-
> place. I would support nearly all as important reforms if proposed
> in a legislative chamber or a constitutional convention. In apprais-
> ing them as judicial rulings, however, I find it necessary to ask
> whether an excessive price was paid by enlarging the sphere and
> changing the nature of constitutional adjudication.[159]

---

155. *See* R. BERGER, GOVERNMENT BY JUDICIARY (1977); A. BICKEL, THE MORALITY OF
CONSENT 120-23 (1975); P. KURLAND, WATERGATE AND THE CONSTITUTION (1978); L. LUSKY,
BY WHAT RIGHT? (1975).
156. 39 U.S.C. §§ 3005-3007 (1970 & Supp. V 1975).
157. 15 U.S.C. §§ 41-77 (1976).
158. L. HAND, THE BILL OF RIGHTS 70 (Harvard University Press 1958).
159. A. COX, THE ROLE OF THE SUPREME COURT IN AMERICAN GOVERNMENT 102 (1976).

The question I leave with you, then, is whether the American body politic would have been stronger or weaker had the Court abstained from supplying us with its personal preferences and left the state and national legislatures to determine those public issues on which there was no certain constitutional mandate under the first amendment's religion clauses. I urge only, contrary to the prevailing views within legal academia, that there is more than one side to the argument.

[5]

8

RELIGION, PUBLIC MORALITY, AND CONSTITUTIONAL LAW

DAVID A. J. RICHARDS

The proper balance between moral pluralism and community is, I believe, a pervasive interpretive issue in American constitutional law in the constitutional jurisprudence of state neutrality required by the religion clauses, free speech, and constitutional privacy. State abridgements of religious liberty, for example, are justifiable, if at all, only on a strong showing of neutral state purposes.[1] In a recent book, *Toleration and the Constitution*,[2] I develop a general position on the role of history, interpretive conventions, and political theory in constitutional interpretation in general and try to show the interpretive fertility of this approach in terms of a unified theory of the value of constitutional neutrality pervasive in the interpretation of the religion clauses, free speech, and constitutional privacy. My analysis here elaborates an aspect of that argument, namely, how interpretations of religion-clause neutrality, shifting over time, can be plausibly understood in terms of an approach to constitutional interpretation that takes seriously the distinctive role of a certain kind of moral and political theory in making the best interpretive sense of our history and our changing interpretive conventions. On that basis, I make some correlative suggestions about how to understand comparable shifts in the interpretation of neutrality argument fundamental to the modern law of free speech and constitutional privacy. My larger theme is that the distinctively American constitutional commitment to liberties of religion, speech, and privacy self-consciously embodies an associated theory of constraints on state power that radically departs from traditional conceptions of enforceable public morality.

I. LOCKEAN TOLERATION AND THE RELIGION CLAUSES

The religion clauses of the First Amendment both use and elaborate the theory of religious toleration classically developed both in John Locke's *Letters Concerning Toleration*[3] and Pierre Bayle's contemporary *Philosophique Commentaire*.[4] Importantly, that theory incorporates interdependent critical and constructive aspects.[5]

The crux of Locke's and Bayle's critical attack on the theory and practice of Augustinian religious persecution[6] is its conception of a justly enforceable criterion for the erring conscience, namely, the Augustinian argument that conscience may be subject to criminal law when it expresses a willful failure to accept evident religious truths. Everyone, however, has a conviction of the truth of her or his beliefs, on the basis of which dissenting beliefs will be regarded as willful failures to acknowledge evident religious truths. Accordingly, the argument will justify universal persecution, which neither a just God nor the law of nature could have intended. At bottom, one theological system, among others equally reasonable, is made the measure of enforceable truths.

Such a biased conception of enforceable rational truth corrupts, in turn, the conception of just freedom of the person. The putatively irrational person is supposed, for that reason, to be unfree, marred by a disordered will. A judgment of unfreedom, alleged as the ground of coercive persecution, in fact viciously degrades the freedom that for Locke and Bayle, is the inalienable right of conscience: Conscience is made hostage to the judgments of others. The moral nerve of the argument for the right to conscience is that persons are independent originators of claims and that the demands of ethics and of an ethical God are only both known and practically effective in our lives when persons' right to conscience is appropriately respected. Otherwise, the demands of ethics are confused with public opinion or popular taste.

The association of religious conscience with ethical imperatives is, of course, pervasively characteristic of the Judeo-Christian tradition and its conception of an ethical God acting through
history.[7] Locke and Bayle are religious Christians in this tradition. They regard themselves as returning Christianity to its
ethical foundations, reminding Christians, for example, of the
toleration of the early patristic period.[8] Disagreements in speculative theology, which had grounded Augustinian persecutions for heresy, were, for them, patent betrayals of essential
Christianity; they disabled people from regulating their lives by
the simple and elevated ethical imperatives of Christian charity.

Thus, Locke's and Bayle's deepest criticism of Augustinian
persecution was its corruption of religion, politics, and ethics,
and the motivation of their arguments for the inalienable right
to conscience is a new and constructive interpretation of what
ethics is, and how it connects to religion and politics. Locke
thus linked a free conscience to the autonomous exercise of the
moral competence of each and every person, as a democratic
equal, to reason about the nature and content of the ethical
obligations imposed on persons by an ethical God[9] and thought
of these obligations as centering on a core of minimal ethical
standards reflected in the Gospels.[10] And ethics, for Bayle, as
for Kant, is only a vital force in one's life when one independently acknowledges its principles oneself and imposes them on
one's life.[11] Bayle, who rejoiced in paradox, puts the point
bluntly: Beliefs in speculative religious truths did not insure
salvation. Such beliefs were often brigaded with the gravest irreligion, that is, barbarous failures of ethical obligation and
Christian charity, i.e., religious persecution; moreover, disbelief
in such truths, even atheism, was consistent with decent conduct.[12] The very point of respect for conscience, for Locke and
Bayle, is to ensure that each and every person is guaranteed
the moral independence to determine the nature and content
of ethical obligations. State enforcement of sectarian religious
beliefs taints this inalienable moral freedom by its enforcement
of speculative theological disagreements that distort the central
place of this democratic conception of ethics in what both regarded as true religion.

This new conception of ethics is, for Locke and Bayle, motivated by what they take to be the distinctive vision of God in

the Judeo-Christian tradition—God as personal and supremely ethical.[13] We come to know this personal God, in part, through the realization of our ethical nature, our creative moral powers of rationality and reasonableness, as persons, made in his image, in relation both to him and all persons. On this conception, religion does not embed us in ontological hierarchies characteristic of many of the world's cultural traditions,[14] but actually makes possible, indeed liberates a respect for persons expressive of our rational and reasonable freedom. The right to conscience has the focal role that it has in a just polity because it makes possible moral self-government.

This conception—that ethical independence and the right to conscience are mutually supportive—leads to a radical departure in political principle from other political traditions, namely, Locke's principle that sectarian religious ends are not a legitimate state concern.[15] Locke's principle was naturally opposed as undermining public morality and political stability, especially when it was later elaborated to include disestablishment in Virginia and under the First Amendment of the United States Constitution.[16] Political experience theretofore had associated religion with state coercive and other support, so that many wondered how a state could be stable when all religions were independent of it. Bayle and Locke responded that a peaceful civility can be restored only when religious persecution is abandoned; persecution itself creates the instabilities of intractable, sectarian conflict.[17] Indeed, their argument suggests that the older view of enforceable public morality, itself the product of religious persecution, was itself morally corrupt.

We should understand this claim of moral corruption in the content of a central puzzle for Christians and democrats like Locke: How is it that a religion like Christianity, a religion for Locke of democratic equality and civility, had long been associated in the West with the legitimation of antidemocratic institutions like hereditary monarchy? The question is particularly poignant for Locke and the Lockean revolutionary Americans a century later since they believed that, in fact, a properly understood Protestant Christianity supplied the ethics of personal self-government that made possible the theory and practice of democratic self-government. How, for millenia, could Christianity have thus betrayed its essential emancipatory purposes, degrading just human freedom into acceptance of morally arbitrary hierarchies of privilege and power? It is a distinguishing feature of the American democratic tradition that it chose to answer the question not in the terms of a Voltairean religious skepticism hostile to religion as such, a view that gravitates to the familiar British and European practice of a latitudinarian, established church that tames and civilizes religion to state purposes, along the lines of Rousseau's Erastian conception of civil religion.[18] Rather, American thought derives from an alternative analysis of how Christianity had itself been politically corrupted from its essential purposes by its role as an established church, thus suggesting an internally religious as well as ethical basis for attack on the very idea of an established church.

Thomas Jefferson, author of the Virginia Bill for Religious Freedom, thus argued, under the influence of both Kames[19] and Bolingbroke,[20] that the history of Augustinian intolerance in the West has corrupted Western ethics, including a proper understanding of the ethics of the Gospels, by speculative theology.[21] Indeed, Jefferson's commitment to the eighteenth-century theory of a moral sense gave a more potent sense to Locke's and Bayle's argument that Augustinian intolerance corrupted both religion and ethics.[22] The violation of the right to conscience was not construed, by Jefferson among others, as a corruption of the moral sense itself.[23] Jefferson's radical analysis of this moral corruption is associated with a radical cure envisaged neither by Locke nor Bayle, namely, an attack on established churches as such. Jefferson, in contrast to Locke, expressly elaborates the underlying moral ideal of respect for conscience to include not only free exercise, but any form of religious qualification for civil rights or any compulsion of tax money for support of religious beliefs, even one's own. For Jefferson, the very idea of an established church, associating state power with the support of sectarian religious belief, was the historical root of the corruption of Christianity from its essential emancipatory purposes: The dependence of religion on state power "tend only to beget habits of hypocrisy and meanness, are a departure from the plan of the holy author of our religion . . . and . . . hath established and maintained false religions over the greatest part of the world and through all time".[24]

On this view, Christianity fulfills its essential purposes of moral self-government and thus makes possible political self-government when persons, free of all state incentives, are guaranteed the ultimate right and responsibility as democratic equals to acknowledge, express, and revise the ultimate organizing aims of their personal and moral lives. A religion of democratic equality becomes the vehicle and support of such equality only when its independence of state power enables persons as democratic equals to understand and act on its ethics of democratic equality.

The upshot of both the critical and constructive aspects of the argument for religious liberty is, as Locke clearly saw, a politically operative distinction between the state's legitimate pursuit of state purposes broadly neutral among all forms of conscience and the illegitimate use of state power to either reinforce or endorse sectarian conscience. Bayle, though not a contractarian in his political theory, proposed a strikingly contractarian way of drawing distinction:

> "I would ask him first to hold himself aloof from his own personal interest and the manners of his country and then to ask himself this question: If a certain custom were to be introduced into a country where it has not been in usage, would it be worthy of acceptance after a free and critical examination."[25]

Locke's more explicitly contractarian argument defines neutrally acceptable state purposes as:

> "[c]ivil interest . . . life, liberty, health, and indolency of body; and the possession of outward things, such as money, lands, houses, furniture, and the like".[26]

The legitimate exercise of state power is thus limited to the pursuit of certain general goods that all persons would want as conditions of whatever else they might want. The idea is not that these goods define what makes a life ultimately valuable. Rather, state pursuit of such ends defines the limits of legitimate state power precisely because these goods do not themselves define ultimate questions, but are the all-purpose goods consistent with the kind of interpretive independence on such questions that respect for the inalienable right to conscience requires.[27] The Lockean theory of toleration would allow state power to forbid religious rituals involving child sacrifice (the taking of life, a general good) whereas a state prohibition on animal sacrifices (the taking of animal life not being a general good) might be forbidden.[28] Justifiability by neutral state purposes is thus to be interpreted by reference to a background theory of general goods, i.e., as the terms of secular justification for coercive state power acceptable to all persons committed as a normatively pluralistic community to the inalienable right to conscience as a background right.

The religion clauses of the First Amendment to the United States Constitution are clearly shaped by the Lockean argument to even more radical effect than Locke envisaged. James Madison, the architect of the First Amendment and the central Virginia advocate of successful passage of Jefferson's Bill for Religious Freedom, ensured that the First Amendment not only protect Locke's interest in religious free exercise, but also Jefferson's elaboration of Lockean argument to prohibit state establishments of religion.[29] Both the free-exercise and anti-establishment clauses clearly deploy the Lockean distinction between legitimate and illegitimate state purposes. Any infringement of the religious liberty of free-exercise can be justified, for example, only by a compelling secular state purpose,[30] and the anti-establishment clause demands that the state not support any form of sectarian religious teaching but pursue only neutrally acceptable secular purposes.[31]

Contractarian political theory has a powerful role to play in understanding these constitutional provisions in so far as a defensible form of contemporary contractarian theory best expresses their motivating conception. As I argue at length elsewhere, a contractarian theory that gives focal place to our moral powers of rationality and reasonableness meets that test.[32] This theory naturally enables us to understand and interpret the religion clauses as a coordinated protection of the inalienable right to conscience, the right to form, express, and revise our highest order interests in a rational and morally reasonable life.[33] The free-exercise clause thus protects expression of religious belief and ritual from state coercion; and the anti-establishment clause protects the formation and revision of ultimate personal and moral views from any state incentives. Both clauses limit state power in either area to the neutrally acceptable secular purposes defined by contractarian theory.[34]

II. THE SCOPE OF RELIGIOUS LIBERTY

In order to understand how contractarian theory assists the task of interpreting the religion clauses, I examine here one abstract issue of moral and political theory that directly bears on a range of interpretive questions in religion clause jurisprudence, namely, the proper interpretation of constitutional neutrality. The issue at stake is the interpretive connection between religion clause jurisprudence and background conceptions of the nature of ethics. For example, background assumptions about the nature of ethics—Locke's theological ethics[35] versus the moral-sense theory of the American Enlightenment[36]—are an important source of interpretive disagreement over Lockean principles of toleration, and thus over the meaning of the religion clauses. Jefferson's refusal to follow Locke in excluding Catholics and atheists from the protection of the Virginia Bill for Religious Freedom reflects his own background assumptions,[37] and many later historical shifts in the interpretation of these clauses pivot on similar changes in thought. When Justice Story, for example, dubbed Protestant Christianity the de facto established church of the United States, he assumed that Protestantism was a just proxy for ethics itself. Accordingly, Story found no violation of constitutional neutrality in state imposition of prayers or Bible reading in public schools, or prosecutions for blasphemy, or exclusion of atheists from public office.[38] If we today take constitutional objection to such practices, this must turn on background shifts in our ideas of whether Protestant Christianity can any longer justly be regarded as a proxy for ethics as such.

These disagreements do correspond to the moral motivations of the argument for universal toleration stated contemporaneously by Locke and Bayle: The motivation of their argument for the inalienable right to conscience is, as we have seen, a new interpretation of what ethics is, namely, an ethics of the moral independence of democratic equals, and how it connects religion to democratic politics. However, because both Locke and

Bayle understand moral independence as a quest for an ethical God's uncompromisable demands, they exclude atheists from the scope of universal toleration.[39] Though atheists may act morally, as Bayle clearly acknowledges,[40] they lack the appropriate epistemic attitude of mind open to ethical demands, the uncompromisable demands of a personal and ethical God.[41] And the exclusion of Catholics from toleration is directed not against their worship (Bayle condemns such coercion and much else),[42] but against what Locke and Bayle took to be their commitment to intolerance and their seditious advocacy of the overthow of legitimate Protestant government.[43]

Accordingly, the sense of the political theory of toleration is linked to a cognate moral philosophy of democratic ethics by the very structure of the argument for toleration. Interpretation of the religion clauses, including the scope of toleration, will turn on how these background questions of political theory and moral philosophy are resolved.

We may, indeed, map a range of alternative positions on the scope of religious liberty onto their associated theories of democratic ethics—for example, the Massachusetts theocrats, Locke and Bayle, moral-sense theorists, and contemporary moral philosophers. The Massachusetts theocrats supposed natural knowledge of ethics to be corrupted by the Fall and associated ethical knowledge with reading the Bible in a certain highly specific way.[44] Locke and Bayle believed that we may come to know ethics by our natural reason inferring God's existence and his will for us; they believed that the Bible both assists and is assisted by such inquiry into ethical knowledge.[45] Moral-sense theorists argued that we know what is ethically right by our uncorrupted moral sense independent of God's will, a sense confirmed, however, by a proper reading of the Bible and reenforced by belief in an afterlife.[46] Contemporary moral theory—whether deontological, utilitarian, or intuitionist—standardly analyzes ethical reasoning independently of religious reasoning or belief in an afterlife.[47] Presumably, all these ethical theories, in the order roughly arranged, will dictate a correspondingly broader inclusive ambit for universal toleration: from belief in God and reading the Bible a certain way (the Massachusetts theocrats), to belief in God and reading the Bible (Locke and Bayle), to belief in God (some moral-sense views), to belief in God as well as agnosticism and atheism (other moral-sense views and contemporary moral theories).

Attitudes about Bible interpretation are a useful historical guide to the enlarging ambit of toleration, and an important background issue in controversies over religion clause jurisprudence in the United States. We should put these controversies in the context of the historical tradition they reflect and elaborate. Both Locke and Bayle, for example, are religious Christians in the Protestant tradition, a tradition in search of a pure Christianity of the Bible, to which one alone looked for guidance, *sola scriptura*.[48] But the metainterpretive diversity encouraged by humanism and the Reformation also unleashed diversity in styles of Bible interpretation (Erasmus, La Peyrere, Richard Simon, and Spinoza).[49] Both Locke and Bayle took seriously the wide range of disagreements over Bible interpretation that reasonable persons could, in view of this metainterpretive diversity, entertain; indeed, they conceived of respect for the right to conscience, the ground of universal toleration, as facilitating the exercise of reasonable judgment, including both epistemic and practical rationality.[50] So understood, the essence of their argument for toleration is that the state may not itself dictate standards of Bible interpretation (as Catholic intolerance did),[51] but must allow the exercise of the independent epistemic and practical rationality of persons as democratic equals in adopting, expressing, and revising standards on their own. All reasonable persons, once afforded opportunity to study the Bible, must believe in God and must believe that the Bible is the word of God; but they must be allowed rationally and reasonably to determine by their own standards what the truth is. This freedom alone ensures a pure religion and a practical ethics. Elisha Williams, a kinsman of Jonathan Edwards, makes precisely this point in his 1744 defense of conscience and toleration so typical of the evolving American normative consensus on these matters, gravitating to the unique American constitutional commitment to anti-establishment principles.[52]

Locke and Bayle, as well as Elisha Williams, implicitly concede that universal toleration must extend much further if rational and reasonable judgment, guaranteed the right to conscience, achieves their underlying ethical aims: an ethics of the moral competence of democratic equals. While Catholic standards of Bible interpretation cannot be enforced by law, persons' reasonable adoption of such standards must be respected if it is consistent, as it certainly is, with a tolerant respect for the rights of others. Once conceptions of moral reasonableness are, under the impact of moral-sense theory, not linked to God's will, respect for independent rational and reasonable judgment may not require either belief in God in general or in the Bible in particular. Jefferson, for example, believed in a deist God, in an afterlife, and, like Locke, in the essential ethical wisdom of the gospels, suitably edited (see the Jefferson Bible).[53] But apparently his lifelong study of and interest in pagan ethics led him to doubt that the cultivation and exercise of moral reasonableness required such belief.[54] An acute sensitivity to issues of reasonable metainterpretive diversity about ethics and its sources led Jefferson to believe that the argument that Christian ethics was superior to pagan ethics was *an argument* with which reasonable persons could disagree.[55] The implicit premise of this argument is that rational and reasonable persons might realize and express personal and ethical integrity through beliefs other than Christian focussing on the Bible, religious beliefs, or beliefs in an afterlife.[56] If rational and reasonable persons could realize their integrity through other kinds of beliefs and other texts besides the Bible, respect for conscience must be accorded them. The conception of the scope of universal toleration thus expands for Jefferson to include not only Catholics but atheists.

If this was so in Jefferson's historical context, contemporary notions of universal toleration can hardly be less generous. Undoubtedly, the nineteenth-century American consensus on religion-clause jurisprudence reflected an understanding of ethics closer to Locke's than to Jefferson's. This is the consensus that Justice Story articulated when he appealed to the de facto establishment of Protestant Christianity in the United States, and justified state impositions of prayers and Bible reading in the public schools, blasphemy prosecutions, and excluding atheists from public office. But the nineteenth and twentieth centuries saw a number of developments in Bible criticism and in science, sharper demarcation between religious and ethical claims, and even criticism of religion on ethical grounds. These developments have, I believe, irretrievably undermined Justice Story's conception.

To summarize a long and complex story: Developments in historiography and Bible criticism have permanently eroded any monolithic conception of the essential beliefs and sources of Protestant Christianity.[57] Developments in science have further expanded such metainterpretive diversity, for example, over how to reconcile the epistemic claims of science, such as evolution, with traditional Bible interpretation.[58] Correlative with the radical metainterpretive diversity regarding essential religious beliefs and sources, a more critical appreciation is accorded the autonomy of ethics,[59] motivated by our need for a common ethical basis in the face of radical metainterpretive diversity, that is, for an ethics of equal respect centering on all-purpose general goods. Indeed, an autonomous ethics may be required from an internally religious perspective if it better expresses, as it may, the ethical motivations of a religion in which our moral powers fully express themselves in an ethics of equal respect for all persons whose dignity is the image of God in us.[60] From this perspective, the ethical independence even of the unbeliever may better express the spirit of ethically prophetic religion than the attitude of the conventional religious believer whose views mirror, and do not ethically examine, the often callous inhumanity of conventional morality.[61]

Furthermore, some influential contemporary perspectives criticize religion itself as ethically repressive, and claim that alternative nontheistic, or even atheistic, views are more expressive of realizing a community of equal respect.[62] Such a conception would, if true, turn the traditional exclusion of atheists from universal toleration on its head; advocacy of religion, not atheism, would be excluded from universal toleration.

None of these developments requires us to say that belief in God or in the truth of the Bible is false, or that any of the alternative propositions claimed is true. But they do establish the general line of Jefferson's thought: Persons may realize their personal and ethical dignity, expressing their moral powers of rationality and reasonableness, through belief in any of these propositions. Our conception of reasonable metainterpretive diversity, in the exercise of our freedom of conscience, has widened, if anything, beyond Jefferson's idea of reasonable arguments and sources. The scope of universal toleration must be correspondingly larger.

This kind of analysis clarifies the shifting scope of universal toleration over time and cognate constitutional arguments about the meaning and application of the constitutional neutrality commanded by the religion clauses of the first Amendment. For example, consistent with the analysis here proposed, the anti-establishment clause has been interpreted to forbid any form of state endorsement of religious teaching, for example, state-endorsed prayers in the public schools,[63] or adaptation of the curriculum to sectarian religious belief as in the creationism controversies.[64] And an important thread of religion clause jurisprudence suggests that the central right protected by the religion clauses cannot be confined to conventional forms of theistic belief.[65]

This analysis may clarify as well larger themes of moral pluralism and community, explaining how and why an interpretive dynamic of universal toleration has powerfully motivated an internal linkage of a more generous moral pluralism and a more encompassing and fair-minded conception of the legitimate scope of moral community. Constitutional interpretation here, and in the cognate areas of free speech and constitutional privacy, expresses a critical reflection on the enduring strands of arguments of principle and how they should be elaborated over time consistent with their motivating political and moral theory. So to interpret our constitutional law is also to interpret our history, but not slavishly or stupidly. Indeed, interpretive reflection may make possible an illuminating understanding of the contradictions of our constitutional tradition, a tradition with the most complete guarantees of religious liberty yet capable, as John Stuart Mill bitterly observed, of the most savage religious persecution (of the Mormons).[66] Such reflection may enable us to see otherwise unconnected developments in the jurisprudence of the religion clauses, free speech, and constitutional privacy as a self-critical coming to terms with contradiction and incoherence, indeed as motivated by an integrity of common arguments and principles. I briefly exemplify this program by an examination of the current jurisprudence both of free speech and constitutional privacy.

III. THE SCOPE OF FREE SPEECH

The interpretive structure of the current law of free speech in the United States tends to enlarge the class of communications protected by the free speech and press clauses of the First Amendment and to forbid a state restriction on communications aimed at what is said, a content-based restriction on speech, unless there is a clear and present danger of some very grave harm. The modern law of free speech is remarkable both for its expansion in the scope of protected speech and its highly demanding requirements for satisfaction of the clear and present danger test. Each development is, I believe, clarified by the contractarian analysis here proposed.

We begin by noting that the judiciary has sharply eroded or contracted the traditional understanding that a range of communicative utterances (clearly "speech" in any reasonable sense of that term) is exempt from protection by the values of free speech. The traditional list included subversive advocacy,[67] fighting words,[68] libels both of groups and individuals,[69] obscenity,[70] commercial advertising,[71] and the like. The modern Supreme Court has now reexamined and recast such traditional exemption of these forms of speech from free speech protection: Subversive advocacy[72] and group libel[73] are now fully protected, and much that was traditionally fighting words,[74] obscene,[75] and advertising[76] is now more fully protected than previously.

I believe this expansion in the scope of free speech protection rests on the same kind of shift in the application of constitutional neutrality already examined in the area of religion-clause jurisprudence. For the same reason that no form of distinction among forms of conscience (religious or nonreligious) appears any longer consistent with equal respect for moral independence, traditional exclusions from free speech protection now compromise the kind of equal respect for communicative integrity that constitutional values of free speech command in service of freedom of conscience itself. American constitutional law has come to understand, for example, that neutrally applicable protections of free speech cannot exclude subversive advocacy, for this advocacy is often precisely the kind of independent expression of ultimate social, political, and moral criticism essential to respect for the diverse forms of moral independence in a pluralistic society.[77] Even the traditional scope of the idea of the obscene has, I believe, been eroded in the face of a range of forms of legitimate moral pluralism in styles of sexuality and life unthinkable in the morally homogeneous and sexually repressive society that dictated the way in which puritanical reformers in Britain and the United States enforced Victorian sexual morality through the obscenity laws.[78] If that sexual morality is now conscientiously debated in society at large, as itself arguably immorally repressive and unjust, the traditional scope of the obscene must now appear no longer neutral because of a shift in underlying assumptions similar to the reasons that the traditional scope of religion-clause jurisprudence is no longer neutral.[79]

Correlative with the expanding scope of constitutionally protected speech, the Supreme Court has been increasingly demanding in the showing of a clear and present danger required for a content-based restriction on protected speech. The Court has thus moved from its highly deferential tendency test,[80] to a less deferential but still weak test of aggregate expectable harm,[81] to its current quite demanding requirements of very grave harms both highly probable and not rebuttable by the normal pattern of dialogue and discourse in society at large.[82] This modern interpretation of a clear and present danger is, I believe, the elaboration in free speech jurisprudence of the test for legitimate state action first stated by Jefferson in his Virginia Bill for Religious Freedom as a criterion for interfering in religious liberty: "that it is time enough for the rightful purposes of civil government for its officers to interfere when principles break out into overt acts against peace and good order", and that the normal course for rebuttal of noxious belief, consistent with respect for the right to conscience, is "free argument and debate."[83] Jefferson formulates this test as a way of insuring that mere objection to a certain system of religious belief cannot of itself justify abridgement of exercise of that belief, for democratic majorities will often confuse their unhappiness with and disapproval of the claims of an unfamiliar religion with a threat of secular harms. Accordingly, the state must limit any restrictions on religious belief to cases where there are such secular harms, for example, Locke's example of a religious ritual of child sacrifice. But the same pattern of intolerance familiar in unjust religious persecution occurs as well in censorship of speech, and the modern Court has correctly understood that the same protections of moral independence fundamental to our Jeffersonian conceptions of religious liberty apply, as a matter of principle, to free speech as well. The lesson of the McCarthy witchhunts is, as the name suggests, precisely the common wrong of and remedy for religious and political persecution.[84]

IV. CONSTITUTIONAL PRIVACY

Finally, the same erosion of the traditional understanding of legitimate moral debate—that we have seen in the areas of religious liberty and free speech—explains as well the development in modern American constitutional law of the constitutional right to privacy. My understanding of the constitutional right to privacy is that it centrally protects from state coercive interference the right to form intimate relations of which the traditional exemplar was, of course, the marriage relation.[85] That right was, I believe, quite clearly one of the reserved unenumerated rights protected by the Ninth Amendment, the Privileges and Immunities Clause of Article IV, and, eventually, the Privileges and Immunities Clause of the Fourteenth Amendment.[86] However, the need to protect this constitutional right, as a live constitutional issue, arose in the relatively recent modern era when the traditional understanding of constitutionally neutral moral argument eroded in ways we have already seen in the areas of religious liberty and free speech. When the Supreme Court validated the criminal prosecution of Mormon polygamy in *Reynolds v. United States*,[87] as consistent with the constitutional guarantee of religious free-exercise in the First Amendment, it did so on grounds that assimilated the moral neutrality of the prohibition of bigamy to the prohibition on the murder of children or one's wife in a religious sacrifice or ritual. That decision could not, I believe, be decided with the same ease today precisely because our moral views of family law are so profoundly in dispute among feminists and society at large. My larger point is not the rightness or wrongness of

Reynolds then or now, but the kind of reigning American consensus on the morality of marriage relations at the time of *Reynolds* which made almost any prohibition applicable to marriage
relations appear based on constitutionally neutral, not sectarian, grounds and thus justly enforced at large. On this view,
the constitutionally required burden for abridging a fundamental right like marriage was satisfied for the same reasons
that abridgement of the right of religious free-exercise was satisfied, and thus arguments of constitutional privacy were not
elaborated.

The development of the right to constitutional privacy under
American law reflects the erosion of the belief in the neutrality
of such moral prohibitions. When the Supreme Court recognizes the constitutional right to privacy in *Griswold v. Connecticut*,[88] it protects the right of married couples to use contracep-
tives because any justification for the criminal prohibitions of
contraceptive use appeared then clearly sectarian, and so not
neutral. Such laws could not be justified by any plausible argument of secular harms either to others or to self. To the contrary, contraceptive use enabled married couples to limit population growth in ways politically desirable to society at large,
and advanced the rational good of married couples in general
and married women in particular through enabling them better to control reproduction and to explore the sexual dimension of personal relations in a humanely fulfilling way. In this
context, the traditional moral condemnation of contraception
as a kind of homicide against the unborn (St. Thomas)[89] must
appear as a metaphysically non-neutral view that cannot justly
be enforced on society at large. The perceptions underlying the
view are simply not the broadly shared premises that leave the
state neutral among competing sectarian interpretations of various general goods. Rather, the enforcement of such perceptions through prohibitions of contraception use enlists the state
in the support of sectarian conscience in a core area of the just
moral independence of both women and men in the exercise
of constructive moral powers defining permanent value in living. Since the moral justification for the prohibition of contraception appeared non-neutral, it became invalid, and the Supreme Court understandably extended the constitutional right

to privacy to protect a traditionally recognized fundamental right.[90]

Both the empirical and normative components of many traditional moral views, about contraception and the like, may once have commanded broad consensus, embracing the most tolerant and enlightened people. From the perspective of such uncontroversial beliefs, state prohibitions even of central human rights like conscience, speech, and privacy are justifiable to all reasonable persons,[91] and are thus constitutionally adequate justifications for abridgements even of fundamental rights. Often, however, empirical and normative assumptions become subject to much reasonable criticism on grounds of empirical mistake or changing social circumstances or new elaborations of central principles of fairness or humanity. The previous universal consensus about these beliefs is shattered, and so too is the justifiability of their constitutional neutrality as the basis for abridgement of fundamental rights. What once were the normative assumptions common to all forms of reasonable conscience are now the subjects of sectarian debate and division. Their enforcement through law is hence the functional equivalent of the injustice that Locke and Bayle identified as the imposition of speculative theology through law: the invention of orders and hierarchies that corrupt and degrade the essentially human moral powers for self-government. In short, coercive laws no longer satisfy the constitutionally required burden of neutral justification for abridgement of fundamental rights, and a right like constitutional privacy is properly elaborated in our law, and properly applied to contraceptive use.

The Supreme Court's later elaboration of the constitutional right to privacy (its application to abortion[92] and pornography use in the home,[93] its failure of application to consensual homosexuality)[94] is, of course, enormously controversial, and I cannot discuss such disputes here.[95] My more abstract interpretive point is that the constitutional right to privacy is a principled elaboration of and argument over the impact of background shifts in the understanding of constitutional neutrality in the area of traditionally recognized fundamental rights, here the right to marriage, elsewhere the right to conscience and free speech.

V. CONCLUSIONS

The general theme that unites these developments in the constitutional jurisprudence of religious liberty, free speech, and constitutional privacy is the impact of the enlarging scope and understanding of legitimate moral pluralism on a constitutional tradition centrally committed to toleration for forms of conscience, speech, and ways of life that do not impose secular harms on others. That impact is, I have suggested, the consequence of a central contractarian commitment of American constitutional law to the inalienable right to conscience, viz., to our self-determining moral powers of rationality and reasonableness.[96]

This way of connecting politics, religion, and ethics was historically original, linking, as it does, constitutional guarantees of basic liberties of conscience, speech, and privacy to respect for exercise of moral powers essential to self-government. Persons, on this view, are no more naturally or necessarily embedded in hierarchies of privilege and power than they are fatalistically chained to some metaphysical order of being. Rather, a just society is so structured as to allow persons to live in a cooperative community fully expressive of their rational and reasonable freedom, a community in which self-respect and respect for others are complementary resources of personal, moral and political life.

A just community, thus understood, must continually review and revise its conceptions of the scope of neutrally enforceable state power in light of these values. Otherwise, traditional assumptions of the natural order of things (for example, of women's role) may, on critical reflection, express yet another hierarchy of domination corrupting to a decent respect for our constructive moral powers. The constitutional command of neutrality expresses, I have suggested, this imperative and this constraint on the coercive power of the state to enforce traditional morality. Our examination of the constitutional jurisprudence of religious liberty, free speech, and constitutional privacy shows how this command is naturally sensitive to the ways in which the scope of legitimate ethical debate has opened to include critical debate about traditional morality that bears upon

Religion, Public Morality, and Constitutional Law   171

certain fundamental rights. Much of traditional morality will
not bear upon these rights, and much that does will survive the
analysis, for example, the prohibition of intrafamilial murder
or rape or violence, all of which are secular harms that satisfy
the constitutional burden required for state interference even
in sensitive areas of intimate relations. But we retain legitimate
state prohibitions not because they are traditional, but in service of the ethics of self-governing moral freedom which, I have
suggested, is the distinctive morality of constitutional liberty.

NOTES

1. See, e.g., *Sherbert v. Verner*, 374 U.S. 398 (1963); *Wisconsin v. Yoder*,
   406 U.S. 205 (1972).
2. David A. J. Richards, *Toleration and the Constitution* (New York:
   Oxford University Press, 1986).
3. See *The Works of John Locke* (London: Thomas Davison, 1823), vol.
   6.
4. Pierre Bayle, *Philosophique Commentaire sur ces paroles de Jesus Christ
   "Contrain-les d'entree"*, *Oeuvres Diverses de Mr. Pierre Bayle* (A la Haye:
   Chez P. Husson et al., 1727). vol. 2, pp. 357–560 (hereinafter *Philosophique Commentaire*).
5. For a fuller analysis, see Richards, *Toleration and the Constitution*,
   pp. 89–98.
6. Ibid., pp. 86–88.
7. For the distinctive force of this conception in the Old Testament's
   narrative style and sharp repudiation of different conceptions of
   divinity in surrounding cultures, see Herbert Schneidau, *Sacred
   Discontent: The Bible and Western Tradition* (Baton Rouge: Louisiana
   State University Press, 1976); Dan Jacobson, *The Story of Stories*
   (New York: Harper and Row, 1982); Robert Alter, *The Art of Biblical Narrative* (New York: Basic Books, 1981).
8. See, e.g., Bayle, *Philosophique Commentaire*, pp. 387–88.
9. See, in general, John Colman, *John Locke's Moral Philosophy* (Edinburgh: Edinburgh University Press, 1983).
10. See John Locke, *The Reasonableness of Christianity*, ed. I. T. Ramsey
    (Stanford: Stanford University Press, 1958).
11. Bayle, *Philosophique Commentaire*, pp. 367–72, 422–33.
12. See Walter Rex, *Essays on Pierre Bayle and Religious Controversy* (The
    Hague: Martinus Nijhoff, 1965), pp. 51–60, 62–65.
13. On the importance of this conception in shaping Old Testament
    narratives and revulsion against surrounding religions, see

172   DAVID A. J. RICHARDS

Schneidau, *Sacred Discontent*; Jacobson, *Story of Stories*. On the impersonality of India's concept of the divine, see Arthur Danto, *Mysticism and Morality* (New York: Harper, 1973), pp. 40–41. On the personality of the Western conception of the divine and its broader cultural significance for Western ethics, politics, and science, see Denis de Rougemont, *Man's Western Quest*, trans. Montgomery Belgion (Westport, Conn.: Greenwood, 1973).

14. Van Leeuwen thus notes peculiarly Western anti-ontocratic concerns. See, in general, Arend Th. van Leeuwen, *Christianity in World History*, trans. H. H. Hoskins (New York: Scribners, 1964). Cf., William Albright, *From the Stone Age to Christianity* (Garden City, N.Y.: Doubleday Anchor, 1957).

15. The statement of this principle is the subject of the first *Letter Concerning Toleration, Works of John Locke*, pp. 5–58.

16. For example, opposition to total disestablishment of the Anglican Church of Virginia, led by Patrick Henry and Richard Henry Lee, centered on the idea that some form of multiple establishment was necessary to preserve public morality in the state. See H. J. Eckenrode, *Separation of Church and State in Virginia* (New York: Da Capo Press, 1971), p. 74.

17. For Locke, see *Works of John Locke*, pp. 7–9; for Bayle, see Bayle, *Philosophique Commentaire*, pp. 415–19.

18. See Jean Jacques Rousseau, *The Social Contract* in *The Social Contract and Discourses*, trans. G. D. H. Cole (New York: Dutton, 1950), pp. 129–41.

19. See Henry Home Kames, *Essays on the Principles of Morality and Natural Religion*, ed. R. Wellek (New York: Garland Publishing, 1976), pp. 136–49.

20. See Lord Bolingbroke, *The Works of Lord Bolingbroke* (London: Frank Cass, 1967), vol 3, pp. 373–535.

21. See Adrienne Koch, *The Philosophy of Thomas Jefferson* (Gloucester, Mass.: Peter Smith, 1957), pp. 9–39. For Jefferson's own linkage of religious persecution with moral and religious corruption, see Thomas Jefferson, *Notes on the State of Virginia*, ed. William Peden (Chapel Hill: University of North Carolina Press, 1955), pp. 159–61; and the Preface to Bill for Religious Freedom, in *The Papers of Thomas Jefferson, 1777–1779*, ed. Julian Boyd (Princeton: Princeton University Press, 1950), vol. 2, pp. 545–46. In his later life, Jefferson subscribed to Joseph Priestley's views on the corruption of true Christianity. See, in general, Dickinson Adams, ed., *Jefferson's Extracts from the Gospels* (Princeton: Princeton University Press, 1983), pp. 14–30; Jefferson's own attempts at Bible criticism were actuated by the desire to distinguish the gold from the dross.

Religion, Public Morality, and Constitutional Law 173

22. Both Shaftesbury and Hutcheson, who shape the moral-sense theory of the age, specifically deny that the concept of ethics depends either on God's will or on divine punishment. See, e.g., Third Earl of Shaftesbury (Anthong Ashley Cooper), *An Inquiry Concerning Virtue, British Moralists*, ed. L. A. Selby-Bigge (New York: Dover, 1965), pp. 15–16, 23–24, 45–47; Francis Hutcheson, *An Inquiry Concerning the Original of our Ideas of Virtue or Moral Good, British Moralists*, ed. L. A. Selby-Bigge (New York: Dover, 1965), vol. 1, pp. 71–72, 79, 85–86, 90–92, 122–23, 125. Since the experience of ethics is defined by an independent moral sense, the very content of such ethics depends on the exercise of this natural sense, in terms of which we define our concept of a good and just God, not conversely. Accordingly, the corruption of this moral sense will corrupt, in turn, our capacity to know God's will. Since for Locke, in contrast, knowledge of ethics requires knowledge of God's will, not conversely, only corruption of specifically religious truth would corrupt ethics. For eighteenth-century believers in the theory of the moral sense, corruption of ethics itself is the root of all other corruptions.

23. See note preceding.

24. Jefferson, Preface to Bill for Religious Freedom, p. 545.

25. *The Great Contest of Faith and Reason: Selections from the Writings of Pierre Bayle*, ed. Karl Sandberg (New York: Frederick Ungar, 1963), pp. 45–46.

26. *Letter Concerning Toleration, Works of John Locke*, p. 10.

27. See John Rawls, "Social Unity and Primary Goods," in *Utilitarianism and Beyond*, eds. Amartya Sen and Bernard Williams (Cambridge: Cambridge University Press, 1982), pp. 159–85.

28. See *Letter Concerning Toleration, Works of John Locke*, pp. 33–34.

29. See, in general, Thomas Curry, *The First Freedoms: Church and State in America to the Passage of the First Amendment* (New York: Oxford University Press, 1986), pp. 134–58, 193–222.

30. See, e.g., *Sherbert v. Verner*, 374 U.S. 398 (1963).

31. See, e.g., *Lemon v. Kurtzman*, 403 U.S. 602 (1971).

32. I defend the proposition that contractarian theory is the best such theory in David A. J. Richards, *Toleration and the Constitution* (New York: Oxford University Press, 1986). See also John Rawls, *A Theory of Justice* (Cambridge: Harvard University Press, 1971); "Kantian Constructivism in Moral Theory," *Journal of Philosophy* 77 (1980): 515. Cf., David A. J. Richards, *A Theory of Reasons for Action* (Oxford: Clarendon Press, 1971).

33. See, in general, Richards, *Toleration and the Constitution*, pp. 121–62.

34. Ibid.

174   DAVID A. J. RICHARDS

35. See, in general, Colman, *Locke's Moral Philosophy.*
36. See note 22.
37. For Locke's exclusions, see Locke, *Works of John Locke*, vol. 6, pp. 45–47 (Catholics); p. 47 (atheists). For Bayle's comparable exclusion, see Bayle, *Philosophique Commentaire*, pp. 410–15 (Catholics); p. 431 (atheists). In contrast, Jefferson's Bill for Religious Freedom makes no exception for Catholics or atheists, and Jefferson's notes on Locke make clear that the omission is intended. Pointing to the Lockean exceptions, Jefferson states: "But where he stopped short, we may go on," Jefferson, Preface to Bill for Religious Freedom, p. 548.
38. See Joseph Story, *Commentaries on the Constitution of the United States*, excerpted in *Church and State in the United States* in *Papers of the American Historical Association*, by Philip Schaff (New York: Putnam, 1888), vol. 2, no. 4, pp. 128–30.
39. See note 37.
40. See Rex, *Essays on Pierre Bayle*, pp. 51–60, 62–65, and text accompanying.
41. For Bayle, like Kant, acting in accord with ethics, as atheists could, must be distinguished from acting on ethical motives properly understood, as Bayle believed atheists could not.
42. For example, Bayle insists that Catholics should not be subject to stigma, nor should their possessions be threatened, nor should their right to bring up their children according to their beliefs be disturbed. See Bayle, *Philosophique Commentaire*, p. 412.
43. See note 37.
44. See, for example, Perry Miller, *Orthodoxy in Massachusetts 1630–1650* (Cambridge: Harvard University Press, 1933).
45. See notes 9–12, and accompanying text.
46. See note 22.
47. Among deontological theories, see Alan Gewirth, *Reason and Morality* (Chicago: University of Chicago Press, 1978); Rawls, *A Theory of Justice;* Richards, *A Theory of Reasons for Action;* David Gauthier, *Morals by Agreement* (Oxford: Clarendon Press, 1986). Among utilitarian theories, see R. M. Hare, *Moral Thinking* (Oxford: Clarendon Press, 1981); Richard Brandt, *A Theory of the Good and the Right* (Oxford: Clarendon Press, 1979). Among intuitionist theories, see W. D. Ross, *The Right and the Good* (Oxford: Clarendon Press, 1930); H. A. Prichard, *Moral Obligation* (Oxford: Clarendon Press, 1949).
48. See Norman Sykes, "The Religion of Protestants," in *The Cambridge History of the Bible*, ed. S. L. Greenslade (Cambridge: Cambridge University Press, 1963), vol. 3, pp. 175–98.
49. See Louis Bouyer, "Erasmus in Relation to the Medieval Biblical

Tradition," in *The Cambridge History of the Bible,* ed. G. W. H. Lampe (Cambridge: Cambridge University Press, 1969, vol. 2, pp. 492–505, and Richard Popkin, *The History of Scepticism from Erasmus to Spinoza* (Berkeley: University of California Press, 1979), pp. 214–48.

50. Bayle, for example, quite clearly brings to Bible interpretation standards of moral reasonableness which he will not allow that an ethical God could have violated. See Bayle, *Philosophique Commentaire,* pp. 367–72. And Locke brings to the Bible as much as he finds in the Gospels, the minimum of ethical reasonableness. See Locke, *The Reasonableness of Christianity.*

51. See, e.g., *Works of John Locke,* vol. 6, pp. 26, 145, 194, 366 (express comparison of intolerance to the Pope's infallibility), 401, 407, 411, 412, 517, 531, 532; Bayle, *Philosophique Commentaire,* p. 438. Bayle also condemns assumptions of infallibility, p. 438.

52. See Elisha Williams, *The Essential Rights and Liberties of Protestants* (Boston: Kneeland and Green, 1744), p. 33.

53. See *Jefferson's Extracts,* Adams.

54. On Jefferson's religious and ethical views, see ibid., Introduction, pp. 3–42. Cf., Adrienne Koch, *Philosophy of Thomas Jefferson,* pp. 1–43.

55. See *Jefferson's Extracts,* Adams, pp. 3–42. Jefferson's attempt to integrate the study of classical moralists with the enlightened ethics of the Gospels reflects the tensions between classical and Christian sources characteristic of the metainterpretive diversity of the Reformation and the Enlightenment. See, in general, Peter Gay, *The Enlightenment: An Interpretation* (New York: W. W. Norton, 1966), vol. 1: *The Rise of Paganism,* pp. 207–419.

56. For historical background on the seventeenth-century debates over an afterlife, see, in general, D. P. Walker, *The Decline of Hell* (Chicago: University of Chicago Press, 1964).

57. See, e.g., Jerry Brown, *The Rise of Bible Criticism in America, 1800–1870* (Middletown, Conn.: Wesleyan University Press, 1969); Stephen Neill, *The Interpretation of the New Testament 1861–1961* (New York: Oxford University Press, 1966); Nathan Hatch and Mark Noll, *The Bible in America* (New York: Oxford University Press, 1982); James Barr, *The Bible in the Modern World* (London: SCM Press, 1973). On the resulting divisions within Protestantism, see William Hutchison, *The Modernist Impulse in American Protestantism* (Cambridge: Harvard University Press, 1976); Martin Marty, *Righteous Empire* (New York: Dial Press, 1970); Ernest Sandeen, *The Roots of Fundamentalism* (Chicago: University of Chicago Press, 1970); George Marsden, *Fundamentalism and American Culture* (New York: Oxford University Press, 1980). On the erosion of distinc-

tions between believers and unbelievers, see Martin Marty, *Varieties of Unbelief* (Garden City, N.Y.: Anchor, 1966); idem, *The Infidel: Freethought and American Religion* (Cleveland: World Publishing, 1961).

58. See, in general, Charles Gillispie, *Genesis and Geology* (Cambridge: Harvard University Press, 1951); John Greene, *The Death of Adam* (Ames: Iowa State University Press, 1959). On the response to Darwin by American religion, see Sidney Ahlstrom, *A Religious History of the American People* (New Haven: Yale University Press, 1972), pp. 766–72.

59. See, in general, Gene Outka and John Reeder, *Religion and Morality* (Garden City, N.Y.: Anchor, 1973); Paul Helm, ed., *Divine Commands and Morality* (Oxford: Oxford University Press, 1981). Cf. Philip Quinn, *Divine Commands and Moral Requirements* (Oxford: Clarendon Press, 1978); Basil Mitchell, *Morality: Religious and Secular* (Oxford: Clarendon Press, 1980).

60. Cf., Gordon Allport, *The Individual and His Religion* (New York: Macmillan, 1950).

61. See, in general, Marty, *Varieties of Unbelief*.

62. See, e.g., Kai Nielsen, *Ethics Without God* (Buffalo, N.Y.: Prometheus Books, 1973). Cf., David Muzzey, *Ethics as a Religion* (New York: Frederick Ungar, 1951).

63. See, e.g., *Engel v. Vitale*, 370 U.S. 421 (1962); *Abington School Dist. v. Schempp*, 374 U.S. 203 (1963); *Wallace v. Jaffree*, 105 S.Ct. 2479, 466 U.S. 924 (1985).

64. See *Epperson v. Arkansas*, 393 U.S. 97 (1968); *McLean v. Arkansas Board of Education*, 529 F. Supp. 1255 (E.D. Ark. 1982).

65. See *United States v. Ballard*, 322 U.S. 78 (1944); *Torcaso v. Watkins*, 367 U.S. 488 (1960); *United States v. Seeger*, 380 U.S. 163 (1965). But cf. *Wisconsin v. Yoder*, 406 U.S. 205, 216 (1972). For commentary, see Richards, *Toleration and the Constitution*, pp. 129–33, 141–46.

66. See John Stuart Mill, *On Liberty*, ed. Alburey Castell (New York: Appleton-Century-Crofts, 1947), pp. 92–93.

67. See, e.g., *Gitlow v. New York*, 268 U.S. 652 (1925).

68. See, e.g., *Chaplinsky v. New Hampshire*, 315 U.S. 568 (1942).

69. See, e.g., *Beauharnais v. Illinois*, 343 U.S. 250 (1952).

70. See *Roth v. United States*, 354 U.S. 476 (1957).

71. See *Breard v. Alexandria*, 341 U.S. 622 (1951).

72. See *Brandenburg v. Ohio*, 395 U.S. 444 (1969).

73. See *Collin v. Smith*, 578 F.2d 1197 (1978), *cert. den.*, 439 U.S. 916 (1978).

74. See, e.g., *Gooding v. Wilson*, 405 U.S. 518 (1972).

75. See, e.g., *Miller v. California*, 413 U.S. 15 (1973).

76. See, e.g., *Virginia Pharmacy Board v. Virginia Consumer Council*, 425 U.S. 748 (1976). But see *Posadas de Puerto Rico Associates v. Tourism Company of Puerto Rico*, 478 U.S.—(1986).

77. For fuller discussion, see Richards, *Toleration and the Constitution*, pp. 178–87.

78. For fuller discussion, see David A. J. Richards, "Free Speech and Obscenity Law: Toward a Moral Theory of the First Amendment," *U. Pa. L. Rev.* 123 (1974): 45.

79. For fuller discussion, see Richards, *Toleration and the Constitution*, pp. 203–9.

80. Under this test, it sufficed that dangerous speech, for example, subversive advocacy, might have some tendency to frustrate legitimate state purposes. See, e.g., *Schenck v. United States*, 249 U.S. 47 (1919).

81. This test focussed on the result of discounting the prospective harm by its judged improbability, so that even subversive advocacy with very little probability of being effective could be abridged if the prospective harm, for example, the overthrow of constitutional government in the United States, were so grave that the low probability multiplied by the very grave harm would be a large amount. This was, of course, the theory that allowed the Supreme Court to legitimate abridgement of the advocacy of the American Communist Party: while the likelihood of success was admittedly infinitesimal, the harm was so grave as to justify abridgement under the applicable test of aggregate expectable harm. See *Dennis v. United States*, 341 U.S. 494 (1951).

82. See *Brandenburg v. Ohio*, 395 U.S. 444 (1969).

83. *Papers of Thomas Jefferson*, p. 546.

84. If, as I have suggested, the background right to conscience must today be interpreted to include all forms of conscience (theistic, agnostic, and atheistic), then suppression of Marxism is itself a kind of religious persecution in the constitutionally condemned sense: One of the great secular religions of the modern age is unjustly suppressed by law. On Marxism as a religion or heretical anti-religion, see Joseph Needham, *Science in Traditional China* (Cambridge: Harvard University Press, 1981), pp. 122–31.

85. See Kenneth Karst, "The Freedom of Intimate Association," *Yale L.J.* 80 (1980): 624.

86. See Richards, *Toleration and the Constitution*, pp. 232, 256.

87. *Reynolds v. United States*, 98 U.S. 145 (1878).

88. *Griswold v. Connecticut*, 381 U.S. 479 (1965).

89. Thomas Aquinas elaborates Augustine's conception of the exclusive legitimacy of procreative sex in a striking way. Of the emission of semen apart from procreation in marriage, he wrote:

178 DAVID A. J. RICHARDS

"[A]fter the sin of homicide whereby a human nature already in existence is destroyed, this type of sin appears to take next place, for by it the generation of human nature is precluded." Thomas Aquinas, *On the Truth of the Catholic Faith: Summa Contra Gentiles,* trans. Vernon Bourke (New York: Image, 1956), pt. 2, chap. 122(9), p. 146.

90. For fuller discussion, see Richards, *Toleration and the Constitution,* pp. 256–61.
91. Cf., T. M. Scanlon. "Contractualism and Utilitarianism," in *Utilitarianism and Beyond,* pp. 103–28.
92. *Roe v. Wade,* 410 U.S. 113 (1973).
93. *Stanley v. Georgia,* 394 U.S. 557 (1969).
94. *Doe v. Commonwealth's Attorney,* 403 F. Supp. 1199 (E.D. Va. 1975), *aff'd without opinion,* 425 U.S. 901 (1976); *Bowers v. Hardwick,* 54 U.S.L.W. 4919 (decided June 30, 1986).
95. I discuss these issues in Richards, *Toleration and the Constitution,* pp. 261–80.
96. Does the way of thinking I here defend depend on contractarian theory in contrast to other political theories (for example, utilitarianism)? I argue that contractarian theory, suitably understood, is the best way to understand these issues in Richards, *Toleration and the Constitution.*

Part II
Beyond Strict Neutrality

[6]

CHURCH, STATE, AND MORAL VALUES: THE LIMITS OF AMERICAN PLURALISM

JAMES HITCHCOCK*

I
INTRODUCTION

Through most of its history America has been perceived as a predominantly religious nation, with relatively high rates of church attendance, numerous public expressions of piety, and a general assumption that civic and private virtue depend on religious belief. The 1950's marked perhaps the peak of that diffuse religiosity, when the idea of religious belief and observance was maximally honored, often apart from commitment to any of its specific forms. Billboards urged citizens to "Attend church this week," as though church-attendance were a self-evidently good thing and as though it made little difference which church one attended, or why.

Although this kind of social piety might be thought mere conformism, and as such lacking in substance, it was intended to symbolize certain realities. For one thing it was intended to affirm that America was a nation of church-going and God-fearing people, an affirmation of national commitment that transcended particular differences or particular examples of infidelity. For another, it was an affirmation of the belief that morality itself, the basis without which any civilized existence would be impossible, depended upon religion. Thus it was essential to affirm that commitment as a way of affirming one's belief in the social contract itself.

Although moral values are notoriously elusive of investigation, it also appears to be the case that until the 1960's Americans held to a fairly general consensus on such values, a consensus which was celebrated in political and civic rhetoric, extolled from a wide variety of pulpits, honored in the mass media, and to a great extent perpetuated through formal education, both public and private. This consensus included as its key factors the self-evident rightness of patriotism, self-discipline, hard work, self-reliance, family stability, personal honesty, and sensual self-restraint. However dishonored in practice, these virtues received consistent public affirmation, and were usually thought of as based on religious belief.

From the beginning there has always been a fundamental ambivalence in America about the degree to which the society is and should be what is now called "pluralistic," that is, how wide a diversity of beliefs and practices are and may be tolerated. That such ambivalence has been present from the beginning is evident to anyone with even minimal knowledge of early American history. School children

* Professor of History, St. Louis University.

Law and Religion

learn that the early settlers of New England came seeking religious freedom. As they get a little older they also learn that those same settlers denied religious freedom to others.

The temptation is to dismiss the Puritans as hypocrites. But in their own minds they were totally consistent—there was a moral obligation to tolerate religious truth, which not even kings could abridge; there was no obligation, and indeed no right, to tolerate religious error. Put in more modern and more secular terms, the earliest American settlers affirmed the desirability of greater freedom than existed in the Old World, yet believed with equal conviction that society had to rest on a common moral consensus. At various times in history this consensus has been thought to exclude Quakers, Catholics, Jews, and other religious groups. Sooner or later, however, excluded groups have been understood in such a way as to permit them to be part of the consensus. Although most Americans would probably say that there is full religious freedom in the country, certain practices dictated by religious beliefs are in fact outlawed—polygamy, snake-handling, and the withholding of medical treatment from sick children are the most obvious examples.

Whether rightly or wrongly, most Americans prior to the 1960's probably perceived a fundamental moral consensus underlying a variety of religious denominations unequalled in world history in terms of number and diversity of beliefs. Equally important, this consensus was assumed to embrace even the majority of those who had no real religious belief. Relatively few public figures would admit to such a condition, and nominal church affiliation—often with liberal groups such as the Unitarians—was a way of concealing it. Direct attacks on the broadly conceived "Judeo-Christian ethic" were rare, except perhaps in relatively protected and insulated environments such as college campuses.

The 1960's and 1970's saw a definite decline in church membership and attendance, sometimes a very sharp decline.[1] More important than the numerical fluctuation, which has tended towards a rather irregular historical pattern, has been the fact that a secular way of life is now more respectable in America that at perhaps any time in the twentieth century—understanding secularism first in the narrower sense of rejection of institutional religion and then in the broader sense of making no claim of being guided by the teachings of the historical religions. Not only do public figures now find it unnecessary to claim religious affiliation; in certain segments of society such claims are becoming increasingly rare. A frankly secularist stance enjoys a prestige equal to that of religious belief.

It would, however, be a mistake to understand what has happened in America since about 1960 as merely a division between the churched and the unchurched. The division, within each denomination, between what are often called, borrowing the vocabulary of politics, "liberal" and "conservative" elements, has been equally important. Although such divisions, in one form or another, have been a part of American religious life almost from the beginning, they took on unusual sharpness

---

1. For a discussion of church membership and religious practice, *see* D. KELLY, WHY THE CONSERVATIVE CHURCHES ARE GROWING 8 (1973) and D. HOGE & D. ROOZEN, UNDERSTANDING CHURCH GROWTH AND DECLINE, 1950-78 (1979).

and deepening passion after 1960. To cite merely a few examples—the changes in
the Roman Catholic Church either mandated by the Second Vatican Council of
1962–65 or implemented in its name, the decision of the Episcopal Church to
ordain women to the priesthood and to authorize a new edition of the *Book of
Common Prayer,* disagreements within major Protestant bodies over the exact nature of the authority of Scripture and the extent of its inerrancy, and possibly
widening divisions within Judaism over the authority of traditional religious laws
and practices.

In most of these cases it could be argued with cogency than the more "liberal"
groups came to be perceived as having perhaps more in common with secularists
outside their framework of formal religion than with the "conservatives" within
their own churches. Liberals have tended to emphasize a political agenda, for
example, which is critical of the American economic system and of America's role
in world affairs, an agenda shared in large measure with the secular left. Religious
liberals have tended to support, quite strongly, feminism, the movement for homosexual rights, and much of what goes under the name of the "sexual revolution."
One major divergence between themselves and the religious conservatives is precisely their attitudes toward secular movements of social change, liberals being
inclined to recognize these as actual manifestations of the divine will, conservatives
seeing them as frontal assault on the Judeo-Christian ethic. Thus in 1980 certain
religious leaders could join with proclaimed secularists like the television producer
Norman Lear in issuing a public warning against the organization called the Moral
Majority.[2] The warning was issued in response to the widespread impression that,
as a new decade began, there was a "swing to the right" in which religious
conservatives were once against asserting what they regarded as traditional American values which had been transgressed.

The liberal critique of American society is in large measure the claim that,
while based on the ideal of total openness or "pluralism," in practice it has always
been more closed and monolithic than it should be. To what degree America was
intended originally to be totally "open" is itself an open question. Through much
of the nineteenth century there were legal restrictions on personal freedom which
today would be regarded as intolerable, slavery being only the most obvious example. Among the Founding Fathers the commitment to civil liberties was not as
complete as in retrospect civil-libertarians find it useful to believe.[3] However,
history aside, it is the essence of the liberal position that the story of America is the
story of the gradual extension and unfolding of that pluralism, the full encom-
passment of more and more diverse groups and hitherto proscribed beliefs and
behavior. Liberty is regarded as capital which cannot simply be allowed to lie secure
but must always be expanded, often with considerable elements of risk. Although
many would have difficulty expressing the moral sources of that imperative, liberals are generally convinced that there exists a moral obligation on America to
broaden continually the limits of its tolerance. So far as racial, ethnic, and religious

---

2. A national letter went out over Lear's signature (copy in possession of the author).
3. L. LEVY, JEFFERSON AND CIVIL LIBERTIES: THE DARKER SIDE (1963).

groups are concerned this point has, at least in principle, been won completely. It has now been extended to other categories of people, such as women as a group, who are assumed to have specific rights which must be guaranteed apart from the guarantee of rights to all citizens; to cultural minorities like homosexuals; and to all those who profess "deviant" ideas or ways of life. Both the reality of and the potentiality for social conflict in these areas is, if anything, greater than it was with respect to struggles for racial equality.

In general the liberal response to this conflict is to insist that it is based on a misapprehension, which in turn is based on fear and insecurity. The purpose of an extended pluralism, the liberal argument runs, is simply to extend the rights of citizenship to all Americans, to remove all vestiges of inequality and injustice. America means equality, so the argument runs, and only when the rights of everyone are fully protected are the rights of anyone really secure. Resistance to this is then deemed to originate from one of two causes—simple bigotry, the wish to keep others in an inferior status; or unfounded fear that the extension of some people's rights will result in the constriction of one's own.

Probably not since the days of slavery has American politics confronted issues with moral roots running so deep as those now on the political agenda. Questions like abortion, the relationship between men and women, and personal sexual behavior are not easily dealt with in a political context, and instinctively politicians in times past have tried to evade questions likely to touch such deep nerves. But the commitment to a steadily expanding pluralism makes confrontation with such questions unavoidable. With most traditional struggles over equality won at least in principle, the new frontiers necessarily are defined in places hitherto inaccessible to political intrusion.

This new phase of the struggle for equality will of necessity test the limits of American pluralism in ways they have never been tested before. This will occur (and indeed is already occurring) in part because it raises issues that go to the heart of deeply held and fundamental moral beliefs which cannot be easily compromised and where the mutual respect, which makes democratic dialogue possible, is often lacking. (Abortion is an obvious example. Some people regard it as one of a woman's most basic rights, others as the deliberate killing of a helpless human being. In such circumstances there is not much room for "statesmanlike" solutions.)

Another test of the limits of pluralism is the question as to what unifying principle remains at the heart of a society as that society becomes more and more diverse, especially in terms of accepted moral values. A society can tolerate a certain number of positions which are antithetical to each other. Is there a limit beyond which these antitheses become socially destructive? The moral revolution since 1960 has tended to call into question, systematically, virtually one by one, every settled belief from the past. It has now become a political question whether a social order can survive based on no moral consensus. (To cite only the most obvious question, what motivates people to obey the law, and to what extent, in the absence of such a consensus?)

Thirdly, it is necessary to ask the question whether society can be indefinitely pluralistic, indefinitely tolerant of all points of view, while still maintaining genuine equality among them all. At some point does the legitimization of some positions necessarily require the constriction of others? It will be the purpose of this paper to argue that, where fundamental values are involved, this is precisely the case, and the question, which touches many areas of social life, will be considered primarily from the point of view of those issues which touch directly or indirectly on religious belief and practice.

II
THE WALL OF SEPARATION

The separationist clause of the First Amendment is admittedly very general in nature, using only ten words, and as such is subject to a number of possible interpretations. For some time after the ratification of the Constitution some of the states continued to maintain relationships between church and state which later constitutional doctrine would regard as unacceptable.[4]

Thomas Jefferson's phrase, "wall of separation of church and state" was first used, in passing, by the Supreme Court in 1878,[5] then resurrected after many decades of neglect in 1947.[6] Since the latter date it has come to be thought of as the governing metaphor in the area of church-state relations, and it has come to be the purpose of much litigation in that area of constitutional law to ferret out systematically all signs of public support of religion.

Oddly, however, in an age when few traditional assumptions have been left unchallenged, there has been relatively little discussion of why an absolute wall of church-state separation is necessary. It remains one of the few basic principles still treated as self-evidently true, even though it is far from self-evident that the First Amendment mandates such a doctrine.

Mark DeWolfe Howe argued a double tradition of church-state separation in American history: one essentially secular, deriving from Jefferson and James Madison, and seeking to protect the public weal from the intrusion of religion; the other older, derived from colonial figures like Roger Williams, wanting to insure maximum freedom for the churches without government interference. Howe argued that the first strain has generally governed separationist thinking.[7]

Judging from the rhetoric both of some of the Founding Fathers and of later court decisions, commitment to the separationist dogma has its origins in the Enlightenment of the eighteenth century, an age highly conscious of the seemingly "irrational" passions which religion could stir up, still suffering from the aftermath of religious wars which had been common in the previous two centuries, persuaded

---

4. *See, e.g.,* A. STOKES, CHURCH AND STATE IN THE UNITED STATES (1950) (3 vols.); C. ANTIEAU, A. DOWNEY, & E. ROBERTS, FREEDOM FROM FEDERAL ESTABLISHMENT: FORMATION AND EARLY HISTORY OF THE FIRST AMENDMENT RELIGION CLAUSES (1964); and S. COBB, THE RISE OF RELIGIOUS LIBERTY IN THE UNITED STATES (1902).

5. Reynolds v. United States, 98 U.S. 145, 164 (1878).

6. McCullom v. Board of Educ., 333 U.S. 203, 231 (1948).

7. M. HOWE, THE GARDEN AND THE WILDERNESS 6-7 (1962).

that organized religion was almost the natural enemy of freedom.[8] The principal
motive for absolute separation was to protect society from destructive religious
quarrels, which were deemed uniquely intense and dangerous.

Justice Hugo Black articulated the same viewpoint in 1952:

> It was precisely because Eighteenth Century Americans were a religious people
> divided into many fighting sects that we were given a constitutional mandate to
> keep Church and State completely separate. Colonial history had already shown
> that, here as elsewhere, sectarians entrusted with governmental power to further
> their causes would sometimes torture, maim, and kill those they branded "heretics,"
> "atheists," or "agnostics."[9]

Justice Felix Frankfurter had similarly warned that "the public school must keep
scrupulously free from entanglement in the strife of sects,"[10] and Justice Robert
Jackson had written, "If we are to eliminate everything that is objectionable to any
of these warring sects or inconsistent with any of their doctrines, we will leave
public education in shreds."[11] In cases involving religion, the courts have tended to
employ "sect" as a favorite synonym for organized religion, implying factionalized
conflict.

If, however, the peculiar horror in which the courts seem to hold religious
conflict can be seen as a holdover from eighteenth century history and attitudes, it
has assumed the character of an unquestioned assumption of eternal validity. Thus
Chief Justice Warren Burger could write in 1969:

> Ordinarily political debate and division, however vigorous or even partisan, are
> normal and healthy manifestations of our democratic system of government, but
> political division along religious lines was one of the principal evils against which
> the First Amendment was intended to protect.[12]

A statement of this kind automatically invites the question "why." In an age
when the acceptable limits of political controversy have broadened considerably,
when freedom of speech is deemed necessarily to include the expression of many
divisive and potentially inflammatory ideas, it is not clear why disagreement along
religious lines should be held in peculiar horror. Arguably, in the America of the
1980's political divisions along the lines of race, economic status, even perhaps
gender, are actually and potentially more divisive than religious divisions. Furthermore, it hardly seems consistent with the governing spirit of liberal democracy
to inhibit certain expressions of belief because these might be potentially divisive.
Supposedly such "divisiveness" is not only the price paid for a real democracy but
almost in a sense the very essence of that democracy, and it ought not to be the
business of the courts to protect society from such disruptions.

At present it remains unproven that religious division constitutes a uniquely
dangerous threat to political stability and, if it indeed is, that it is of such magni-

---

8. *See, e.g.,* R. HEALY, JEFFERSON ON RELIGION AND PUBLIC EDUCATION 162, 211, 216-19, 225 (1962).
9. Zorach v. Clauson, 343 U.S. 306, 318-19 (1952).
10. McCullom v. Board of Educ., 333 U.S. 203, 216-17 (1948).
11. *Id.,* at 235
12. Lemon v. Kurtzman, 403 U.S. 602, 622 (1971).

tude as to require systematic vigilance by the courts against it. Both assumptions, however, seem to lie behind the strict separationist position which the courts have accepted in large measure.

The "wall of separation" is often presented as a high constitutional principle which, perhaps reluctantly, the courts must apply even when regrettable inconveniences occur. Thus it is argued, for example, that if children attending a rural parochial school on a cold winter's morning are given a ride on a public-school bus, the entire American tradition of church-state separation is endangered.

It is worth noting that the pragmatic liberal mind does not ordinarily countenance what seem like harsh conclusions in support of abstract principles. That mind in fact prides itself on its ability to adjust principle (including law) to social reality. For this reason alone it is unlikely that abstract principle of itself governs the strict separationist position. In practice it appears that much of that position has been carved out in response to pressures from sources which regard either organized religion in general or specific religious groups as undesirable social institutions. To an extent greater than is generally realized, the separationist doctrine rests on anti-religious foundations.

That Thomas Jefferson and some other of the Founding Fathers felt this hostility is well known.[13] However, it was built into law over the years in sometimes surprising ways—not until 1978 did the Supreme Court invalidate a Tennessee law, for example, prohibiting clergymen from holding public office.[14]

The personal views of the judges are scarcely irrelevant to the question. As indicated by his statement above, Justice Black, for one, seems to have regarded religious believers as uniquely likely to torture, maim, and kill in the name of their beliefs and thus to be needful of restraint from so doing. His son revealed that the Justice regarded people who attended church as "hypocrites" and had a particular dislike of the Catholic Church. (As a young lawyer in Alabama, Black successfully represented a Methodist minister accused of killing a Catholic priest. The defendant's guilt was not seriously in doubt, but Black exploited the anti-Catholic sentiments of the jurors.[15])

In several of the cases involving the question of public aid to religious schools, the principle has been enunciated that the character of those schools is itself objectionable. In *Lemon v. Kurtzman*,[16] for example, Justice William O. Douglas stated that, while it was the purpose of the public schools to educate, it was the purpose of Catholic schools to indoctrinate.[17] His source for this sweeping statement was a book by a fundamentalist Protestant author claiming to make an exposé of the Catholic Church. The book claimed, among other things, that

---

13. *See, e.g.,* HEALY, *supra* note 8.

14. McDaniel v. Paty, 435 U.S. 618 (1978).

15. H. BLACK JR., MY FATHER, A REMEMBRANCE (1975); V. HAMILTON, HUGO BLACK: THE ALABAMA YEARS (1972).

16. 403 U.S. 602 (1971).

17. *Id.,* at 635.

Catholic priests and religious teachers are not allowed to think, that parochial schools represent a dangerous "foreign" influence in the United States, and that they produce a disproportionate number of gangsters and juvenile delinquents. The author concluded by recommending that Catholics not be allowed to teach in public schools or hold high public office.[18] In his extra-judicial writings Douglas revealed that he was influenced by the anti-Catholic polemicist Paul Blanshard.[19]

The suspicion that teachers in religious schools cannot be relied on to teach even secular subjects in a proper manner was expressed by Chief Justice Burger and Justice Black in *Lemon*,[20] bringing from Justice White the observation that nothing in the judicial record actually showed that secular subjects were being taught improperly.[21] Justice Jackson wrote in *Everson v. Board of Education*[22] "[o]ur public school, if not a product of Protestantism, at least is more consistent with it than with the Catholic culture and scheme of values."[23]

Prior to World War II church-state cases before the Supreme Court were relatively rare. There was a spate of conscientious-objection cases at the start of World War II. Since then, beginning in 1947, there has been a steady flow of church-state cases, immeasurably broadening the scope of constitutional law in this area. In general the courts have tended towards a strict separationist position.[24]

The leading historian of the phenomenon has noted that for the most part these cases were carefully chosen and prepared and were designed to establish sweeping constitutional principles. Often they did not grow out of genuine social conflicts so much as from the desire of the plaintiffs to make a philosophical point. While skilled constitutional lawyers usually represented the plaintiffs, defendants' lawyers, especially where public agencies like school boards were concerned, rarely had much experience in constitutional matters and not infrequently had no particular commitment to the positions they were defending. In addition, strict separationists were generally on the offensive, acting as plaintiffs in 53 of 67 major church-state cases between 1951 and 1971.[25]

Three organizations played important roles in the long-term separationist strategy: the American Civil Liberties Union (A.C.L.U.), the American Jewish Congress (A.J.C.), and Protestants and Other Americans United for Separation of Church and State (P.O.A.U.), now Americans for Separation of Church and State.[26] In all three cases, besides constitutional principle, participants were at least sometimes motivated by antipathy to the Catholic Church and by the belief that Catholic schools are a pernicious influence in society. P.O.A.U. is the most obvious case— dating back many years it had warned Americans, frequently in tones of alarm,

---

18. L. BOETTNER, ROMAN CATHOLICISM 360-63, 364, 368, 370, 379-80 (1962).
19. W. DOUGLAS, THE BIBLE AND THE SCHOOLS 50 (1966).
20. Lemon v. Kurtzman, 403 U.S. 602, 618, 635-36 (1971).
21. *Id.*, at 667.
22. 330 U.S. 1 (1947).
23. *Id.*, at 23.
24. F. SORAUF, THE WALL OF SEPARATION: THE CONSTITUTIONAL POLITICS OF CHURCH AND STATE 9, 19, 21 (1976).
25. *Id.*, at 30-33, 89, 106-11, 165, 349-50.
26. *Id.*, at 31-33.

that the Catholic Church constituted a threat to democracy and that Catholics could not be good Americans.[27] (Its rhetoric has moderated in recent years.) In one case brought by the A.C.L.U., the plaintiff was a woman who believed that religious education deforms minds in the same way that Chinese foot-binding deformed women's feet.[28] Leo Pfeffer, counsel for the A.J.C. and probably the most effective separationist lawyer over the past thirty years, admits to a personal dislike of Catholic schools, which he regards as undemocratic.[29]

It is arguable that the strict separationist position, which was only adopted by the courts after World War II, represents the triumph of those who regard organized religion as an actual or potential danger to the Republic. As such it is not an even-handed application of some principle of neutrality so much as it is the enshrining in law of a particular philosophy.[30]

III
Separation versus Liberty

As it applies to religion, the First Amendment contains two clauses, the second, ensuring free exercise of religion, being only slightly shorter than the first. If the extent of the separationist clause is in some doubt, the extent of the free-exercise clause is not. From the beginning of the United States it has been clear that there were to be no restrictions of religious liberty except in very extreme cases, such as the Mormon practice of polygamy in the nineteenth century.

Liberal opinion has generally held that the two clauses are perfectly complementary to each other, that the separation clause is in fact a necessary prerequisite of the free-exercise clause, since church-state entanglement would itself pose a serious threat to religious liberty. However, in practice it has often been necessary for the courts to choose between them, and a judicial policy of remaining vigilant against church-state entanglement in practice often means the willingness to impose, or to allow others to impose, burdens on the free exercise of religion.

The dilemma would be less acute under a regnant judicial philosophy which regards the interpretation of the Constitution as a narrow and technical matter, in which it is the business of the judges to expound the law as written, whatever practical consequences might flow from that. However, for many years the reigning judicial philosophy has concerned itself quite consciously with the real or potential social affects of court decisions. The frequency with which the courts have shown a willingness to permit disabilities in the exercise of religious freedom, for the sake of maintaining strict separation, indicates what is often a deliberate choice on the judges' part.

---

27. For an example of P.O.A.U. rhetoric, see C. Lowell, The Great Church-State Fraud (1973). For a sample and refutation of such rhetoric over the span of a decade, see L. Creedon & W. Falcon, United for Separation: P.A.O.U. Assaults on Catholicism (1959).

28. Sorauf, supra note 20, at 135.

29. Pfeffer, The "Catholic" Catholic Problem, Commonweal, Aug. 1, 1975, at 302-03.

30. See the article by Francis Canavan in this issue, The Pluralist Game, 44:2 Law & Contemp. Prob., Spring 1981, at 23.

The most obvious example is public aid to religious schools. It would be difficult to show that concrete harm comes to the body politic as a result of such aid, or that such aid necessarily would deprive religious schools of their independence. Countries with political structures comparable to the United States— Canada, Australia, and the Netherlands, for example—have maintained such aid programs for many years without serious ill effect.

The strict separationist argument rests rather on abstract principle—that such aid is in itself bad, because it violates a self-evident principle. But the evident correctness of the principle is precisely what is in question. When it does not rest on abstract principle the argument against such aid is usually based on the fact that some people object to the use of their taxes for purposes of which they disapprove or in which they do not believe. But the Constitution provides no guarantee that one's taxes will only be used in ways compatible with one's beliefs. Given the immense size and complexity of the federal budget, virtually any taxpayer could discover numerous uses of tax money of which he or she morally disapproves. It appears to be only in the area of religion that the courts have recognized a quasi-right of taxpayers to object to specific uses of their tax money.

Court decisions with regard to school aid have been somewhat inconsistent. However, in general they have tended to forbid all direct or indirect forms of such aid at the primary and secondary levels, while allowing it for the most part at the level of colleges and universities.[31] During the period when these cases were under litigation, and particularly since about 1965, many private religious schools, especially those under Catholic auspices, closed because of financial pressures. If it is assumed that church-operated schools are an important exercise of religious freedom, if it is assumed that by operating schools the churches are performing a vital social service, and if it is recognized that parents who send their children to religious schools are also taxpayers, it would seem that the state has a compelling interest in seeing to it that these schools are as good as they can be and are not starved for funds. The courts have in general tended to hold that people cannot effectively exercise their rights if they lack the financial means to do so (thus, for example, the provision of free legal services for indigent defendants). In the area of religion, however, it often appears that the courts, from a separationist standpoint, take a certain satisfaction in permitting as many financial burdens as possible to develop. The general tendency in modern society is for the state to find ways of aiding institutions which, even though private, are deemed worthy of survival, a pattern which prevails from hospitals to zoos and includes symphony orchestras and groups which provide contraceptive and abortion services. Religious schools almost alone remain outside this pattern, often because they are regarded as social institutions which should not survive or whose survival should be made difficult.

Along with school aid, the question of religious observances in the public

---

31. The principal Supreme Court cases are: Everson v. Board of Educ., 330 U.S. 1 (1947); Board of Educ. v. Allen, 392 U.S. 236 (1967); Lemon v. Kurtzman, 403 U.S. 602 (1971); Committee for Public Educ. & Religious Liberty v. Nyquist, 413 U.S. 756 (1973); Meek v. Pittenger, 421 U.S. 349, *reh. denied*, 422 U.S. 1049 (1975); Wolman v. Walter, 433 U.S. 229 (1977); Roemer v. Maryland Pub. Works Bd., 426 U.S. 736 (1976).

schools has provided the bulk of the church-state cases of the past thirty-five years. While there have been some seeming inconsistencies, in general the courts have systematically banned all overt religious instruction, along with prayers, readings from Scriptures, and religious symbolism. Reluctantly, they have allowed, under certain circumstances, children in public schools to be released from regular classes in order to attend religious instruction off school premises.[32]

The religious elements banned from the schools have usually been studiously non-denominational in character. Thus the courts have ruled not only against the favoring of any particular religion but against the favoring of religion in general. The schools are to be scrupulously neutral where matters of religion are concerned.

How neutral they can be in practice is something which will be discussed later. There are, however, certain other aspects of this position which are questionable. Beginning in 1948, it has been a consistent claim by plaintiffs in separationist suits that their rights are violated if religious observances, however generalized, are imposed on them. One such early case, for example, held that even though children receiving religious instruction in a public school left the regular classroom, those who remained behind were subjected to embarrassment and possible harassment.[33] However, on other occasions the Supreme Court has specifically said that, in the words of Justice Jackson, "If we are to eliminate everything which is objectionable to any of these warring sects or inconsistent with any of their doctrines, we will leave public education in shreds."[34] It sometimes appears in court decisions that there exists a constitutional right on the part of non-believers to be protected from unpalatable impositions of religious beliefs, but no corresponding right on the part of believers to be protected from ideas which they find offensive.

The strict separationist position also seems incompatible with prevailing trends in modern education. It was more defensible when schools were regarded as having a primarily technical role—they were to teach young people skills like reading, writing, and arithmetic, which could be seen as divorced from larger questions of meaning and value. Now, however, schools tend to stress "total" education and are seen as institutions which shape young people in myriad ways, of which the strictly academic is only a part. Furthermore, it has been a general tendency in modern education to hold that children should not be insulated from controversial and even disturbing aspects of reality.

Given these views of education, any system which resolutely excludes religion is already an anomaly. If the schools are regarded as helping to shape the child's total world, then the exclusion of religion cannot help but shape a religionless world. At the most formative period of their lives, children are in effect taught that religion is unimportant or even perhaps false. They are habituated in modes of thinking and feeling in which religion plays no part. Although the school may

---

32. The principal Supreme Court cases are: McCollum v. Board of Educ., 333 U.S. 203 (1948); Zorach v. Clauson, 343 U.S. 306 (1952); Engel v. Vitale, 370 U.S. 421 (1962); Abington School Dist. v. Schempp, 374 U.S. 203 (1963).
33. McCollum v. Board of Educ., 333 U.S. 203 (1948).
34. *Id.*, at 235.

deliberately seek to introduce the child to "controversial" subjects, religion cannot be one of these. The very exclusion itself has major symbolic importance.

Several remedies are proposed. One is that religion be taught as an academic subject, rather like geography. But in practice this does not appear to be very common and in any case does not have much bearing on an education which seeks to prepare children for "life."

More common is the assertion that religious education is properly the business of the family and the church. But this begs the question. Parents send their children to school precisely because they feel incompetent to educate them at home. And although strong family practice is probably an essential prerequisite for instilling religious belief in a child, in many homes this practice may be relatively inarticulate and unsophisticated. Churches have access to children for only a very few hours a week, not in any way comparable to the time they spend in school. There are many functions currently performed by the schools that might be performed adequately by other agencies. When any of these is in fact relegated to other agencies, the school is conveying to the child the idea that such is not really important.

Cases in which strict separationism has been applied in such a way as seemingly to limit religious freedom have become fairly common: Currently under appeal to the Supreme Court is a case in which a federal circuit court permitted a student organization to use campus facilities for a Bible-study group.[35] A district court[36] had originally upheld the university's decision to forbid such use. At another state university, student religious groups are restricted in the number of meetings they may hold on campus and are required to pay rent for the facilities, conditions not imposed on other student groups. A state court upheld such restrictions and granted university authorities the right to impose prior restraint on such meetings, on the grounds that there was a "clear and present danger" of violation of the establishment clause.[37]

Such cases have arisen at a time when the overwhelming tendency of courts, and of universities and colleges themselves, has been to expand the limits of student freedom and to hold that all manner of "controversial" opinions have a right to be heard. They have also arisen in an atmosphere in which the tendency of courts has been to protect constitutional freedoms not only in narrowly procedural ways but also by seeking to identify substantive violations of freedom which may seem technically legal. The trend in church-state cases seems to go contrary to both these tendencies.

IV

PUBLIC NEUTRALITY

The theory of separationism holds that the state is and must be neutral in matters of religion. But, as suggested previously, such neutrality is difficult to attain

---

35. Chess v. Widmar, 635 F.2d 1310 (8th Cir. 1980), *cert. granted,*—U.S.—(1981).
36. Chess v. Widmar, 480 F. Supp. 907 (W.D. Mo. 1979).
37. Dittman v. Western Washington University, No. C79-1189W (W.D. Wash., Feb. 28, 1980).

in practice. There can be little doubt that present separationist safeguards do insure government neutrality among religious groups—public policy does not seem to favor Christians over Jews, for example, or Catholics over Protestants. However, it is a more substantial question whether public policy can and does maintain effective neutrality between religion and unbelief, between professed theism and other kinds of faith which can be thought of as competing with it.

To maintain that such neutrality is possible seems to require postulating that public policy is somehow arrived at in a "value-free" manner. Yet it would be difficult to show any policies which are in fact completely neutral. At the lowest level, certain policy decisions may be purely functional in that they merely involve choices as to how to achieve particular goals. Yet the goals themselves, at a higher level of policy-making, cannot be "value-free." Certain values may be assumed to be commonly shared throughout the body politic. However, it is one of the arguments of this paper that such common assumptions are becoming fewer in number. Furthermore, even within the framework of common assumptions, important value judgments must often be made which involve sharp conflict.

A classic example, already alluded to, was the Supreme Court's 1878 decision outlawing polygamy as practiced by Mormons in the Western United States. On one level the decision was clearly a limitation on religious freedom. The Court reached its decision by positing the existence of an over-riding value—the welfare of society required the support of a stable, legal family in the traditional sense, which polygamy would tend to undermine. (The court also made a distinction, which proved not to be very useful, between freedom of religious beliefs on the one hand and religious actions on the other, which might be restricted by law.[38]) The court assumed a commonly held value—the legally established nuclear family— which was one of the givens of American society. Today there are many people who would reject that given, and it seems likely that a similar case today might be decided quite differently.

The common liberal argument for pluralism at this point asserts that the law merely expands the limits of permissible belief and behavior. In the process no one suffers; people may find certain ideas distasteful or invalid, but they are not required to accept them, merely to tolerate them. With regard to polygamy, for example, some people might be permitted in law to practice it, but others could still enter into traditional marriages.

Such a philosophy is totally out of step with the overwhelming tendency of modern government, however, which seems almost inevitably set on a course of expansion of powers and expansion of the ways in which it intervenes in the lives of its citizens. The minimal government envisioned by classical conservative theory might conceivably claim the kind of neutrality which pluralism postulates. The modern, activist, liberal, welfare state cannot be neutral and does not aim to be.

Public education, as already discussed, is a prime case in point. No responsible educator would deny that education involves the making of countless value judgments—in establishing curricula, choosing teachers, mandating textbooks, set-

---

38. Reynolds v. United States, 98 U.S. 145 (1878).

16   LAW AND CONTEMPORARY PROBLEMS   [Vol. 44: No. 2

ting goals, etc. Many of these judgments involve moral choices which may be controversial. The very absence of religion is, as already argued, a judgment of this kind. Contrary to the beliefs of many people, the courts and the schools have decided that education is best carried out with no religious component at all.

One of the relatively few instances in which opponents of strict separationism have taken the offensive in litigating constitutional questions has been recent cases in which Protestants of the type generally called fundamentalist have sued school districts to force the inclusion of biblical accounts of creation alongside the theory of evolution in their curricula or, alternatively, to present evolution as merely a theory rather than a fact. Plaintiffs contend that the teaching of evolution alone violates their religious beliefs and also violates the required neutrality of the state.[39]

A more widespread and perhaps more sensitive area of conflict is over sex education in the public schools. Such programs have become all but universal and perhaps arouse more public controversy than any other aspect of education. The standard argument in favor of such programs is that they are indeed neutral—they merely impart information to students which is deemed appropriate for students to have. But the very existence of such programs involves a value judgment, since some parents oppose them on moral grounds and assert that sex education belongs to the domain of the family. Others would approve such programs, but only if they included explicit moral guidance about sexual behavior. In reality, it appears that many such programs aim at shaping children's values and attitudes with regard to sex. The general assumption behind such programs is that being "sexually active" in a variety of ways is normal and healthy for young people and that the schools should help them to do so safely and without guilt.[40] Such aims conflict directly with the moral and religious beliefs of many parents, who thus perceive the schools as directly undermining their own attempts to inculcate values in their children. Legal challenges to such programs have generally been unsuccessful. It is not even clear that courts will recognize a general right of exemption from such programs for children whose parents disapprove.[41] In any case, in some of its earlier decisions, the Supreme Court seemed to say that it is insufficient merely to exempt certain children from programs which violate their consciences, since this may single them out for ridicule and harassment.[42]

If the public schools are the most obvious place where values clash, they are by no means the only cockpit. Abortion is another classic example. The liberal position—that those who oppose abortion are free not to engage in it, while those who approve it may do so—simply begs the question, since in the minds of anti-abortionists they are being asked to countenance the massive taking of human life. A possible compromise over the abortion issue would be to permit abortions to be

---

39. Epperson v. Arkansas, 393 U.S. 97 (1968); Daniel v. Walters, 515 F.2d 485 (6th Cir. 1975).
40. For a critique of such programs, *see* Horner, *Is the New Sex Education Going Too Far?*, New York Times Magazine, Dec. 7, 1980, at 137–48.
41. *See, e.g.,* Cornwell v. State Board of Educ., 428 F.2d 471 (4th Cir.), *cert. denied,* 400 U.S. 942 (1970).
42. *See, e.g.,* McCollum v. Board of Educ., 333 U.S. 203, 227, 232 (1948).

performed by private agencies but to keep the state scrupulously neutral. Virtually no one, however, finds this acceptable. Pro-abortionists generally wish to see major governmental support for the practice—it is regarded as an integral part of health care, as well as an important tool in population control, and as such should be promoted by publicly funded agencies both domestically and abroad. The modern welfare state simply cannot remain neutral on such issues.

Recognizing this, suit was brought in federal court to invalidate the so-called Hyde Amendment whereby Congress forbids most expenditures of public funds for abortions. The major grounds for the suit was the claim that the law violated church-state separation because it enacted the principles of particular religions, notably the Roman Catholic Church. Under the so-called "divisiveness" doctrine, the claim was made that any legislation which could be shown to have been influenced primarily by religious believers was invalid because of its tendency to promote religious conflict in society. Plaintiffs went to the length of reading the mail of the congressional sponsor of the legislation, to determine the religious affiliation of those who wrote to him, and of submitting an affidavit about his personal religious practices. The Supreme Court ultimately rejected the argument.[43]

Had it won acceptance, it would have had immensely far-reaching consequences, since a great deal of legislation (for example, the Civil Rights Act of 1964)[44] could be shown to have been passed as a result of strong religious pressures. At some level the divisiveness doctrine—the argument that certain kinds of state action are forbidden simply because they tend to create religious controversy—is recognized by the Supreme Court, however. It was enunciated by Chief Justice Burger in one of the school-aid cases.[45] The very fact that the issue is raised tends to demonstrate the impossibility of the state's neutrality in matters of basic values.

Another point of conflict between the professed neutrality of the state and its actual commitment to certain values is the question whether policies to which the state is in principle committed may be enforced with regard to religious institutions which claim exemption either in terms of religious freedom or church-state separation. The Supreme Court, by a narrow margin, has ruled that the National Labor Relations Board does not have jurisdiction over teachers in religious schools. The Catholic hierarchy argued in the case that to permit such a thing would be to permit the government to intervene in disputes which might be of a purely religious nature, e.g., a decision to dismiss a teacher for failing to teach Catholic doctrine.[46] A Protestant school has successfully argued in a state court that regulations imposed on the school by the state effectively interfered with religious freedom by restricting the school's right to set its curriculum and hire teachers in

---

43. Harris v. McRae, 448 U.S. 297 (1980) (copy of plaintiff's brief in possession of the author).

44. For the importance of religious influence on legislation, see J. ADAMS, THE GROWING CHURCH LOBBY IN WASHINGTON (1970). The Civil Rights Act is considered at 1-3.

45. Lemon v. Kurtzman, 403 U.S. 602, 622 (1971).

46. NLRB v. Catholic Bishop of Chicago, 440 U.S. 490 (1979).

18   LAW AND CONTEMPORARY PROBLEMS   [Vol. 44: No. 2

accordance with its religious mission.[47] Largely unlitigated, at least at the federal level, is the question whether religious institutions, contrary to their professed beliefs, would be prohibited from discriminating against classes of persons specially protected by law, for example, by excluding women from the ranks of the clergy or refusing to hire homosexuals as teachers.

It is worth noting that certain strict separationists do not altogether regard the wall as excluding both sides equally. Leo Pfeffer, for example, notes that church and state historically have sought to dominate each other, with the state usually successful.[48] He also argues that some of the Supreme Court's decisions of the past thirty years have made the "liberalization" of the Catholic Church more likely by making parochial schools harder to maintain, thus helping those in the Church who seek a "congregational" polity independent of hierarchical control. Pfeffer believes all religions, partly as a result of court decisions, are fated to become irresistibly secularized.[49]

V

DEFINITION OF RELIGION

Through most of American history, questions of church-state relations have been fairly easy to define because there were few problems as to what constituted a church. However, the First Amendment does not mention "church" but rather "religion." Implicitly, therefore, it seems as though the amendment does not only apply to formally organized groups which designate themselves as churches. America has always been fruitful in producing new religions, and in the past twenty years there has been a vast proliferation of them, the constitutional import of which is not clear.

Insofar as newer religious movements can be readily identified as such there is no problem, since presumably they have the same rights and are subject to the same restraints as older and more established churches. The problem emerges with respect to movements which may not declare themselves to be religions, and may in fact even deny that they are, but which others understand to be. An issue has arisen which respect to the movement called Transcendental Meditation, whose proponents claim that it is merely a technique for recollection and self-exploration, while critics claim it is a religion actually or potentially in conflict with other religions. Thus far Federal courts have upheld the critics.[50]

A potentially much more divisive issue is over the "religion" of Secular Humanism. Many religious believers are convinced that there exists such a philosophy, which is antithetical to theism, dismissing the latter's claims as illusory and hence as

---

47. Sheridan Road Baptist Church v. Michigan Dept. of Educ., Cir. Ct., Mich., No. 80-26205-AZ (Dec. 8, 1980).

48. L. PFEFFER, CHURCH, STATE, AND FREEDOM 727 (1953).

49. L. PFEFFER, GOD, CAESAR, AND THE CONSTITUTION: THE COURT AS REFEREE OF CHURCH-STATE CONFRONTATION 49, 231, 250, 253, 348 (1975).

50. Malnak v. Yogi, 592 F.2d 197 (3d Cir. 1979).

personally and socially damaging to those who accept them. Secular Humanism also advocates an approach to life in which human beings are encouraged to rely entirely on their own powers and to live and act as though no divine being governs the universe. Finally, certain practical consequences tend to flow from these theoretical beliefs—for example, Secular Humanists tend to reject the traditional, strict Judeo-Christian moral code with regard to sex and to advocate "free" and "open" attitudes towards sexuality which are morally objectionable to many religious believers.[51]

However, it is not the contention of critics that Secular Humanism is merely the doctrine of a particular organization having relatively few members. They rather contend that it is a widely held philosophy of life shared by many people, not all of whom would even be familiar with the name. For purposes of the First Amendment the contention is that Secular Humanism often functions as the governing philosophy of many public schools and other public agencies and that it is not subject to the same restraints in the name of separation that organized churches are. Thus, the argument runs, religious believers suffer violation of their rights by having an alien and unacceptable philosophy imposed on them. Thus far the courts have shown no inclination to accept this argument.[52]

That the courts should take the argument more seriously is suggested by the fact that the Supreme Court, in establishing the criteria for valid conscientious objection from military service, has itself declared Secular Humanism to be a religion, entitled therefore to the same considerations and protections as all other religions. In one such case the Court ruled that:

> We believe that . . . the test of belief "in a relation to a Supreme Being" is whether a given belief that is sincere and meaningful occupies a place in the life of its possessor parallel to that filled by the orthodox belief in God of one who clearly qualifies for exemption.[53]

If Secular Humanism is indeed a religion for the Court's purposes, and if religion is to be understood as the Court thus understands it, it seems to follow that very difficult and profound questions are raised with respect to the duty of the state to be vigilant against Secular Humanist intrusions into the public order in the same way it is required to be vigilant against theistic intrusions. It is noteworthy that no less a personage than Leo Pfeffer argues that the courts have indeed enshrined Secular Humanism as the official creed.[54]

The issue raises once again the anomaly discussed in relation to the unexamined assumptions of the strict separationists, namely, why it is to be assumed that theistic creeds alone, of all the schools of thought which contend with each other in modern society, are to be singled out for special exclusions.

---

51. A convenient summary of secular humanist doctrine is found in AMERICAN HUMANIST ASSOCIATION, HUMANIST MANIFESTO I & II (1953, 1973).

52. See, e.g., Hobolth v. Greenway, 52 Mich. App. 682, 218 N.W.2d 98 (1974); Medeiros v. Kiyosaki, 52 Haw. 436, 478 P.2d 314 (1970).

53. United States v. Seeger, 380 U.S. 163, 165-66 (1965). See also Torcaso v. Watkins, 367 U.S. 488, 495 (1961).

54. Issues That Divide: The Triumph of Secular Humanism, 1977 J. OF CHURCH & STATE 203-05.

20   LAW AND CONTEMPORARY PROBLEMS   [Vol. 44: No. 2

VI
PERSONAL CONSCIENCE VERSUS PUBLIC POLICY

Instinctively the liberal mind tends to uphold individual rights, especially those based on conscience, when these conflict with law or government policy. A long tradition holds that individual rights must be scrupulously respected, and even dissent from law must be accommodated as much as possible.

It remains uncertain, however, how far the courts will go in permitting dissent on religious grounds from firmly established law or public policy. Historically the Supreme Court has gone fairly far in upholding the right of Jehovah's Witnesses, for example, not to be compelled to salute the American flag[55] or of Amish parents not to be forced to send their children to public schools.[56] However, as one constitutional scholar has somewhat cynically suggested, the courts have a record of solicitousness towards religious beliefs perceived as marginal and dissenting while tending towards strictness and vigilance with respect to "mainline" beliefs.[57]

An acute area of conflict has been the growing tendency of some Protestants to establish their own schools. Such establishments have come under attack by various government agencies, including the Internal Revenue Service (charging improper claims of tax exemption) and state departments of education demanding control of accreditation. The results so far have been rather mixed. In each case, however, the supporters of the schools in question claim that conscience, particularly relating to freedom of religion, forbids them to enroll their children in public schools.[58] More radical yet is the contention of some parents that the moral character of existing schools requires them to educate their children at home, in accord with their own beliefs. Again the judicial results have been mixed.[59]

Parents have also brought suit to overturn compulsory sex-education courses in public schools, on the grounds that such courses violate the religious and moral beliefs of the parents. Such claims have been disallowed.[60]

The practice of "deprogramming" of recruits to various religious sects also raises questions of religious freedom which are far-reaching in their consequences. On the one hand the state seems to have a clear obligation to protect those who are tricked or coerced into joining groups which suppress their freedom, as in the notorious case of the People's Temple of Rev. Jim Jones. However, in the nature of things it is extremely difficult for the state to determine when an individual has indeed been subjected to techniques which negate personal freedom, and the very attempt to do so may have a "chilling" effect on religious liberty. Once the state takes it upon itself to judge when religious conversions are genuine and when the result of forced means, there would be no end to the necessary interference in

---

55. Board of Educ. v. Barnette, 319 U.S. 624 (1943).
56. Wisconsin v. Yoder, 406 U.S. 205 (1972).
57. W. BERNS, THE FIRST AMENDMENT AND THE FUTURE OF AMERICAN DEMOCRACY 77-79 (1976).
58. *See, e.g.,* Kentucky State Bd. v. Rudasill, 589 S.W.2d 877 (Ky. 1979).
59. *See, e.g.,* Michigan v. Noble, No. 5791-0115-A (1979).
60. Note 35, *supra.*

matters of conscience and religious liberty.[61] It is also worth noting in this connection that some modern sceptics believe that all religious commitment is by definition irrational and therefore might be subject to automatic suspicion and review.

Attempts to "deprogram" members of religious cults are often brought by the members' parents, and the whole area of parental authority is a sensitive one in which the ground appears to be shifting. It is also a subject closely intertwined with personal religious liberty, as indicated in the instances cited above in which parents object on grounds of principle to what is taught in the public schools. The Supreme Court has already ruled that minor children have a right to contraceptive and abortion services without their parents' consent,[62] a ruling which offends the consciences of many parents not only in its substance but also in the way that it seems to establish the authority of the state above that of the parent in a highly sensitive and important area of life—the nurture of children. Some parents with traditional beliefs fear that the state will indefinitely expand the scope of children's rights so as to minimize parental authority, especially in the crucial area of moral values, and that the state will commit itself to certain policies, *e.g.*, the encouragement of sexual activity among the young, that will directly conflict with parents' own values.

VII
Summary

As American society, often led by its courts, has greatly widened the limits of permissible belief and behavior over the past twenty years, it has not simply enriched the "pluralism" which has always been a feature of that society. In the nature of things the decision to tolerate certain hitherto disapproved ideas or actions has often required tightening restrictions on ideas or actions previously considered orthodox. An indefinitely elastic pluralism is not possible. Expansions in some areas are likely to cause contractions in others.

In particular the unofficially privileged place which organized religion has traditionally enjoyed in American life has been eroded, often with active judicial effort towards that end. The urge to ensure that non-belief does not suffer in comparison with belief has often led to practical and theoretical restrictions being placed on religion itself. The classical doctrine of strict separationism rests on an assumption that the state can and must be neutral. But in practice this is impossible. Values are necessary for the functioning of any society, and if they are not consciously adopted and publicly acknowledged they will be smuggled in surreptitiously and often unconsciously. Values are always in real or potential conflict, and the state inevitably favors some values over others.

---

61. Alexander v. Unification Church of America, 634 F.2d 673 (2d Cir. 1980); Peterson v. Sorlien, 299 N.W.2d 123 (Minn. 1980).

62. Planned Parenthood of Missouri v. Danforth, 428 U.S. 52 (1976). Note, however, that the Court has recently limited *Danforth*. Although it remains unconstitutional to legislate an irrevocable power to parents to forbid their daughter's abortion, a state may require parental notification, when possible, of an abortion to be performed on a dependent unmarried minor. H. L. v. Matheson, 49 U.S.L.W. 4255 (U.S. March 24, 1981) (No. 79-5903).

[7]

Concepts and Compromise in First Amendment Religious Doctrine

Phillip E. Johnson†

The first amendment's religion clauses have perplexed commentators and Supreme Court Justices for some time.[1] The difficult body of doctrine derived from these clauses seems to consist of contradictory principles, vaguely defined tests, and eccentric distinctions. Present legal doctrines cannot even claim the support of history with much plausibility. Despite the customary invocation of James Madison and Thomas Jefferson, whose views on this subject were complex and in any event not necessarily shared by the other Framers, scholars know that the present doctrinal approach stems from post-World War II Supreme Court decisions.[2] In an important sense, contemporary doc-

---

† Professor of Law, Boalt Hall School of Law, University of California, Berkeley. A.B. 1961, Harvard University; J.D. 1965, University of Chicago.

My colleagues Michael Smith and Jesse Choper encouraged my interest in this subject in the course of many stimulating conversations, and my student assistant Mark Ryland also provided valuable critical input.

1. "Candor compels acknowledgment . . . that we can only dimly perceive the lines of demarcation in this extraordinarily sensitive area of constitutional law." Lemon v. Kurtzman, 403 U.S. 602, 612 (1971). *See also* Committee for Pub. Educ. v. Regan, 444 U.S. 646, 662 (1980); Tilton v. Richardson, 403 U.S. 672, 677-78 (1971).

2. For a recent treatment of the historical background of the religion clauses, see R. CORD, SEPARATION OF CHURCH AND STATE (1982), which disputes the "strict separationist" interpretation previously advanced in L. PFEFFER, GOD, CAESAR AND THE CONSTITUTION (rev. ed. 1967).

Professor Mark De Wolfe Howe wrote that in the religion cases, "[T]he Court has too often pretended that the dictates of the nation's history, rather than the mandates of its own will, compelled a particular decision. By superficial and purposive interpretations of the past, the Court has dishonored the acts of the historian and degraded the talents of the lawyer." M. HOWE, THE GARDEN AND THE WILDERNESS 4 (1965). The historical evidence is debated in the majority and dissenting opinions in Marsh v. Chambers, 103 S. Ct. 3330 (1983) and Lynch v. Donnelly, 104 S. Ct. 1355 (1984).

The practices of the early Presidents are cited by people on both sides of the religion debate. For example, proponents of the "wall of separation" theory emphasize that Presidents Jefferson and Jackson refused to issue proclamations of National Days of Thanksgiving, whereas adherents of the "benevolent neutrality" theory note that Presidents Washington, Adams, and Madison (as well as more recent presidents) issued numerous such proclamations, expressing the nation's gratitude to God and imploring Him for His blessing. *See Lynch*, 104 S. Ct. at 1360. James Madison, the principal drafter of the establishment clause, was a member of the committee that selected a chaplain to open the sessions of the First Congress with prayer, and he voted for the bill authorizing payment of the chaplain. *See Marsh*, 103 S. Ct. at 3333 n.8. On the other hand, his "Detached Memoranda," written after his retirement from politics many years later, disapproved the practice. *Id.* at 3343-44. Even President Jefferson negotiated a treaty with the Kaskaskia Indians, one condition of which was a pledge by the United States to support a Catholic priest in his priestly duties, and Jefferson repeatedly supported federal land grant trust laws that subsidized

trine has reversed the original understanding and literal meaning of the first amendment. What was intended to keep the federal government (Congress) out of church-state relations has become a mandate allowing the federal government (i.e. the federal courts) to regulate those relations in every detail.[3]

That in some sense the federal government and the states ought to be "neutral" in religious matters is undisputed, but there is significant disagreement over how benevolent that neutrality should be and how rigorously it ought to be enforced. Practically everyone agrees that government ought not to take sides between Catholic, Protestant, and Jew. It is not equally clear, however, that government can or should be neutral as between atheism and theism,[4] nor is it clear whether neutrality implies strictly excluding sectarian symbols from public ceremonies or displays.[5] The Supreme Court seems at times to treat any government assistance to religious activities as a forbidden establishment, yet at other times, it requires governments to take extraordinary

---

missionaries to spread their religion to the Indians. *See* R. CORD, *supra*, at 17-47. As rector of the University of Virginia, Jefferson supported on-campus religious instruction by sectarian divinity schools. *See* McCollum v. Board of Educ., 333 U.S. 203, 245 n.11 (1948) (Reed, J., dissenting).

Whatever one might conclude from the conflicting statements and actions of the early Presidents, the judiciary did not interpret the establishment clause to require strict separation of government and religion until Everson v. Board of Educ., 330 U.S. 1 (1947). "Before that time, the Supreme Court readily upheld government actions concerning religion that seem highly problematic by present standards." Smith, *The Special Place of Religion in the Constitution*, 1983 SUP. CT. REV. 83, 86.

3.

The application of the religion clauses to the states through the due process clause of the fourteenth amendment, the movement from a government of closely limited powers to the affirmative state, and the gradual expansion of our understanding of the nature of religion, have combined to work a fundamental transformation in the question of how religious groups and interests should be treated. In this context, the religion clauses, which for the framers represented relatively clear statements of highly compatible goals, have taken on new and varied meanings that frequently appear to conflict.

L. TRIBE, AMERICAN CONSTITUTIONAL LAW 812 (1978).

4. "We are a religious people whose institutions presuppose a Supreme Being." Zorach v. Clauson, 343 U.S. 306, 313 (1952) (opinion of Douglas, J.). *Cf.* Lynch v. Donnelly, 104 S. Ct. 1355, 1381 (1984) (Brennan, J., dissenting) (footnote and citation omitted):

While I remain uncertain about these questions, I would suggest that such practices as the designation of "In God We Trust" as our national motto, or the references to God contained in the Pledge of Allegiance can best be understood . . . as a form of "ceremonial deism," protected from Establishment Clause scrutiny chiefly because they have lost through rote repetition any significant religious content.

The phrase "under God" in the Pledge of Allegiance is, however, a recent addition.

Professor Howe argued that the constitutional separation of church and state reflected more the evangelical faith of Roger Williams than the skeptical rationalism of Thomas Jefferson, and that this separation, understood from an evangelical perspective, "endorsed a host of favoring tributes to faith—tributes so substantial that they have produced in the aggregate what may fairly be described as a *de facto* establishment of religion." M. HOWE, *supra* note 2, at 11.

5. *See* Lynch v. Donnelly, 104 S. Ct. 1355, 1360-61 (1984).

measures to accommodate unusual religious practices.[6] Despite the most determined efforts of the Justices and the scholars, no single logical framework seems capable of explaining the law.

Many areas of constitutional law are unsettled, of course, but in most areas the uncertainty concerns how far the Constitution requires us to go in a particular direction. In the religion clause area, even the general direction is often difficult to ascertain. For example, if a state decided to experiment with school vouchers as an alternative to the public schools, it could not know whether it would be constitutionally obligated to allow those vouchers to be used at religious as well as secular private schools, or whether it would be constitutionally forbidden to do so; whether it would have the discretion to decide the matter either way without constitutional violation; whether it would be required to give religious schools less money than secular schools to avoid subsidizing the explicitly religious aspects of the curriculum; or whether it would be forbidden to use the voucher alternative altogether because whatever it did with respect to religious schools would be unconstitutional.[7] The Supreme Court's recent decision in *Widmar v. Vincent*[8] illustrates the conceptual chaos that pervades this area of the law. A Christian student group at the University of Missouri had been using a room on campus for worship meetings. University officials stopped the practice, citing a state constitutional provision that the state courts had held to require a stricter "separation" of church and state than that mandated by the establishment clause of the federal constitution.[9] The students, on the contrary, claimed that it was a violation of *their* rights under the free exercise clause to refuse to allow student religious groups to use campus facilities on the same basis as secular student organizations. They also argued that this singling out of religious activities for special adverse treatment violated their rights to equal protection of the laws and freedom of speech, because it distinguished among student meetings on the basis of the content of their speech.

The federal district court agreed with the university administration that providing a room was an impermissible establishment of religion.[10] The court of appeals disagreed, siding with the students.[11]

---

6. *Compare, e.g.*, McCollum v. Board of Educ., 333 U.S. 203 (1948) *and* Committee for Pub. Educ. v. Nyquist, 413 U.S. 756 (1973) *with, e.g.*, Sherbert v. Verner, 374 U.S. 398 (1963).

7. *See* Mueller v. Allen, 103 S. Ct. 3062 (1983) (upholding state tax deduction for limited educational expenses at private and public schools); Widmar v. Vincent, 454 U.S. 263 (1981) (holding that to deny student religious group use of facilities generally open to other student groups violates first amendment); Committee for Pub. Educ. v. Nyquist, 413 U.S. 756 (1973) (disapproving tuition grants for low-income parents who send children to nonpublic schools).

8. 454 U.S. 263 (1981).

9. *Id.* at 275-76.

10. Chess v. Widmar, 480 F. Supp. 907 (W.D. Mo. 1979), *remanded*, 635 F.2d 1310 (8th Cir. 1980), *aff'd sub nom.* Widmar v. Vincent, 454 U.S. 263 (1981).

11. Chess v. Widmar, 635 F.2d 1310 (8th Cir. 1980), *aff'd sub nom.* Widmar v. Vincent, 454 U.S. 263 (1981).

820 *CALIFORNIA LAW REVIEW* [Vol. 72:817

Both decisions are equally rational in terms of conventional constitutional law. Providing facilities such as meeting rooms certainly aids the religious activity, much as if the state were to make a direct cash grant to pay the rent on a church building.[12] Yet, one can hardly describe as "neutral" a state policy that provides meeting rooms to Republicans, communists, musicians, and stamp collectors, but denies similar facilities to religious groups.[13] Such discrimination seems to imply that religion is a peculiarly disfavored activity.

The Supreme Court eventually decided the case on free speech grounds, ruling that worship is a form of communication and invoking the familiar principle that a state may not ordinarily favor one speaker over another on the basis of the content of their speech.[14] The decision thus held the state constitution's ban on aid to sectarian activities unconstitutional as applied.

Justice White, in dissent, was gravely troubled by the Court's willingness to categorize worship as speech for constitutional purposes.[15] He pointed out that the Supreme Court itself has gone to great lengths to exclude this particular type of speech from the public school classroom.[16] When the Supreme Court decides that a school teacher may not lead her class in reciting the Lord's Prayer but may lead it in reciting the Pledge of Allegiance,[17] or when the Court decides that a state may not require the posting of the Ten Commandments on classroom walls although it certainly could require the posting of the ten amendments of the Bill of Rights,[18] it is certainly making distinctions based on the religious content of the speech or writing. The majority's decision in *Widmar* thus called into question an entire body of doctrine.

First amendment religion doctrine is radically indeterminate in three ways. First, there are what I would call the *characterization* issues, illustrated by *Widmar*.[19] A particular disputed issue can often be characterized in two or more different ways: for example, as an establishment clause problem, a free exercise problem, or a free speech prob-

---

12. *See* Tilton v. Richardson, 403 U.S. 672 (1971) (establishment clause forbids use of federally subsidized university facilities for religious purposes).

13. "The University's policy singles out and stigmatizes certain religious activity and, in consequence, discredits religious groups." *Chess*, 635 F.2d at 1317 (footnote omitted).

14. Widmar v. Vincent, 454 U.S. 263, 277 (1981).

15. *Id.* at 284-86 (White, J., dissenting).

16. *Id.*

17. *Compare* Engel v. Vitale, 370 U.S. 421 (1962) *with* West Va. State Bd. of Educ. v. Barnette, 319 U.S. 624 (1943). Although religious dissenters may have a right to refuse to salute the flag or recite the Pledge of Allegiance, such patriotic ceremonies are not banned from classrooms.

18. *See* Stone v. Graham, 449 U.S. 39 (1980).

19. Widmar v. Vincent, 454 U.S. 263 (1981).

lem. The constitutional outcome depends largely, though not entirely, on the characterization option that one selects; and, as *Widmar* and other cases show, no neutral principles govern this determination.

After the characterization decision has been made, a second source of indeterminacy arises when the Court applies a subjective test to determine whether the practice is forbidden, permitted, or required. For example, in free exercise cases, the Court "balances" the individual's or group's interest in the religious practice against the government's interest in regulating the behavior. Similarly, if the issue is characterized as one involving establishment of religion, the Court then considers whether the challenged practice involves a forbidden religious purpose, has a primary effect of advancing or inhibiting religion, or threatens to foster an excessive government "entanglement" with religion. But as with the characterization issue itself, these subjective-test concepts are not really helpful in explaining where to draw the line between what government may and may not do in support of religious institutions or practices.

Third and finally, there is no accepted definition of "religion" for constitutional purposes, and no satisfactory definition is likely to be conceived. The significance of this definitional gap has generally been overlooked because most Supreme Court cases have dealt with Christian groups and practices that are concededly "religious." But first amendment law is based upon an assumption that there is something important about "religious" practices that differentiates them from "secular" practices and entitles (or subjects) them to special constitutional treatment. To the extent that we are unable to identify any factor which distinguishes the religious from the secular, we call into question whether that special treatment is necessary or even rational.

The first three Parts of this Article develop further this theme of indeterminacy, explaining and illustrating the three areas of uncertainty just summarized. Part IV then explores the ideological considerations that might motivate the Justices to exercise their opportunities to manipulate doctrine in one direction rather than another.

I

THE CHARACTERIZATION ISSUE

Judges and commentators have often observed that the free exercise and the establishment clauses look in opposite directions, so that a direct conflict may arise if one is allowed to intrude into territory properly belonging to the other.[20] What is less frequently noted is that many significant problems can be categorized so as to fall under the

---

20. *See* Walz v. Tax Comm'n, 397 U.S. 664, 668-69 (1970); L. TRIBE, *supra* note 3, at 815;

rule of *either* the establishment clause or the free exercise clause, depending upon which we would prefer to have govern the situation.

A. Aid to Religious Private Schools

A good example of this characterization problem is the perennially controversial question of whether it is a forbidden "establishment of religion" for a state legislature to provide some assistance to religious schools, or the students in them, as part of a general program of assistance to private education. If we view the transfer of funds to religious schools (with or without the parents or students as a conduit[21]) in isolation, the program seems to be providing a special benefit to religious activity, and thus it is at a minimum constitutionally suspect. That is precisely how the federal district court viewed the use of facilities for student worship in *Widmar*.[22] On the other hand, we could equally logically focus on the state educational program as a whole and view the tuition grants or whatever as a rough attempt to "equalize" the treatment of those parents and students who desire a religious education with those who prefer a secular education. In that case we would understand the state's action not as an attempt to benefit religion, but as an attempt to avoid disadvantaging or discriminating against it.

Relatedly, it has long been assumed that parents have a right under the free exercise clause to send their children to religious schools if they can do so at their own expense.[23] It is not obvious that the religious liberty of the children is always furthered by allowing their parents to choose a sectarian education,[24] or that a "compelling interest" could not be found to justify a law requiring all children to go through the socializing experience of public education.[25] Nonetheless, the parental right is well established and not controversial.

Granted that premise, it is difficult to understand how it can be impermissible for a state to make the same option available to everyone

---

Choper, *The Religion Clauses of the First Amendment: Reconciling the Conflict*, 41 U. Pitt. L. Rev. 673, 690-92 (1980).

21. For establishment clause purposes, Supreme Court holdings indicate that it makes some difference if the state channels the aid to religious schools through individual parents. *See* Mueller v. Allen, 103 S. Ct. 3062, 3069 (1983).

22. "[T]his Court finds that a university policy permitting regular religious services in university-owned buildings would have the primary effect of advancing religion." Chess v. Widmar, 480 F. Supp. 907, 915-16 (W.D. Mo. 1979), *remanded*, 635 F.2d 1310 (8th Cir. 1980), *aff'd sub nom.* Widmar v. Vincent, 454 U.S. 263 (1981).

The issue, of course, is whether one characterizes the policy as a policy permitting religious services or as a policy permitting student activities generally.

23. Wisconsin v. Yoder, 406 U.S. 205, 213-14 (1972); *cf.* Pierce v. Society of Sisters, 268 U.S. 510 (1925) (holding Oregon statute requiring children between the ages of eight and sixteen to attend public schools unconstitutional).

24. *See Yoder*, 406 U.S. at 241-46 (Douglas, J., dissenting).

25. *See id.* at 237-41 (White, J., concurring).

by tuition tax credits, grants, or other forms of aid to private schools. Looked at that way, the question should *not* be whether it is a permissible activity for the state to provide aid to religious schools, but whether the Constitution permits a state (or even conceivably requires it) to give the poor the kind of opportunities for educational choice that the rich and middle class currently enjoy.

The issue in the assistance-to-schools cases is analogous to that involved in *Widmar*, except that much more is at stake. The problem is that government is simultaneously forbidden from giving substantial assistance to religious activities and from discriminating against religious activities. When the question is whether religious organizations should be allowed to receive funding or use facilities on the same basis as secular organizations, the principles of "no assistance" and "no discrimination" come into conflict.[26]

One can deny the existence of the conflict by denying that "religious" and "secular" educations are the appropriate things to be compared. A person taking this view would probably prefer to label the public schools of the United States as "neutral" rather than "secular." Our public schools do not endorse any particular religious position— Christianity, Judaism, Islam, or whatever—nor do they preach atheism, as the schools in the Soviet Union are said to do. The schools avoid controversial religious questions not because the school authorities have concluded that those questions are not important, but rather because they think religious instruction is best carried on in homes or churches free of governmental involvement. From this viewpoint, the only way to be neutral about religion is to ignore the subject altogether.[27]

Whether schools that avoid the topic of religion altogether are thereby "neutral" towards religion is debatable. For one thing, the schools have to teach subjects—biology in particular—which touch directly upon matters of religious controversy. A textbook that teaches that the human species evolved gradually over millions of years from simple life forms is anything but neutral from the viewpoint of Biblical literalists. Courses in social living, "values clarification," and sex education also produce religious controversy, because opinions about sexual morality and other ethical issues are so closely related to religious beliefs.[28]

---

26. The conflict between the "no assistance" and "no discrimination" principles was apparent even in the first Supreme Court decision on aid to parochial schools. *See* Everson v. Board of Educ., 330 U.S. 1, 16-18 (1947).

27. *See infra* note 115 and accompanying text.

28. *See* Eger, *The Conflict in Moral Education: An Informal Case Study*, Pub. Interest, Spring 1981, at 62.

For example, is heterosexual, life-long marriage the ideal sexual relationship to which all others are unfavorably compared, although others may be legally tolerated, or should various "living together" arrangements, including homosexual liaisons, be regarded as equally acceptable alternatives? Should pregnant teenagers be encouraged to consider abortion as a morally respectable alternative to raising the child or offering it for adoption? No matter how hard the schools try to straddle that sort of question, they are drawn irresistibly towards either reinforcing the traditional religion-based sexual morality without explaining its theological foundation, or towards emphasizing informed personal choice as the ultimate criterion.[29]

The point here is not that the public schools are doing something wrong in teaching evolutionary biology, or stressing the practical problems of teenage sex (i.e., contraception and disease prevention) rather than its ultimate morality. The schools ought to teach their students what they need to know, whether or not the teaching touches on controversial subjects. But what do the students need to know, and what do they need to be warned against? One's religious commitments necessarily affect how one answers those questions. To put the point another way, what matters is not so much what the schools do or do not explicitly teach their students about religion, but what assumptions about the nature of humanity and the purpose of life guide the school authorities in planning the curriculum and administering the life of the school.[30] Although it is possible to be more or less fair minded about such matters, there is no such thing as a dead-center neutrality in comparison to which all other positions are partisan.

B.   Unemployment Compensation

Characterization problems also arise in other contexts. For example, the Supreme Court held in *Sherbert v. Verner*[31] that the free exercise clause requires states to pay unemployment compensation to Seventh-Day Adventists who refuse to accept employment that requires Saturday work. By contrast, critics such as Dean Choper have argued that not only was this result not required by the free exercise

---

29. *See* Kasun, *Turning Children into Sex Experts*, PUB. INTEREST, Spring 1979, at 3. For a further exchange on the sex education controversy, see Crosbie, *Sex Education: Another Look*, PUB. INTEREST, Winter 1980, at 120; Kasun, *More on the New Sex Education*, PUB. INTEREST, Winter 1980, at 129.

30. For example, in a relatively permissive society, public schools are also likely to be permissive. Religious schools attract many students (or parents) by offering a more structured and disciplined learning environment. A school does not have to be religious in order to be strict, of course, but many religious schools do stress discipline. Perhaps a firm commitment to a set of beliefs—whether or not labeled as religious—predisposes school authorities to be firm with their students.

31. 374 U.S. 398 (1963).

clause, but it actually violates the establishment clause by giving to Saturday worshipers a privilege that would be denied to persons who refuse to accept Saturday employment for nonreligious reasons.[32]

The difference in characterization depends upon what is compared with what. Dean Choper compared the position of strict Saturday worshipers with that of persons who prefer not to work on Saturday for nonreligious reasons.[33] From his perspective, the former group received a benefit that the latter group did not. The Supreme Court majority, on the other hand, thought it more appropriate to compare the situation of Saturday worshipers with that of Sunday worshipers, whose freedom to refuse work on Sunday was solidly protected by law.[34] Because it would involve little added expense or inconvenience to the state to make an adjustment for Saturday worshipers, the Court saw doing so as a fair-minded attempt to equalize the treatment of persons adhering to different creeds.

As in the aid-to-schools cases, one could resist this logic by describing Sunday as the "neutral" day of rest recognized by the state for secular purposes, rather than as a day set apart because of its significance to orthodox Christians. On that basis, the Supreme Court has held that states may forbid businesses to operate on Sunday,[35] and to the extent that businesses are closed on Sunday, the question of willingness to work on that day will not arise. Where Sunday work is permitted, on the other hand, a policy of strict neutrality requires that both religious and nonreligious persons who refuse to work on Sundays be treated alike for unemployment compensation purposes, and that persons who refuse to work on other days for religious reasons be given no special dispensation. By granting no religious exemptions at all, the state can avoid having to answer thorny hypothetical questions such as how it should treat an eccentric group that requires its members to refuse to work on Wednesdays. In practice, Saturday worshipers and not Sunday worshipers would probably have to accept employment on their day of worship, due to Sunday closing laws and related customs, but at least the law would be formally neutral if not equal in effect, and the state could avoid the quagmire of individualized exceptions for religious claims.

II
THE SUBJECTIVE TESTS

Although it is an important first step, the characterization decision

---

32. Choper, *supra* note 20, at 690-92.
33. *Id.* at 691.
34. Sherbert v. Verner, 374 U.S. 398, 406 (1963); *see also* Choper, *supra* note 20, at 692-95.
35. McGowan v. Maryland, 366 U.S. 420 (1961).

does not necessarily control the outcome of a religion case. If we find that a state regulation or command burdens someone's free exercise of religion, then that burden must be justified by a "compelling state interest" that cannot be satisfied in some other, less intrusive manner. If we decide instead that we are dealing with a possibly forbidden establishment of religion, then the benefit is nonetheless constitutional if the questioned act can pass a three-part test formulated by the Supreme Court in *Lemon v. Kurtzman*:[36] it must have a secular purpose, its principal or primary effect must be one that neither advances nor inhibits religion, and it must not foster " 'an excessive government entanglement with religion.' "[37]

At times, however, the Court disregards the *Lemon* test in establishment clause cases if its application would lead to inconvenient outcomes. A leading example is *Marsh v. Chambers*,[38] where a six-to-three majority allowed the Nebraska Legislature to continue its long-standing practice of paying a Protestant clergyman to open each day of the legislative session with a nondenominational prayer "in the Judeo-Christian tradition."[39] Legislative prayer seems like a clearcut endorsement of theistic religious belief, despite the effort to avoid sectarian controversy, but the Supreme Court found constitutional support for the practice in a tradition dating back to the Continental Congress and the founding of the nation.[40] Perhaps the holding can best be explained by adding a fourth element or exception to the *Lemon* test: ceremonial governmental religious pronouncements are not unconstitutional if they are sufficiently "traditional," and if they are not made in the public schools.

The *Lemon* test has been ridiculed because of the seemingly absurd lines that the Supreme Court has drawn in its name, especially in the area of public aid to religious schools. One example is particularly notorious: the Supreme Court has permitted states to provide free secular textbooks to parochial school students, but has forbidden as an establishment of religion the furnishing of "instructional materials," such as maps.[41] There is nothing about the *Lemon* test itself, however,

---

36. 403 U.S. 602 (1971).

37. *Id.* at 612-13 (quoting Walz v. Tax Comm'n, 397 U.S. 664, 674 (1970)). The *Lemon* test is also sometimes discussed in free exercise cases, when the issue is whether a religiously motivated individual or group should have an exemption from some broadly applicable regulation. *See, e.g.*, Wisconsin v. Yoder, 406 U.S. 205, 234 n.22 (1972). If granting that exemption would run afoul of the test used to determine when assistance to religion violates the establishment clause, then we would have a perfect standoff between the two clauses. The free exercise might conceivably require what the establishment clause forbids.

38. 103 S. Ct. 3330 (1983).

39. *Id.* at 3336 (footnote omitted).

40. *Id.* at 3333-36.

41. *See generally* Wolman v. Walter, 433 U.S. 229 (1977).

that required the Supreme Court to draw the line where it did rather than somewhere else. The problem with the *Lemon* test is not that it requires drawing lines, but rather that its three concepts—religious purpose, religious effect, and entanglement—do not help us to decide where the lines should be drawn. At the same time, they create further characterization problems. Finally, it is not clear why these concepts are even relevant.

A. Religious Purpose or Effect

Consider, for example, the difficulty of making sense out of the crucial distinction between *religious* purpose or effect and *secular* purpose or effect. Governments usually act out of secular motives, even when they are directly aiding a particular religious sect. An atheistic ruler might well create an established church because he thinks it a useful way of raising money, or of ensuring that the clergy do not preach seditious doctrines.[42] In democratic societies, elected officials have an excellent secular reason to accommodate (or at least to avoid offending) groups and individuals who are religious, as well as groups and individuals who are not. They wish to be re-elected, and they do not want important groups to feel that the community does not honor their values.

Moreover, it is generally acknowledged that religious belief influences behavior, whether for better or for worse. A government might have excellent secular reasons for opposing sects that forbid their members to perform military service or that require racial segregation. For similar reasons, the state might want to support sects that teach their adherents to obey the laws or respect the equality of all races. If establishing a religion had no secular purpose, secular rulers would rarely be attracted to the idea.

Clearly, then, it is difficult to tell religious and secular purpose apart, or to say which effect is primary and which secondary. But beyond that, it is difficult to understand why it is necessarily unconstitutional for legislation to have the purpose or effect of assisting religious practice generally, when the Constitution itself gives a special status to religion. The free exercise clause itself can be said to have the purpose and effect of allowing the citizenry to practice their religion freely. Can it be unconstitutional for government to assist the citizens to exercise

---

42. King Henry VIII disestablished the Church of Rome and established the Church of England because he wanted to divorce his wife and seize the property of the monasteries. Presumably, equally secular motives or effects would not justify an American Congress in establishing a national church. Perhaps establishing a church has an inherently religious *purpose* even when the *motive* is secular, but then the definition of religious purpose seems to be circular: an act has a religious purpose if it aids religion in an unconstitutional manner.

their constitutional rights under the free exercise clause? But such assistance seems to have the purpose and effect of aiding religion!

The perennial problem of public financial assistance to religious schools can once again be used to illustrate the point. Suppose that a state legislature appropriates money which is to be transferred directly to religious schools to subsidize their operations, complete with a preamble announcing that the statutory purpose is to assist parents to exercise their constitutional rights under the free exercise clause, specifically to ensure that their own children receive a religious education.[43] Whether that purpose is termed "religious" or "secular" is entirely a matter of semantic choice. The legislation purposely assists religious activity, but it also purposely assists people to exercise a right guaranteed by that secular document, the Constitution. One effect of this assistance might be that more youngsters will have religious beliefs than would otherwise be the case. But that is also a likely effect of the free exercise clause itself. Perhaps there are excellent reasons for limiting the permissible forms of state aid to religious educational institutions. The point here is that discussing "religious purpose" and "religious effect" is not a useful way of identifying those reasons or deciding what the limitations ought to be.

The notion that it is wrong for legislation to have the purpose or effect of assisting religion only makes sense in terms of an assumed "neutral" starting point that defines what advantages or disadvantages religion ought to have. When the federal government supplies chaplains for the armed services, it clearly means to assist the military personnel to practice their various religions. Even Justices who take a strict "wall of separation" approach to most establishment issues find the military chaplain program acceptable, because they see it as compensation for the difficulties the government creates by removing military personnel from their former environments.[44] Provision of routine public services like sewers and fire protection to church-related structures is also rarely questioned, and nobody proposes to deny the use of subsidized public transportation to people who are going to church.[45] Even very substantial aid in the form of tax exemptions for churches and other religious institutions like hospitals and schools is acceptable to most of the Justices, because it can be viewed as treating them like

---

43. A state would be much more likely to justify such a subsidy on the ground that it compensated the schools for the purely secular societal benefit of education in secular academic subjects. Dean Choper, among others, has argued that subsidies to religious schools are justified if they do not exceed the secular benefits of the education to the community. *See* Choper, *supra* note 20, at 675, 679-80. The hypothetical in the text is meant to state a more difficult example.

44. *See* Marsh v. Chambers, 103 S. Ct. 3330, 3346 (1983) (Brennan, J., dissenting).

45. *See* Mueller v. Allen, 103 S. Ct. 3062, 3073 (1983) (Marshall, J., dissenting).

other similar charitable and educational institutions.[46]

Measures that have the effect of aiding religious practices or institutions—as all the stated examples do—become controversial only when people perceive them as going beyond a conventionally accepted norm. Until we know where that norm is located, the test of religious purpose or effect is meaningless. Once we have set that norm, *it* measures the appropriate level and forms of public aid for religion, and we can dispense with the *Lemon* criteria altogether. The constitutionality of subsidies to religious schools or employment of either legislative or military chaplains must turn on the nature of the subsidized activity rather than the subjective purpose of the legislators who voted for the appropriation. Clearly, then, the tests that look to religious purpose or effect do not explain the distinctions that the Court has drawn.

B.   Entanglement

There are equally difficult problems with "entanglement," the third branch of the *Lemon* test. Entanglement in this context seems to have at least two distinct connotations. In the more literal sense, it means simply "excessive involvement." It is undesirable for the state to become deeply involved in the government or regulation of religious institutions, because such involvement itself may curtail religious freedom or involve the state in controversies with which it is not competent to deal.[47] For this reason, the Supreme Court has insisted that states permit religious organizations a greater degree of self-government than would be required in the case of secular organizations such as corporations, labor unions, or charities.[48]

A second and more important meaning of entanglement seems to be "divisiveness." Religious issues are considered to be particularly likely to arouse strong passions and enmities, especially when one faction or another sees the possibility of enlisting the state to further its cause.[49] To avoid bitter controversies over what the state's role should be, the state should avoid matters touching on religion to the greatest extent possible.[50] It is in this sense of divisiveness that entanglement is

---

46. The issue of tax exemptions for church property used solely for religious worship should have been an extremely difficult one for the Supreme Court, because houses of worship do not provide the kind of "secular benefit" that religious schools and hospitals do. Nonetheless, only Justice Douglas dissented from the decision upholding those benefits in Walz v. Tax Comm'n, 397 U.S. 664, 700 (1970). Possibly the Court was influenced by the fact that many more religious denominations were threatened by the prospect of denial of tax exemptions than were affected by the denial of subsidies for religious schools.

47. *See generally* Laycock, *Towards a General Theory of the Religion Clauses: The Case of Church Labor Relations and the Right to Church Autonomy*, 81 COLUM. L. REV. 1373 (1981).

48. *Id.*

49. *Id.* at 1393-94; *see also* L. TRIBE, *supra* note 3, at 866-67.

50. *See, e.g.*, Lemon v. Kurtzman, 403 U.S. 602, 622-24 (1971).

most often used in the cases.

Justification of an active judicial role overseeing state involvement with religion on the basis of a policy of avoiding divisive entanglements rests upon two problematic factual assumptions. One is that religious disputes and religious people are particularly contentious, so that state involvement in religious matters is more likely to breed bitter conflicts than state involvement in such matters as the distribution of wealth or civil rights. Undoubtedly, religious conflicts have led to wars and persecutions, as have conflicts over secular ideologies like fascism and communism. What is problematic is whether, in conditions of contemporary American society, matters such as school prayers, legislative chaplains, and Christmas displays are more hotly disputed than many secular matters with which state legislatures deal routinely.[51]

The second problematic assumption is that courts alleviate divisiveness when they take an issue away from the voters and legislators and decide it on the basis of a constitutional principle. This is a most implausible idea, and such evidence as exists seems to be against it. Many of us find it easier to accept being outvoted by a majority of our fellow citizens or their representatives than by a handful of judges. Legislative battles over the issue of legalized abortion seem to have become *more* bitter and divisive since the Supreme Court attempted to preempt the issue in *Roe v. Wade*.[52] The very act of deciding a dispute on the basis of some abstract legal principle rather than on the give-and-take of legislative compromise tends to identify more clearly one side as the winner and the other side as the loser, with the result of increasing the bitterness of the loser.

One sure way to encourage conflict on any subject is to encourage people to think that what seem to be minor irritations are in reality violations of some sacred principle for which they have a duty to fight. The Supreme Court's decision in *Lynch v. Donnelly*,[53] involving the constitutionality of a community's tradition of including a crèche or nativity scene in its otherwise secular Christmas display, illustrates the tendency of expansive judicial remedies to generate conflict that might not otherwise occur. The crèche had been part of the annual display for at least forty years. The district court found that no controversy existed over it, until local members of the American Civil Liberties Union brought a lawsuit to enjoin its display.[54] Nonetheless, the dis-

---

51. *See* Smith, *supra* note 2, at 97.
52. 410 U.S. 113 (1973).
53. 104 S. Ct. 1355 (1984).
54. Donnelly v. Lynch, 525 F. Supp. 1150, 1180 (D.R.I. 1981), *aff'd*, 691 F.2d 1029 (1st Cir. 1982), *rev'd*, 104 S. Ct. 1355 (1984).

trict court,[55] and the dissenting opinion in the Supreme Court by Justice Brennan,[56] found the divisiveness engendered by the lawsuit itself to be evidence that the Christmas display posed a danger of divisive entanglement, noting that the calm that had prevailed prior to the lawsuit might merely have reflected a feeling on the part of dissatisfied individuals that it would be futile to oppose the majority.[57]

No doubt a sense of futility is a possible explanation for the absence of recorded complaint, but that fact also demonstrates that, by encouraging persons who are easily offended by religious symbolism to believe that the courts stand open to remedy their complaints, the courts foster divisive conflicts over religion. Similarly, by encouraging citizens and legislators to believe that aid to religious schools is a matter to be decided on the basis of abstract constitutional principles rather than by compromise and accommodation, the Supreme Court may well have made such disputes more bitter than they otherwise would be. That consideration does not necessarily mean that the Court has acted wrongly because justice, not domestic peace, is the primary aim of constitutional adjudication.[58] American society might be more peaceful if the Supreme Court stopped enforcing constitutional rights altogether.

III
THE DEFINITIONAL PROBLEM: WHAT IS "RELIGION"?

First amendment religion law proceeds on the assumption that "religious" activity can and should be treated differently from otherwise similar activities, sometimes to religion's benefit and sometimes to its detriment. For example, religious statements and practices are sometimes exempted from government regulations that apply to other forms of speech or conduct, but as a rule religion is excluded from public institutions such as the schools. Accordingly, an organization may gain or lose privileges depending upon whether it is classified as reli-

---

55. *Id.*

56. Lynch v. Donnelly, 104 S. Ct. 1355, 1374 (1984) (Brennan, J., dissenting).

57. *Id.*

58. The discussion of entanglement in Lemon v. Kurtzman, 403 U.S. 602 (1971), is particularly perplexing. The majority opinion by Chief Justice Burger praises the enormous contribution that private religious schools have made to our national life, and observes that taxpayers have saved "vast sums" due to their existence. *Id.* at 625. Nonetheless, public aid to these schools has such "divisive political potential" that allowing such aid would tend to polarize state politics, and thus "to confuse and obscure other issues of great urgency." *Id.* at 622-23.

But if religious schools enormously benefit our national life and save taxpayers vast sums of money, why do proposals to assist them arouse such passionate opposition? Is it likely that the opponents of subsidies take so benign a view of religious education? When has public controversy over aid to religious schools actually caused this destructive polarization, and what other issues has it confused or obscured? Above all, who is to blame for this unfortunate state of affairs—the supporters of the subsidies or the opponents?

gious or secular. The practice of Scientology became the Church of Scientology in part to protect the organization's E-meters and other therapeutic devices and practices from regulation by the Food and Drug Administration.[59] The cult of Transcendental Meditation, though clearly derived from Hindu religion, sought classification as a therapeutic science in part because it wanted to promote its meditation techniques in the public schools.[60] On what principle are we to assign groups to one category or the other?

The fact is that no definition of religion for constitutional purposes exists, and no satisfactory definition is likely to be conceived. According to an important article by Dean Choper,[61] "the scope of religious pluralism in the United States alone has resulted in such a multiplicity and diversity of ideas about what is a 'religion' or a 'religious belief' that no simple formula seems able to accommodate them all."[62] Professor Greenawalt's article in this Symposium carries a similar message: no factor or set of factors has been found that satisfactorily distinguishes "religion" from philosophy or ideology.[63]

Most Americans probably imagine that religion inherently has something to do with the concept of a creator God. But some faiths commonly called religions—Buddhism, for example—have no such doctrine.[64] In addition, a number of famous Christian theologians have attempted to "demythologize" their religion by removing all the explicitly supernatural elements that may be uncongenial to the world view of twentieth century rationalists.[65] Many persons who think of themselves as Christians conceive of God more as an abstract ideal of goodness or "ground of all being" than as a personal being who makes pronouncements to humanity. By contrast, persons who believe that the universe is in some sense rationally ordered, and that there is an objective standard of right and wrong independent of human opinion, may think of themselves as agnostics or atheists because they find the idea of God as an "old man in the sky" to be incredible. The differences among these groups may be more a matter of preferred vocabulary than substance. It would be odd indeed if the Constitution were

---

59. *See* Founding Church of Scientology v. United States, 409 F.2d 1146 (D.C. Cir.), *cert. denied*, 396 U.S. 963 (1969). The E-meter is a skin galvanometer used in some Scientology rituals to measure a person's emotional responses to questions. It is believed that through proper interpretation of the E-meter readings, one can determine the mental and spiritual condition of a subject. *Id.* at 1153.

60. Malnak v. Yogi, 440 F. Supp. 1284 (D.N.J. 1977), *aff'd*, 592 F.2d 197 (3d Cir. 1979).

61. Choper, *Defining "Religion" in the First Amendment*, 1982 U. ILL. L. REV. 579.

62. *Id.*

63. Greenawalt, *Religion as a Concept in Constitutional Law*, 72 CALIF. L. REV. 753 (1984).

64. *See* Torcaso v. Watkins, 367 U.S. 488, 495 n.11 (1961); *see also* Johnson, *Do You Sincerely Want to be Radical?*, 36 STAN. L. REV. 247, 288 n.106 (1984).

65. This point is well developed in L. TRIBE, *supra* note 3, at 826-27.

read to treat persons very differently on the basis of whether they used or avoided the word "God" in expressing their understanding of the fundamental order or disorder of the universe.

A.   The Seeger *Dilemma*

It is therefore not surprising that the Supreme Court, on the rare occasions when it has been asked to say anything about the definition of "religion" or "religious belief," has indicated that the category must be open ended. In *United States v. Seeger*,[66] the Court held that draft exemptions granted to persons who oppose participation in all war "by reason of their religious training and belief" must be extended to pacifists who hold any sincere and meaningful belief that "occupies a place in the life of its possessor parallel to that filled by the orthodox belief in God of one who clearly qualifies for the exemption."[67] In another decision, the Court observed that the religion clauses prohibit government support of "those religions based on a belief in the existence of God as against those religions founded on different beliefs," noting that "[a]mong religions in this country which do not teach what would generally be considered a belief in the existence of God are Buddhism, Taoism, Ethical Culture, Secular Humanism and others."[68]

Such formulations make the category of "religion" seem so all-inclusive that it is doubtful whether any system of beliefs that people treat as important can be excluded. Perhaps this is as it should be, because it may be inherently arbitrary to distinguish among beliefs about what is fundamentally real and important on the basis of whether they are conventionally designated as "religious" or not. Consider, for example, Professor Greenawalt's suggestion that, if nonreligion is not religion, government endorsement of atheism might not violate the establishment clause.[69] This possibility is consistent with the ordinary language usage of the term religion. It does seem peculiar, however, that a constitutional clause supposedly dedicated to religious neutrality could be read to permit the government to endorse one side of a religious issue but not the other, particularly when the clause literally forbids not just an "establishment of religion" but rather "a law respecting an establishment of religion."

Thinking this way leads one to a paradox. If the first amendment

---

66. 380 U.S. 163 (1965); *see also* Welsh v. United States, 398 U.S. 333 (1970).

67. *Seeger*, 380 U.S. at 165-66, 176, 184. The *Seeger* opinion purports to be interpreting the Selective Service Act, but the interpretation is so strained that commentators have assumed that the Court had constitutional considerations in mind.

68. Torcaso v. Watkins, 367 U.S. 488, 495 & n.11 (1961).

69. Greenawalt, *supra* note 63, at 793-94. Greenawalt concludes that whatever the relevant constitutional clause, government sponsorship of either religion or antireligion ought to be disfavored. *Id*. at 794.

is supposed to prevent government from favoring one religion over another, or from favoring religion over nonreligion or vice-versa, then how do we explain the special constitutional status for religion that the first amendment itself mandates? Does the first amendment violate itself, by giving "religion" special immunities and disabilities? Or, if we avoid this problem by construing "religion" so broadly that the term includes all deeply felt beliefs, do we create an impossibly long list of things that government must not "establish" and whose free exercise government must not hinder?

To some people the most important thing is God; to others it may be the categorical imperative, the pleasure or pain that humans (and animals?) feel, human rights, national glory, the U.S. Constitution, the free market, the class struggle, the battle of the sexes, the liberation of an oppressed racial or ethnic group, the love of power or fame, the life of the mind, artistic or athletic excellence, the bottle, or the needle. If the appropriate set is beliefs about ultimate reality, as the Supreme Court majority seems to have thought in *Seeger*,[70] then those opinions about that reality that we conventionally label as "religious" seem to constitute an arbitrarily defined subset.

B. Two Definitions or One?

Some scholars have suggested that the term "religion" ought to be defined differently for different purposes. Professor Tribe did not even attempt an overall definition in his treatise, but contented himself with the suggestion that nontheistic creeds or philosophies that are both arguably religious and arguably nonreligious should be protected by the free exercise clause, but should be free of the restrictions of the establishment clause.[71] An individual who refused to comply with a law because of a strong moral belief that would not be religious under a narrow definition would be entitled to have his defense considered under the free exercise clause, but a school board could provide for the teaching of that same belief in the public schools without running afoul of the establishment clause. Although the first amendment uses the word "religion" only once, Tribe thought this dual definition necessary if the establishment clause was not to become "an awful engine of destruction" that would invalidate legislation whose purpose or effect was to advance such arguably religious values as " 'human dignity, equality, national destiny, freedom, enlightenment, and morality' . . . especially if the legislation was the result of pressure by church or religious

---

70. *See* United States v. Seeger, 380 U.S. 163, 176, 184, 186 (1965).

71. L. TRIBE, *supra* note 3, at 828-33.

groups."[72]

Even if one is willing to allow a term that is used only once in the Constitution to have two definitions, Professor Tribe's approach has the objectionable effect of permitting those groups and persons whose beliefs are both arguably religious and arguably not religious to claim the benefits of the free exercise clause without incurring the burdens of the establishment clause.[73] In other words, they could have it both ways, which happens to be the classic definition of unfair preference. Members of traditional, "indisputably religious" churches could hardly be expected to see the dual definition as anything but legalistic flim-flam in the service of nontheistic religious ideology. Indeed, if the Supreme Court were to endorse Tribe's reasoning, it would lend support to the claim of some religious fundamentalists that the public schools and other governmental agencies are currently establishing a form of secular religion.

C. Getting Along Without a Definition

Dean Choper grasped the other horn of the dilemma in his own attempt to define religion for constitutional purposes. He defined "religious belief" as necessarily involving "extratemporal consequences," so that a conscientious objector's claim would only be defined as religious if the objector believed that he would be punished in the afterlife for participating in war.[74] This definition has practically nothing to do with how the word religion has been used either in ordinary language or in Supreme Court opinions; Choper chose it solely because he felt that an individual should not be able to claim an exemption from a legal obligation (such as military service or compulsory school attendance) on free exercise grounds, unless he feared punishment in the afterlife if he complied.[75]

The important thing is not the definition itself, however, but the limited use Choper makes of it. The definition has practical effect *only* in free exercise clause cases, where in fact Choper contemplates that relief from generally applicable laws would rarely be granted.[76] For establishment clause issues, the definition of religion is unimportant to

---

72. *Id*. at 831 (quoting Galanter, *Religious Freedom in the United States: A Turning Point?*, 1966 WIS. L. REV. 217, 266).

73. Greenawalt, *supra* note 63, at 814.

74. Choper, *supra* note 61, at 597-601.

75.
[A]lthough there is no sure method of proving it scientifically as an empirical matter, intuition and experience affirm that the degree of internal trauma on earth for those who have put their souls in jeopardy for eternity can be expected to be markedly greater than for those who have only violated a moral scruple.
Id. at 598.

76. *See* Choper, *supra* note 20, at 696-700.

Choper, because he concludes that government has a general constitutional obligation, independent of the establishment clause, to be ideologically neutral with respect to religious and secular creeds alike.[77] Without such a general obligation of governmental neutrality, Choper's definition would have the disturbing consequence of permitting the government to "establish" any doctrine, whether or not conventionally labeled as religious, provided the doctrine did not relate to extratemporal consequences.[78] In effect, Choper is attempting not so much to define religion as to find a way of getting along without a definition.

Given the difficulty of framing a satisfactory definition of religion, there is much to be said for trying to treat the "establishment" problem under some more general doctrine. If there really is no clear-cut difference between religious doctrines and nonreligious doctrines, then why not require government to be neutral about *all* doctrines? As Choper puts it, the public schools may offer courses about "Dewey or Hegel— or Keynes or Friedman, or Luther or Christ—" but for government to attempt to convince its citizens of the ultimate truth of the teaching of *any* of these thinkers would be "ideological partisanship" that ought to be unconstitutional wholly apart from the establishment clause.[79] But could the schools—or other agencies of government—even try to convince people that it is wrong to cheat and steal, or to practice racial discrimination? What is needed, Choper concludes, is a coherent first amendment doctrine capable of distinguishing " 'narrow partisan ideologies' (which government may not subsidize or promote) from . . . 'widely shared and basically noncontroversial public values'—such as the inherent dignity of the individual and the essential equality of all human beings— (which the state may aid or sponsor)."[80] Abandoning the futile attempt to distinguish "religion" from ideology or philosophy leads us back to Professor Tribe's fear that the establishment clause might become an "awful engine of destruction" directed at government efforts to promote values that are themselves thought to have a constitutional basis.[81] As constitutional law expands to include a growing list of "fundamental values," should *it* be described as an established national civil religion or philosophy? Among the fundamental doctrines of our judicially defined constitutional philosophy are racial equality

---

77. *See* Choper, *supra* note 61, at 610-11.

78. "For example, the public schools might have voluntary programs of prayers to God seeking only worldly assistance, or state funds might be granted to a modern Protestant sect whose beliefs excluded salvation." *Id*. at 610.

79. *Id*. at 612.

80. *Id*.

81. *See supra* text accompanying note 72.

and integration (including intermarriage),[82] a right to privacy (encompassing contraception and abortion),[83] and an incompletely defined principle of sexual equality (despite the failure of the Equal Rights Amendment).[84] These doctrines are not narrowly partisan, but they are not basically noncontroversial either.

Judicial decisions do not compel anyone to believe in anything, of course, but they certainly express an emphatic official endorsement of the moral or philosophical premises on which they rest. May the government expend public resources—in the schools or elsewhere—to encourage people to respect values which the courts have endorsed as fundamental to the American "concept of ordered liberty"?[85] Unless we can justify distinguishing religion from philosophy or whatever, then the U.S. Commission on Civil Rights, to name a single example, is engaged in establishing something indistinguishable from a religion.

D. Case-by-Case Adjudication

Concluding that none of the attempts to formulate a constitutional definition of religion has been satisfactory, Professor Greenawalt writes in this Symposium that the attempt to settle upon any one definition is misconceived.[86] He argues that religion is such a complex subject that no single definition is likely to be satisfactory, and we must therefore proceed by the familiar common law method of case-by-case analogical reasoning.[87] If we start with institutions or beliefs that are indisputably religious and compare doubtful cases of religion to the conceded ones, we can set each doubtful case on one side of the line or the other and gradually create a body of case law that can substitute for a true definition.[88]

Deciding each case by analogy is certainly a viable option, one which the courts have used often enough. But everything depends upon what we choose as the point of comparison from which to analogize. If we compare each doubtful case to the Episcopal Church, few philosophies will qualify as religions because they will lack the ceremonial superstructure. Yet if we compare the doubtful cases to the sort of

---

82. Bob Jones Univ. v. United States, 103 S. Ct. 2017 (1983).

83. Roe v. Wade, 410 U.S. 113 (1973).

84. Mississippi Univ. for Women v. Hogan, 458 U.S. 718 (1982). This case, which held the exclusion of qualified males from the School of Nursing of a state-supported university unconstitutional, was decided July 1, 1982, the day after the ratification period for the Equal Rights Amendment expired.

85. *See* Palko v. Connecticut, 302 U.S. 319, 325 (1937), *overruled on other grounds by* Duncan v. Louisiana, 391 U.S. 145 (1968).

86. Greenawalt, *supra* note 63, at 763.

87. *Id.*

88. *Id.* at 769 n.60.

philosophy of life that the Supreme Court found to be religious in *Seeger*,[89] everything that anyone believes in strongly will be a religion. Curiously, it is possible that some conventional churches would *not* be "religious" under the *Seeger* test, at least for their members who belong for cultural or social reasons and for whom the church is not a matter of "ultimate concern."

If we retain a creative tension between the points of comparison, each case will be an opportunity for creative reformulation. How we resolve the doubtful cases is not terribly important anyway, according to Greenawalt, because the subjective tests used to decide establishment and free exercise claims are sufficiently flexible that we can avoid "inapt" conclusions.[90] The Rastafarians may be a religion, for example, but we do not have to let them smoke marijuana;[91] neither do we need to allow a mendicant cult to keep its members' children out of school so that they can beg on the streets.[92] Even if racial equality and feminism are in some sense religious doctrines, government can easily find a secular reason for promoting them.

My intention is not to denigrate the work of Tribe, Choper, or Greenawalt. Each did his best to work out a solution to an intractable problem, and each advanced our understanding of just how intractable the problem is. Government must endorse *some* values, and does so every day. This is particularly true in public schools, which are as important as they are largely because we believe or hope that they can motivate children to improve upon the values of their parents. Most people want our schools to teach children that it is wrong to cheat on tests, that it is wrong to treat people as intrinsically inferior because of their skin color or ethnic background, that it is wrong to limit arbitrarily the options available to people because of their sex, and that it is right to develop one's own capacity so that one can make a contribution to the community instead of becoming a burden upon it. A public school that tried to be neutral about all such matters would be making the case for private education.

All-pervasive public neutrality cannot be the answer, nor can the answer be one that distinguishes between "clearly" and "arguably" religious philosophies to the advantage of one as opposed to the

---

89. *See* United States v. Seeger, 380 U.S. 163 (1965).

90. Greenawalt, *supra* note 63, at 770; *see also id.* at 762.

91. *See* Whyte v. United States, 471 A.2d 1018 (D.C. 1984).

92. In Wisconsin v. Yoder, 406 U.S. 205, 222-26 (1972), the Court held that the Amish could withdraw their children from school after the eighth grade. The key element in the case was that the Amish continued to educate their children "vocationally" in a manner likely to prepare them to function in ordinary society should they eventually leave the Amish community. The Court did not endorse the general notion that parents can remove their children from school by a simple invocation of some "religious" belief.

other—unless some further justification can be advanced for the preference. Absent a better solution, we may well have no alternative but to decide cases by analogy as they arise, comforting ourselves with the thought that by defining something as "religion" we are not really committing ourselves to anything, because the subjective tests we employ from that point on give us more than enough maneuvering room to avoid any outcomes that we happen not to like.

A body of constitutional law certainly *can* be built upon that basis. The question is whether it ought to be. If first amendment law is based upon an arbitrary distinction between religion and every other form of belief, why should the Supreme Court continue to employ the first amendment religion clauses to strike down legislation? The inability to define religion is not simply a problem that sometimes arises in particular cases; rather, it reflects a fundamental gap in first amendment theory. How can we say anything about religion if we do not know what it is?

IV
IDEOLOGY AND COMPROMISE

The preceding sections of this Article have attempted to establish the point that Supreme Court decisions in the religion area cannot be justified on the basis of the abstract legal concepts discussed in the opinions, because too much freedom exists in characterizing the issues and applying the subjective tests. Moreover, the doctrinal objectives are inherently contradictory, providing at once both a special legal position for religion and a principle that the law is not supposed to favor or disfavor religious belief. Finally, we have no principled definition of religion, and hence no way to justify treating religious beliefs differently from other beliefs. Doctrinally, first amendment religion law is a mess.

Still, the fact that the constitutional doctrine is at times muddled and internally inconsistent does not necessarily mean that it is intolerable. On the contrary, the very fact that the holdings do not fit any abstract pattern may indicate that the Court is steering a careful path between undue preference for religion (conventionally defined) and undue hostility to it. One major objective of the first amendment is to keep the public peace on religious issues, and one way of doing this is for every religious and antireligious group to feel that the government is neither squarely on its side nor squarely on the other side. It is not good for *anyone* if a major ideological or social group becomes persuaded that the government consistently rejects its values or symbols. A body of decisions that is meant to keep the peace between strong contending factions may seem incoherent to those who wrongly suppose that the Court's purpose is to put into effect some abstract doctrinal principles.

If we judge our constitutional law regarding religion on the basis of its acceptability to persons of widely differing religious opinions rather than its conceptual coherency, it looks a great deal better. For example, parents who desire a religious education for their children have a constitutional right to select this alternative.[93] The state may not provide direct cash subsidies or tuition grants for such schools, but it may, if it chooses, provide free secular textbooks, bus transportation, and a certain measure of tax relief for educational expenses.[94] Church and church-school property may be exempt from property taxes,[95] and donations to religious institutions are exempt from income tax,[96] which makes it relatively painless for well-to-do patrons to provide scholarship money for low-income students. Private schools tend to be less expensive to operate per student than public schools, in part because they do not have to support elaborate administrative structures and in part because they may not need to pay teachers as much.[97] All these circumstances contribute to reducing the financial burden on parents who choose a religious education. Greater and more direct public subsidies would reduce the financial burden still more, but possibly at the cost of inviting more intrusive regulation of the schools' curriculum and administration.[98] Persons favoring religious education have as much reason to fear basic change in the present legal compromise as to welcome it.

At the same time, establishment clause doctrine has given substantial support to the values of those who want a secular education and who do not want to be taxed to pay for religious alternatives. The religious intrusions that people seem to find most offensive—teacher-led prayers and Bible readings in the classroom—have been banned,[99] and

---

93. *See id.* at 213-14; *supra* note 23 and accompanying text.

94. *See* Mueller v. Allen, 103 S. Ct. 3062 (1983).

95. *See* Walz v. Tax Comm'n, 397 U.S. 664 (1970).

96. *See* Bob Jones Univ. v. United States, 103 S. Ct. 2017 (1983).

97. *See* M. FRIEDMAN & R. FRIEDMAN, FREE TO CHOOSE 154-60 (1980).

98. It is frequently argued that religious schools must be protected from government subsidies in their own interest because their independence would be threatened by the regulation that tends to accompany the subsidies. After the decision in *Bob Jones University*, it appears that the existence of tax deductions can also be an invitation to government regulation. If tax deductions can be taken away from schools that practice racial discrimination, then why can they not be taken away from schools that practice religious or sexual discrimination as well? Even in the absence of "tax subsidies," states can and do regulate private schools, including religious schools. We should, therefore, be careful not to overestimate the degree to which the independence of religious schools is protected by any constitutional doctrines. Nevertheless, it is likely that regular appropriations bills for direct subsidies would inspire legislators to think about regulating religious schools more frequently than they do now.

99. School Dist. v. Schempp, 374 U.S. 203 (1963); Engel v. Vitale, 370 U.S. 421 (1962).

the majority of voters who favor allowing some prayer have been unable to overturn the ban.[100] Some public assistance does go to private schools, many of which are religious, but the fact that the aid is limited and indirect seems to reduce the degree to which it is offensive to persons who would prefer no aid at all. Apparently, it is not so much the dollar amount of the aid that generates resentment as whether the aid is provided in a way that seems to associate the state with a particular religious practice.[101]

Public endorsement of controversial religious symbols outside the classroom has also been strictly limited. The exceptions are sufficiently limited that they prove the rule. The significant thing about the holding of *Lynch v. Donnelly*[102] from this viewpoint is not that the Court allowed the city to continue including a nativity scene in its Christmas display, but that the vote was so close and the decision justified on such narrow grounds.[103] Militant secularists do not win all the battles, but they too have reason to view the overall situation with at least partial satisfaction.

The free exercise cases are also easier to understand as exercises in political compromise rather than as a working out of abstract constitutional concepts. Regulations of general applicability that are quite reasonable as applied to most people may require some unusual individuals or groups to violate their most deeply held beliefs. Where an exemption can be given without substantially impairing the state or federal government's interests, the Court can invoke the free exercise

---

100. There is evidence that approximately 80% of the public favors allowing some form of school prayer. *See* Smith, Book Review, 72 CALIF. L. REV. 908, 913-14 (1984) (reviewing H. MCCLOSKY & A. BRILL, DIMENSIONS OF TOLERANCE: WHAT AMERICANS BELIEVE ABOUT CIVIL LIBERTIES (1983)). In the 1984 Term, the Supreme Court will consider the constitutionality of legislation providing for silent prayer in public schools.

101.

> Because of the symbolic role of elementary and secondary education—because of the special place that such education has in our society—the Court has been particularly careful to avoid government programs that would provide economic aid directly and conspicuously to elementary and secondary parochial schools. . . . [Every] dollar spent on police or fire protection for church-affiliated schools and colleges is a dollar released from their budgets, and hence a dollar they are free to spend on religious activity. But the provision of such secular services is not offensive because no one perceives police or fire protection as part of the educational enterprise. Such aid goes to institutions not as schools but as parts of the general public. Similarly, aid for secular programs in all colleges, including those with church affiliation, is generally perceived as assistance to non-religious activities. But the moment aid is sent to a parochial school as such, it is widely seen as aid to religion. The number of dollars released for religious purposes may be identical; the symbolism, and hence the constitutional result, is not.

L. TRIBE, *supra* note 3, at 843-44.

102. 104 S. Ct. 1355 (1984).

103. "[G]iven the Court's focus upon the otherwise secular setting of the Pawtucket crèche, it remains uncertain whether absent such secular symbols as Santa Claus' house, a talking wishing well, and cut-out clowns and bears, a similar nativity scene would pass muster under the Court's standard." *Id.* at 1370 n.1 (Brennan, J., dissenting).

clause to require the exemption. Avoiding unnecessary confrontations over issues of basic principle is an important part of the art of democratic government.

Cases like *Sherbert v. Verner*[104] and *Wisconsin v. Yoder*[105] tend to trouble the legal mind because they involve a mild form of discrimination on religious grounds, and because they involve subjective judgments about how sincere a particular group is, how important various beliefs or practices are to it, and how adversely the public interest will be affected by a special exemption. In *Yoder*, the Court's opinion left no doubt that the decision turned largely on the respect the Justices had for the Old Order Amish and their long historical struggle to preserve their distinctive way of life. The opinion warned that other groups with different characteristics should not necessarily expect similar treatment.[106] It is not easy to achieve this kind of outcome by a neutral application of legal concepts; rather, what the Court did looks more like an act of prosecutorial discretion or executive clemency. Legal scholars struggle to justify what the Court does on neutral principles; but perhaps it would be more honest simply to acknowledge that the Court occasionally gives a deserving party a break.

Behind the compromising and interest balancing that characterizes the constitutional law of religion lies a major ideological issue. Are the prevailing religious beliefs beneficial on the whole to a pluralistic democratic society, or are they something that we tolerate and endure despite their social costs? Would it be desirable if fewer people held theistic beliefs, or at least held them less passionately? In some quarters, religious belief (at least in the traditional sense) is associated with persecution, obscurantism, and social strife, and the religious groups most prone to these evils are thought to be the ones most likely to seek government support.[107] On the other hand, there are many others who consider Judeo-Christian religious belief to be an important positive force in building the values of a democratic citizenry, and who associate *loss* of religious faith with a permissiveness that tends to undermine private and civic virtue. The social value of religion in general is an extremely complex topic, of course, but people do tend to have attitudes about it. Consciously or unconsciously, those attitudes affect how we apply subjective tests, or how we choose to characterize constitutional questions.[108] The state ought to maintain a "wall of separa-

---

104. 374 U.S. 398 (1963).
105. 406 U.S. 205 (1972).
106. *Id.* at 235-36.
107. Smith, *supra* note 100, at 915-16.
108. For an illuminating discussion of the personal views of various Supreme Court Justices about religion, and the extent to which those views influenced their attitudes towards the religion clauses, see Smith, *supra* note 2, at 105-23. Smith draws a useful distinction between corporate

tion" between itself and creeds which are prone to encourage intolerance and ignorance. "Benevolent neutrality" is a more appropriate paradigm for dealing with creeds that promote virtues that help to maintain the health of the republic, or are at least harmless.

Of course the category "religion" incorporates creeds with a variety of vices and virtues, and we may well feel differently about the category as a whole, depending upon which examples we have in mind. Some legal issues characteristically involve specific kinds of religion. For example, the Supreme Court first invoked the "wall of separation" metaphor against aid to religious schools in a context where the only schools receiving the aid were Roman Catholic,[109] and at a time when many Americans regarded the Catholic church as a semitotalitarian menace to their liberties. Paul Blanshard's influential book *American Freedom and Catholic Power*,[110] characterized the Catholic church as an antidemocractic "state within a state,"[111] which aimed to impose its own law upon Catholics and non-Catholics alike.[112] Blanshard saw the Catholic schools as substantially inferior to the public schools academically, with teaching assigned to undereducated and overdisciplined nuns who were primarily concerned with indoctrinating the children to be obedient to the Church and its priests.[113] Because the Church required Catholic parents to send their children to parochial schools or suffer denial of absolution for their sins, attendance at those schools was not truly a matter of personal or family choice.[114] All other American religious groups were satisfied with the public schools and their education, according to Blanshard;[115] only the Catholic hierarchy de-

---

religion and individual religion. Many Justices sympathetic to individual religion were or are intensely suspicious of "corporate religion," particularly the Roman Catholic Church. Not surprisingly, those Justices who tend to regard corporate religion as greedy, totalitarian and intellectually backward have tended to be activist in interpreting the first amendment to forbid government assistance to religion. *Id*. at 105-13.

109. *See* Everson v. Board of Educ., 330 U.S. 1 (1947).

110. P. BLANSHARD, AMERICAN FREEDOM AND CATHOLIC POWER (1949). To illustrate the work's influence, more than 100,000 copies of the book were sold in the first nine months following publication. *Id*. at copyright page.

111. *See id.* at 4.

112. *Id*. at 3-4.

113. "[Teaching nuns] are never allowed to forget that they are primarily religious missionaries whose chief mission is the inculcation of the Catholic faith." *Id*. at 69.

114. *Id*. at 65.

115.

The attitude of most non-Catholic Americans toward public support for Catholic schools might be summed up in this fashion: The Catholic people have been offered the same free, democratic schools that have been offered to everybody else. If they do not wish to join the rest of the American community, that is their affair. Methodists, Baptists, Jews, and nearly everybody else except Catholics belong to the great fraternity of American public education. The Catholic people have not been blackballed; they have been elected to full membership, but their priests have persuaded them to stay away from the meeting. They should not pretend that they are being discriminated against. Method-

manded something different—and "un-American."[116]

The point here is not to examine the extent to which Blanshard's polemic was a caricature of the Catholic church in 1949. However fair or unfair, *American Freedom and Catholic Power* stated a view of the Catholic hierarchy that was widespread among Americans at the time of the cases that set establishment clause doctrine on its present course—a time when the possible election of a Catholic president aroused the deepest fears. To the extent that they accepted Blanshard's account as substantially true, judges would understandably be attracted to a constitutional theory that disfavored public subsidies for nonpublic schools. Granted Blanshard's premises, or even somewhat less extreme ones, it was simply a matter of self-preservation for non-Catholics to interpret the Constitution in a manner likely to hamper, rather than encourage, the anticonstitutional plans of the Catholic hierarchy.

Attitudes toward both the Catholic church and its schools have changed a great deal since the 1940's, reflecting such developments as the reforms of the Second Vatican Council and the election of a Catholic President. Today, the Catholic schools are staffed primarily with lay teachers rather than nuns, and a high percentage of the pupils in some cities are non-Catholics whose parents were presumably attracted by the quality of the education rather than by any program of religious indoctrination.[117] Some studies have compared the performance of the Catholic schools very favorably to that of the public schools in educating low-income minority pupils in inner-city areas.[118] If these studies are reliable, the Catholic schools are performing a service of enormous value to the society as a whole.

Attitudes toward the public schools have also changed. Most non-Catholic Americans may have been satisfied with the public schools in 1949, but clearly they are satisfied no longer. Widely publicized problems of violence, drug use, and low academic achievement have motivated many parents to search for alternatives, whether secular or religious. In many places, enrollment at Protestant Christian schools has increased enormously, and there is serious discussion of "voucher" plans which would permit students to attend private schools at public

---

ists, Baptists and Jews cannot collect public funds for their schools. Neither can Catholics. We must treat everybody alike.
Id. at 88.

116. Blanshard urged "continuous and scientific inspection of all parochial schools to see that the standard requirements of the state are maintained, that classes are taught in the English language, and that textbooks do not distort history, science and sociology in an un-American manner for the benefit of the hierarchy." *Id*. at 304-05. He described Catholic schooling as based on "a whole philosophy of education that is alien to the American outlook." *Id*. at 65.

117. For statistics and references on this point, see Laycock, *supra* note 47, at 1387 n.119.

118. *See id*. at 1387 n.118.

expense.[119] These developments are controversial. Many persons are no more enthusiastic about Protestant Fundamentalism than Paul Blanshard was about the Catholic church, and to some degree the enthusiasm for private education may be related to court-ordered racial integration.[120] The point here is not to decide whether public assistance for private education is ultimately a good or a bad idea, but merely to note that the context in which the constitutional issues arise has changed enormously since the 1940's. To the extent that programs of aid to private education are seen as meeting a widespread desire for alternatives to publicly administered education, permitting religious schools to participate may seem more like avoiding discrimination against religion, rather than creating a religious establishment.[121]

CONCLUSION

It is no contradiction to say that the constitutional law of religion reflects both ideological bias, and an attempt at "neutral" compromise among conflicting ideological viewpoints about religion. Fortunately, one widely shared ideological premise in American society is that all-out religious conflict must be avoided, which implies that we should make strenuous efforts to avoid identifying government squarely with any religious position, including antireligion. Government must seem to be evenhanded about religious disputes. What it does may coincide with the wishes of some groups and thwart the plans of others, but this coincidence must seem to be the outcome of neutral principles or fair-minded interest balancing, rather than conscious partisanship on the part of judges. The emphasis upon neutrality is not necessarily deceptive. Most judges want to be fairminded and to arrive at a solution that seems reasonable from as many points of view as possible. To say that they are influenced by ideology is not to say that they are ideologues.

There is never only one possible compromise, and neutrality can be more or less benevolent, depending upon what we think we are being neutral about. We may have to be "neutral" with respect to anach-

---

119. *See* J. COONS & S. SUGARMAN, EDUCATION BY CHOICE (1978); M. FRIEDMAN & R. FRIEDMAN, *supra* note 97, at 150-75.

120. For illuminating discussions of the racial aspects of the growth in Christian schools, see Rabkin, *Behind the Tax-Exempt Schools Debate*, PUB. INTEREST, Summer 1982, at 21; Skerry, *Christian Schools versus the I.R.S.*, PUB. INTEREST, Fall 1980, at 18.

121. Groups whose real interest is to protect the public schools from competition can be expected to continue to invoke the establishment clause as a useful weapon for protecting their economic interests. In California Teachers Ass'n v. Riles, 29 Cal. 3d 794, 632 P.2d 953, 176 Cal. Rptr. 300 (1981), the California Supreme Court ruled that the state constitution's ban on aid to sectarian schools prohibited a state program providing free textbooks for private schools. *Cf.* Wolman v. Walter, 433 U.S. 229 (1977). Although most of the schools that received the textbooks had some religious affiliation, I am confident that the teachers' union that brought the lawsuit was primarily interested in protecting the jobs of its members from private sector competition.

ronistic superstitions that serve the interests of fanatics and unscrupulous power seekers, but we can seek the definition of neutrality that least facilitates their advancement. We may have to avoid "establishing" groups that promote moral truths and serve the cause of liberty rightly understood, but we do not have to erect unnecessary obstacles for their beneficial activities. Inherited legal doctrine and social convention restrict the choices that a lawyer is likely to consider legitimate; ideological preference governs the exercise of choice among alternatives perceived as legitimate.[122]

We ought not to be shocked at the frank acknowledgment that our attitudes about religious truth and the social value of prevailing religious practices influence how we choose to interpret the Constitution's mysterious phrases. Ideology organizes reality for use, and we cannot decide what to do about law or anything else without relying on some picture of reality, incomplete and distorted though it may inevitably be. One vital component of our ideology is the extent to which it permits us to consider that radically differing groups may each be glimpsing a part of reality through their own distorting lenses. Ideological bias is not itself inconsistent with fair adjudication; on the contrary, it provides an indispensable starting point for the inquiry into what fairness means in a particular context. What we need to fear is not ideology but ideological blindness, including the blindness that takes the form of imagining that one's own views are derived logically from premises acknowledged by all reasonable persons.

---

122. When Professor Mansfield refers to a "constitutional philosophy," he may mean the same thing that I call "ideological preference." Mansfield, *The Religion Clauses of the First Amendment and the Philosophy of the Constitution*, 72 CALIF. L. REV. 847 *passim* (1984). I am uncertain about this because Mansfield does not explain how the constitutional philosophy is generated or whether it is something distinct from the philosophies of particular Justices who participate in writing opinions. Using his language, I would say that each Supreme Court Justice has a philosophical perspective which he or she employs when deciding cases. A constitutional philosophy arises because a number of Justices happen to agree on certain principles over a period of time, and implicitly rely upon those principles in writing opinions. The constitutional philosophy is likely to change as new members are appointed to the Court, or as continuing Justices change their ways of thinking. Perhaps it would be more accurate to speak of a "Supreme Court philosophy," because the constitutional philosophy is not derived in any direct way from the document whose authority it invokes.

[8]

THE CONSTITUTION OF RELIGION

by Mark Tushnet*

INTRODUCTION

The constitutional law of religion is "in significant disarray."[1] States may subsidize the purchase of books by students at religious schools, but they may not subsidize the purchase of globes.[2] States may engage in ritualistic invocation of religious norms, but they may not attempt to inculcate the norms that give sense to the rituals.[3] Exempting from the Social Security system those who oppose participation for reasons based on religion threatens the integrity of the tax structure,[4] while exempting the same people from the education system does not substantially affect *its* integrity.[5] Forms of aid to nonpublic schools that are indistinguishable in economic terms are distinguished in legal

---

* Professor of Law, Georgetown University Law Center; J.D., M.A., Yale University.

1. Pepper, *The Conundrum of the Free Exercise Clause—Some Reflections on Recent Cases,* 9 N. KY. L. REV. 265, 303 (1982). *See also* Johnson, *Concepts and Compromise in First Amendment Religious Doctrine,* 72 CALIF. L. REV. 817, 839 (1984) ("Doctrinally, first amendment religion law is a mess."). For compilations of the confusions in the law, see Choper, *The Religion Clauses of the First Amendment: Reconciling the Conflict,* 41 U. PITT. L. REV. 673, 680-81 (1980); Note, *Rebuilding the Wall: The Case for a Return to the Strict Interpretation of the Establishment Clause,* 81 COLUM. L. REV. 1463, 1463-66 (1981).

2. *Compare* Meek v. Pittenger, 421 U.S. 349, 372 (1975) (subsidy of globes unconstitutional) *with* Board of Educ. v. Allen, 392 U.S. 236, 248 (1968) (subsidy of textbooks constitutional). A distinction between loans and purchases seemed viable until the Supreme Court decided Committee for Pub. Educ. & Religious Liberty v. Regan, 444 U.S. 646, 650 (1980), which for the first time approved a direct financial grant to religious schools.

3. *Compare* Marsh v. Chambers, 463 U.S. 783, 788 (1983) (prayers in legislature constitutional) *with* Stone v. Graham, 449 U.S. 39, 42-43 (1980) (posting of Ten Commandments in school classrooms unconstitutional). Because the Court in *Marsh* made it dispositive that the practice of legislative prayer had a sufficient historical pedigree, 463 U.S. at 786-92, it did not address the argument that legislative prayer differs from the posting of the Ten Commandments because legislators are more mature than school children. *See, e.g.,* Marsa v. Wernik, 86 N.J. 232, 430 A.2d 888 (1981) (nondenominational invocation or silent meditation at start of council meeting did not violate establishment clause), *appeal dismissed and cert. denied,* 454 U.S. 958 (1981).

4. *See* United States v. Lee, 455 U.S. 252, 260 (1982).

5. *See* Wisconsin v. Yoder, 406 U.S. 205, 234 (1972). *See also* Marshall, *Solving the Free Exercise Dilemma: Free Exercise as Expression,* 67 MINN. L. REV. 545, 548-53 (1983) (discussing *Wisconsin v. Yoder* and *United States v. Lee*).

terms, with the Court taking the position—rejected in other contexts—that here form matters more than substance.[6] The list could go on, especially if one were to include the tests commentators have offered to impose order on the subject, but the general point is clear enough: Contemporary constitutional law just does not know how to handle problems of religion.

This article examines the sources of this ignorance and the resulting disarray. My thesis is that the social relations of our society do not now provide the support needed for a concept of politics into which religion would comfortably fit.

Part I of this article surveys the contemporary constitutional law of the religion clauses to describe the existing doctrinal confusion. Part II then identifies two principles that appear to underlie the Supreme Court decisions: the "reduction" principle and the "marginality" principle. As my labels suggest, these principles express the difficulties of fitting religion into categories of constitutional law. Finally, Part III of the article discusses the role of religion in the two traditions of political theory that pervade the Constitution, liberalism and republicanism. It suggests that a reconstituted law of religion might draw on the the republican tradition to alleviate existing intellectual disarray by providing to nonbelievers as well as believers a view of the law that affirms the connectedness that religious belief mobilizes and that liberalism denies.

I. Confusion in the Law of Religion: An Analytic Survey

Perhaps it is not surprising that the Supreme Court has not developed a satisfactory case law of the religion clauses. Membership on the Court changes, as do the issues presented to it by litigants responding to the legislative product of shifting political coalitions. But it is surprising that no one has been able to make overall sense of the religion clauses under a unifying doctrinal or theoretical approach.

---

6. *Compare* Mueller v. Allen, 463 U.S. 388 (1982) (facially neutral form of tuition tax credit constitutional) *with* Committee for Pub. Educ. & Religious Liberty v. Nyquist, 413 U.S. 756 (1973) (another form of tuition tax credit unconstitutional). *Compare also* Flast v. Cohen, 392 U.S. 83 (1968) (taxpayer has standing to challenge the donation of money to religious organization under the establishment clause of the first amendment) *with* Valley Forge Christian College v. Americans United for Separation of Church & State, Inc., 454 U.S. 464 (1982) (taxpayer lacks standing to challenge donation of land and buildings to religious organization).

A. Doctrinal Approaches

Doctrinal development falls between two polar positions, strict neutrality and strict separation. These polar positions are weakened both by their lack of coherence and by their extremely undesirable consequences.[7] Philip Kurland, the most articulate proponent of a doctrine of strict neutrality, admits that it has not been adopted by the Court,[8] though the rhetoric of neutrality is widely used by commentators. Under Kurland's proposal, "religion may not be used as a basis for classification for purposes of governmental action, whether that action be the conferring of rights or privileges or the imposition of duties or benefits."[9]

There are three major difficulties with the strict neutrality doctrine. The first is that strict neutrality prohibits governments from accommodating their secular programs to the objections of religious believers. A state may not exempt a person from military service or jury duty even if those obligations severely intrude on a believer's sense of the proper balance between secular demands and divine commands. Nor may a state enact antidiscrimination laws that require nonbelievers to adjust their behavior to take account of the religious beliefs of others. Kurland's proposal is troubling not just because the Court has gone further than merely permitting accommodations and has required them in some instances,[10] but also because it is hard to see why a legislature cannot be nice to believers at least to the extent of exempting them from severe burdens. The doctrine of strict neutrality

---

7. Intermediate positions also lack coherence, though, largely because their proponents have been unable to identify, in a noncontroversial way, what makes various outcomes desirable or unattractive to substantial numbers of people. *See infra* note 26 and accompanying text.

8. *See* Kurland, *The Irrelevance of the Constitution: The Religion Clauses of the First Amendment and the Supreme Court*, 24 VILL. L. REV. 3, 24 (1978) ("[T]he proposition that the religion clauses were not separate mandates . . . [but rather] should be read as stating a single precept . . . met with almost uniform rejection.").

9. Kurland, *Of Church and State and the Supreme Court*, 29 U. CHI. L. REV. 1, 5 (1961).

10. *See* Wisconsin v. Yoder, 406 U.S. 205 (1972); Sherbert v. Verner, 374 U.S. 398 (1963). The scholarly consensus is that the Constitution often permits, and sometimes—at least when the adjustments of secular programs are modest and burdens on conscience severe—compels the accommodations prohibited by strict neutrality. *See, e.g.,* Clark, *Guidelines for the Free Exercise Clause*, 83 HARV. L. REV. 327, 345 (1969); Dodge, *The Free Exercise of Religion: A Sociological Approach*, 67 MICH. L. REV. 679, 706-07 (1969); Giannella, *Religious Liberty, Nonestablishment, and Doctrinal Development: Part I. The Religious Liberty Guarantee*, 80 HARV. L. REV. 1381, 1399-402 (1967); Marcus, *The Forum of Conscience: Applying Standards Under the Free Exercise Clause*, 1973 DUKE L.J. 1217, 1235-36; Pfeffer, *Religion-Blind Government*, 15 STAN. L. REV. 389, 392-400 (1963). *Contra* Choper, *supra* note 1, at 691; Garvey, *Freedom and Equality in the Religion Clauses*, 1981 SUP. CT. REV. 193, 198.

704   CONNECTICUT LAW REVIEW   [Vol. 18:701

finds its justification in the argument that such a way of being nice, which is normatively attractive, is indistinguishable from other ways of being nice—such as subsidizing the salaries of ministers—which are not at all attractive. But the argument only shows that something is wrong in our understanding of the relationship between government and religion.

The second difficulty with the doctrine of neutrality is that it is easy for legislatures to draft facially neutral statutes that raise serious questions about religious freedom. In *Epperson v. Arkansas*,[11] for example, the Court invalidated a state law prohibiting the teaching of evolution. The court purported to find that the law, though neutral as to religion on its face, was motivated by impermissible religious purposes.[12] Yet the evidence of religious motivation was actually quite weak,[13] and elsewhere the Court has said that support of legislation because it is consistent with one's religious belief is not a ground for invalidation.[14] As a religion case,[15] *Epperson* seems best explained on the ground that its subject matter was a religiously sensitive one,[16] and that legislation on such sensitive matters is highly suspect. This explanation does not strengthen the neutrality argument, however, because the category of religiously sensitive issues is open-ended and its content is likely to be affected by subjective evaluations.[17]

---

11.   393 U.S. 97 (1968).

12.   *Id.* at 107-09.

13.   *Id.* at 112-13 (Black, J., concurring) ("I find it difficult to agree with the Court's statement that 'there can be no doubt Arkansas has sought to prevent its teachers from discussing the theory of evolution because it is contrary to the belief of some that the Book of Genesis must be the exclusive source of doctrine as to the origin of Man.' It may be instead that the people's motive was merely that it would be best to remove the controversial subject. . . .").

14.   Harris v. McRae, 448 U.S. 297, 319-20 (1980).

15.   One might be tempted to treat *Epperson* as a free speech case, but doing so raises substantial questions about the scope of a state's ability to determine the curriculum it prescribes in public schools, and ultimately about the constitutionality of compulsory education. *See infra* notes 101-02 and accompanying text.

16.   Such legislation is analogous to what have been called "race-specific" statutes. *See* Sunstein, *Public Values, Private Interests, and the Equal Protection Clause*, 1982 SUP. CT. REV. 127. *See also supra* note 7.

17.   For example, should statutes authorizing schools to have a moment of silence or restricting the availability of abortions be treated as religiously sensitive? Professor Laurence Tribe initially offered a version of this approach, Tribe, *Foreword: Toward a Model of Roles in the Due Process of Life and Law*, 87 HARV. L. REV. 1, 21-25 (1973), but later retracted his analysis, arguing that it failed to give enough weight to the interest that religiously motivated people have in participating in politics to advance their religiously based views. *See* L. TRIBE, AMERICAN CONSTITUTIONAL LAW 928 (1976). It might be possible to reconstruct the analysis by isolating a particular category of "religion-sensitive" cases to which it applies. Yet the abortion example suggests one serious problem with that category: Perhaps abortion was a religion-sensitive subject in 1973, but the rise

Finally, facial neutrality is insufficient because there are no nonarbitrary ways of defining the categories over which to assess neutrality. The problem is most evident in the law of aid to nonpublic education.[18] *Mueller v. Allen*[19] upheld a facially neutral program of tax credits for expenses associated with going to school. These expenses were mostly tuition for nonpublic, largely sectarian, education.[20] A state can achieve the same results by enacting a program of tax credits only for tuition in nonpublic schools, and defending it on the ground that the total package of state programs supporting education is neutral: One part of the package is the tax-credit statute, and another is the system of tax-financed subsidies given to public schools. Yet, the course was held unconstitutional in *Committee for Public Education & Religious Liberty v. Nyquist*,[21] where, despite the existence of a massive state subsidy program for public schools, the Court struck down a statute providing tax credits to parents of children in private (and thus largely sectarian) schools.[22] No one has successfully explained why simply splitting the package into its components, one of which is not neutral on its face, makes it unconstitutional.[23]

At the pole opposite to strict neutrality, the doctrine of strict separation suffers from similar defects. That doctrine prohibits any interaction whatsoever between the institutions of government and those of religion.[24] But a careful definition of subject matter inevitably produces such an interaction. Again the usual example is aid to education, where strict separation, defined as nonsupport for sectarian education, reduces

---

of organized secular opposition to abortion has made it difficult so to confine the topic.

18. The example of aid to education also illustrates how the concept of neutrality encourages manipulation in defining a statute's impact. To assess impact, a court must identify the relevant subject on which the program at issue has an effect. But the subject matter can be described narrowly or broadly, whichever is needed to produce the desired neutral result: If "aid to nonpublic education" is too narrow, then the court can describe the same subject matter as "aid to education" or "aid to socially-beneficial nonprofit organizations." Some parts of Walz v. Tax Comm'n, 397 U.S. 664 (1970), in which the Court upheld exemptions for churches from property taxes, suggest this analysis. For a different perspective on *Walz*, see *infra* text accompanying notes 138-39.

19. 463 U.S. 388 (1983).

20. *Id.* at 391.

21. 413 U.S. 756 (1973).

22. *Id.* at 792-94. *See infra* notes 106-15 and accompanying text for further comparison of the statutes at issue in *Mueller* and *Nyquist*, and analysis of these decisions in the context of the reduction principle.

23. *See* Giannella, *Religious Liberty, Nonestablishment, and Doctrinal Development: Part II. The Nonestablishment Principle*, 81 HARV. L. REV. 513, 519-20 (1968); Johnson, *supra* note 1, at 822-23.

24. *See, e.g.,* L. PFEFFER, CHURCH, STATE, AND FREEDOM 133-159 (1953).

the economic incentives to send children to sectarian schools.[25] Yet that reduction is itself a form of interaction. Even more troubling than this analytical difficulty are some practical consequences of the doctrine of strict separation. It would seem to preclude incidental and indirect support for churches, even when this support—such as subsidized rates for government-provided police and fire services—is widely available to nonreligious organizations. And, like the doctrine of strict neutrality, the doctrine of strict separation does not permit, much less require, the adjustment of secular rules to believers' requests for exemptions.

Between the polar positions of strict neutrality and strict separation is the typical doctrinal form of all legal compromises: Decision makers are to balance all the relevant factors, such as the values of neutrality and separation, burdens on conscientious religious belief, altruistic desires to accommodate religious belief, the costs of accommodation, and, so it seems, whatever else they want to put into the balance. Although precise formulations vary, these intermediate approaches have the defects of all balancing tests.[26] The "relevant considerations" are defined so generally that the weight a decision maker gives to any particular consideration is left almost entirely open. The effect is that balancing tests are inevitably driven by the results sought to be reached.

B. *Theoretical Approaches*

General theoretical analyses of the religion clauses are no more helpful than doctrinal ones. The three most prominent theoretical analyses apply originalism, moral philosophy, and political pluralism in the context of the religion clauses.

1. Originalism

At least since *Everson v. Board of Education*,[27] the dominant originalist position has been that historical evidence provides support for strict separation: The framers of the first amendment wanted strict separation, and the framers of the fourteenth amendment applied that approach to the states. Yet there is other evidence of the framers' intent that would give a different meaning to the religion clauses. Originalist strict separation cannot account for the indisputable fact

---

25. *See* Giannella, *supra* note 23, at 574-75; Johnson, *supra* note 1, at 822-23.
26. *See* Tushnet, *Anti-formalism in Recent Constitutional Theory*, 83 MICH. L. REV. 1502, 1508-18 (1985).
27. 330 U.S. 1 (1947).

that most framers explicitly understood that the religion clauses were designed to bar the national government from certain actions, including interference with existing establishments of religion in the states.[28] Nor can originalist strict separation explain why the framers and their contemporaries acted shortly after the adoption of the first amendment to link government and religion by subsidizing missions for native Americans and authorizing days of thanksgiving.[29]

Apart from the general difficulties with the originalist theory of incorporation of the Bill of Rights into the fourteenth amendment, there are some problems specific to the absorption of the religion clauses. The language of the due process clause, which protects people against deprivations of life, liberty, and property, is not well-suited to encompass those interests protected by the establishment clause; although the right to free exercise of religion is a "liberty," the guarantee against establishment does not protect anything readily characterized as a personal liberty or as property.[30] In addition, to the extent that the framers of the first amendment sought to protect state establishments against national action, it is not entirely consistent to say that the amendment is now applicable *to* the states. Finally, the originalist stance about incorporation of the religion clauses is weakened by the fact that, within a decade of the adoption of the fourteenth amendment, substantial political forces promoted the adoption of the Blaine Amendment as a means of applying the protection of the free exercise and establishment clauses to the states.[31]

These difficulties with originalist strict separation have led others to urge a different originalist position. Justice Rehnquist's dissent in *Wallace v. Jaffree*,[32] relying on the work of Robert Cord,[33] argued that the best originalist analysis viewed the religion clauses as authorizing governments to take a stance of what has been called benevolent neutrality toward religion.[34] Governments could not favor one sect or de-

---

28. *See* L. TRIBE, *supra* note 17, at 816-17.

29. *Id.* at 820.

30. These difficulties are most apparent in the Court's decisions on standing in establishment clause cases. *See, e.g.*, Doremus v. Board of Educ., 342 U.S. 429 (1952) (taxpayers do not have standing to challenge state law providing for reading from Old Testament at opening of each public school day because they lack direct and particular financial interest).

31. In Abington School Dist. v. Schempp, 374 U.S. 203 (1963), Justice Brennan responded to this argument in a fundamentally unresponsive way by saying that the argument came "too late in the day." *Id.* at 257 (Brennan, J., concurring).

32. 105 S. Ct. 2479, 2508-17 (1985) (Rehnquist, J., dissenting).

33. R. CORD, SEPARATION OF CHURCH AND STATE (1982).

34. 105 S. Ct. at 2509-15 (Rehnquist, J., dissenting) (citing Cord, 105 S. Ct. at 2515).

nomination over another, but could encourage religion as against nonreligion or anti-religion. Yet this proposal suffers from the standard problems of any originalist position.[35] First, social change means that we cannot infer from the framers' endorsement of benevolent neutrality by the institutions of 1789 that they would endorse benevolent neutrality by today's institutions. For example, the framers might think that the reach of government is so much greater now that benevolent neutrality poses greater risks to important values than it did in 1789. In addition, religious pluralism has become so much more pervasive that the very notion of neutrality among denominations may no longer make sense. For example, denominations differ on what counts as a prayer,[36] there may be no such thing as a nondenominational prayer under modern conditions. Finally, as with all originalist inquiries, Cord's theory produces evidence that underspecifies doctrine. Although Cord finds evidence supporting benevolent neutrality, that same evidence supports both neutrality among Christian denominations (or at least among mainstream religions) and separation except in situations of extraordinary national need.[37]

2. Moral Philosophy

A second theoretical analysis of the Constitution looks to moral philosophy to tell us what rights the Constitution protects. A rights-based theory of the religion clauses fairly readily produces some version of the free exercise clause, because religious belief is something that a right to conscience or intellectual freedom ought to protect.[38] But I have not seen a persuasive rights-based defense of the establishment clause that is not parasitic on free exercise: Establishment claims, in this view, are disguised ways of arguing that the practice at issue will coerce people into adhering to or abandoning some religious beliefs. For example, the rights-based analysis says that the vice of school prayers

---

35. *See* Abington School Dist. v. Schempp, 374 U.S. at 237-42 (Brennan, J., concurring). *See also* Tushnet, *Following the Rules Laid Down: A Critique of Interpretivism and Neutral Principles*, 96 HARV. L. REV. 781, 787-92 (1983). Justice Rehnquist's proposal also has at least one distinctive problem, that of dealing with the denomination that endorses strict separation: No program that is not one of strict separation can be neutral as to that denomination.

36. *See* Marsh v. Chambers, 463 U.S. 783, 819-21 (1983) (Brennan, J., dissenting) (categorizing the widely varying positions taken by different denominations on the propriety of collective prayer).

37. *See also* Tushnet, Book Review, 45 LA. L. REV. 175 (1984) (reviewing R. CORD, SEPARATION OF CHURCH AND STATE (1982)).

38. *See also infra* note 172 and accompanying text.

is that children will be forced to pray. One might challenge this argument by asking for evidence that coercion actually occurs (which converts the argument into a direct free-exercise argument), as did Justice Stewart in *Abington School Dist. v. Schempp.*[39] But the rights-based defense might respond with the assertion that detecting the presence of coercion on a case-by-case basis is so difficult that the practice at issue must be flatly prohibited. In this manner, the rights-based theory treats the establishment clause as a prophylactic against free exercise violations.

There are several difficulties with the rights-based theory. First, it is unclear how we are to use a rights-based theory to decide how much coercion is too much. Determining that any coercion at all is too much of course returns us to the problems of the strict separation approach.[40] Second, the rights-based theory does not explain the psychosocial theory of coercion that underlies the prophylactic view of the establishment clause. Finally, a rights-based approach seems likely to deprive the establishment clause of any meaning independent of the free exercise clause, and the free exercise clause of any meaning independent of the free speech clause.

3.   Political Pluralism

A third theoretical analysis of the religion clauses relies on the interaction between the religious pluralism of the United States and its pluralistic political system.[41] The theory begins with the observation that there is tension between the free exercise and establishment clauses. A legislature that exempts people from a general regulation because of their religious beliefs might violate the establishment clause,[42] but its failure to provide an exemption might violate the free exercise clause. Similarly, in a society pervaded by government subsi-

---

39.   374 U.S. at 316-20 (Stewart, J., dissenting).

40.   Because governmental acts pervade our society, the government inevitably structures its institutions in ways that influence—and therefore to some degree coerce—some people to act in ways inconsistent with or in tension with their religious beliefs. Thus, some degree of coercion is inevitable, and if the existence of any coercion at all violates someone's rights, the rights-based approach is strict separationist. *See supra* notes 24-25 and accompanying text.

41.   The pluralist analysis given here is a version of the theory of "representation reinforcing review" associated with John Ely. *See generally* J. ELY, DEMOCRACY AND DISTRUST (1980).

42.   *See* Laycock, *Towards a General Theory of the Religion Clauses: The Case of Church Labor Relations and the Right to Church Autonomy*, 81 COLUM. L. REV. 1373, 1414-15 (1981) (arguing that the exemption in *Sherbert v. Verner* caused non-Sabbatarians to subsidize Seventh Day Adventists through their contributions to the unemployment compensation fund); Choper, *supra* note 1, at 691-92. *See also* 26 U.S.C. § 1402(g) (1982).

dies of secular activities, failure to subsidize the alternative desired by religious believers might violate their free exercise rights.[43] The pluralist theory, which has been offered most recently by Justice White,[44] does not deny that one could devise doctrines to resolve specific instances of the free exercise/establishment clause tension. But it is skeptical about the availability of an overarching doctrine that would do so for all instances, and it is confident that such a doctrine would be undesirably complex.

The pluralist theory offers an alternative to complex theories that attempt to reconcile the tension. It argues that where religion is involved, legislatures have relatively broad discretion to select a policy that reasonably promotes free exercise values at the expense of establishment clause ones, and vice versa.[45] Pluralism justifies this conclusion by arguing that in a religiously diverse society, the contention among religious groups and that between religious groups and secular ones, with shifting alliances and overlapping cleavages, will produce a public policy that is unlikely to pose serious threats to the values promoted by the religion clauses.[46] Thus, courts need only police the perimeters of public policy affecting religion to guard against unreasonable regulations that work to the severe detriment of one segment of a religiously diverse society.[47]

---

43. See Giannella, *supra* note 23, at 522-26.

44. See, e.g., Widmar v. Vincent, 454 U.S. 263, 288-89 (1981) (White, J., dissenting). *See also* Thomas v. Review Bd., 450 U.S. 707, 720-27 (1981) (Rehnquist, J., dissenting); Sherbert v. Verner, 374 U.S. 398, 418-23 (1963) (Harlan, J., joined by White, J., dissenting).

45. Thus, a university may prohibit prayer meetings or allow them as *it* chooses; a state may subsidize religious education but need not do so.

46. Alternatively, the religion clauses might be treated as creating broad outer boundaries for a set of values, and their proper interpretation would require that each generation be allowed to decide for itself how to accommodate those values within the limits set by the clauses. Under this view, pluralism assures that the accommodation will respect those limits.

47. On the limits of reasonableness, see Widmar v. Vincent, 454 U.S. at 287 (White, J., dissenting) (university could not bar students from saying grace before meals).

The pluralist theory also offers a justification for the establishment clause branch of Kurland's religion clause theory because religious pluralism would require legislatures to structure their programs using criteria that are neutral as to religion. The pluralist process that would produce such programs is unlikely to threaten serious erosions of establishment clause values. A more likely result is legislative paralysis, an inability to come up with a neutral program at acceptable levels of cost. The recently adopted Equal Access Act, Pub. L. No. 98-377, 98 Stat. 1303 (1984) (to be codified at 20 U.S.C. § 802(a)), provides a useful example, although the operative political constraint was not concern over costs. The Equal Access Act was designed to ensure that student religious groups would be allowed to use school facilities. The Act as adopted provides that schools that create "limited open forums" as defined in the Act may not discriminate against students who wish to conduct meetings "on the basis of the religious, *political, philosophical or other content* of the speech at such meetings." *Id.* at § 802(a) (emphasis added). The emphasized

Pluralist theories of constitutional law are subject to powerful empirical challenges. Problems arise because communities in the United States are not homogeneous as to religion, nor are religious groups represented in substantial numbers in every community.[48] Rather, the distribution of denominational membership is uneven, with concentrations of groups in different communities. Where there is only a small minority on some issue regarding religion, and if that minority believes that other issues are more important, pluralist bargaining may not fully take that group's interest into account: Its members will be outnumbered on the religious issue, and unwilling to withhold their votes on other important issues to extract concessions on the religion one.[49] Pluralist bargaining would also fail if the group was completely marginal to the community, so that no one else would find it politically profitable to trade support for the group's position on religious issues in exchange for its support on other issues.[50] In the context of the religion clauses, the empirical challenge to a pluralist theory seems well-founded. Christians outnumber adherents of other religions by a wide margin, and even expanding our view to include the so-called "Judaeo-Christian tradition" leaves many religious groups outside the pluralist process.

Justice O'Connor has begun to develop a version of the pluralist theory. She advocates inquiring into whether the governmental action at issue communicates a message "to nonadherents that they are outsiders, not full members of the political community," and communicates an accompanying message "to adherents that they are insiders, favored members of the political community."[51] Justice O'Connor's emphasis on symbolic messages is problematic for two reasons. First, her approach would have judges decide the symbolic content of the government's messages. But judges will always be broadly representative of the general population, and will be susceptible to all the distortions of interpretation that membership in the majority entails.[52] Sec-

---

words were added to reduce the political opposition to the Act; they also dilute its particularly religious content. *See also infra* note 95 and accompanying text. Such dilution may not be a socially desirable outcome, but it is not one with which Kurland's theory, or indeed the Constitution, is concerned.

48. If communities were homogeneous, no one would bother to question a community's decisions, and if there were enough adherents of each religion in every community, the pluralist bargaining process might work well.

49. This statement describes the political stance of many American Jews.

50. This is the political position of organized secularists and such outcast "cults" as the Reunification Church ("Moonies").

51. *See* Lynch v. Donnelly, 465 U.S. 668, 688 (1984) (O'Connor, J., concurring).

52. For example, Justice O'Connor articulated her own approach in concurring with the

ond, it is not clear why symbolic exclusion should matter so long as "nonadherents" are in fact actually included in the political community.[53] Under those circumstances, nonadherents who believe that they are excluded from the political community are merely expressing the disappointment felt by everyone who has lost a fair fight in the arena of politics. Symbolic exclusion after actual inclusion might matter if the nonadherents become so disheartened by their losses that they withdraw from politics altogether, but this prospect seems remote enough under presently foreseeable circumstances to make a prophylactic approach as questionable here as it is in the rights-based analysis of the establishment clause.[54]

II. FURTHER CONFUSION IN THE LAW OF RELIGION: A PRAGMATIC SURVEY

The foregoing survey of doctrinal and theoretical approaches to the religion clauses shows that we lack a satisfactory overall concept of those clauses. It is important now to develop a map of the Supreme Court's present understanding of religion and the Constitution. Two principles explain, though they do not justify, much of what the Supreme Court has done about religion.[55] The first is what I call the *re-*

Court's decision to find no establishment clause violation in the public sponsorship of a creche; she concluded that the practice "cannot fairly be understood to convey a message of government endorsement of religion." *Id.* at 694. This came as a surprise to most Jews, whose views on this issue turn out to be "unfair" in Justice O'Connor's eyes. *See* Tribe, *Constitutional Calculus: Equal Justice or Economic Efficiency?* 98 HARV. L. REV. 592, 611 (1985) ("One cannot avoid hearing in *Lynch* a faint echo of the Court that found nothing invidious in the Jim Crow policy of 'separate but equal.' "). One could use stronger words. Indeed it is difficult to believe that the *Lynch* majority would have reached the same result had there been a Jew on the Court to speak from the heart about what public displays of creches really mean to Jews. At the same time, of course, Jews have always known that they were strangers in the land, and have taken succor from that fact. *Lynch* reminds us of that, and distressing as it may be to have it brought home, we may profit from learning the lesson again. *See also* Kurland, *The Religion Clauses and the Burger Court,* 34 CATH. U.L. REV. 1, 13 (1984) (*Lynch* is "sleazy"); Van Alstyne, *Trends in the Supreme Court: Mr. Jefferson's Crumbling Wall—A Comment on* Lynch v. Donnelly, 1984 DUKE L.J. 770, 781-87.

53. It seems worth noting that in Aguilar v. Felton, 105 S. Ct. 3232, 3244-45 (1985) (O'Connor, J., dissenting), Justice O'Connor emphasized that a long record of nonindoctrination in religious matters by public school employees sent into parochial schools to provide remedial services was enough to overcome concern that indoctrination would occur. This seems to parallel a record of actual inclusion in the face of concerns about symbolic exclusion.

54. *See supra* notes 38-40 and accompanying text.

55. These principles should be taken as ones that provide order to the description of the Supreme Court's decisions rather than as ones that I believe are normatively appropriate. With one notable exception, see *supra* note 52, I have tried to exclude from my discussion arguments in favor of or against the fundamental normative merit of these principles, although I do indicate

duction principle: Religious belief is reduced to ordinary belief, protected by the free speech guarantees of the first amendment but no further because of its special character as religious belief. The second is what I call the *marginality* principle: To the extent that religious belief has an irreducible core, it is protected only to the extent that providing protection has no socially significant consequences.[56] An examination of how the reduction and marginality principles operate with respect to both religion clauses demonstrates that most of the Court's religion clause decisions rest on a set of ideas that do not view religion as a serious form of human endeavor.

A. The Reduction Principle

Religious belief is, of course, a kind of belief. The free expression clause of the first amendment protects the general class of beliefs, and thus necessarily protects religious belief as well. The reduction principle insists that religious belief is indistinguishable from other types of belief, so that neither the free exercise nor the establishment clause constrains governmental action any differently than does the free speech clause. The operation of the reduction principle has frequently been noted in free exercise cases.[57] Its operation in establishment clause cases, on the other hand, has only recently emerged.[58]

1. Operation of Reduction in Free Speech Cases

The reduction principle divides the religious beliefs and activities into three components: the belief itself, the body of ritual activities that accompany belief, and the impact of belief-motivated actions—including rituals—on secular interests. Then, for deciding free exercise issues, the reduction principle applies to each of these components the tests that have been developed to deal with problems of free speech. For example, just as the government may not burden "mere" political belief unconnected to otherwise undesirable social consequences,[59] the

---

analytical difficulties they create.

56. I am not sure that these principles are analytically distinct. Once religion is largely reduced to ordinary belief, what is left may necessarily be marginal. But I have found that using two labels makes exposition easier.

57. *See supra* note 10.

58. *But see* Choper, *Defining "Religion" in the First Amendment,* 1982 U. ILL. L. REV. 579, 610-12; Laycock, *supra* note 42, at 1383-84 (1981).

59. *See* Yates v. United States, 354 U.S. 298 (1957) (Smith Act construed not to penalize abstract belief as distinguished from advocacy of unlawful action).

government may not burden religious belief standing alone.[60] Moreover, according to the reduction principle, the rituals associated with belief are forms of symbolic speech and are to be tested by the standards developed in symbolic speech cases. Finally, advocates of the reduction principle point out that all speech has some effect on governmental interests unrelated to the suppression of speech, and that the Supreme Court has developed a number of rules that require governments to accommodate those interests to the interest in free expression.[61] The reduction principle thus requires application of similar rules when actions motivated by religious belief affect secular governmental interests.[62]

The reduction principle had its origins in the 1940s, when the Court, emerging from its confrontation with the President over New Deal economic legislation, began to develop a new constituency by enforcing limitations on government that were attractive to civil libertarians.[63] In a series of cases involving local efforts to regulate proselytizing by Jehovah's Witnesses, the Court articulated a set of rules about what governments could do.[64] Two characteristics of these cases suggest the Court was groping toward the reduction principle. First, as has been widely noted,[65] the Court in these early cases did not distinguish between the protections provided by the free speech clause and those provided by the free exercise clause. Instead it invoked the entire first amendment as the basis for its decisions.[66] Second, when it did address the free exercise clause separately, the Court drew on the same distinction between belief and action that it made in free speech cases.[67]

---

60. *See* U.S. CONST. art. IV (no religious test to be imposed for public office); Torcaso v. Watkins, 367 U.S. 488 (1961) (no religious test for state Notary Public commission).

61. *See, e.g.,* Kovacs v. Cooper, 336 U.S. 77 (1949) (governmental ban on loud or raucous noise emitted by sound-amplifying vehicles not infringement on free speech right); Schneider v. Irvington, 308 U.S. 147 (1939) (free speech guarantee invalidates municipal ban on handbill distribution designed to prevent littering of public streets).

62. For extensive articulation and defense of the reduction principle, see Marshall, *supra* note 5. *See also* Choper, *supra* note 58, at 581-82; Clark, *supra* note 10, at 336-37.

63. *See generally* Cover, *The Origins of Judicial Activism in the Protection of Minorities,* 91 YALE L.J. 1287 (1982).

64. *See* Martin v. Struthers, 319 U.S. 141 (1942) (door-to-door advertising may not be banned by city ordinance); Cox v. New Hampshire, 312 U.S. 569 (1941) (ban on parading without city permit upheld as valid time, place and manner regulation); Lovell v. Griffin, 303 U.S. 444 (1938) (ban on leafletting without city permit invalid infringement on free speech).

65. *See, e.g.,* Kurland, *supra* note 9, at 36-44; Marshall, *supra* note 5, at 562-64.

66. *Cf.* Kurland, *supra* note 9, at 40.

67. In Cantwell v. Connecticut, 310 U.S. 296 (1940), Justice Roberts wrote that free exercise "embraces two concepts,—freedom to believe and freedom to act. The first is absolute, but in the

A later example of the operation of the reduction principle is provided by the Sunday closing cases.[68] In upholding Sunday closing statutes against a free exercise challenge, Chief Justice Warren's plurality opinion in *Braunfeld v. Brown*[69] distinguished between direct and indirect burdens on religion,[70] a distinction again part of the law of free expression at the time.[71] More interesting is Chief Justice Warren's formulation of the general test for free exercise claims:

> [I]f the State regulates conduct by enacting a general law within its power, the purpose and effect of which is to advance the State's secular goals, the statute is valid despite its indirect burden on religious observance unless the State may accomplish its purpose by means which do not impose such a burden.[72]

Minor stylistic alterations aside, this test is structurally the same as the one stated for symbolic speech in *United States v. O'Brien*:[73]

> [A] government regulation is sufficiently justified if it is within the constitutional power of the Government; if it furthers an important or substantial governmental interest; if the governmental interest is unrelated to the suppression of free expression; and if the incidental restriction on alleged First Amendment freedoms is no greater than is essential to the furtherance of that interest.[74]

The reduction principle reached its fullest application in *Widmar v. Vincent*,[75] where, in a case crying out for free exercise treatment, the Court adopted a free expression analysis instead. In *Widmar*, the University of Missouri denied a group of students permission to conduct its prayer meetings in University buildings even though the buildings were

---

nature of things, the second cannot be." *Id.* at 303-04. This distinction is exactly the one the Court expressed contemporaneously in labor picketing cases. *See, e.g.,* Thornhill v. Alabama, 310 U.S. 88, 104-06 (1940).

68. Gallagher v. Crown Kosher Super Mkt., 366 U.S. 617 (1961); Braunfeld v. Brown, 366 U.S. 599 (1961); Two Guys From Harrison-Allentown, Inc. v. McGinley, 366 U.S. 582 (1961); McGowan v. Maryland, 366 U.S. 420 (1961).

69. 366 U.S. 599 (1961).

70. *Id.* at 605-06.

71. *See, e.g.,* Konigsberg v. State Bar, 366 U.S. 36, 49-51 (1961); Adler v. Board of Educ., 342 U.S. 485, 492-93 (1952).

72. 366 U.S. at 607.

73. 391 U.S. 367 (1968).

74. *Id.* at 377.

75. 454 U.S. 263 (1981).

available to nonreligious organizations for their meetings.[76] A free exercise analysis would treat this as a simple case of discrimination based on religion. The Court's free speech analysis treated it as an instance of content-based restriction of speech, which could be justified only by a compelling state interest. Religion entered the Court's analysis by the back door, as the Court rejected the University's claim that it had a compelling interest in avoiding the appearance of an establishment of religion. As William Marshall has said, "Because few activities are more profoundly religious than prayer, *Widmar* suggests that there is no core religious activity exclusively protected by the free exercise clause."[77]

Widmar shows that there is substantial overlap between free speech law and the results one would expect under free exercise law. The reduction principle would make the overlap complete. This argument is weakened, however, by two prominent cases that seem irreconcilable with the reduction principle.[78] In *Sherbert v. Verner*,[79] a Seventh Day Adventist was denied state unemployment benefits when she refused to make herself available for employment if it entailed Saturday work hours. Such a refusal did not constitute good cause for turning down "suitable work" under the regulations, so benefits were withheld.[80] The Supreme Court held that this denial violated her rights under the free exercise clause.[81] Similarly, in *Wisconsin v. Yoder*,[82] the Court held that the free exercise clause required states to exempt from the operation of their compulsory education laws the children of Amish parents whose religion forbade attendance at school after the eighth grade.[83]

In these cases the free exercise clause required states to create exemptions from general regulatory statutes. The free speech clause requires states to create exemptions as well; a person seeking to use a

---

76. *Id.* at 265.

77. Marshall, *supra* note 5, at 559-60. Much of this argument depends on the scope one gives to notions of symbolic speech: A ritual sacrifice might or might not be symbolic speech, but could perhaps receive free exercise protection no matter how it was regarded. *See* Frank v. State, 604 P.2d 1068 (Alaska 1979) (free exercise protection for illegal killing of cow moose during native Indian funeral ritual overrides state interest in game management).

78. *See* Greenawalt, *Religion as a Concept in Constitutional Law*, 72 CALIF. L. REV 753, 777-88 (1984).

79. 374 U.S. 398 (1963), *followed in* Thomas v. Review Bd., 450 U.S. 707 (1981).

80. 374 U.S. at 400-01.

81. *Id.* at 422.

82. 406 U.S. 205 (1972).

83. *Id.* at 219.

park for her company's softball tournament may be subjected to requirements that could not be imposed on a person seeking to use the park for a demonstration.[84] Yet it seems unlikely that, in a variation of the *Sherbert* case, the free speech clause would be held to require unemployment compensation for a person whose *political* beliefs caused her to be fired and prevented her from finding further employment in the private sector.[85] Similarly, the Court in *Yoder* carefully emphasized that the Amish had a long tradition of opposition to advanced education precisely to distinguish them from "hippie" types whose opposition to such education was political.[86] Thus, substitution of free speech analysis for free exercise analysis under the reduction principle does not work well in these two cases.

Proponents of the reduction principle can handle these cases in either of two ways. First, they can argue that *Sherbert* and *Yoder* were wrongly decided. Because *Yoder* so openly relies on an invidious comparison between religious beliefs and other beliefs,[87] repudiating it might not be unattractive. Repudiating *Sherbert* is more difficult, because the burden on belief seems both severe and not really necessary.[88] Thus, the second way to salvage the reduction principle is to expand the class of exemptions under the free speech clause: If a Seventh-Day Adventist is entitled to unemployment compensation notwithstanding that her religious beliefs prevented her from complying with the qualifying regulations, so too is a person who is unable to follow the regulations due to her political beliefs.[89] The fuzziness of the law of exemptions under the free speech clause is such that this expansion would entail no major doctrinal revisions. The courts could tinker a bit with the characterization of the interests that go into the balance, and create exemptions that are at present unavailable.

---

84. *See* Murdock v. Pennsylvania, 319 U.S. 105 (1943) (press, speech and religion privileges protected from indiscriminate license tax imposed on all commercial door-to-door solicitors); Martin v. Struthers, 319 U.S. 141 (1943) (exempting those engaged in religious and speech activities from ban on door-to-door soliciting).

85. The employers might be liable under the civil rights acts for a private conspiracy to deprive her of her political rights. Arguably the state's decision to construe its unemployment statutes to make political grounds "cause" for discharge would be unconstitutional under the circumstances hypothesized. But that was unlikely when *Sherbert* was decided, and is even more unlikely now. *See, e.g.,* Rendell Baker v. Kohn, 457 U.S. 830 (1982).

86. 406 U.S. at 235; *see* Kurland, *The Supreme Court, Compulsory Education, and the First Amendment's Religion Clauses,* 75 W. VA. L. REV. 213, 237-38 (1973).

87. *See* 406 U.S. at 215-16; *see also supra* note 86 and accompanying text.

88. This is the consensus of the commentators. *See, e.g.,* Clark, *supra* note 10, at 337-38.

89. *See* Marshall, *supra* note 5, at 586-87.

Yet tinkering with free speech law to preserve the reduction principle is a bit disquieting. In part the suggestion is troubling because it is unlikely that the Court as presently composed will expand free speech exemptions, except perhaps in largely innocuous situations.[90] But there is a more fundamental difficulty: The reduction principle denies what the text of the first amendment affirms, that there is a distinction between religion and other forms of expression.[91] Justice White, dissenting in *Widmar*, attempted to describe the distinction. He would have distinguished between "verbal acts of worship and other verbal acts," so that "the Religion Clauses [would have] independent meaning in circumstances in which religious practice took the form of speech."[92] The majority, on the other hand, criticized the distinction between worship and speech on three grounds.[93] First, the distinction did not explain when verbal acts, such as singing, reading, and teaching, acquired religious content so as to transform them from speech into worship. Further, courts could not intelligibly "inquire into the significance of words and practices" to determine whether a reading from the Bible was speech or worship.[94] Finally, the distinction between worship and speech was weakened because "religious speech designed to win religious converts" was protected by the free speech clause, and there was no difference between such speech and "religious worship by persons already converted."[95]

Justice White described the distinction between worship and speech but did not examine it in detail. The majority's criticisms indicate how it could be given content. The key is the difference between proselytizing and worshipping. Proselytizing is directed from within a

---

90. *See, e.g.*, Brown v. Socialist Workers '74 Campaign Comm., 459 U.S. 87 (1982) (Socialist Workers Party exempted from state statutes requiring names and addresses of campaign contributors because "reasonable probability" of harrassment of contributors shown by party).

91. I do not offer this as a criticism based on an "antiredundancy" canon of constitutional interpretation, though I confess to finding it striking that Marshall, *supra* note 5, in presenting the most recent extensive advocacy of the reduction principle, does not address the redundancy issue. I offer the observation in support of the argument, developed below, that religion is peculiar in ways that contemporary liberalism finds difficult to understand.

92. 454 U.S. at 285, 284 (White, J., dissenting). Verbal acts of worship include "offering prayer, singing hymns, reading scripture, and teaching biblical principles." *Id.* at 283.

93. *Id.* at 269-70 n.6.

94. *Id.* at 270 n.6.

95. *Id.* (citing Heffron v. International Soc'y for Krishna Consciousness, Inc., 452 U.S. 640 (1981). Justice White conceded this third point. *Id.* at 285 (White, J., dissenting). Marshall, *supra* note 5, at 579, argues that, in a Meiklejohn-type theory of free expression, religious speech is at least not entitled to greater protection than political speech because it does not directly contribute to the process of political deliberation.

community of believers to outsiders, whereas worship occurs among the community of believers. Proselytizing invites others to join an already-constituted group; worshipping is the means by which the group affirms its existence as a group. Similarly, praying and singing hymns are means by which believers affirm to each other and to their god their participation in a community set apart from others. Teaching scripture differs from teaching about the Bible because participants in the former activity open themselves to inspiration and participation in a church in ways that participants in the latter activity need not. Worship differs from speech, then, by manifesting a commitment to a community less encompassing than the whole society.[96]

It is clear that this distinction between speech and worship captures something deeply important about religion. Yet the reduction principle rejects any such distinction. The reduction principle is attractive precisely because it allows the law of religion to gloss over the fact that religious communities necessarily stand apart from, and in many ways stand in opposition to, the wider community of which they are a part.[97] As I argue below, that fact threatens some fundamentals of the liberal tradition.

---

96. The perspective here is essentially that of Durkheim, but in order to make my major points I need adopt only such a general perspective, without addressing the controversial details of Durkheim's own work. For similar perspectives on recent religious phenomena in the United States, see Bellah, *The New Religious Consciousness and the Crisis of Modernity*, in THE NEW RELIGIOUS CONSCIOUSNESS 333 (1976); Johnson, *The Hare Krishna in San Francisco, id.* at 31, 41, 44-45; Tobey, *The Summer Solstice of the Healthy-Happy-Holy Organization, id.* at 5, 14-15. For similar perspectives in legal commentary, see Valente, *Aid to Church Related Education—New Directions Without Dogma*, 55 VA. L. REV. 579, 604-05 (1969); Note, *The Sacred and the Profane: A First Amendment Definition of Religion*, 61 TEX. L. REV. 139, 158-59 (1982).

97. This description of religion's distinctiveness can be challenged from two directions. First, it might be said that it ignores religious traditions emphasizing the direct contact between the believer and God, religious traditions celebrating isolated monastic existence, and the deist tradition in which communal worship is replaced by rationalist appreciation of God's role in the world. Yet the anchorite's isolated worship is religious rather than eccentric because it is located in a tradition of discourse to which other believers have access. *See* Africa v. Pennsylvania, 662 F.2d 1025 (3d Cir. 1981) (MOVE sect not a religion under the first amendment because it did not address "fundamental and ultimate questions," was not "comprehensive," and did not have the defining "structural characteristics" of a traditional religion); Brown v. Pena, 441 F. Supp. 1382 (S.D. Fla. 1977) (worship entailing consumption of cat food not a religion; pantheism not a religion). Talk about a person's relation to God can be coherent only in a socially located discourse making such talk sensible. However, this point gives weight to the second challenge: All speech, not just religious worship, can be coherent only in socially located discourses. Religion should then be treated as exemplary rather than distinctive. I agree with this challenge. *See supra* note 8, and *infra* notes 171-72.

2. Operation of Reduction in Establishment Clause Cases

In establishment clause cases, the reduction principle means that government support of religion may go as far as its support of speech.[98] In this context, the reduction principle arises indirectly, based on reflection about free speech problems. In *Epperson v. Arkansas*,[99] the Court struck down a statute prohibiting the teaching of Darwinian theories of evolution in the public schools as violating the establishment clause.[100] The opinion resonated with overtones of the proposition that illicitly-motivated statutes are unconstitutional. Because that proposition was inconsistent with then-prevailing views of the role of motivation in constitutional adjudication,[101] observers sought to reconstruct *Epperson* as a free speech case.[102] However, doing so raised a host of troubling issues. The difficulty lay in the fact that the only speaker involved in *Epperson* was the teacher performing duties required by state law. It was not easy to determine the proper limitation on the government's power to speak—that is, to prescribe the curriculum for its employees—given the wide range of activities in which various government agencies distribute to the public views and information that affect the political process.

Two solutions were offered to resolve the problem of government speech. One commentator argued that, because government speech was analogous to government support of religion, the courts should enforce a fairly rigid set of rules prohibiting an establishment of speech to parallel what the author took to be the stringent prohibitions of the establishment of religion clause.[103] This view was quickly rejected; the proposed restrictions were thought to prohibit too many worthwhile activities, and the problem was seen as amenable to a milder solution.[104] A consensus emerged around the second solution, which essentially left government speech free of judicial control.[105] This solution

---

98. Of course it may go no further. But, as shown below, that does not turn out to be a significant limit on the government's power. Under these circumstances, the reduction principle might be called an "escalation" principle.

99. 393 U.S. 97 (1968).

100. *Id.* at 109.

101. *See* United States v. O'Brien, 391 U.S. 367, 383 (1968) (fundamental principal that court will not strike down otherwise constitutional statute on basis of allegedly illicit legislative motive).

102. *See, e.g.,* M. YUDOF, WHEN GOVERNMENT SPEAKS 217-18 (1983).

103. Kamenshine, *The First Amendment's Implied Political Establishment Clause*, 67 CALIF. L. REV. 1104 (1979).

104. *See, e.g., infra,* note 105.

105. Shiffrin, *Government Speech*, 27 UCLA L. REV. 565 (1980); M. YUDOF, *supra* note 102.

rested on a pluralist analysis of American politics. According to that analysis, contending interest groups shape the development of public policy, including public policy about government speech. Given a rough balance of forces in the pluralist struggle, troubling forms of government speech are unlikely to occur with sufficient frequency to constitute a problem to which courts can profitably direct their attention.

Offered as an *alternative* to the establishment clause solution, the pluralist analysis of government speech in fact reproduces the solutions suggested by the pluralist theories of the establishment clause. The establishment clause solution to the problem of political speech would have escalated the constraints on such speech to what its proponents thought was the high level set by the establishment clause. The pluralist theories reduce the constraints on the establishment of religion to the level set by pluralist politics.

The Supreme Court's decision in *Mueller v. Allen*[106] illustrates this reduction in operation. Ten years earlier, the Court had held unconstitutional a New York statute that provided tuition tax credits to parents who sent their children to private schools, the vast majority of which were affiliated with religious organizations.[107] *Mueller* upheld a Minnesota statute that allowed parents to deduct certain expenses of sending their children to school, whether public or private.[108] Because parents whose children attend public school rarely have substantial actual expenses, the primary beneficiaries of the statute were parents with children in private schools and the large majority of these were, as in New York, sectarian. The Supreme Court distinguished the New York statute on the ground that the Minnesota statute "neutrally provide[d] state assistance to a broad spectrum of citizens."[109]

Of course the New York statute was also neutral on its face. It provided its tax benefits not only to parents in sectarian schools but also to those with children in any private schools. What distinguishes the cases is not neutrality, but the breadth of the statutory classifica-

---

For a review of the latter, see Tushnet, Book Review, 1984 WIS. L. REV. 129.

106.   463 U.S. 388 (1983).

107.   Committee for Pub. Educ. & Religious Liberty v. Nyquist, 413 U.S. 756 (1973).

108.   463 U.S. at 391. This deduction was limited to actual expenses for tuition, textbooks, or transportation, up to $500 (grades kindergarten through six) or $700 per child (grades seven through twelve).

109.   463 U.S. at 398-99. The Court also stated that aid provided through parents rather than directly to the schools "reduced the Establishment Clause objections." *Id. But see* Committee for Pub. Educ. & Religious Liberty v. Regan, 444 U.S. 646, 658 (1980) (acknowledging that the New York and Minnesota statutes were indistinguishable on this ground).

tion. Yet it remains to be shown why the classification "parents" is broader in some relevant sense than the classification "parents with children in private schools." Obviously, there are more people in the former class. However, New York provides massive subsidies through its expenditure system to parents whose children attend public schools. Thus, both forms of subsidies taken together constitute a system of subsidies to parents, just as in Minnesota.[110] Further, the relevance of numbers alone is obscure. In New York, enough parents of children in public schools were willing to subsidize the smaller group of parents with children in private schools to create a majority in favor of the statute.[111]

The Court in *Mueller* expressly rejected an alternative measure of breadth by refusing to look beyond the face of the statute to the actual fiscal impact of the benefits provided.[112] The Court seems to have determined by intuitive judgment that the classification was broad enough. Such a judgment may have been shaped by an equally intuitive theory of the interaction between religious pluralism and the political process.[113] A statute whose classifications are neutral is likely to provide benefits to a relatively large number of people because religious and nonreligious interests will bargain in the political process. Such benefits are likely to have a significant fiscal impact. That impact in itself is likely to reduce the number of occasions in which statutes that threaten establishment clause values can be enacted.[114]

---

110. *See supra* notes 18-23 and accompanying text.

111. 413 U.S. at 773.

112. *Mueller,* 463 U.S. at 401. Tracing benefits through the tax system is indeed difficult, and the results will vary from year to year depending on how carefully parents with children in public schools keep records supporting their claimed deductions. Further, the Court was concerned that it could not develop standards to distinguish broad fiscal impacts from narrow ones. *Id.*

113. After distinguishing the New York statute, the Court stated that "the attenuated financial benefits flowing to parochial schools [did not threaten] the evils against which the Establishment Clause was designed to protect." *Id.* at 399. Those evils were strife based on religion. Further, the Court quoted an earlier statement by Justice Powell that "[t]he risk . . . of deep political division along religious lines is remote. . . ." *Id.* (quoting Wolman v. Walter, 433 U.S. 229, 263 (1977) (Powell, J., concurring in part, concurring in the judgment, and dissenting in part). The risk was remote because of religious pluralism.

114. The pluralist analysis is filled with judgments about how the political process is likely to work, and the Court's refusal to examine actual fiscal impact in *Mueller* indicates that it is unwilling to entertain empirical challenges to the wider set of political judgments involved. Yet there is something to be said for the pluralist analysis. Some states might adopt statutes like Minnesota's, and in a federal system that might well be acceptable. By contrast, devising a national tuition tax credit system stated in sufficiently neutral terms to attract political support and thereby withstand judicial scrutiny may be quite difficult, precisely because of the rather large fiscal impact of such a program. Discussions of proposals to adopt a national tuition tax credit plan illus-

There is more than a little irony in the development of the reduction principle. The establishment clause reduction was first invoked to increase restrictions on government speech, but a more complete theory of government speech led to the use of establishment clause reduction to decrease restrictions on government support of religion.[115] Moreover, the reduction principle eliminates from the first amendment any specific concern for religion as a distinctive human activity. As discussed below, the marginality principle has much the same effect.

B. *The Marginality Principle*

1. Operation of Marginality in Free Exercise Cases

In free exercise cases, the operation of the marginality principle is expressed in the rule that emerged from *Sherbert v. Verner:*[116] The state must accommodate its general regulatory programs to the religious beliefs of its citizens.[117] The required degree of accommodation is to be determined by balancing the religious interest against the regulatory interest, each measured in an appropriate way. The effort to measure and balance these interests produces the rhetoric of the marginality principle.

The rhetorical strategy of proponents of free exercise exemptions is to minimize the impact of the exemption on the governmental interest. They do this by emphasizing that the religious practice has minor social consequences. In *Sherbert,* for example, the Court carefully noted how few Seventh Day Adventists there were in the locality and suggested that only rarely would a Sabbatarian be unable to get a job that could accommodate her schedule.[118] Likewise, as indicated earlier, the education exemption in *Yoder* was confined to the special case of

---

trate the problem with the latter approach. *See Hearing on S. 2673 Before the Senate Comm. on Finance,* 97th Cong., 2d Sess. (July 16, 1982). To keep the fiscal impact within acceptable bounds, the Finance Committee scaled back the Reagan Administration's proposals, primarily by eliminating a provision making the credit refundable to those whose incomes were so low as to make them unable to benefit from a pure tax credit. However, eliminating that feature makes the program beneficial only to the relatively well-to-do, which undermines the political attractiveness of the proposal.

115. An analogue in free speech law, both in one of its messages and in the necessary qualifications, is the "clear and present danger" test, which can be read as allowing suppression of speech just at the point of its effectiveness. *See* Tushnet, *Deviant Science in Constitutional Law,* 59 Tex. L. Rev. 815, 817-18 (1981).

116. 374 U.S. 398 (1963).

117. This rule cannot readily be accounted for by the reduction principle.

118. 374 U.S. at 399 n.2.

the Amish.[119] According to proponents of exemptions, the relevant measure is the incremental impact of the exemption at issue on the governmental interest.[120] As is evident from the cases above, careful definition of the incremental impact will always show that the religious practice plays a marginal role in the accomplishment of social goals.

On the other side of the argument, opponents of free exercise exemptions engage in a related manipulation of the balance. Instead of focusing on the incremental impact of the particular exemption sought, however, they focus on the cumulative impact of that and analogous exemptions. The cumulative impact can always be made significant, particularly if one throws into the balance the difficulties of administering a scheme with numerous exemptions. Thus, in *United States v. Lee*,[121] the Court refused to exempt Amish employers from the social security tax, saying that "[u]nlike the situation in *Wisconsin v. Yoder*, it would be difficult to accommodate the comprehensive social security system with myriad exceptions flowing from a wide variety of religious beliefs."[122]

Cases involving statutory accommodations of religious belief express similar judgments about the marginality principle: Once again, the law can take religion into account only because, and to the extent that, it is not socially significant.[123] Thus, the Court in interpreting Congress's requirement that employers accommodate their practices to the religious beliefs of their employees has demanded only *de minimis* adjustments, that is, accommodations that have only the most minor impact on the employers' business decisions.[124] And in *Estate of Thornton v. Caldor, Inc.*,[125] the Court held that a broader statutory

---

119. *See supra* note 86 and accompanying text.

120. *See, e.g.*, Clark, *supra* note 10, at 331-33.

121. 455 U.S. 252 (1982).

122. *Id.* at 259-60. An alternative explanation of the Court's distinction between *Yoder* and *Lee* is that it believed that exemptions from taxes give people incentives to misrepresent their religious beliefs in ways that exemptions from public education do not, and that determining the sincerity with which a person holds a religious belief is administratively difficult in the tax context. *See* Freed & Polsby, *Race, Religion, and Public Policy*: Bob Jones Univ. v. United States, 1983 SUP. CT. REV. 1, 24-26. I find the second of these propositions implausible, given the Court's willingness in other contexts—such as religion-based conscientious objection to compulsory military service—to authorize inquiries into sincerity. The first proposition imposes a rather rationalistic frame on assertions of religious belief.

123. This argument does not deny that exemptions are significant in alleviating the pressures felt by individual believers, but it does claim that the Constitution requires that individual burdens be alleviated only if doing so is not socially significant.

124. Trans World Airlines v. Hardison, 432 U.S. 63 (1977).

125. 105 S. Ct. 2914 (1985).

accommodation violated the establishment clause in part because the statute, by requiring employers to give employees their "Sabbath" off from work, failed to take account of the hardships such an accommodation would cause employers and coworkers.[126]

2. Operation of Marginality in Establishment Clause Cases

Like the reduction principle, the marginality principle emerges less directly in establishment clause cases than in free exercise ones. Nevertheless, the marginality principle lies at the heart of standard establishment clause doctrine. One of the Court's "tests" for detecting an establishment clause violation examines whether legislation has the purpose of advancing or inhibiting religion.[127] Using this test, the Court invalidated Alabama's "moment of silence" statute because its examination of the legislative history persuaded it that the statute's sole purpose was to promote religious observance in the public schools.[128] But the Court strongly hinted that a properly motivated moment of silence statute would be constitutional.[129] The secular purpose requirement thus means that if enough people take religion seriously, they cannot enact their program, but if they favor the same program for other reasons, they can enact it. It seems fair to say that this rule does not accept the view that religion should play an important part in public life.

Mark DeWolfe Howe identified another example of the marginality principle, though he did not give it that label or endorse its operation.[130] He called a number of practices "de facto" establishments of religion.[131] De facto establishments are practices that our society tolerates even though they would be characterized as establishments of religion under any sensible test for establishment. Such practices include tax exemptions for church property,[132] and legislative prayer.[133] Difficulties in determining how to identify de facto establishments and distinguish them from true establishments produce the marginality princi-

---

126. *Id.* at 2918.

127. Lemon v. Kurtzman, 403 U.S. 602, 612 (1971). The other two prongs of the *Lemon* test require that the statute's principal effect must neither advance nor inhibit religion, and that the statute must not foster excessive government entanglement with religions. *Id.* at 612-13.

128. Wallace v. Jaffree, 105 S. Ct. 2479, 2492 (1985). For another application of the purpose branch of the test, see Stone v. Graham, 449 U.S. 39 (1980) (invalidating statute requiring that the Ten Commandments be posted in schoolrooms).

129. *Wallace,* 105 S. Ct. at 2491.

130. M. HOWE, THE GARDEN AND THE WILDERNESS 11 (1965).

131. *Id.*

132. *See* Walz v. Tax Comm'n, 397 U.S. 664 (1970).

133. *See* Marsh v. Chambers, 463 U.S. 783 (1983).

ple in establishment clause cases.

Marsh v. Chambers[134] suggests that de facto establishments might be those created contemporaneously with the Constitution. The Court there upheld the practice of paying the salary of a chaplain who opened legislative sessions with a prayer. Instead of relying on its settled three-part test for evaluating establishment clause claims,[135] the Court emphasized the "unique history" of the practice at issue, noting, for example, that three days after Congress authorized the appointment of chaplains, it approved the text of the first amendment.[136] Yet a "contemporaneous interpretation" approach to de facto establishments is likely to be unsatisfactory. As noted earlier, changes in social institutions make it difficult to be certain that a present-day practice is sufficiently similar to one in use at the time of the framing to warrant characterizing the institutions as the same.[137] For example, property tax exemptions for churches are different in modern society, when major portions of a state's activities are financed by property tax revenues, from what they were two centuries ago, when public activities were much more limited in scope and financed largely by excise taxes.

In *Walz v. Tax Commission*,[138] the Court upheld such tax exemptions by relying on a slightly broader historical approach. The Court mentioned general establishment clause tests, but gave more emphasis to the proposition that "[f]ew concepts are more deeply rooted in the fabric of our national life . . . than for the government to exercise . . . this kind of benevolent neutrality. . . ."[139] This approach avoids the difficulties of contemporaneous interpretation because it views de facto establishments as practices deeply entrenched in our traditions, without regard to the precise time of their origin. Yet a traditionalist definition of de facto establishments is not without its own problems. First, courts must select the tradition to invoke. Consider the question of school prayer. That issue was highly contentious in the late nineteenth century. The first modern state law requiring prayer in public schools was enacted in 1913.[140] Yet, as *Marsh* shows, there is also a tradition of

---

134. *Id.*

135. *See supra* note 127 and accompanying text.

136. *Marsh*, 463 U.S. at 791.

137. *See supra* text accompanying notes 35-37.

138. *Walz*, 397 U.S. at 664.

139. *Id.* at 676.

140. *See* R. DRINAN, RELIGION, THE COURTS, & PUBLIC POLICY 90-91 (1963) (only Massachusetts had statute requiring Bible-reading in public schools before 1913); A. REICHLEY, RELIGION IN AMERICAN PUBLIC LIFE 145 (1985) (in 1946, Bible reading required in 13 states, author-

religiosity in important public institutions. The courts must decide which tradition is more relevant in today's society to the issue of school prayer. Second, any approach emphasizing tradition must take into account the tradition of federalism. Doing so would convert all locally-settled practices into de facto establishments, which probably takes the concept too far. Finally, as the school prayer example indicates, the courts must also decide how much tradition is enough.

Lynch v. Donnelly,[141] the Court's decision upholding the constitutionality of municipal creches, illustrates the difficulties in identifying de facto establishments and suggests that the solution lies in the use of the marginality principle. The Court could not rely directly on a contemporaneous interpretation approach because Christmas did not begin to be widely observed as a national holiday until after the middle of the nineteenth century.[142] But the Court did invoke history: The opinion recited a variety of diverse practices—legislative chaplains, Thanksgiving declarations, displays of pictures with religious subjects in art museums—to show that "the role of religion in American life" has been acknowledged by government since 1789.[143]

The Court then turned to an analysis of the issue before it. Evaluating the municipal creche display "in the proper context of the Christmas Holiday season,"[144] the Court concluded that the creche had the "secular purpose" of "celebrat[ing] the Holiday and . . . depict[ing] its origins."[145] In this conclusion, the word "secular" takes on a curious meaning. The Court did not deny that the creche has a religious meaning; it could not do so without making meaningless its use of the word "celebrate."[146] Rather, the Court determined that the creche is "secular" in the sense that, in its context, it does not really do much to

---

ized in 25 more); Tyack & James, *Moral Majorities and the School Curriculum: Historical Perspectives on the Legalization of Virtue*, 86 TCHR'S C. REC. 513, 519-22 (1985) (describing increase in and controversies over public school Bible reading in 19th and early 20th centuries).

141.   465 U.S. 668 (1984).

142.   *Id.* at 720 (Brennan, J., dissenting). For much of the period before the Civil War, the Alabama legislature routinely met on Christmas. *See* J. THORNTON, POLITICS & POWER IN A SLAVE SOCIETY 82 (1978).

143.   *Lynch*, 465 U.S. at 674-78.

144.   *Id.* at 680. Although it did not precisely identify what that context was, presumably the Court meant to evoke images of a season of generalized good will and commercial promotion. *See id.* at 685 ("display engenders a friendly community spirit of good will in keeping with the season"). *See also id.* at 727 (Blackmun, J., dissenting) ("creche has been relegated to the role of a neutral harbinger of the holiday season, useful for commercial purposes. . . .").

145.   *Id.* at 681.

146.   *See also id.* at 685 (creche has "religious implications"); *id.* at 687 (creche has "religious significance").

promote one religion over another, or even to promote religion in general.[147] The creche is a "passive symbol," acknowledging religion but otherwise not terribly important.[148] The Court's message was that the creche's opponents were taking the issue far too seriously.[149] Thus, the creche is religious—but not very. There is a tradition of religiosity—but not of Christianity. It is all intended to be very soothing.

The *Lynch* Court thus accomplished its goal of easing sectarian tensions by invoking the marginality principle.[150] Some of its examples of the acknowledgement of religion, such as paintings with religious themes in museums, can only mean that religion is not in itself terribly important. Other examples, such as the mandatory presence of the national motto, "In God We Trust" on currency, or the language "One nation under God" in the Pledge of Allegiance, involve the ritualistic employment of religious symbols that few take seriously. If the creche is constitutional because its religious component, while real, resembles the religious components of these other activities, it is constitutional because it is marginal.

In this view, de facto establishments are governmental activities that support what sociologists have called the American "civil religion."[151] The civil religion includes among its elements a diffuse religiosity, captured in the law by Justice Douglas's statement, "We are a religious people whose institutions presuppose a Supreme Being."[152] In

---

147. *Id.* at 681-85.

148. *Id.* at 686.

149. This theme is almost explicit in Justice O'Connor's concurring opinion, which makes dispositive "the message the . . . display actually conveyed." *Id.* at 690. She concluded that this particular creche "was [not] intended to endorse [and did not have] the effect of endorsing Christianity." *Id.* at 694. *See also supra* notes 51-52 and accompanying text.

150. The Court's decisions prohibiting the practice of state-sponsored group prayer and Bible reading in public schools pose a problem for this analysis, because such practice would seem to be consistent with a system of public support for diffuse religiosity. It may be that the state's role in composing the prayer in Engel v. Vitale, 370 U.S. 421 (1962), was too obvious an intrusion of the state into religious matters, and that the use of the Bible in Abington School Dist. v. Schempp, 374 U.S. 203 (1963), was insufficiently diffuse in its religiosity. As the Court saw it, these practices were simply motivated by religious purposes, *see supra* text accompanying note 127, and therefore went beyond the bounds of diffuse religiosity in public life.

151. *See* R. BELLAH, THE BROKEN COVENANT: AMERICAN CIVIL RELIGION IN TIME OF TRIAL (1975). Bellah's own definition of civil religion is that it is a true religion, not "religion in general" or diffuse religiosity. This definition and its use in the United States context are quite controversial and probably lack substantial scholarly support. For a collection of the basic materials, see AMERICAN CIVIL RELIGION (R. Richey & D. Jones eds. 1974). *See also.*Demerath & Williams, *Civil Religion in an Uncivil Society,* 480 ANNALS 154 (1985). For another discussion of diffuse religiosity in constitutional law, see Van Alstyne, *supra* note 52, at 786-87.

152. Zorach v. Clauson, 343 U.S. 306, 313 (1952).

our public life, we are allowed, and may be encouraged, to bolster our positions by reference to a deity.[153] But we cannot derive policy positions from religion; that would make unacceptably concrete the civil religion's generalized religiosity.[154] The pluralist theory of the establishment clause prevents this from happening by providing innumerable locations in which people can create or verify their relationship to a god whom they imagine in many different ways. Although sects differ in the policy conclusions they draw from religion, and some sects oppose public support of religion on theological grounds,[155] pluralist bargaining is likely to eliminate all but the least contentious position. This is precisely the religiosity of the civil religion.[156]

III. RELIGION AND POLITICAL THEORY

Both the analytic survey and the pragmatic one leave us with a law of religion that few should find satisfactory. An examination of the relationship between religion and political theory reveals a similarly unacceptable situation. Constitutionalists today are committed to developing a law of religion even though they do not understand why they have to do so. The Constitution as a whole, and the religion clauses of the first amendment in particular, embody the confluence of two traditions of political theory. The first tradition, that of liberalism, is concerned about threats to individual security and property. In that tradition the state serves to protect individuals from each other. Other institutions,

---

153. Cf. McDaniel v. Paty, 435 U.S. 618 (1978).

154. In an especially dramatic criticism of the influence of concrete religiosity on public life, Anthony Lewis has written: "If there is anything that should be illegitimate in the American system, it is [a President's] use of sectarian religiosity to sell a political program." Lewis, Onward Christian Soldiers, N.Y. Times, Mar. 10, 1983, at A27, col.1.

155. Justice Stevens has emphasized that the tradition of religious opposition to public support of religion is based on the view that such support actually undermines religion. See, e.g., Wolman v. Walter, 433 U.S. 229, 266 (1977) (Stevens, J., dissenting) ("To qualify for aid, sectarian schools must relinquish their religious exclusivity . . . .[and] will be under pressure to avoid textbooks which present a religious perspective on secular subjects, so as to obtain the free textbooks provided by the State."); Roemer v. Board of Pub. Works, 426 U.S. 736, 775 (1976) (Stevens, J., dissenting) (noting "the pernicious tendency of a state subsidy to tempt religious schools to compromise their religious mission without wholly abandoning it").

156. One potential outcome should be noted, though I think it unlikely to occur very often. Sects might agree to support public endorsement of a religious "fair," in which the sects would openly display their diverse views on concrete religious matters. Two points should be noted. First, sectarian opposition to public support of religion may make it difficult to assemble sufficient support for a religious fair. Second, the message of a fair, even one that excludes some sects, is that religiosity in general is worthwhile. Thus, a fair consisting of many religious "booths" still supports no more than the civil religion.

such as the Constitution, are designed to protect citizens from the state. The second tradition, that of republicanism, is concerned about the institutions that shape character. The republican citizen acts to advance the public good, and is induced to do so by institutions—families, schools, churches—that teach him or her that the public good is not always the same as his or her private interest. Yet religion posed a threat to this intellectual world of the liberal tradition because it was a form of social life that mobilized the deepest passions of believers in the course of creating institutions that stood between individuals and the state. Constitutionalists have lost their understanding of the need to fit religion into the constitutional framework because the liberal tradition has so increased its cultural authority that it is difficult to retrieve the republican tradition for purposes of grasping the meaning of the Constitution. We must retrieve both the liberal tradition and the republican one to improve our understanding of the role of religion in the constitutional order.

A. *The Liberal Tradition*

Liberal political theory was shaped by a set of historical circumstances and a set of philosophical problems about the maintenance of social order. Each gave support to efforts, like those embodied in the reduction and marginality principles, to reduce the significance of religion in public life.

The historical origins of modern liberal political theory lay in philosophers' reflections on the emergence of the unified nation-state.[157] In order to create a national entity strong enough to act in the emerging world polity and to expand into the world market, the nation-state had to destroy the power of intermediate institutions standing between the individual and the comprehensive state.[158] In this world order, churches were not only intermediate institutions, but they were closely tied to other local monopolies of power.[159] As property owners, churches were actors in the feudal order. Indeed, the ritual bonds of feudalism were

---

157. *See generally* P. ANDERSON, LINEAGES OF THE ABSOLUTIST STATE (1974); I. WALLERSTEIN, THE MODERN WORLD-SYSTEM (1974). For a summary of the argument as made in liberation theology, see H. COX, RELIGION IN THE SECULAR CITY 93-96, 163-64 (1984).

158. The term "comprehensive state" is obviously metaphorically inappropriate; before the nation-state emerged, there was nothing against which these institutions could stand as intermediaries.

159. Other intermediate institutions were the baronies of feudalism that bound people together by ritualistically created personal ties of reciprocal duty, the guilds that protected local markets against erosion, and the feudal attachments that tied workers to their neighborhoods.

created in conjunction with religious sanctions. As ideological enterprises, churches developed theologies to support the maintenance of whatever secular hierarchies they found in the vicinity. Further, the central religious institution at that time, the Catholic Church, posed a particular obstacle to the nation-state by its claim to universal status. Establishing the secular ruler's power would require diminishing that of the priests.

The philosophical basis for liberal political theory came from a reaction against the theology of Catholicism, which reproduced the problem posed by intermediate institutions. In the religious sphere, Catholic theology insisted on a relationship with three elements: the believer, the church, and God. In the secular sphere, the ideology of the nation-state sought to establish a relationship with only two elements: the subject and the state. Although clever thinkers could no doubt have designed ideological systems that explained and justified this incongruity, the availability of a competing theology made it largely unnecessary to do so. The alternative Protestant theology insisted also on a two-element relationship in which believers could—indeed had to—communicate directly with their God.[160] Thus, ideologists of the nation-state could begin to think of political life and religious life as two harmonious spheres; the direct relationship between believer and God paralleled the direct relationship between subject and state.

As they developed modern liberal theory, political philosophers saw a terrain in which attachment to a universal nation-state had substantially reduced attachment to local institutions and in which their theology allowed them to remain believers while eliminating the church as an intermediate institution. Religion posed a threat to this intellectual world because it was a form of social life that mobilized the deepest passions of believers in the course of creating institutions that stood between individuals and the state.[161] The liberal tradition accommo-

---

160. This is the widely noted significance of the Protestant translations of the Bible into the vernacular. The translations enable believers to grasp their religion without having to learn an esoteric language. *See also* Mead, *The "Nation With the Soul of a Church"* in AMERICAN CIVIL RELIGION, *supra* note 151, at 45, 51 (homology of Protestantism and democracy).

161. *Cf.* Note, *Reinterpreting the Religion Clauses: Constitutional Construction and Conceptions of the Self*, 97 HARV. L. REV. 1468 (1984). Like this article, the note posits that present theories inadequately explain the equilibrium between the establishment and free exercise clauses, but it locates the source of the tensions in an enduring psychological dualism of one's self-conception as an individual and as a member of the community. The note also takes a normative stance, whereas I do not. *See supra* note 55. For a discussion of the role of other intermediate institutions in the constitutional scheme, *see* Tushnet, *Federalism and the Traditions of American Political Theory*, 19 GA. L. REV. 981 (1985).

dated religion by relegating it to the sphere of private life, a sphere whose connections to public life were of essentially no interest.[162] According to liberal political theory as developed by Hobbes and Locke, public policy rested on the aggregation of individual preferences. Those preferences were formed outside the public sphere, and the manner of their formation was not a subject of political analysis: Preferences were exercises of private will, while public life consisted of mechanisms to subject private will to the operation of reason.

In this picture of public life, intermediate institutions have three roles to play.[163] First, they can provide the matrix within which private preferences are formed. Those preferences are then expressed in public life, where they are aggregated with the preferences of other citizens, to create policy. For instance, voters take positions on abortion because of their participation in intermediate institutions such as their churches, their families, and the voluntary associations to which they belong. In this role intermediate institutions are exogenous to public policy; they are impenetrable black boxes within which things happen that affect public policy, but which cannot be the objects of that policy.[164]

Second, intermediate institutions can serve as instruments of public policy. Churches will be tolerated so long as, and to the extent that, they induce believers to act in ways consistent with public policies determined without reference to religious values.[165] In this role, intermediate institutions are not really intermediate; instead, they are parts of the state, like the government bureaucracy or the public school system.

Finally, intermediate institutions can be vehicles of alliance among like-minded people who find that they can better advance their preferences by pooling resources in the effort to influence the development of public policy. Yet the individualist assumptions of liberal political theory make these alliances unstable. Individuals have preferences that co-

---

162. For a brief discussion of the tensions between religious privatism and religious communalities, see Roof & McKinney, *Denominational America and the New Religious Pluralism*, 480 ANNALS 24 (1985).

163. Because the dynamics of economic growth in the United States had particularly strong effects undermining the republican tradition, the development of the church-state relationship in the United States differed from that in other liberal societies. I therefore do not claim that the constitutional law of religion, as discussed in this article, is the only possible result; rather, it describes how the liberal and republican traditions worked out in the United States.

164. For a classic recent expression, see Stigler & Becker, *De Gustibus Non Est Disputandum*, 67 AM. ECON. REV. 76 (1977).

165. *Cf.* Reynolds v. United States, 98 U.S. 145 (1878) (religious belief no defense against criminal prosecution for polygamy), *discussed in* Kurland, *supra* note 9, at 6-8.

incide in some matters and conflict in others. Temporary trade-offs may be possible, but long-term alliances are unlikely. Instability is further promoted by the fact that such alliances provide opportunities for "free riders," who remain outside the alliance but benefit from its activities nonetheless.[166] Even members of the alliance are sometimes able to profit from strategic behavior by defecting to another alliance when the right issue comes along.

In none of these roles does religion serve to shape public policy. Indeed, by treating individual preferences as outside the scope of political analysis, the liberal political tradition excludes religion from public life. It then seeks a theoretical expression for what it has done. The most obvious expression is a theory of strict separation of church and state. The liberal tradition's long-standing and still deeply felt attraction to strict separationist theories demonstrates that such theories fit well with liberal political theory. The reduction and marginality principles together provide a milder expression of the liberal political view: Religion is still largely private, and its intrusion into the public sphere is small and unimportant.

In contrast to these individualist-oriented means of expressing religious belief, however, it is clear that *non*-individualist values are implicit in religious activities. This is illustrated in two ways. The first involves the free rider problem that arises in alliances. The alliance frequently tries to solve the problem by providing its members with benefits other than influence on public policy. Among such selective benefits are the promotion of values inherent in the fact of creating an alliance; the members come to value the alliance not because it allows individual preferences to shape public policy more effectively, but because it allows the experience of solidarity, of mutual action itself.[167] However, at this point the individualist predicates of liberal political theory come under stress. Instead of allowing the more effective expression of exogenously determined individual preferences, intermediate institutions such as churches now begin to shape those preferences. Further, the preferences that take shape are necessarily preferences for nonindividualist experiences.

The second illustration of how nonindividualist values are implicit in religious activities is found in Justice White's argument in *Widmar*

---

166. *See* M. Olson, The Logic of Collective Action (1971).

167. *See* Garet, *Communality and Existence: The Rights of Groups*, 56 S. Calif. L. Rev. 1001, 1009 (1983) ("groups are possibile sites for religious experience").

v. Vincent.[168] There he sought to distinguish worship from speech on the ground that worship is directed within the community of believers, while speech is directed outside. This distinction indicates that rituals take on their meaning because they occur within an intermediate institution. Vis-a-vis the wider society, rituals are a communal activity shared among the believers. They are necessarily not individualist but communal.[169]

A major problem with the liberal tradition's treatment of religion, therefore, is that it cannot account for the separate identification of religion in the first amendment without recognizing the nonindividualist values that are implicit in religious activities. When the liberal tradition takes religion seriously, the result subverts the individualist premises of the very theory into which religion is supposed to fit.[170] Yet by distinguishing between religion and other forms of belief, the first amendment itself contains a nonindividualist principle.[171] It thus signals that the Constitution is not an entirely individualist document. The Constitution's communitarian commitments are an implicit appeal to a tradition of civic republicanism that was more vibrant in the framers' world than it is in ours.[172] This helps explain the incoherence in the

---

168.   454 U.S. 263 (1981); *see supra* notes 92-96 and accompanying text.

169.   For definitions of religion that point in this direction, see Boyan, *Defining Religion in Operational and Institutional Terms*, 116 U. PA. L. REV. 479 (1968); Dodge, *supra* note 10; Note, *Toward a Constitutional Definition of Religion*, 91 HARV. L. REV. 1056 (1978).

170.   The reduction and marginality principles deny to believers that their religious beliefs are different in kind from their own political ones. For definitions suggesting that religious beliefs are not merely "deeper" or about "more fundamental" things than political ones, see Note, *The Sacred and the Profane: A First Amendment Definition of Religion*, 61 TEX. L. REV. 139 (1982); Choper, *supra* note 58, at 581-82. As has been frequently noted, this definition in fact does not distinguish religion from some kinds of political belief, such as political beliefs grounded in comprehensive social theories. *See* Clark, *supra* note 10, at 339-43. The usual example is Marxism and associated bodies of political thought. Another example is liberalism itself, which asks us to take "on faith" a set of assumptions about human nature and capacity. The most dramatic illustration is R. NOZICK, ANARCHY, STATE, AND UTOPIA at ix (1974) (asserting without defense anywhere in the book that "[i]ndividuals have rights, and there are things no person or group may do to them [without violating their rights]."). For a general critique of liberalism on the ground that we need not take its view of human nature, see M. SANDEL, LIBERALISM AND THE LIMITS OF JUSTICE (1982).

171.   *See* Garet, *supra* note 167, at 1013 (need to recognize "a group face of value").

172.   If my argument is correct, we should be able to discover analogous tensions in the law of other intermediate institutions such as families and education. I believe that such tensions can be found. For examples, see Burt, *The Burger Court and the Family*, in THE BURGER COURT: THE COUNTER-REVOLUTION THAT WASN'T 92 (V. Blasi ed. 1983) (families); Frug, *The City As A Legal Concept*, 93 HARV. L. REV. 1059 (1980) (cities and federalism); Note, *Peaceful Labor Picketing and the First Amendment*, 82 COLUM. L. REV. 1469 (1982) (labor unions and picketing); Note, *Labor Picketing and Commercial Speech: Free Enterprise Values in the Doctrine of*

constitutional law of religion: It is founded on a tradition that we no longer fully understand.[173]

B. The Republican Tradition

At the time of the framing, two visions of the social order competed for intellectual dominance. The liberal tradition discussed above was powerful then, and has become even more so. The alternative vision was drawn from the tradition of civic republicanism.[174] That tradition rejected the individualism of liberal political theory. Without denying the importance of a private sphere, the republican tradition insisted that the public sphere consisted of more than the aggregation of exogenously determined and unanalyzable preferences. It also consisted of a search for public policy to advance what citizens believed was the public good. The citizenry was to learn from its institutions that the public good was something other than the aggregation of private preferences. One element of a republican public policy, therefore, was concern that the institutions of social life shape citizens who had an acceptable balance of public-regarding and private-regarding motivations.

Although religious institutions sit uneasily in the liberal tradition, they fit quite comfortably into the republican one. Historically, the proponents of republicanism sought to preserve some of the traditional intermediate institutions against the encroachment of liberal ones. In that sense they were conservatives, although they acknowledged to varying degrees that the changes induced by liberalism were inevitable and, if not carried too far, valuable. As conservatives, republicans understood the role of religion in stabilizing the social order.[175]

Religious institutions fit into the republican tradition for conceptual as well as historical reasons. Citizens must acquire civic responsibility and a concern for the public interest somewhere; if citizens enter the political arena without the appropriate balance of public and pri-

---

Free Speech, 91 YALE L.J. 938 (1982) (same).

173. A full discussion of the role of community as a predicate for the coherence of constitutional law would require a treatment of several topics in free speech: symbolic speech, the implications of the statement in Cohen v. California, 403 U.S. 15, 25 (1971), that "one man's vulgarity is another man's lyric;" and the use of aesopian, metaphoric language to convey implicit political messages. But that discussion is beyond the scope of this article.

174. This account draws on the following: J. POCOCK, THE MACHIAVELLIAN MOMENT (1975); C. ROBBINS, THE EIGHTEENTH-CENTURY COMMONWEALTHMAN (1959); G. WILLS, EXPLAINING AMERICA: THE FEDERALIST (1981); G. WOOD, THE CREATION OF THE AMERICAN REPUBLIC 1776-1787 (1969).

175. Liberals understood this role too, which is why they incorporated into their efforts a challenge to religion. *See supra* text accompanying notes 159-160.

vate concerns, they may misuse public power to advance merely private interests. Intermediate institutions provide a sound location for the inculcation of the appropriate balance of values. As communal organizations in which members are interdependent, giving life to the institution itself, intermediate institutions can provide the experience of acting for the common good. With that experience, members can enter the political arena knowing that they should pursue not only their private interests, but the public interest as well.

The constitutional law of religion is confused because the republican tradition is far less available to us than it was to the framers.[176] I do not mean to suggest that we could rationalize the law of religion by imagining what a revitalized republicanism would do with religion. The republican tradition, as a conservative tradition, insisted on the historicity of institutions and public policy. That very insistence makes it impossible to impose on today's society solutions drawn from a less-than-vital, indeed to some extent imaginary, tradition. In addition, the republican tradition claims that its vision of the polity is completely integrated with its vision of the social order. Citizens in the republican society would have sufficient material wealth to ensure their independence from anyone who might seek to control their actions as citizens. They would be sensitive to the need to maintain a proper balance between public and private goals, and would develop that sensitivity through a system of civic education. The conservative branch of republican thought assumed that the necessary equality in material and intellectual capacity could be accomplished only if the polity were restricted. The democratic revolutions of the eighteenth and nineteenth century have made it impossible to realize the republican vision in its conservative form. Instead, they require that the republic vision be revitalized by large transformations in the social order.

As a starting point for such transformation, Arthur Sutherland's comment on *Engel v. Vitale*[177] suggests one possible view of the relationship between republicanism and the religion clauses. In *Engel*, the Supreme Court held unconstitutional the practice of requiring the recitation in public schools of a "nondenominational" prayer composed by

---

176. L. GOODWYN, DEMOCRATIC PROMISE: THE POPULIST MOMENT IN AMERICA (1976), argues that the populist movement in the late 19th century was an effort to revitalize the republican tradition. A. BRINKLEY, VOICES OF PROTEST (1982), argues that support for Huey Long and Father Coughlin during the 1930s stemmed from a similar desire to revitalize the tradition. Brinkley's argument seems more strained than Goodwyn's, and in any event both arguments attempt to locate the republican tradition in movements that ended in failure.

177. 370 U.S. 421 (1962).

a state agency.[178] As did other commentators,[179] Sutherland thought the case trivial.[180] But his article opens the way to a more subtle understanding of the religion clauses. Sutherland laid the groundwork for this new understanding in his discussion of an intricate question of standing. Because *Engel* involved no coercion of students and, at most, only minor expenditures of public money to support the prayer, it was difficult to discern the deprivation of liberty or property necessary to fit the case within the fourteenth amendment.[181] However, Sutherland recognized that the law of standing was both technical and flexible enough to accommodate the case. Rather than criticizing the Court for finding standing, he used the difficulties as a basis for suggesting that the Court should have exercised a sound discretion to avoid deciding the case.[182]

Sutherland then concluded his article by proposing a brilliant generalization of the question of discretion. Drawing on his experience as a member of a small town's school board, he said that the school board in *Engel* might have solved the problem had it deliberated seriously about the religious contention caused by its use of the prayer and decided to forgo the practice as a matter of discretion, not of constitutional command.[183] The symmetrical point of view is suggested by *Lynch v. Donnelly*:[184] Those offended by the prayer might similarly have exercised a wise discretion to forgo the constitutional challenge they were, in a strict sense, entitled to bring.

In suggesting a reliance on mutual forbearance, rather than the Constitution, as the basis for resolving issues concerning the relationship between government and religion, Sutherland drew on the tradition of civic republicanism.[185] One consequence of a vital republicanism

---

178. *Id.* at 433.

179. *See, e.g.*, Brown, *Quis Custodiet Ispos Custodes?—The School-Prayer Cases*, 1963 SUP. CT. REV. 1, 5-7; Kurland, *The Regents' Prayer Case: "Full of Sound and Fury, Signifying . . ."*, 1962 SUP. CT. REV. 1, 19-22. The case generated great public controversy. *See* Elifson & Hadaway, *Prayer in Public Schools: When Church and State Collide*, 49 PUB. OP. Q. 317 (1985) (reviewing opinion surveys from 1974 and 1980); Way, *Survey Research on Judicial Decisions: The Prayer and Bible Reading Cases*, 21 W. POL. Q. 189 (1968).

180. Sutherland, *Establishment According to* Engel, 76 HARV. L. REV. 25 (1962).

181. *Id.* at 41. *See* Doremus v. Board of Educ., 342 U.S. 429 (1952) (suggesting that more than de minimis expenditures are required to support standing to raise establishment clause claims). *Engel* was decided before Flast v. Cohen, 392 U.S. 83 (1968), temporarily restructured the law of establishment clause standing.

182. Sutherland, *supra* note 180, at 39-45.

183. *Id.* at 52.

184. 465 U.S. 668 (1984); *see supra* notes 141-49 and accompanying text.

185. Communitarian premises can be found elsewhere in the Constitution. I find Madison's

might well be a culture where mutual forbearance prevails. Citizens, in this type of culture, would understand that the public policy was intended to advance the public good. They would recognize that civic actions that generated intense hostility would be unlikely to advance the public good, so they would forbear from taking such actions. These citizens would also see that civic actions designed to promote intensely held values would be likely to advance the public good—even if some individuals thought those actions unwise or even troublesome on grounds of conscience—so they would then forbear from challenging such actions. Such a culture of mutual forbearance would result in a pattern of public actions that superficially resembles the current marginality of religion in public life. But here marginality would not be a principle; rather, it would be a characteristic that citizens would *choose* to give to their public life. Sutherland was exactly right to appeal to discretion rather than to the law of standing as a way to avoid questions of religion and the law.

CONCLUSION

I have argued that the Supreme Court's decisions in religion cases, and commentators' efforts to explain the religion cases, are unsatisfying. As doctrines or theories, the approaches we are offered have neither the coherence nor the normative appeal that we seek from constitutional law. I have also argued that these difficulties occur because we must appreciate the intellectual power of the republican tradition to make sense of the religion clauses, and that our society has developed in ways that make the republican tradition unavailable to us. But invoking the republican tradition to the religious clauses is useful even though the tradition is no longer vital and cannot be made vital without large changes in our social order. It demonstrates that what might otherwise seem to be utopian yearnings to establish a society with a different balance between individualism and community are yearnings that are in fact grounded in the Constitution we have today.

---

defense of federalism in THE FEDERALIST Nos. 45 and 46 (J. Madison) perhaps the most dramatic reliance on those premises in the constitutional tradition. *See also* G. WILLS, *supra* note 174.

[9]

Duke Law Journal

VOLUME 1987   DECEMBER   NUMBER 6

EVOLUTIONISM, CREATIONISM, AND TREATING RELIGION AS A HOBBY

STEPHEN L. CARTER*

Contemporary liberalism faces no greater dilemma than deciding how to deal with the resurgence of religious belief. On the one hand, liberals cherish religion, as they cherish all matters of private conscience, and liberal theory holds that the state should do nothing to discourage free religious choice. At the same time, contemporary liberals are coming to view any religious element in public moral discourse as a tool of the radical right for the reshaping of American society, and that reshaping is something liberals want very much to discourage.

In truth, liberal politics has always been uncomfortable with religious fervor. If liberals cheered the clerics who marched against segregation and the Vietnam War, it was only because the causes were considered just—not because the clerics were devout. Nowadays, people who bring religion into the making of public policy come more frequently from the right, and the liberal response all too often is to dismiss them as fanatics. Even the religious left is sometimes offended by the mainstream liberal tendency to mock religious belief. Not long ago, the magazine *Sojourners*—published by politically liberal Christian evangelicals—found itself in the unaccustomed position of defending the evangel-

---

* Professor of Law, Yale University. A nearly identical version of this essay was delivered at the Third Annual Duke Law Journal Lecture on February 26, 1987. For publication, I have added a sprinkling of footnotes (most of them citations), clarifed a few points that I learned from the question-and-answer session had not been put as precisely as they might have, and reintroduced a brief discussion, deleted at the podium, of the work of Mark Yudof and Bruce Ackerman. I have also inserted three brief references to the Supreme Court's decision in Edwards v. Aguillard, 107 S. Ct. 2573 (1987), which was handed down after my delivery of the Lecture. Comments and criticism following the Lecture led into interesting areas that deserve exploration, and I am particularly grateful for insightful suggestions and other assistance from Enola Aird, Walter Dellinger, Bernard Dushman, Ronald Feenstra, Stanley Fish, Karen Porter, and Jennifer Weidman. Nevertheless, because the essay originated as a lecture, I have elected not to make substantive changes for publication.

ist Pat Robertson against secular liberals who, the magazine sighed, "see[m] to consider Robertson a dangerous Neanderthal because he happens to believe that God can heal diseases."[1] The point is that the editors of *Sojourners,* who are no great admirers of the Reverend Robertson, also believe that God can cure disease. So do tens of millions of Americans. Conservativism, with its deep emphasis on the immutability of certain traditional values, is relatively comfortable with the idea that the values it preserves may have a source beyond the arbitrary moral judgments of fallible humanity. Liberalism, steeped as it is in skepticism, rationalism and tolerance, unfortunately has little idea of how to cope with the millions of people who embrace so absurd a notion. The answer up to now has been to repeat, like a catechism, the language of the Supreme Court in *School District of Abington Township v. Schempp:*[2] "the command of the First Amendment [is] that the Government maintain strict neutrality, neither aiding nor opposing religion."

In this essay, I will suggest that the liberal response—the notion that the government must be "neutral" with respect to religion—bespeaks an underlying uncertainty about, or perhaps even a fear of, the role that religious belief might play in the dialogue that determines public policy. There are many battlegrounds on which liberal politics and religious belief carry on their struggle—prayer in the public schools, reproductive freedom, pornography, and sexual choice are just a handful of examples. But no current controversy poses the issue in quite so subtle and troubling a way as the fight by some states to require students in their public schools to study so-called scientific creationism alongside evolution theory in the biology classroom. By taking the scientific creationism debate as my example, I hope to expose the contradictions at the heart of the liberal theory of neutrality toward religion. In particular, I propose that in its stated zeal to cherish religious belief under the protective mantle of "neutrality," liberalism is really derogating religious belief in favor of other, more "rational" methods of understanding the world. The great risk lying a bit further down this path is that religion, far from being cherished, will be diminished, and that religious belief will ultimately become a kind of hobby: something so private that it is as irrelevant to public life as the building of model airplanes.

I do not so much pass judgment on these consequences as insist that liberals ought to be aware of them, for a theory of law or politics that is afraid to analyze its own consequences is a theory with no right to sur-

---

1. Collum, *The Kingdom and the Power,* Sojourners, Nov. 1986, at 4; *cf.* Shriver, *What Can Liberals and Evangelicals Teach Each Other?,* 104 Chris. Cent. 687, 688 (1987) (arguing that liberal Christians should be less skeptical of beliefs of evangelical Christians).
2. 374 U.S. 203, 225 (1963).

vive. Thus, as I dissect the scientific creationism controversy and analyze the liberal response, my enterprise is not to argue against the liberal theory of religion (for it has much to recommend it), but to count its costs.[3] I am thus less interested in undertaking concrete constitutional analysis than in exploring the instincts that form the background for the widespread insistence, recently ratified by the Supreme Court as constitutional dogma,[4] that the first amendment must be read to prohibit the teaching of scientific creationism. To begin my exploration I will consider the problem of scientific creationism itself, before drawing back to consider what the controversy teaches about liberal law and politics.

I. THE CREATION SCIENCE CONUNDRUM

What we have come to call creation science or creationism or, the term that I use here, scientific creationism, is less a clear theory than a reaction to a theory. Scientific creationism, when sketched without reference to the Bible, is defined primarily through its disagreements with both classical Darwinian evolutionary theory and modern gene-based evolutionary theory. Evolutionists posit an earth billions of years old in which higher forms of life evolved from lower, and lower forms of life quite likely evolved from the inanimate, a world in which mutation is beneficial and new species are sometimes created. Creationists posit instead a much younger world in which life in nearly all of its forms came upon the world quite suddenly, a world in which mutation is harmful, and in which no important new species appear.[5] I describe the creationist theory as a reaction more than a theory because the scientific evidence the creationists put forth, while occasionally calling into question the conclusions of evolutionists, only rarely does anything to bolster the claims of creationism.[6]

---

3. Mine is not, of course, the first effort in this direction, and much of the work is recent. *See, e.g.,* McConnell, *Accommodation of Religion,* 1985 SUP. CT. REV. 1 (arguing that pluralism and liberty should define church and state relationship); Tushnet, *The Constitution of Religion,* 18 CONN. L. REV. 701 (1986) (arguing that republican tradition must play important role in religion clause interpretation).

4. *See* Edwards v. Aguillard, 107 S. Ct. 2573 (1987) (holding Louisiana Balanced Treatment for Creation-Science and Evolution-Science in Public Instruction Act, which forbids teaching of evolution without accompanying instruction in creation science, invalid under establishment clause).

5. Henry Morris, in an all-too-brief but still interesting table, has laid out many of these differences. H. MORRIS, SCIENTIFIC CREATIONISM 13 (public school ed. 1974); *see also* P. KITCHER, ABUSING SCIENCE: THE CASE AGAINST CREATIONISM 41 (1982) (same table); Cracraft, *The Scientific Response to Creationism,* in CREATIONISM, SCIENCE, AND THE LAW: THE ARKANSAS CASE 138 (M. La Follette ed. 1983) (attacking creationism's central "scientific" assertions).

6. A detailed but critical recounting of much of the evidence on which creationists rely is in P. KITCHER, *supra* note 5, at 30-44, 55-123. A more sympathetic assessment of the evidence against evolution, by a critic of creationism, is G.R. TAYLOR, THE GREAT EVOLUTION MYSTERY (1983). An account by a prominent creationist of the case against evolution is D. GISH, EVOLUTION? THE

Although creationists are quick to point out that many of those who support their view of the origin of earth and of life hold advanced degrees in the sciences,[7] it would, I suspect, be an error to suppose that many creationists came to their views by a careful study of scientific evidence. The liberal critic may be right to say that creationism is bad science. But why should that issue be the crucial one? Creationists are not irrational merely because they are unscientific. Creationism was not created from thin air; creation theory developed as a consequence of the preferred hermeneutical method of many Christian fundamentalists for understanding the world. This hermeneutical approach is best expressed by the combination of the following propositions drawn from the Articles of Affirmation and Denial adopted in 1982 by the International Council on Biblical Inerrancy: (1) "the normative authority of Holy Scripture is the authority of God Himself"; (2) "the Bible expresses God's truth in propositional statements, and . . . biblical truth is both objective and absolute"; (3) "since God is the author of all truth, all truths, biblical and extrabiblical, are consistent and cohere, and . . . the Bible speaks truth when it touches on matters pertaining to nature, history, or anything else"; and (4) "Genesis 1-11 is factual, as is the rest of the book."[8]

Critics of scientific creationism may doubt the validity of these propositions, but there is hardly any room for doubt that those who profess them are sincere. And once the adherent of this literalist hermeneutic states these propositions, what chance is there that the theory of evolution is correct? Virtually none. Evolution is just a theory, scientific creationists insist, and must, as a theory, be open to challenge. And challenge it they do, pointing to mountains of exceptions and inexplicable transitions.[9] To the Biblical literalist, however, the most important evidence against evolution theory is not the complexity of the fossil record or the troubling matter of falsification, but the beginning of the Book

---

Fossils Say No! (public school ed. 1978). There is, of course, a considerable risk in arguing from a gap in the evidence to a certainty that a theory is wrong, "because the frontiers of knowledge often move quite rapidly." Consequently, "[i]t never pays to base a philosophical position on what scientists do not know." J. Trefil, The Moment of Creation: Big Bang Physics From Before the First Millisecond to the Present Universe 178 (1983).

7. See Note, *Freedom of Religion and Science Instruction in Public Schools*, 87 Yale L.J. 515, 517 n.13, 555 n.198 (1978). This note was authored by Wendell Bird, then a law student, who has subsequently become the most important creationist legal theorist. He argued and lost Edwards v. Aguillard, 107 S. Ct. 2573 (1987), in the Supreme Court of the United States.

8. *The Chicago Statement on Biblical Hermeneutics*, reprinted in A Guide to Contemporary Hermeneutics: Major Trends in Biblical Interpretation 21, 22-25 (D. McKim ed. 1986).

9. See generally D. Gish, supra note 6 (arguing that fossil record does not support major claims of evolutionary theory); H. Morris, supra note 5 (arguing that evolutionary change is too slow to be reasonable and occurrence of small variations fails to prove essential change into highe life form).

of Genesis, comprising, as one creationist has written, "eleven chapters of straightforward Bible history which cannot be reinterpreted in any satisfactory way."[10]

I emphasize these points because I believe that critics often overlook that there is a nontrivial hermeneutic and a rational application of it behind the creationist rejection of evolutionary theory.[11] The creationist position is no mindless assault on modernism in general or on secular science in particular, although obviously it contains elements of hostility to both. Nor do the "equal time" statutes necessarily represent officially authorized proselytizing. It is something of a commonplace in liberal theory to treat the parental attempts to control the school curriculum as though the parents are trying to impose their own religious beliefs on others, but I very much doubt that this vision is a realistic one. More likely, the parents are frightened of the conflict between religious authority on the one hand, and the authority of secular society—as represented by the schools—on the other.

These parents, very devout and very worried, are trying to protect the core of their own beliefs. It is not that the parents want the public schools to proselytize in their favor; it is rather that they do not want the schools to press their own children to reject what the parents believe by calling into question a central article of their faith. The response of the Christian fundamentalist to evolutionary theory may thus be more consistently viewed as a reaction to a fear of indoctrination: religion demands one intellectual position, and the state seeks to command another. Liberalism is curiously intolerant of what certainly may be viewed as a classic case of conscience interposed before the authority of the state. Nor have the consciences of the protestors been formed without any thought. They understand quite well that the hermeneutic they have chosen has interpretive implications, not just for the Bible, but for the entire natural world, and devout literalists understand and accept them. The creationist parents are not a superstitious rabble. They are independent thinkers who insist on a right to their own means for seeking knowledge of the world, and they deny the right of the state to tell their children that their worldview is wrong.

On this vision, a public school curriculum perceived as secular and modernist is a grave and obvious threat to the efforts of parents to raise their children in their religious belief with its hermeneutical implications.

---

10. D. WATSON, THE GREAT BRAIN ROBBERY 46 (1976).

11. Christian fundamentalists, in fact, insist that their faith itself is based on reason, rejecting both the modern liberal notion that an unexplained "leap of faith" is needed to explain religious belief, and the popular understanding of a sharp separation between the task of religion and the task of science. *See* H. COX, RELIGION IN THE SECULAR CITY 53-59 (1984).

Thus, the question that moves the debate—who shall control the education of children?—is starkly posed. Liberalism may insist that the public schools should be neutral on questions of religious belief, but the parents will no doubt protest that this insistence is simply window dressing for something more sinister. What the schools are offering, the parents will charge, is not a neutral curriculum, but one that can only call into question—or place into ridicule—their most cherished religious beliefs. For those whose Biblical hermeneutic insists on literalism and inerrancy, the tension between a disdainful science and an unchallengeable core belief is plain.

One early response to the tension was the effort to ban the teaching of Darwinian evolution. Many have forgotten that in the *Scopes* case[12] this ban was justified not as a means of protecting a particular religious view from contradiction, but rather as a way of easing the move toward modernization of the science curriculum in the public schools of Tennessee. In affirming the conviction of Mr. Scopes for teaching evolution theory, the state supreme court held that the legislature could make the judgment that popular prejudice would make a sophisticated science curriculum impossible unless, at least for the short term, the curriculum omitted all discussion of the origin of humanity.[13] This justification might have been a smokescreen, but if sincere, it was neither foolish nor venal. It might even represent a compromise between the demands of some citizens for a modern science course for their children, and the insistence of others that the state not trivialize their core religious beliefs.

I do not mean this to be taken as a call to ban the teaching of evolution, but only as a suggestion that the ban might, in some set of historical circumstances, have represented wise policy. Of course, historical circumstances may change, and by the time the Supreme Court, in *Epperson v. Arkansas*,[14] brushed aside a ban on the teaching of evolution as a plain violation of the establishment clause, the statutes still on the books in many states apparently were not being enforced. The tension, however, had not died. With the political rebirth of the Christian fundamentalist movement beginning in the mid-seventies, the objection of parents to what their schools were teaching took on a new form, driven by a new insight: in a political world emphasizing rationality and pluralism, the effort of parents to protect their children from what they considered antireligious indoctrination by the state would have to present itself as both rational and pluralistic. By calling their interpretive conclusions "sci-

---

12. *Scopes v. State,* 154 Tenn. 105, 117-18, 289 S.W. 363, 366 (1927).
13. *Id.*
14. 393 U.S. 97, 107-09 (1968).

ence," the parents chose a fresh face that would, they hoped, survive constitutional scrutiny.

The courts, however, have viewed this fresh face as a subterfuge. The Supreme Court, in *Edwards v. Aguillard,* [15] has rejected entirely the effort to make creation theory a part of the science curriculum, but the judicial hostility predates *Edwards.* Certainly, there was little sympathy in the forceful opinion of Judge Overton in *McLean v. Arkansas Board of Education,* [16] the first federal court case dealing with the merits of a facially neutral statute requiring equal classroom time for evolution and creation. The court faced the difficulty of adapting the Supreme Court's establishment clause precedents to a situation that the Justices who wrote them could never have envisioned: the state's endorsement of a theory whose proponents base their particular version of truth on their religious beliefs.

I will not in these brief remarks analyze the court's opinion in detail, but there is one point that does bear mention, because it illustrates the contradiction within liberal constitutional doctrine on religious belief. According to the Supreme Court, one requirement of the establishment clause is that a statute's "primary effect must be one that neither advances nor inhibits religion." [17] In *McLean,* the court found that the equal time statute failed this test, and the analysis on this point is intriguing: "The facts that creation science is inspired by the Book of Genesis and that Section 4(a) [of the Act] is consistent with a literal interpretation of Genesis," the judge argued, "leave no doubt that a major effect of the Act is the advancement of particular religious beliefs." [18]

The conclusion may well be right, but the analysis is surely imprecise. To see why, one may suppose that Albert Einstein had stated publicly that his theories of general and special relativity were "inspired" by his musings on some sacred text. Suppose further that the state mandated the teaching of his theories through a statute that was "consistent with a literal interpretation" of his sacred text. These are not reasons to refuse to teach in school what he has discovered, unless one is prepared to assert what I assume the court in *McLean* would not—that nothing consistent with any religious belief may be taught.

Judge Overton did not rest his opinion only on the consistency of scientific creationism and a particular religious belief; he also relied on expert testimony to conclude that scientific creationism could not pass

---

15. 107 S. Ct. 2573 (1987).

16. 529 F. Supp. 1255 (E.D. Ark. 1982), *aff'd,* 723 F.2d 45 (8th Cir. 1983).

17. Lemon v. Kurtzman, 403 U.S. 602, 612 (1971) (citation omitted).

18. 529 F. Supp. at 1266.

the establishment clause test because *it was not science.*[19] I will not labor this point, which has been the subject of much comment elsewhere,[20] except to suggest that while I am sure that such was never Judge Overton's intention, the establishment of a test of this nature risks creating a new interpretive rule in which the operative question is not whether a curriculum furthers religion, but whether it masquerades as science when it is not. It is as though the command of the first amendment is not to cherish religion, but to cherish science.[21]

From the beginning, the constitutional case against creationism seemed bound up inextricably with the scientific case against it. This seems to me a profoundly mistaken course. A statute simply cannot be said to further religion on the ground that a majority of scientists do not believe that it furthers science. So what if the "scientific" case for creationism is appallingly shoddy and naive? What has this to do with constitutionality?

We live in a world in which epistemology may sometimes reflect religious belief—a world in which religious belief may move people to decide, quite sincerely, whether to accept or reject both moral and factual propositions. Consequently, there is little except the conflict with science to distinguish religiously motivated legislation requiring the teaching of creation theory from religiously motivated legislation to implement the Biblical injunction "Thou shalt do no murder"—or religiously motivated legislation in response to the Roman Catholic bishops' call for a more equitable sharing of the nation's wealth. A prohibition of murder, like a forced redistribution of wealth, might be religiously motivated; but only the teaching of creationism conflicts with natural science.

I do not mean by any of this to suggest that *McLean* was wrongly decided, but rather to raise the question of why liberalism insists—as it surely does—that the decisions in *McLean* and in *Edwards* are right. Liberals are most comfortable, I suspect, treating the question as a purely constitutional one, without deep implications for liberal theory or religious belief. But reducing the problem to one of constitutional interpretation slips around the heart of the matter without ever piercing through. For the underlying question remains: why is it that contemporary liber-

---

19. *See id.* at 1267-72.

20. *See, e.g.,* Laudan, *Commentary on Ruse: Science at the Bar—Causes for Concern,* in CREATIONISM, SCIENCE, AND THE LAW: THE ARKANSAS CASE, *supra* note 5, at 161-66 (complaining that prohibiting creationism because it is unscientific "leaves many loopholes for the creationists to exploit").

21. Steven Goldberg has deduced from the Constitution's language and history what he calls the "implied science clause," which holds that "Congress may legislate the establishment of science, but shall not prohibit the free exercise of scientific speech." Goldberg, *The Constitutional Status of American Science,* 1979 U. ILL. L.F. 1, 1.

alism, which proclaims the freedom of individual conscience, values conscience less when an individual chooses to discover the world through faith rather than through reason? What is it about religious belief that liberalism so fears?

II. LIBERALISM AND RELIGION

Let's go back a step: the rule prohibiting religiously motivated instruction in public school classrooms is a commonplace of liberal, political, moral, and constitutional dialogue. It is supported by the charming notion that autonomous individuals have the right to make up their own minds about which religious belief to accept, or whether to accept any at all, and that the state may not, through placing its imprimatur on one set of religious beliefs, implicitly cast doubt on the others. Liberalism recites its catechism: the government must "maintain strict neutrality."

"Neutrality" has become a political and constitutional buzzword, a term—so constitutional theorists tell us—embodying the twin requirements that the government neither encourage one religious belief nor discourage another. This vision of the sort of freedom from orthodoxy that the Constitution protects, and the kind of imposition of belief that it forbids, possesses so obvious an appeal that it would be a shame to let it go untested.[22] But in order to test the neutrality principle, it is necessary first to understand why liberalism is so troubled by public moral discourse rooted in religious belief.

I will begin by disposing of one relatively uninteresting response. I have in mind the argument that the neutrality principle fosters religious pluralism. Of course it does so at its core, by prohibiting the imposition of someone's religious ritual or belief on someone else. But the proposition that the state must be neutral in order to foster plurality of religious belief has no bearing on the question of whether the state can ever act on the basis of the religious motivation of legislators or constituents. In a nation that prides itself on cherishing religious freedom, it is something of a puzzle that a Communist or a Republican may try to have his worldview reflected in the nation's law, but a religionist cannot; that one whose basic tool for understanding the world is empiricism may seek to have her discoveries taught in the schools, but one whose basic tool is Scripture cannot; that one whose conscience moves him to doubt the validity of the social science curriculum may move to have it changed, but

---

22. A wave of recent scholarship has already tested this neutrality principle, and found it wanting. *See, e.g.,* McConnell, *supra* note 3, at 8-13 (asserting that first amendment permits government action to facilitate religious liberty without regard to nonreligious activities); *cf.* Edwards v. Aguillard, 107 S. Ct. 2573, 2595 (1987) (Scalia, J., dissenting) (arguing that state must sometimes act affirmatively to remove threats to religious liberty).

986   *DUKE LAW JOURNAL*   [Vol. 1987:977

one whose religious conviction moves her to doubt the validity of the natural science curriculum may not. If a statute prohibits pornography, it is not immediately clear why the judgment on its constitutionality should turn on whether the legislators said "This is morally necessary to help end the degradation and oppression of women" or "This is morally necessary to please our God." The statute would in either case have the same effect on purveyors of pornography. Neither legislative justification, moreover, would have any effect on the ability of all citizens to pursue their own religious beliefs. If the statute itself inhibited religious belief, then neither of these justifications might be sufficient to save it. In short, something more than the desire to foster religious pluralism is needed to explain why liberalism so fears religious motivation.

The best explanation for the fear of public action motivated by religious belief rests on the reliance of liberalism on dialogue and rationality as indispensable components of its political theory, and the often unstated premise of many liberal theorists that reasoning and religious belief are mutually exclusive means for understanding the world.

The primacy of reason has been the theme of any number of liberal critiques of society in the past few years. Mark Yudof, for example, not long ago brought forth a book-length analysis of the ways in which officially sanctioned speech can become officially sanctioned indoctrination, and of possible paths by which the legal system can help citizens to resist.[23] But why does any of this matter? Because, Professor Yudof explains, "The ideology of democratic government posits the existence of autonomous citizens who make informed and intelligent judgments about government policies, free of a state preceptorship that substantially impedes individual choice and consent by selective transmission of information."[24] People need information so that they can make up their minds in a manner that is "informed" and "intelligent"—in other words, rational.

A similar understanding must move Bruce Ackerman, who has devoted a book to demonstrating a conception of liberalism resting on dialogue among citizens.[25] What matters most in the liberal state, Professor Ackerman insists, is not the efficacy with which its government structure aggregates private preferences into policy, but rather the validity—as demonstrated in conversation—of the reasoning that undergirds the policy. Nor will just any conversation do: in order to qualify as *liberal* conversation, the dialogue must be governed by concepts of neutrality

---

    23. M. YUDOF, WHEN GOVERNMENT SPEAKS: POLITICS, LAW, AND GOVERNMENT EXPRESSION IN AMERICA (1983).
    24. *Id.* at 32.
    25. B. ACKERMAN, SOCIAL JUSTICE IN THE LIBERAL STATE (1980).

and rationality.[26]

These and other theories share in common a vision that an earlier generation of liberal theorists perhaps left ambiguous: that the key to liberalism is dialectic, and that intelligent, informed citizens can engage in rational conversations and reach rational results. By necessary implication, it follows that state action that interferes with this dialogue is impermissible.[27]

Liberals display a single-minded fanaticism in upholding the right to freedom of speech (even when the speech might lead to destruction of their ideals) because speaking—which always implies the possibility of convincing others—is at the heart of liberal politics. The liberal is essentially an optimist, a believer in the underlying goodness of humanity. The liberal believes in persuasion: we can persuade the hostage-takers that their efforts are counterproductive, we can persuade the Soviet Union to abandon its affection for expensive weapons, we can persuade the segregationist to let a black family live next door, we can persuade the South Africans to move toward pluralism, we can persuade everyone who is wrong to do what is right. The modern liberal, in short, is essentially a Kantian: the liberal believes that reason is the most important human faculty, and that amenability to reason is the trait that distinguishes humans from the rest of creation.

---

26. *Id.* at 11-12, 34-45.

27. Interestingly, both Professor Ackerman and Professor Yudof are quick to dismiss religious dialogue, although they are concerned with different aspects. For Professor Yudof, what is crucial is that the state not interfere, through an endorsement of a particular religious belief, with the freedom of citizens to make up their minds independent of official indoctrination. M. YUDOF, *supra* note 23, at 164-65. For Professor Ackerman, the question of what God thinks is logically irrelevant to liberal policy analysis, because it is not neutral and nonverifiable even if neutral. B. ACKERMAN, *supra* note 25, at 40-41, 280-82. Professor Yudof does not consider the possibility that religious parents and their children might see the curriculum as it now exists as an actively indoctrinating one; Professor Ackerman does not consider the sensitivity of dialectic to the preconceptions of the interlocutors, who might, for example, *know* that Genesis is true in the same way that Professor Ackerman knows that no citizen, "regardless of his conception of the good . . . is intrinsically superior to one or more of his fellow citizens." *Id.* at 11; *cf. id.* at 281 (Neutrality means that no one may claim "privileged access to the meaning of the universe."). Both these omissions illustrate a fundamental principle of contemporary hermeneutics: what you see depends a good deal on where you are standing. *See* D. HOY, THE CRITICAL CIRCLE: LITERATURE, HISTORY, AND PHILOSOPHICAL HERMENEUTICS 48-51 (1978) (arguing that psychoanalysis as a method of interpretation "is an inquiry in which the objectivity of the interpretation cannot be determined independently of the value or use of the interpretation").

I do not wish to carry my doubts about the adequacy of their treatments of religious belief too far, because a liberal analysis of religion is not the main point of what either Professor Ackerman or Professor Yudof proposes. More important is their shared image of patient, rational dialogue among citizens, and the faith that this image demonstrates in the power of reason. It is this faith that is at the center of modern liberal theory, and it is this faith that is threatened when citizens' public political posture turns on private religious belief.

Without this faith in the ability of individual humans to recreate themselves and their world through dialogue, without this trust in the power of reason to move others to action, liberalism becomes an impoverished philosophy: either a simple-minded majoritarianism, in which preferences are aggregated formally (if inefficiently) through a legislative process, and in which those who lose in that process are without recourse; or a variant of Leninism, because it has nothing behind it but an insistence on one set of values as the correct one, and a willingness to back that conviction with all the power of the state. In short, without a faith in the faculty of reason, liberalism has nothing whatever to recommend it.

This faith is reflected, for example, in David A. J. Richards's recent reformulation of the Constitution's religion clauses.[28] Because of the richness of what Professor Richards proposes, it is worth considering his analysis in some detail, both for what he has to say about the nature of liberal society, and because of the way his analysis illustrates some of the inevitable inconsistencies in the neutrality principle.

The underlying theme of the free exercise and establishment clauses, Professor Richards tell us, is "toleration" of the conclusions dictated by conscience. "[J]udgments of true belief are for good reason forbidden as the measure of universal toleration," and "comparable judgments about the acceptability of things believed should be similarly suspicious."[29] I assume Professor Richards to be putting the case that all religious belief is presumptively the result of an exercise of the faculty of moral judgment—a faculty which, in classical liberal analysis, rests on reason—and therefore dismissing the contention that some religious beliefs, because irrational, are not acceptable.

Thus, the primacy of reason and religious toleration would seem to merge nicely, and so they do in his theory, until he faces the problem of the establishment clause, or, as Professor Richards would have it, the "Antiestablishment" clause. Resting his argument here, as elsewhere, on the primacy of reason in settling matters of individual conscience, Professor Richards paraphrases Jefferson's functional justification for the establishment clause: "Since conscience is an inalienable human right, the formation and revision of conscience in accord with religious teaching must be completely disassociated from state power . . . ."[30]

So far, well and good—but look what happens when Professor Richards moves on to confront the claims of the creationists. Ever meticu-

---

28. D. RICHARDS, TOLERATION AND THE CONSTITUTION (1986).
29. *Id.* at 138.
30. *Id.* at 147.

lous, he tries, before refuting them, to state the arguments for equal time in their strongest terms. Unlike the flat prohibition on the teaching of Darwinian theory, he notes, what the creationists demand "is not a sectarian exclusion of a neutral educational good, but a more equal dialogue among points of view on scientific truth, method, and inquiry."[31] Nevertheless, he rejects the dialogue, because it "is not an intrascientific dispute relevant to the educational mission of a science curriculum."[32] Instead, he explains: "Creationist science is not science in the sense that is of interest to the educational mission of the public schools."[33] Why isn't it? Because "[i]t is not training in a neutral method of critical inquiry, expressive of our capacities of epistemic rationality, whose educational importance is training our capacities of critical rationality to follow reason wherever it leads, upsetting and challenging beliefs and preconceptions."[34] This observation is the key to the entire analysis presented by Professor Richards, and to understanding the core of the liberal objection to scientific creationism. I pause to make two points about it.

Note first the crucial assumption Professor Richards is making about the tools that are needed for life in liberal society and those that can be disregarded. "Critical rationality" is the faculty that the schools ought to promote; students should be trained to challenge "beliefs and preconceptions." One need not quarrel with this vision of what citizens will need in their lives to recognize that it is a profoundly secular one, and one that almost in so many words throws down the gauntlet before the religious. "Send us your children," the schools proclaim, "and we will send them back to challenge your most cherished beliefs."

The other problem with responding to scientific creationism by claiming that it necessarily runs counter to the need to develop the critical faculties is that the objection is probably beside the point. Quite likely it would be possible to design a creation science curriculum fitting that description—one that would help develop critical faculties.[35] Even

---

31. *Id.* at 153.
32. *Id.*
33. *Id.* at 154.
34. *Id.*
35. The Supreme Court impliedly endorsed this proposition (or at least left it open) even as it rejected scientific creationism in the form challenged in Edwards v. Aguillard: "We do not imply that a legislature could never require that scientific critiques of prevailing scientific theories be taught." 107 S. Ct. 2573, 2582 (1987). Further, the state might "validly" require classroom instruction in a "variety of scientific theories about the origins of humankind" if "done with the clear secular intent of enhancing the effectiveness of science instruction." *Id.* at 2583. This much, perhaps, Professor Richards would accept, although "enhancing the effectiveness of science instruction" was precisely the justification offered by the State of Tennessee for the ban on the teaching of Darwinian evolution tested in the *Scopes* case. *See supra* text accompanying note 13.

were that task impossible, it is difficult to imagine that Professor Richards seriously wants to ban from the public school classroom whatever does not encourage critical thinking or challenge beliefs and preconceptions. Surely very little of the public school curriculum—as taught to and as understood by students—could fit that description.[36] I recall from my own childhood being taught in a public school of the District of Columbia, as though there were no room for debate on the matter, that the slaves in the antebellum South were essentially happy and had no desire to be free. That example admittedly is anecdotal, but the scientific creationists, whatever the other inadequacies of their method, are demons at tracking down others.

Undoubtedly aware of this possibility, Professor Richards goes on to distinguish scientific creationism in a second, more interesting way. The point of scientific creationism, he contends, "is to show how its view of the truth of the Bible *could* be rendered consistent with the scientific record."[37] To permit its teaching would be to allow "distortion of a neutral educational good by a substantive conception of sectarian religious belief."[38] This, too, might be true, although it fails to consider the possibility that the legislators voting in favor of a scientific creationism curriculum *really believe,* for whatever complex set of reasons, that they are voting to offer an alternative vision of scientific truth. The scientific conclusions of the legislators might be at odds with the consensus of scientists working in the field, but if the legislators in good faith believe that they are promoting the critical faculties, in the same way that they are when offering other science courses, then it is difficult to see why Profes-

---

36. "It is not possible for educators to convey only information; for information itself, and the manner of its selection and presentation, will lead to socialization to widely accepted values." M. YUDOF, *supra* note 23, at 53. To illustrate the point, Professor Yudof quotes Bertrand Russell:

> It is not altogether true that persuasion is one thing and force is another. . . . Consider what we do to our children. We do not say to them: "Some people think the earth is round and others think it is flat; when you grow up, you can, if you like, examine the evidence and form your own conclusion." Instead of this we say: "The earth is round." By the time our children are old enough to examine the evidence, our propaganda has closed their minds, and the most persuasive arguments of the Flat Earth Society make no impression.

Id. (quoting B. RUSSELL, POWER: A NEW SOCIAL ANALYSIS 368-69 (1938)). It is not really a response to say that the Flat Earth Society deserves to be ignored; the issue is not one of truth, but of the ability of individuals to decide truth for themselves. Although children are taught critical thinking, they must be taught some axioms, too, and when they are, indoctrination occurs. That the indoctrination may be perceived by the indoctrinator as truth does not make it any less indoctrination.

37. D. RICHARDS, *supra* note 28, at 154. In support of this proposition, Professor Richards cites only the work of critics of scientific creationism. *See id.* at 154 n.199.

38. *Id.* at 154.

sor Richards ought to object.[39]

Professor Richards' test, moreover, would require the judge faced with the scientific creationism case or a similar one to continue along the path on which the court in *McLean* took the first, shaky steps: finding a definition of science, and testing the so-called science curriculum against that definition. On this approach the possible religious motivation behind the teaching of creation theory alongside evolution theory becomes less important than the issue of whether scientific creationism is or is not science. Down this metaphysical slope await all the obstacles that I have mentioned, not the least of them is one which should give Professor Richards pause: suddenly science, not conscience, holds primacy in human affairs, or at least in the supposedly neutral education of children. Scientists deserve our applause, our support, and our thanks for all the technological progress that has vastly improved our lives and for all the fresh advances we can expect in the future. But no matter how great our veneration of the scientific enterprise, its conclusions ought never serve as the critical test in constitutional interpretation.

But that path I have already criticized, so let me return for a final time to the views of Professor Richards. Toward the end of his discussion, he concludes that keeping scientific creationism out of the classroom—preventing the state from reinforcing, as Professor Richards would have it, "a substantive conception of sectarian religious belief"— is ultimately justified because of a philosophy aimed at nurturing the individual conscience in its critical rational judgments.[40] Religion, he says, is contrary to this philosophy of criticism. One may fairly dispute his claim that the philosophy he prefers "no more sanctifies the secular than it attacks the religious,"[41] but that is hardly the point. The point, I think, is that Professor Richards, reflecting the mainstream liberal objection, is in effect throwing up his hands and saying, "But one cannot rea-

---

39. As J. Thomas Cook has pointed out, even a decision to make one's self believe a thing may be reached and carried out through the faculty of reason. *See* Cook, *Deciding to Believe Without Self-Deception,* 84 J. PHIL. 441, 441 (1987). And even if the belief systems of the legislators are disliked, one may challenge the logic or the possibility of inquiring into the motivation of the legislators at all. *See* Edwards v. Aguillard, 107 S. Ct. 2573, 2605-07 (1987) (Scalia, J., dissenting). This is an old debate among constitutional scholars, and leading theorists have grappled for decades with the problem of legislative motivation. *See, e.g.,* A. BICKEL, THE LEAST DANGEROUS BRANCH 208-21 (1962) ("[I]f the . . . legislative leaders declare, not that the statute is to have this or that effect, but that one effect among many is the one that chiefly motivates them, how can that be imputed to every member of a legislative majority?"); J. ELY, DEMOCRACY AND DISTRUST 136-45 (1980) ("[I]t would be next to impossible for a court responsibly to conclude that a decision was affected by an unconstitutional motivation whenever it is possible to articulate a plausible legislative motivation for the action taken . . . ." (footnotes omitted)).

40. D. RICHARDS, *supra* note 28, at 154-55.

41. *See id.* at 155.

son with these religionists!" It is that intuition—the understanding that
religion and reason exist in tension with one another—which bottoms the
liberal discomfort with public religious argument. In the end, we come
back to the beginning: those who believe that God can heal disease *are*
dangerous primitives. They are primitive because they do not celebrate
reason as the path to knowledge of the world. They are dangerous because if they do not celebrate reason, they may not be amenable to reason, and anyone not amenable to reason is a threat to liberal society.

III. COPING WITH FAITH: RELIGION AS HOBBY

Suppose now the case which, depending on point of view, is either
the best or the worst: suppose that every member of the legislature accepts the hermeneutic of a literally inerrant Bible. Suppose that the same
legislature now examines the curriculum. The legislators are furious to
learn that only evolution theory is offered in the science classroom. The
liberal critic might say that the legislators are furious because evolution
runs counter to the teachings of their religion, but to make that the end
of the matter is simplistic. Yes, the teachings of evolutionary theory are
doubtless contrary to what the legislators hear in church and read in the
Bible, but they are more than that, too. To the devout fundamentalist
who accepts the principles of literalism and inerrancy, evolution theory is
not simply contrary to religious teachings; it is *false.* Nor is it false in
some intuitive or metaphysical sense. Based on the interpretive tools
with which members of the legislature are accustomed to understanding
the universe, it is *demonstrably* false.

The liberal, convinced that the legislative tools are bad ones and that
the tools of science are superior, might shift into epistemology, contending that science deals with *knowledge* about the natural world, and is
based on evidence, whereas religion is simply a system of *belief,* based on
faith. One may criticize the implicit balancing of the relative merits of
empirical evidence and spiritual faith, and many have done so.[42] But I
am not even sure why the legislators should concede the initial proposition, that one involves knowledge and the other does not. Here, I am put
in mind of Wittgenstein, who observed:

> But I might also say: It has been revealed to me by God that it is so.
> God has taught me that this is my foot. And therefore if anything
> happened that seemed to conflict with this knowledge I should have to

---

42. One of the most cogent criticisms was voiced by William James in his Gifford Lectures:
[I]f we look on man's whole mental life as it exists, on the life of men that lies in them apart
from their learning and science, and that they inwardly and privately follow, we have to
confess that the part of it of which rationalism can give an account is relatively superficial.
W. JAMES, THE VARIETIES OF RELIGIOUS EXPERIENCE 72 (1902).

regard *that* as deception.[43]

This, of course, is precisely the logic that motivates many Christian fundamentalists to oppose the teaching of evolution or support the teaching of creation theory. They are informed by God's revelation; no artifice of mortal man can contradict that; and any "evidence" that the revelation is incorrect is either erroneous or deceptive.

This is the worldview of Christian fundamentalists. This is more than what they believe. In any sensible use of the word, this is what they *know*. Their fury that their children are taught in school something contrary to what they know to be true is like the fury of the black parents when my eighth-grade history teacher told us about the happiness of the slaves. There is no apparent reason to take the fury of the creationist parents less seriously, once one grants their right to their own epistemological choice.

If on the other hand the liberal refuses to accept the claim that the devout religionist knows rather than simply believes, then the argument that religion is nevertheless cherished stumbles near the edge of a frightening and perhaps unbridgeable precipice, yawning with the prospect of the humiliating dismissal of what liberal thought claims to cherish. If the arguments of the parents offended by the teaching of evolution are entitled to less weight than the arguments of the parents offended by the teaching of racist history, the reason must surely be that the second set of arguments is clothed in an appeal to liberal rationality and the first is not. The black parents, perhaps, can "prove" the racist history wrong; whereas the "proofs" offered by the creationist parents are irrational, which is to say, crazy.

The psychology of liberalism probably makes this diagnosis inevitable, because liberalism distinguishes sharply between facts and values in a way that religion does not. The liberal celebration of the freedom of individuals to pursue their desires rests on the presumption that they first agree on the characteristics of the world in which they live, and only subsequently decide how to value them. But as Roberto Unger has written, "The contrast of understanding and evaluation is foreign to the religious consciousness, for its beliefs about the world are simultaneously descriptions and ideals."[44] Liberalism rests critically on that contrast, and no simple call upon a principle of neutrality toward religion can hide the implicit tension. The question for the future of liberalism, then, is whether the tension between religion and reason is to be ignored, or cele-

---

43. L. WITTGENSTEIN, ON CERTAINTY 47e para. 361 (D. Paul & G. Anscombe trans. 1969).

44. R. UNGER, KNOWLEDGE AND POLITICS 157-58 (1975); *see also id.* at 41 ("Wherever liberal psychology prevails, the distinction between describing things in the world and evaluating them will be accepted as the premise of all clear thought.").

brated, or softened. A different possible future lies beyond each of those choices.

If the tension is ignored—if liberalism continues paying lip-service to a principle of "neutrality" while in effect permitting official indoctrination in a philosophy that runs contrary to deeply held religious beliefs—then what is left for the parents who want to rear their children in a belief in Biblical inerrancy? One possibility is exit: the parents might try, after the example of the Amish, to have their children excused from the objectionable instruction.[45] This solution, however, has three obvious difficulties. First, by being forced to be the ones to opt out, to act differently from their classmates, the children whose parents oppose the teaching of evolution risk all the psychological trauma usually cited by liberals as the reason that an opting-out privilege cannot save the constitutionality of organized prayer in the public school classroom. Second, there is a dramatic slippery slope problem, as one imagines parents removing their children from one course after another because of conflict with religious knowledge, until, finally, the children are no longer receiving any education apart from home instruction. Third, as we know from *Mozert v. Hawkins County Public Schools,*[46] when parents do try to remove their children from objectionable courses of instruction, the state may try to keep the children in class. By refusing to excuse the children from instruction, the school would be telling the parents what Justice Douglas implied in his partial dissent in *Wisconsin v. Yoder:*[47] your children's education is not yours to choose.

It may be, then, that the tension cannot be resolved within a liberal politics that claims to cherish both religion and reason. Perhaps to cherish both is impossible, and if it is, the liberal state might make a second choice, the choice for candor, the choice to celebrate the tension, by being open about the lurking contempt for any serious effort to gain knowledge through religious belief. The tools of secular science and rationalism, liberals might announce, are the proper tools for understanding the universe and the tools of religious belief are not. The state is free to indoctrinate through use of its schools, and except within certain

---

45. *See* Wisconsin v. Yoder, 406 U.S. 205 (1972) (approving in narrow circumstances the right of parents to exclude their children on religious grounds from secondary public education).

46. 647 F. Supp 1194 (E.D. Tenn. 1986) (rejecting state's effort to force students to use textbooks offensive to parents' religious views), *rev'd sub nom.* Mozert v. Hawkins County Bd. of Educ., 827 F.2d 1058 (6th Cir. 1987), *cert. denied,* 56 U.S.L.W. 3569 (1988).

47. *See* 406 U.S. 205, 244-45 (1972) (Douglas, J., dissenting in part) ("While the parents, absent dissent, normally speak for the entire family, the education of the child is a matter on which the child will often have decided views . . . . It is the student's judgment, not his parents', that is essential . . . ."); *see also* B. ACKERMAN, *supra* note 25, at 139-63 (challenging notion that parents should have plenary discretion over education of their children).

narrow limits, the parents are not free to shield their children from the state's effort to wean them from the religion of their parents. The parents may try to educate their children in their religion at home and in the church, but if the parents fail, even if they fail in part because the state insists on teaching something different, there is no one to whom a complaint fairly may be directed. Nor would this be simply a policy proposal; in a liberal politics of candor, this might be fundamental law.

The third possibility is an effort to transcend these difficulties, and perhaps to transcend liberalism itself, by softening the tension inherent in the liberal principle of neutrality toward religion. The softening would imply doing what many critics have already proposed: finding ways to take seriously the deep religious feelings that motivate so many Americans in their daily lives.[48] To take religious motivation seriously would not necessarily imply permitting the religious to impose their religious doctrines on the rest of society; it would suggest meeting policy proposals on their own grounds, rather than dismissing them because of the religious motivations of their supporters, a dismissal that carries with it an all but explicit ridicule of religious belief itself. A softened liberal politics would not insist on reason as the only legitimate path to knowledge about the world, and if, in the end, only one path were taught in school, at least it would not be taught as though no other path were possible. I will confess that I have not worked out the details of a liberal politics that would acknowledge and genuinely cherish the religious beliefs that for many Americans provide their fundamental worldview; but my sense is that a liberal politics that tries to do this is a liberal politics more likely to survive the resurgence of religious belief.

And yet.

And yet one may respond, no, this analysis is all wrong, the neutrality principle is an excellent one to preserve, and in its practical operation, it possesses the additional virtue of being in accord with intuition. But it is that very intuition that should finally be troubling, for that is the intuition that says of religious belief, "Yes, we cherish you—now go away and leave us alone." It is an intuition that makes religion something that is believed in privacy, not something that is paraded; and if religion *is* paraded, it is this same intuition that assures that it will likely be dismissed. This intuition says that Pat Robertson is stupid or fanatical in believing that God can cure disease, and the same intuition makes sure that everyone understands that his belief is a kind of mystic flight from hard truths—it has nothing to do with the real world. The same intui-

---

48. The weakness of the third possibility is reflected in Mark Tushnet's suggestion that "[w]hen the liberal tradition takes religion seriously, the result subverts the individualist premises of the very theory into which religion is supposed to fit." Tushnet, *supra* note 3, at 734 (footnote omitted).

tion tells the religious that those things that they know to be true are wrong or irrelevant; that they cannot serve as the basis of policy; that they cannot even be debated in the forum of public dialogue on which liberalism depends.

The intuition says, in short, that religion is like building model airplanes: something quiet, something private, something trivial—and not really a fit activity for intelligent, public-spirited adults. This intuition, then, is one that in the end must destroy either religion or liberal theory. That is a prospect that can please only those who hate one or the other or both.

Part III
The Problems of Conscientious Objections

[10]

RELIGION, CONSCIENCE AND LAW[1]

The idea of the religiously motivated man being forced to decide between his country and his God is a theme current throughout history. Modern society tends to be called "plural"—there is room for men of all faiths peacefully to follow their chosen paths, or so it is said. However, law, and criminal law in particular, is not plural—it is singular and thus, given the vast field of social conduct that the law now attempts to regulate, clashes are inevitable. Those who commit crimes at the behest of their religious beliefs are of special interest since what they have perceived as their predominant duty has taken them beyond the boundary of the law. In addition, religious belief and observance are features that our society, if not our law, advances as a generally recognised "good" and in our context it is a "good" in conflict with other "goods", such as that individuals should be protected from the harm of others, that the general viability of society should be advanced and, more controversially, that individuals should be prevented from harming themselves.

This paper sets out to describe some of the possible clashes between the dictates of a religious conscience and the law and to explain how such problems have been traditionally treated in the case-law and by Parliament. The idea of religious freedom as a good advanced by the law is then developed by the suggestion that possible conflicts with religious observances can alter the very definitions of particular crimes. Religious belief in the context of criminal intent is then subjected to additional scrutiny and finally the ideas of religion as a good and religious belief influencing the formation of criminal intent come together in a discussion of religion and dishonesty.

Clashes between Religious and Legal Obligation

Whilst it is not possible to catalogue all of the potential clashes that may occur in this area it is useful to consider some of the widely different situations that can arise.

A frequently discussed[2] possible conflict is where a priest is ordered, under the threat of the law of contempt of court, to disclose information that he has learned in confidence. The comments of Lord Denning M.R. in 1963[3] that the "clergyman is [not] entitled to refuse to answer when directed to by the judge . . .," represent the

---

1 For some aspects of this topic, see Lewis, "The Outlook for a Devil in the Colonies. A Colonial viewpoint on Witchcraft, Homicide and the Supernatural" [1958] *Crim. L.R.* 661; Glanville Williams, *Criminal Law: The General Part* (2nd ed. 1961), 748–750, and *Textbook of Criminal Law* (1978), 88–91; *Russell On Crime* (12th ed. 1964), 76–77 and *Kenny's Outlines of Criminal Law* (19th ed. 1966), 59–60.

2 See, *e.g.*, Lindsay, (1959) 13 *N.I.L.Q.* 160; The Archbishops' Commission on *Church and State* (1970), 58–60; *Eleventh Report of the Criminal Law Revision Committee on Evidence (General)* (1972; Cmnd. 4991), paras. 272–275 and Cross, *Evidence* (5th ed. 1979), 295–6.

3 *A.-G. v. Mulholand; A.-G. v. Foster* [1963] 2 Q.B. 477, 489.

strict legal position, and the Criminal Law Revision Committee[4] feel
that as the problem presents no serious numerical difficulty in practice,
the law should remain as it is, especially as there will be situations
where the administration of criminal justice outweighs the conscience
of priests. The modern legal position has tightened of late and can be
compared with a rather more generous support of such confidentiality in
the mid-nineteenth century. Thus in one case where an accused
murderer had spoken with a prison chaplain, Alderson B. stated—

> I think these conversations ought not to be given in evidence. The principle upon
> which an attorney is prevented from divulging what passes with his client is because
> without an unfettered means of communication the client would not have proper
> legal assistance. The same principle applies to a person deprived of whose advice
> the prisoner would not have spiritual assistance. I do not lay this down as an
> absolute rule; but I think such evidence ought not to be given.[5]

Whilst the modern law will find little time for the learned baron's logic,
his sentiment may yet command appeal.

Other problems may arise with regard to the administration of
justice; thus, for example, if a juryman were to discuss the case he is
trying with his bishop[6] or adviser on religious matters, in order to get
spiritual guidance on it, a clear contempt would be committed.[7]

The most fertile area for controversy, however, lies in the clashes
between non-Christian cultures (now much grown within the United
Kingdom) and the dominant culture, and also between the "fringe"
Christian groups and the law, as the following examples illustrate. The
difficulty of the Sikh turban and the wearing of motor-cycle helmets has
been solved and will be discussed presently. Other problems remain.
Thus, there have been cases in which Sikhs have been convicted of
carrying offensive weapons[8] when showing their kirpans in public.

---

4 *Eleventh Report* (1972; Cmnd. 4991), para. 274.
5 *R.* v. *Griffith* (1853) 6 Cox C.C. 219. At the time of *R.* v. *Hay* (1860) 2 F. & F. 4, the
   existence of such a privilege seemed open to argument. However, its existence was
   denied in *Wheeler* v. *Le Marchant* (1881) 17 Ch.D. 675, at 681, and in *Normanshaw* v.
   Normanshaw and Meashan [1893] L.T. 468. For the developments in Eire, see *Cook* v.
   Carroll [1945] I.R. 515. In *D.* v. *National Society for the Prevention of Cruelty to
   Children* [1978] A.C. 171, Lord Edmund-Davies stated at p. 245: ". . . where a
   confidential relationship exists . . . and . . . disclosure would be in *breach of some
   ethical or social value* involving the public interest the court has a discretion to uphold a
   refusal to disclose relevant evidence provided it considers that, on balance, the public
   interest would be better served by excluding such evidence. . . ." Thus, *Griffith* may
   still give support to an argument based upon *policy* that a priest's obligation of
   confidence should not be breached.
6 See *The Daily Telegraph*, 8th August 1978. See also *Hellfinch Properties Ltd.* v. *Newark
   Investments Ltd.*, *The Times*, 21st July 1981, where Slade J. had to consider whether a
   threat by a rabbinical court to excommunicate an Orthodox Jew for taking a matter to a
   civil court could constitute a contempt.
7 A juryman may not be excused from serving if such service conflicts with his religious
   observances although: "He may . . . be excused at the discretion of the judge on the
   grounds of . . . conscientious objection to jury service. . . ." *Practice Note* [1973]
   1 All E.R. 340.
8 Contrary to the Prevention of Crime Act 1953.

(The kirpan is a short dagger—one of the five symbols of Sikhhood). The views of traditional Muslim religious leaders on what constitutes the correct chastisement of the children in their charge do not always coincide with what is now generally accepted as moderate. The legal obligation on parents to ensure that their children attend school has also produced its difficulties.[9] The Rastafarian view on smoking marijuana, which some commentators[10] have described as a key part in the evolution of their doctrine, is in inevitable collision with Western drug laws.

The Orthodox Position: the Child Neglect Cases

The traditional stance with regard to the interaction between religious and legal obligation is to be found in a series of decisions concerning a now faded nineteenth-century sect known as the Peculiar People. Basing their belief on biblical injunctions to trust in the power of prayer when it comes to curing illness, they were disinclined to call in the medical man when either they or their families fell sick. In a number of cases parents had omitted to call in a doctor when their child was seriously ill with the result that the severe illness or deaths of these children gave rise to a chain of cases, starting with *R. v. Wagstaffe*.[11] In this case the fourteen-month-old child of two members of the sect became ill and the parents, preferring prayer to orthodox medicine, chose not to call in a doctor. The child subsequently died and the parents were prosecuted for gross-negligence manslaughter at common law. Given the legal duty of care that exists between parents and their young children, the question was whether the parents had in their conduct shown that degree of negligence which would justify the intervention of the criminal law. Willes J. took a broad approach to the problem; in his direction to the jury he said that a duty of care in such circumstances could be carried out in more than one way and that history certainly justified a course of action, in such circumstances, based upon reasonable religious belief. The jury acquitted the defendants. At this stage it is important to notice what it is that *Wagstaffe* decided: an essential element of gross-negligence manslaughter is a course of action that is, objectively judged, so negligent as to justify the intervention of the criminal law. If a religiously motivated series of acts,

---

9 Thus, see *The Times*, 10th April 1981, where it was reported that a Jehovah's Witness chose to go to prison for seven days rather than send his son to a school where he would come into contact with objectionable books. Under s. 39(2)(b) of the Education Act 1944, a parent does not commit an offence if he fails to send his child to school on any day exclusively set apart for religious observance by the religious body to which he (the parent) belongs.

10 See Yawney, *Herb and the Chalice: The Symbolic Life of the Children of Slaves in Jamaica* (1972). Minority religious cultures that use prohibited drugs have tested the extent of religious liberty in the United States of America; see, *e.g.*, Campbell and Witmore, *Freedom in Australia* (1966), 212–213, and Thomas Szaz, *Ceremonial Chemistry. The Ritual Persecution of Drugs, Addicts and Pushers* (1974), 126–129 and 198–199 (the U.S.A. Peyote Church).

11 (1868) 10 Cox C.C. 530, per Willes J.: ". . . the question, however, is whether the prisoners held the belief they hold honestly. . . ." See also *R. v. Hines* 13 Cox C.C. 114 n.

or omissions, is considered by the jury to be sufficiently careful, then there is no offence. *Wagstaffe* does not establish that religious motivation where there has been sufficient lack of care, viewed objectively, constitutes an excuse: it was already clear at that time that such motivation in itself did not create an excuse.[12]

Alarm at the acquittal in *Wagstaffe* led to Parliament's creation of the statutory offence of wilful child neglect.[13] Thus, the relevant law was now not only concerned with death but also with other forms of injury. In addition the *actus reus* now involved neglect, as defined by statute—

> . . . wilful neglect to provide adequate . . . medical aid . . . whereby the health of such child shall have been or shall be likely to be seriously injured. . . .

In *Downes*,[14] a member of the sect was convicted of the statutory offence through his failure to call in the physician to treat his child, who was suffering from inflamed lungs. Lord Coleridge C.J. considered[15] that the father's religious beliefs explained his motive but this in itself did not provide an answer to the question of his guilt which depended on his intention. On the basis that he had, because of his religious motivation, intentionally neglected his child, Downes was convicted.

In the briefly reported decision of *Morby*,[16] the child of Peculiar People had died as a result of lack of orthodox medical treatment. Here the parents were convicted of unlawful-act manslaughter but this conviction was set aside by the Court of Crown Cases Reserved because of the lack of sufficient evidence given at the trial.

Finally there is the well-known case of *Senior*,[17] again an unlaw-

---

12 Thus, in *R. v. Sharpe* (1857) 7 Cox C.C. 214, the defendant had moved a corpse from a burial ground for reasons of filial and religious duty. The court expressed some unwillingness in confirming his conviction and only a nominal penalty was imposed on the defendant out of respect for his sincere motive.

13 S. 37 of the Poor Law Amendment Act 1868. See Lewis, "The Outlook for a Devil in the Colonies", *op. cit.*, pp. 668–670.

14 (1875) 1 Q.B.D. 25. Lord Coleridge C.J. stated that he had "grave doubts" whether the same result would have been reached had the case been a prosecution for gross-negligence manslaughter at common law. This case is probably wrongly decided on its facts: see *R. v. Sheppard* [1980] 3 All E.R. 899, 914 (Lord Keith of Kinkel) and Glanville Williams, *Criminal Law: The General Part*, 143–144. Thus Downes, because of his state of mind, did not anticipate that medical aid was necessary and so could not be said to have wilfully refused it. He may, of course, be said to be oblivious to a risk that would be obvious to an ordinary man. In *R.v. Caldwell* [1981] 2 All E.R.961, it was stated that a reckless state of mind (when an essential element of a statutory offence) can encompass "failure to give any thought to whether there was any risk in circumstances where, if any thought were given to the matter, it would be obvious that there was." In situations like that in *Downes*, it is hard to say that he has failed to consider the matter albeit he has reached what may be regarded as an unreasonable conclusion.

15 (1875) 1 Q.B.D. 25, 30.

16 (1882) 15 Cox C.C. 35.

17 [1899] 1 Q.B. 283.

ful-act manslaughter prosecution based on a similar failure by a father, who was a Peculiar Person and who had lost several children from illness in the past, to provide medical aid for his sick child. On the basis that "medical aid and medicine were such essential things for the child that reasonably careful parents in general would provide them . . .", a position which the law now deemed to be necessary whatever the particular parent's belief, the defendant's failure to provide them constituted the unlawful act and he was thus guilty of manslaughter, under the interpretation of the unlawful act doctrine then in force. The case is still regarded as the leading example of the proposition that religious motive in itself is no defence to what otherwise constitutes a breach of the criminal law, for[18]—

> To permit this [as a defence] would be to make the professed doctrines of religious belief superior to the law of the land, and in effect permit every citizen to become a law unto himself.[19]

It should be made clear that by "motive" one is describing a reason for the act where there exists a realisation that the act will or may result in prohibited consequences. Where one's religious beliefs are so predominant that one has no foresight at all of such consequences, one cannot be said to have committed the crime intentionally, nor recklessly where a subjective realisation of the likelihood of the prohibited consequences is included in that term. Where a man's entire set of religious values leads him (perhaps because of cultural differences between the main group in the country and his own) to consider the position that his child is in, and then to suppose that the only thing that is proper in the circumstances is prayer, then this may constitute a lack of any intention *wilfully to neglect* the child.[20] On the other hand, as seems to follow from *Sheppard*,[21] if the parent does appreciate that an ordinary parent would be under a duty to call in the doctor,[22] but he believes that despite this it is in the child's better interests for prayer to be used instead, the offence has been committed.[23] The position may be contrasted with a failure to appreciate the duty, not out of indifference to the child's state but through a belief about the correct way of carrying out the duty, where no offence would seem to have been committed.[24]

---

18 *Reynolds* v. *U.S.* 98 U.S. 145 (1878).
19 This principle was referred to, *obiter*, in discussion of a doctor's liability for the death of his patient where he had refused to give medically necessary treatment (here, an abortion) out of his religious conviction, in *R.* v. *Bourne* [1939] 1 K.B. 687, 693. See the Abortion Act 1967, s. 4.
20 Glanville Williams, *Textbook of Criminal Law* (1978), 89.
21 [1980] 3 All E.R. 899.
22 Under s. 1(1) of the Children and Young Persons Act 1933.
23 See the comments of Lord Diplock, [1980] 3 All E.R. 899, 905–906.
24 Commenting on *Senior*, Lord Diplock, at p. 905, notes: "So here there was not any question of the accused parent being unaware that risk to the child's health might be involved in his failure to provide it with medical aid. He deliberately refrained from having recourse to medical aid with his eyes open to the possible consequences to the child's physical health". On the facts, it has been suggested in *Russell* that the defendant could have been convicted of common law gross-negligence manslaughter: *Russell on Crime* (12th ed. 1964), 76.

These cases provide useful examples of general principles that may come into play when religion and law are in conflict. Motive in itself is no defence. However, the religious setting of the crime may be relevant in considering whether either the requisite *mens rea* has been formed, for example, has the defendant's religious belief been so overwhelming as to make him fail to appreciate the consequences of his acts,[25] or whether, as seems to be the explanation of *Wagstaffe*, the action of the defendant is proscribed by law.

Exemptions

One commonly employed solution to such clashes is the enactment of an exemption to the requirement of the law, either in favour of a defined religious group or for all groups sharing a particular belief on religious grounds. Examples of the former include: special provisions for Jewish workers under the factories legislation;[26] the allowance of Jewish and Muslim methods of ritual slaughter;[27] and the release of members of the Sikh religion from the legal obligation to wear crash helmets while riding motor-cycles.[28] Examples of the latter can include all members of a particular class, such as regular ministers of religion,[29] or it can extend to all conscientious belief, including that formed on other than religious grounds.[30]

A well-known exemption that has developed over the past one hundred and thirty years is the taking of the oath in a court of law.[31] It is now possible to swear in any lawful manner, following either the Christian or Jewish form, or the prescribed mode of any recognisable religion.[32] In one case, in the 1930s, a defendant was permitted to swear by Apollo. Anyone who either believes that it is wrong to take a religious oath, or, alternatively, who has no religion,

---

25 Which may be the correct interpretation of the facts in *Downes*.
26 Factories Act 1961, s. 109.
27 Slaughterhouses Act 1974, s. 36(3). See also Slaughter of Poultry Act 1967, s. 1(2). When a large contract was made by the Libyan authorities for the killing of meat in the ritual Muslim manner in Northern Ireland, there were protests on the ground that the exemption to the law was merely designed to assist the indigenous Muslim population, see *The Times*, 10th and 11th July 1980.
28 Motor-Cycle Crash Helmets (Religious Exemption) Act 1976. Regulations passed in 1973 had made it obligatory for all motor-cyclists to wear crash helmets and the Divisional Court had taken the view that these regulations were not *ultra vires* in that they were "[not] so unfair and [do not] bear so severely on the Sikh community and any others whose religion may require them to keep their heads covered. . . .": *R.* v. *Aylesbury Crown Court, ex parte Chahal* [1976] R.T.R. 489, 492.
29 The status of priest or regular minister of religion has always been an alternative to conscientious objection for exemption from compulsory military service; see, *e.g.*, National Service Act 1948, sch. 1, para. 2 and *Walsh* v. *Lord Advocate* [1956] 3 All E.R. 129.
30 *E.g.*, Abortion Act 1967, s. 4.
31 For an account of the development of the modern law on oaths, see Edward Royle, *Radicals, Secularists and Republicans* (1980), 266–268.
32 Oaths Act 1978, s. 1, (applied to Northern Ireland by s. 8(3)). See D. Schofield and O. Nath Channon, "Oaths of Hindu, Sikh and Muslim Witnesses" (1974) IV *New Community* 409.

may take a solemn affirmation instead.[33] The current law states that the exemption will apply to "any person who objects to being sworn",[34] and thus it is now sufficient for the witness to object—there being no need to inquire into the *bona fides* of his religious beliefs.

The use of exemptions confirms the proposition that conscientious objection is not in itself sufficient for the effect of the criminal law to be nullified. Their use can also create special problems as was shown by the debate over the Sikhs and the motor-cycle helmets.[35] Who is and who is not entitled to the special treatment, that is, what is a Sikh?[36] Will not particular provision for one defined group lead to inevitable jealousy in others? How does one balance religious tolerance on the one hand with the policy of the criminal law on the other? The Government's position on this third issue was summed up thus—

> The need for road safety provisions is of tremendous importance. The Bill is based on religious tolerance and that, too, is an important and vital part of our society. . . . There is no possibility of a compromise on this difficult choice. . . . [I]f Parliament concludes that in this case religious tolerance outweighs road safety and equality, the Government will accept that decision. . . .[37]

It is unrealistic not to accept that such is the position whenever any major exemption is granted.

Statutory Interpretation

Ronald Dworkin has pointed out—

> In the United States, at least, almost any law which a significant number of people would be tempted to disobey on moral grounds would be doubtful—if not clearly invalid—on constitutional grounds as well. . . .[38]

How should a judge in this country approach a law that is disobeyed because of strong religious conviction?

It may be that the law in question is repugnant to the court because of an alteration of public opinion. Thus, in *Kennedy*,[39] a number of

---

33 Oaths Act 1978, s. 5.
34 Under the previous law, the court had to be satisfied that a witness came under a particular exemption. For an example of a rather illiberal approach by a judge at first instance, see *R.* v. *Clark* [1962] 1 All E.R. 428.
35 See *H.C. Debs.* 1975–76 session, Standing Committee F, 23rd June 1976. Similar points have been made about the exemption from the Sunday trading law for members of the Jewish religion: see St. J. A. Robilliard, "No Crime on Sunday?" [1980] *Crim. L.R.* 496, 497–498.
36 A familiar problem in prisons: see St. J. A. Robilliard, "Religion in Prison" (1980) 130 *N.L.J.* 800–801.
37 *H.C. Debs.*, 1975–76 session, Standing Committee F, 23rd June 1976, col. 11.
38 Ronald M. Dworkin, "On Not Prosecuting Civil Disobedience" *New York Review of Books*, 6th June 1968. Glanville Williams, *Criminal Law: The General Part*, 749–750, has cautioned: "Few will deny that on the gravest issues the law may rightfully make its sanction prevail over sincere religious belief; but there must be general agreement that a conflict between law and a strongly held conviction needs anxious thought."
39 (1902) 20 Cox C.C. 230.

Protestant clergymen had attempted to bring a private summons under section 34 of the Roman Catholic Relief Act 1829, which imposed a heavy penalty on anyone who became a Jesuit within the United Kingdom. The magistrate refused to issue the summons and a Divisional Court of the King's Bench held that this was not an improper exercise of his discretion and that in the light of the history of the section it was proper for the magistrate to allow the Crown alone to bring prosecutions. Of the members of the court, Darling J. went so far as to state—

> I think a magistrate may claim and may exercise a wider discretion in the case of proceedings under such statutes as this one is, statutes banishing people for their opinions, than any other statute that I am acquainted with which appear on the Statute books. Whatever may be the reason why they are passed, they were statutes which persecute opinions and Acts that are, to my mind, against the genius and spirit of this age.[40]

What reason may there be for saying that a statute seems to be unfair as regards a particular religious group or is against the "genius and spirit" of our age, and so should be strictly construed, or, if a statutory instrument, declared *ultra vires*?

Firstly, the principles of administrative law would seem to frown on rules that fall with severity on particular groups whilst, at the same time, seem to smile on legitimate special treatment in their favour. Lord Russell C.J.'s pronouncements on the first of these matters in *Kruse* v. *Johnson*[41] are too well known to be repeated here, while support for the latter approach is found in *Dodd* v. *Venner*,[42] where a Divisional Court of the King's Bench found no difficulty in deciding that a by-law, which provided that the Jewish method of ritual slaughter was exempt from a requirement of stunning animals intended for slaughter, was not *ultra vires*.

Secondly, the United Kingdom adheres to a number of international covenants that protect religious freedom[43] and thus a statute or statutory instrument should be read in the light of the presumption that Parliament does not intend to breach its international obligations.

Thirdly, it has been argued,[44] although as yet with little success,

---

40 *Ibid.*, p. 239.
41 [1898] 2 Q.B. 91, 99–100.
42 (1922) 27 Cox C.C. 297.
43 *E.g.*, European Convention on Human Rights and Fundamental Freedoms, Arts. 9 and 14. See also United Nations Universal Declaration of Human Rights (1948), Art. 18; Proclamation of Teheran (1966); Helsinki: Final Act (1975), Art. VII; United Nations International Covenant on Civil and Political Rights (1976), Arts. 18 and 20(1), and United Nations International Covenant on Economic, Social and Cultural Rights (1976), Arts. 2(2), 13(1) and 13(3).
44 The point was made at first instance in *R.* v. *Lemon and Gay News Ltd.* (1977), (unreported), but see Nicolas Walter, *Blasphemy in Britain. The Practice and Punishment of Blasphemy and the Trial of Gay News* (1977). It was not taken up when the case went on appeal.

that modern legislation such as the Race Relations Acts exhibits a general parliamentary wish to be as fair and as non-discriminatory as possible to established minority groups.

Finally, there has been an assumption, repeated in Parliament, the courts and elsewhere,[45] that religious observances and beliefs are always worthy of the most serious respect. Support for this comes from *Graham John*,[46] in 1974. The appellant in that case believed that he had been divinely given certain healing powers which were contained in his blood. When charged with failing without reasonable excuse to supply a specimen of blood for a laboratory test, he claimed that his beliefs did constitute a reasonable excuse. Roskill L.J. approached the issue in the following way—

> It is right to say, of course, that any state of affairs which involves persons committing criminal offences because of beliefs sincerely held by them, is, to put it at its lowest, highly distasteful for any court. Ever since the early or middle part of the 18th century, the courts of this country have prided themselves on the liberality of their approach to matters of conscience. That attitude has continued for the last 200 years at least. Accordingly, any argument such as that to which this court has listened on behalf of the appellant is entitled to and must receive respect. *For a man to be punished for an offence which is committed by reason only of his adherence to his own religion or belief can only be justified if the court is satisfied that the clear intention of the statute creating the offence was in the interests of the community as a whole to override the privileges otherwise attaching to freedom of conscience and belief, which it must always be the duty of the courts to protect and defend.*[47]

The court then went on to decide that the appellant was rightly convicted because: (i) "reasonable excuse" seemed to indicate something objective—something that the courts can judge for themselves, such as a physical illness, and (ii) in any case, because of the severity of the harm that the Road Traffic Acts attempt to avoid, the phrase should be restricted to matters of mental or physical capacity.

As the accused in *John* was relying on his own personal beliefs, and not on those of a substantial religious group, the result was perhaps not too suprising. Equating "reasonable" with "is factually able" is to give a narrow meaning to the word. One remembers that in *Wagstaffe* it was considered that a legitimate course of action based on a sincerely-held religious belief could be reasonable, and that this has had a recent echo in administrative law with regard to the question of whether a religious reason can furnish a reasonable objection to attendance at an inquiry on a particular day.[48] For policy reasons the court in *John* decided that "reasonable excuse" had a far narrower meaning than "conscientious

---

45   The statement by Denning L.J. (as he then was) in *Freedom Under the Law* (1949), 46, is representative of countless others that have been made in recent years on this subject.

46   [1974] 2 All E.R. 561.

47   *Ibid.*, p. 564. Emphasis supplied.

48   *Ostreicher* v. *Secretary of State for the Environment* [1978] 3 All E.R. 82, shows how, to a limited extent, religious belief can be a relevant consideration in the application of the rules of natural justice. Note also *R.* v. *Blaue* [1975] 3 All E.R. 446, 450.

objection" and thus there was no room for a religious objection. In the light of *dicta* in that case, and with some support from *Wagstaffe*, it should be possible, when faced with "reasonable excuse" in other contexts, to weigh the importance of the aim of Parliament against the harm, as described in *John*, that will be caused if a sincere religious belief is ignored.

Belief and Mens Rea

Such incidents as the "child neglect" cases involved find the courts very concerned that religious motivation should afford no defence in law. This leaves the question of *mens rea* untouched. At one time the opinion was popular that peculiar religious beliefs should only ground a defence where they constituted some form of insanity,[49] thus—

> It would be more satisfactory if these instances of fantastic superstitious belief could be approached as insane delusions and treated in accordance with the rules applicable thereto, for some religious delusions are of so extreme a character as to be plain evidence of insanity, and have been held to afford a defence upon that ground. . . .[50]

Modern research into the consequences of religious "indoctrination" suggests[51] that some members of religious bodies may, through group experience, reach the stage at which "reality becomes the present and includes in it elements of supernatural, magical, terrifying thought. . . ." Dr. William Sargant has thoroughly illustrated the means by which religiously-induced states alter mental patterns so that belief and behaviour are changed.[52] The idea of deeming bizarre religious belief to be mental illness is superficially attractive for it is easier to regard certain beliefs as being "mad" rather than to perceive that they may be based on some hitherto unrecognised truth. The mental illness approach, however, is frustrated by evidence[53] suggesting that those who are the most susceptible to the religious conversion process, and even to "possession by demons", are not always mentally unbalanced. A recent manslaughter case,[54] not unique, where during

---

49 E.g., *Russell on Crime*, 76–77; *Kenny's Outlines of Criminal Law*, 60.

50 *Kenny, op. cit.* See also *R. v. Tyler and Price* 8 Car. & P. 616, *per* Lord Denman C.J.: "It is not an opinion which I mean to lay down as a rule of law to be applicable to all cases, that fanaticism is a proof of unsoundness of mind: but there was in this particular instance, so much religious fanaticism – such violent excitement of mind . . . it could hardly be said that he [were he still alive] could be called on to answer for his criminal acts. . . ."

51 Dr. John G. Clark, "Investigating The Effects of Religious Cults on the Health and Welfare of Their Converts" *American Atheist*, May 1977.

52 William Sargant, *Battle for the Mind* (1959) and *The Mind Possessed* (1973). In *Battle for the Mind*, he makes the point that the traditional methods of gaining religious experience by such means as fasting and chanting "modify normal brain functions for religious purposes. . . ." (at p. 79 of the Pan edition 1970).

53 William Sargant, *The Mind Possessed* (1973), 31.

54 See *The Times*, 9th September 1980. In passing sentence, Smith J. declared: "I say straight away I must send you to prison. It is a painful duty because unusually for these courts you are upright Christian men acting, I am satisfied, out of misguided motives and not acting maliciously."

an exorcism two men punched the victim unconscious and kicked and jumped on her whilst attempting to remove the devil, illustrates how insanity[55] is not necessarily always a satisfactory answer to such problems.

A religious belief can, when deeply held, lead the defendant to make a mistaken appreciation of facts or of the probable consequences of his acts. This leads us to the debate between those who thought, as did Professor Kenny, that as mistake in law had to be based on reasonable grounds, no bizarre religious belief could provide support for a reasonable belief, and those who support the view of Glanville Williams[56] that a religiously-induced mistake negativing some part of the *mens rea* should be a defence to any crime requiring such a *mens rea*, but no defence where the crime could be committed negligently, as, for example, in gross-negligence manslaughter. Thus, if a man kills an object believing it to be the devil, he clearly lacks the *mens rea* for murder as he does not intend to kill a reasonable creature. Where, however, the belief has to be reasonably held, as in self-defence,[57] minority religious beliefs (such as he, a witch, is attempting to kill me by witchcraft) would not provide a defence.[58] *Morgan*[59] now clarifies the situation. Thus if a belief, on whatever grounds it is based, negatives an essential mental element of the crime, then there can be no liability. Does this now mean that however bizarre the belief is, it will provide a defence? The belief still has to be held honestly and here lies some measure of control, for, as Hyman Gross points out, if the belief is persisted in contrary to the general experience of the life of the defendant then—

> . . . when the mistaken belief is held only because the accused chose to believe what suited him instead of what quite plainly was the case, how can it be unfair to require him to conform his conduct to the law instead of deluding himself and then violating it?[60]

55 It was not suggested in this case. However in 1976, at Lincoln Crown Court, a man who had killed his daughter believing that she was possessed by the devil, was found not guilty of her murder by reason of insanity. He was suffering from paranoid schizophrenia. In 1981, a man charged with assault, kidnapping, damaging property and unlawfully possessing a firearm with intent to endanger life claimed that he had committed these acts after becoming possessed by the devil: *The Times*, 10th February 1981.

56 In "Homicide and the Supernatural" (1949) 65 *L.Q.R.* 491. Hyman Gross in *A Theory of Criminal Justice* (1979), 220–222, discusses the problem of dealing with attempted harm which, although in fact harmless, is believed by the person using it to be harmful.

57 Glanville Williams, "Homicide and the Supernatural", *supra* fn. 56 at pp. 499–500. See also Law Commission Paper No. 102, *Attempt and impossibility in relation to attempt, conspiracy and incitement* (1980), 52.

58 In "Witch Murder and Mens Rea: A Problem of Society Under Radical Social Change" (1965) 28 *M.L.R.* 46, Seidman points out that a not uncommon feature of African life at that time was ". . . [the] case . . . in which the defendant was tried because he had killed a supposed witch in imagined self-defence against her diabolic craft. With monotonous regularity, courts have convicted, sentenced to death, and—in the same breath—recommended executive clemency."

59 [1976] A.C. 182.

60 Gross, *A Theory of Criminal Justice* (1979), 268.

Mistake of fact must however be distinguished from mistake of law—a belief that a divine law overrides human law[61] does not provide a defence. Whether there should be special treatment for those acting under divine commands instilled from a personality change resulting from a religious conversion is a question which can be asked. Clearly such a person is less responsible than the average man. In any case the plea of a divine command may bring into question the mental stability of the accused.

Religious Fraud

A "pious" fraud may either constitute a crime under the general law or be in breach of the Fraudulent Mediums Act 1951. The obtaining of money or property on the pretext that it will buy, for example, salvation can, *prima facie*, be an offence under the Theft Act; or the common law offence of conspiracy to defraud, or an offence under the Vagrancy Act 1824.

Recent allegations[62] that some of the "new religions" incite their adherents to mislead members of the public with regard to the home to which any contribution that they make will be given, raise questions about honesty. The starting point should be the subjective rather than the objective assessment of the religious belief. Thus, in *United States* v. *Ballard*,[63] the Ballard family claimed to be "divine messengers", stating that they had the power to heal the sick. They had received sums of money as a consequence of these representations. The majority of the Supreme Court held that the correct approach was to examine whether the beliefs were sincerely held by the defendants, while, at the same time, not examining the truth of those beliefs, for—

> Many take their gospel from the New Testament. But it would hardly be supposed that they could be tried before a jury charged with the duty of determining whether those teachings contained false representations. The miracles of the New Testament, the Divinity of Christ, life after death, the power of prayer are deep in the religious convictions of many. If one could be sent to jail because a jury in a hostile environment found these teachings false, little indeed would be left of religious freedom.[64]

Of course, as Jackson J. pointed out in a dissenting judgment, the less believable the jury found the claims in question to be, the more likely they would find the beliefs to be held fraudulently. If the reasoning in *Ballard* is adopted, an appropriation of another's property would not be dishonest if the representor tells the donor all that he

---

61 For a discussion of "commands of God" contradicting the criminal law, see Glanville Williams, *Criminal Law: The General Part* (1st ed. 1953), section 46.

62 See, *e.g.*, 926 *H.C. Debs.*, cols. 1587–1599 (1977); Christopher Edwards, *Crazy for God* (1979) and *Orme* v. *Associated Newspapers Ltd.*, *The Times*, 1st April 1981. In 1980, three defendants were prosecuted for obtaining £12,000 on the basis that they were doctors and possessed magical powers: *Daily Telegraph*, 17th June 1980.

63 322 U.S. 78 (1944).

64 *Per* Douglas J.

honestly believes, even though the belief is bizarre,[65] and recent trends may even indicate that the representor is not dishonest where he deliberately misleads for what he honestly believes is in the better interests of the donor.

It is now clear that dishonesty, as currently defined within the law of theft, is also the essential mental element in common law conspiracy to defraud. One of the noticeable features of the "new religions", whose enthusiasts we are likely to encounter on the street, is that they are often under a rigid discipline enforced by their superiors. Ideas such as "godly deception", that is, a lie about the destination of those funds, told in the belief that it is for the ultimate benefit of the giver, will come from the leaders of groups, and whatever the liability of the superiors in such cases, it is open to argument that a superior order, honestly relied on, will negative dishonesty as regards conspiracy to defraud[66] or offences under the Theft Act.

Street collections are often an important element in the activities of some of the "fringe" groups. Such activity may always be susceptible to laws or by-laws against obstructing the highway and there is also the possibility of a prosecution for begging, contrary to section 3 of the Vagrancy Act 1824. A great many of the religious activities of these groups, whether it be the selling of goods, such as records, in the streets, requests for gifts or even the handing out of leaflets, are in theory in breach of these provisions. There is evidence, however, that many police forces take a tolerant view of these things and will only bring a prosecution where members of the public have been annoyed, shopkeepers inconvenienced or some other harm done.[67] A further comment is needed about section 3 of the Vagrancy Act 1824. This is aimed at those who habitually make their livelihoods by begging and not at those collecting for charity, even though they may partially benefit from the money themselves.[68] Thus, where a member of a religious "community" solicits funds for his group on the street, the small benefit that he may obtain from the sums that he takes in will probably not render him liable for illegal begging under section 3.

Formerly, section 4 of the Vagrancy Act 1824, which prohibits fortune telling, was a serious restriction on spiritualism, especially as it

---

65 See J. C. Smith, *The Law of Theft* (4th ed. 1979), paras. 116–117. Smith believes that the authorities on this point have now gone too far (but see *R.* v. *Landy* [1981] 1 All E.R. 1172) and that the test should be: ". . . [the jury] must find a state of mind to be dishonest if no reasonable man, in the view of the judge, could fail so to find. . . ." This would not seem to answer Jackson J.'s criticism of the majority in *Ballard*. The case where the defendant deliberately misleads the giver (perhaps because he thinks that it is the only way for the giver to be "saved") would seem to be more unreasonable and thus constitutes a belief held less honestly than the case where the defendant tells the giver everything that he believes.

66 See the opinion stated in Civil Service Department, *Legal Entitlements and Administrative Practices: a report by officials* (1979), 17.

67 See 926 *H.C. Debs.*, cols. 1587–1599 (1977).

68 *Mathers* v. *Penfold* (1914) 24 Cox C.C. 642.

was decided in 1921[69] that the offence was committed when one told
fortunes and it mattered not whether or not one had any intention to
deceive, nor did an actual belief in the existence of one's powers
constitute a defence. This decision seems to have been reached on the
basis that no-one can seriously believe in such things;[70] thus in an
earlier consideration of the subject, Denman J. declared—

> It is absurd to suggest that this man could have believed in his ability to predict the
> fortunes of another by knowing the hour and the place of his birth and the aspect of
> the stars at such time. We do not live in times when any sane man believes in such a
> power.[71]

Additional difficulties for spiritualists came from the continued life of
the Witchcraft Act 1735. Thus, the result of *Duncan*[72] seemed to be
that any séance was in peril since the law in effect appeared to assume
that communication with spirits was a pretence and hence illegal. The
wording of the Fraudulent Mediums Act 1951 now means that such
exhibitions are only offences where there has either been an intent to
deceive or the use of a fraudulent device,[73] and to be convicted, the
medium must have acted for either his own gain or that of another. (As
recently as 1975, five people were proceeded against for offences under
section 1 of the Act.) So the 1951 Act has placed fortune tellers and
spiritualists along with all others whose religious or supernatural beliefs
lead them to solicit money. Their culpability rests on their perception
of their beliefs alone; they are not convicted merely because they hold
odd or even fantastic views as viewed by society generally.

Conclusion

   Where a man stands in likely breach of the criminal law out of his
adherence to religious beliefs, it is to be hoped that a court will give
careful thought to a number of issues before it returns a conviction.
What is the policy of this law? Recognising that religious liberty is an
object that the law advances, is it to be outweighed here because, for
example, the prevention of harm to others, including one's own
children, is of more importance than special treatment for one's
conscience? Where the law is paternalistic, (one must wear a motor-cycle
helmet in order to prevent one harming oneself), the necessity of
overbearing conscience may not be so clear. The matter may be so
minor that confidence in the law is confirmed by allowing a special
exception in favour of a group who are, in their own eyes, acting
correctly. Even where the policy of the law does override religious
conscience, the special nature of religious belief will still mean that

---

69 *Stonehouse* v. *Masson* (1921) 27 Cox C.C. 23.
70 See the comment of D. Aikenhead Stroud, (1921) 48 *L.Q.R.* 488.
71 *Penny* v. *Hanson* (1887) 18 Q.B.D. 478, 480.
72 [1944] 1 K.B. 713, and see (1945) 8 *M.L.R.* 158.
73 Fraudulent Mediums Act 1951, s. 1. If *R.* v. *Martin* [1981] *Crim. L.R.* 109 is
    correctly decided, no prosecution of a fortune teller under s. 4 of the Vagrancy Act
    1824 would now seem to be possible.

special attention will have to be paid in ascertaining whether the defendant has formed the requisite mental intent.

There are other issues that may give scope for the development of some of these ideas in the future. Now that the doctrine of provocation has been modified,[74] religious beliefs in this area may come to be important. There again, questions of "supernatural" threats and duress[75] may also come under review. The growth of minority "fringe" religious groups, especially from the United States of America, where these questions have received much attention; new discoveries about the effects of faith, conversion and motivation; the general insistence upon "rights" placed against the ever-increasing army of statutory prohibitions in areas of life, both great and small—all these developments add new zest to a perennial dilemma.

ST. JOHN A. ROBILLIARD*

---

74 How far a religious belief may be considered a "characteristic" under the principle in *R.* v. *Camplin* [1978] A.C. 705 remains to be worked out. In *R.* v. *Newell* (1980) 71 Cr. App. R. 331, the Court of Appeal adopted *McGregor* [1962] N.Z.L.R. 1069 as representing English law on the meaning of "relevant characteristic". In the latter case, North J. stated: "The word 'characteristics' in the context is wide enough to apply not only to physical qualities but also to mental qualities and such more indeterminate attributes as colour, race and *creed*. . . ." At one time, the Law Commission recommended a new defence to murder—a killing under "extenuating circumstances" which could have included religious motivation. The Criminal Law Revision Committee have rejected this suggestion: see [1980] *Crim. L.R.* 538–539.

75 See (1968) 31 *M.L.R.* 84, where *Salaca* v. *The Queen* [1967] N.Z.L.R. 421 is discussed. The defence of duress was raised on the ground that supernatural powers would be invoked against the defendant if he did not marry, and thus commit bigamy. As these threats did not constitute "compulsion by threat of immediate death or grievous bodily harm" (as a statute required), they were not sufficient for the defence to succeed. The present common law may be wider than this: see Law Commission Paper No. 83 (1977), para. 2.7; and thus some supernatural threats may be so grave as to justify the use of the defence.

*   M.A., LL.B., Lecturer in Law, Manchester University.

[11]

CONSCIENTIOUS OBJECTION AND THE FIRST AMENDMENT

INTRODUCTION

THROUGHOUT THE 1960's as United States involvement in the war in Vietnam grew, so did the number of young men drafted to fight in Southeast Asia. For men growing up in the 1960's, the draft was the central fact of their lives, looming over otherwise bright futures like a cloud of napalm. The draft's hovering presence molded plans and decisions—pushing men to enlist in the armed services, to enroll in college, or to emigrate to Canada.

Political disillusionment with the war increased; so did resistance to the draft. Shouts of "Say, hey, L.B.J.! How many people did you kill today?" and "Hell no! We won't go!" shook the nation. Finally, President Nixon ended the draft. Humiliated and spent, the United States withdrew.

For the children of the 1970's, Vietnam and the draft were history, part of an earlier time in which bearded young men and long-haired young women stood on corners handing flowers to passers-by. The children of the Seventies set out efficiently toward their futures in a straight line; no dark mass beyond which they could not see obscured their paths.

Now, on the crest of a renewed patriotism engendered by events in Iran and Afghanistan, the President has reinstated draft registration for nineteen- and twenty-year-old men.[1] If registration comes, can conscription be far behind? Indications are that should reinstatement of the draft follow hard upon the heels of registration, opposition will come more quickly and be more widespread than such opposition has been in the past. "People have under their belt the history of a bad war and the realization that they can say no to a bad war—that that's legitimate."[2]

In the past, each time Congress has authorized a draft it has authorized an exemption from it for conscientious objectors. This exemption has been judicially viewed as acknowledgement by Congress "that liberty of conscience has a moral and social value which makes it worthy of preservation at the hands of the state."[3] The exemption may, however, have a more pragmatic purpose—to serve as a pressure valve to reduce organized opposition to the draft and the war by removing from the ranks of the pacifists many of their most committed and articulate members.[4] The conscientious objector

---

[1] See Presidential Proclamation No. 4771, 45 Fed. Reg. 45247 (July 2, 1980). Discussion of the registration of women is left to other writers.
[2] N.Y. Times, June 15, 1980, § 1 at 19, col. 1.
[3] Stone, *The Conscientious Objector*, 21 COL. U.Q. 253, 269 (1919), quoted in United States v. Seeger, 380 U.S. 163, 170 (1965).

exemption makes it possible for the people who qualify under it to refuse to comply with the law while complying with it.

Given the historical position of the exemption and the purposes it serves, conscientious objector status will probably be retained in any new draft legislation. Strong feeling exists in and out of Congress, however, that the C.O. exemption was abused with the support of the Supreme Court during the Vietnam War. As a result of the exemption, people were getting away with nonmurder. Therefore, Congress will feel pressure to either tighten up or eliminate the conscientious objector exemption in any new draft legislation. If either of these steps is taken, the Supreme Court will inevitably be required to confront constitutional questions it has sought hard to avoid. Indeed, it may well be that only by resurrecting the exemption as the Supreme Court has interpreted it can the constitutional questions be sidestepped or at least postponed.

If Congress were to abolish the C.O. exemption, the question would arise: Is there a constitutional right embodied in the Free Exercise Clause of the first amendment to an exemption from the draft based on conscience? If Congress were to narrow the class of those exempted to, for example, members of established peace churches such as the Quakers, Amish, and Mennonites, the question would arise: Is Congress favoring one religion over another or favoring religion over nonreligion in violation of the Establishment Clause of the first amendment?

Several proposals have been made to eliminate the C.O. exemption and replace it with a national civilian service.[5] Under these plans the registrant or draftee would indicate whether he wanted to fulfill his obligation of national service in military or ' civilian work. Such proposals would eliminate the administrative difficulties of determining who is entitled to exemption from military or combatant service. (The discussion *infra* of the Court's interpretation of the Vietnam era conscientious objector statute should make obvious how difficult such administrative determinations may be.) Such proposals may also be designed to eliminate potential conflict with the Establishment and Free Exercise Clauses of the first amendment. The proposal for civilian national service (particularly during peacetime) raises another constitutional question however: Does it violate the thirteenth amendment prohibition against involuntary servitude? Compulsory civilian service cannot be readily justified, as can a wartime draft, by the existence of Congress' war powers and the Necessary and Proper Clause. To explore

---

[4] It has often been noted that the C.O. exemption, at least since 1940, has favored the educated and articulate.

[5] PRESIDENTIAL RECOMMENDATIONS FOR SELECTIVE SERVICE REFORM, Feb. 11, 1980.

more deeply this thirteenth amendment question, however, is beyond the scope of this comment.

This comment will examine the possible constitutional consequences of the three other probabilities. 1) that Congress will revive the previous C.O. exemption without amendment; 2) that Congress will amend the statute to narrow the exemption; and, 3) that Congress will eliminate the C.O. exemption altogether. An analysis of earlier statutes is necessary to this end.

I. THE STATUTES

Looking at the C.O. exemption from the Civil War through the Vietnam War, one notes that the general tendency has been to broaden the exemption. This liberalizing has been done both by congressional act and (when Congress has been uncooperative) by administrative and judicial interpretation.

The Draft Act of 1864[6] exempted members of religious denominations opposed to the bearing of arms. When men were conscripted during World War I, the Draft Act of 1917 exempted those affiliated with a "well-recognized religious sect or organization . . . whose existing creed or principles forbade its members to participate in war in any form."[7] However, the Secretary of War issued a regulation that authorized exempting those men with "personal scruples against war."[8] In 1940 Congress eliminated from the Selective Service and Training Act the requirement that the conscientious objector be a member of an organized church. It was sufficient that his opposition to war be based on his "religious training and belief."[9] This change was a statutory recognition that conscience derives not from institutional membership but from individual belief. In 1948, however, Congress tightened the language, inserting the requirement that "religious training and belief" stem from the "individual's belief in a relation to a Supreme Being involving duties superior to those arising from any human relation," and excluding objections based "essentially political, sociological, or philosophical views or a merely personal moral code."[10] A 1967 amendment dropped the requirement that the objector believe in a relation to a Supreme Being; it retained, however, the exclusion of "essentially political, sociological, or philosophical views or a merely personal code."[11]

It was under section 6(j) of the 1948 act, with its requirement of belief in one's relation to a Supreme Being, that most of the Vietnam era

---

[6] Ch. 13, § 17, 13 Stat. 6, 9.

[7] Ch. 15, 40 Stat. 76, 78.

[8] SELECTIVE SERVICE SYSTEM MONOGRAPH NO. 11, CONSCIENTIOUS OBJECTION, 40-55 (1950).

[9] Selective Service & Training Act of 1940, Ch. 720, § 5(g), 54 Stat. 885, 889.

[10] Selective Service Act of 1948, Ch. 625, Title I, § 6(j), 62 Stat. 604, 612.

[11] Selective Service Act of 1967, Pub. L. 90-40, 81 Stat. 100, 104.

litigation occurred. The results of this litigation led to the dropping of the requirement of belief in a Supreme Being in the 1967 amendment.

II.   UNITED STATES V. SEEGER

The seminal case for contemporary analysis of the relationship between conscientious objection and the Constitution is *United States v. Seeger*.[12] *Seeger* consolidates the cases of three young men who were denied exemption under section 6(j) on the grounds that their claims were not based upon "belief in a relation to a Supreme Being." Each had expressed skepticism about the existence of a traditional God. Nonetheless, each had couched his description of his beliefs in religious phraseology. Seeger had a "belief in a devotion to goodness and virtue for their own sakes, and a religious faith in a purely ethical creed."[13] The second young man had said he believed in "Godness" which was the "Ultimate Cause for the fact of the Being in the Universe."[14] The third young man had spoken of "the consciousness of some power manifest in nature which helps man in the ordering of his life in harmony with its demands."[15]

As defendants in criminal draft evasion proceedings, the three contended that the statutory definition of religious training and belief as an individual's belief in relation to a Supreme Being was unconstitutional. They argued that the statutory definition violated both the Establishment and Free Exercise Clauses of the first amendment because, (1) it did not exempt nonreligious conscientious objectors and, (2) it discriminated between different forms of religious expression.

The Court, however, refused to take up the constitutional challenge. Instead it narrowed the question before it to one of statutory interpretation: "Does the term 'Supreme Being' as used in § 6(j) mean the orthodox God or the broader concept of a power or being, or a faith, 'to which all else is subordinate or upon which all else is ultimately dependent'?"[16] The Court, turning the legislative history of the 1948 Amendment on its head, held that "Supreme Being" means the latter. It established the following test: "A sincere and meaningful belief which occupies in the life of its possessor a place parallel to that filled by the God of those admittedly qualifying for the exemption comes within the statutory definition."[17]

Only after the Court had established its Parallel Position test to determine whether or not an objector believed in a Supreme Being, did it

---

[12] 380 U.S. 163 (1965).
[13] *Id.* at 166.
[14] *Id.* at 168.
[15] *Id.* at 169.
[16] *Id.* at 174.
[17] *Id.* at 176.

consider the effect of the other limitation added by Congress to section 6(j) in 1948, that the term "religious training and belief" does not include "essentially political, sociological, or philosophical views, or a merely personal moral code." Instead of seeing this latter limitation as Congress' attempt to define what belief in "a relation to a Supreme Being" was *not,* the Court pulled a quick switch. It explained that once it is determined that a belief holds a parallel position to that of orthodox belief it *a fortiori* is not a "merely personal moral code."[18]

In this manner, the Court was able to find that each of the three defendants qualified for conscientious objector status under section 6(j) and avoided the need to handle their constitutional contentions. Had the Court found either that the defendants were atheists (as opposed to theists) or that Congress had intended "Supreme Being" to mean an orthodox God, the Court would have been forced to consider the first amendment questions.

Although the defendants in *Seeger* were found to be covered by the statutory exemption as the Court interpreted it, the test used to catch them in the statutory net did not eliminate the Establishment Clause problems with section 6(j). The Parallel Position test establishes orthodox religion as a norm against which the objector's belief is evaluated. This places orthodox religion in a favored position vis á vis the law, in contravention of the Establishment Clause.[19]

More basically, the Court had earlier ruled that laws which aid religions as against nonbelievers are unconstitutional.[20] It ought to follow from this that conscientious objector status cannot constitutionally be based upon a religious standard, no matter how liberal that standard is. In *Welsh v. United States,*[21] the Court was again asked to hold section 6(j) unconstitutional on this ground, and again, it managed, albeit with somewhat more difficulty, to circumvent the question by deciding the case through statutory interpretation.

III. WELSH V. UNITED STATES

On his application for exemption, Welsh had denied that his beliefs were religious and had said he did not know whether he believed in a Supreme Being. He was denied C.O. status because the government "could find no religious basis for the registrant's beliefs, opinions, and convictions."[22] The government attempted to distinguish *Welsh* from *Seeger* on two grounds.

---

[18] *Id.* at 186.
[19] Bowser, *Delimiting Religion in the Constitution: A Classification Problem,* 11 VAL. U.L. REV. 163 (1977).
[20] Torasco v. Watkins, 367 U.S. 488 (1961).
[21] 398 U.S. 333 (1970).
[22] *Id.* at 338.

First, Welsh more insistently denied that his views were religious. The Supreme Court, however, refused to place such "undue emphasis on the registrant's interpretation of his own beliefs."[23] Although a registrant's characterization of his beliefs as religious should carry great weight, his characterization of his beliefs as nonreligious should not because "very few registrants are fully aware of the broad scope of the word religious as used in § 6(j)."[24] Second, the government maintained that Welsh's objection stemmed from "essentially political, sociological, or philosophical views or a merely personal moral code." The Court sidestepped any problems raised by this wording by interpreting it to mean that those registrants were to be excluded "whose beliefs are not deeply held and those whose objection to war does not rest at all upon moral, ethical or religious principle but instead rests solely upon considerations of policy, pragmatism, or expediency."[25] Through semantic magic the Court found the concepts of politics, sociology, philosophy, and personal morality identical to the concepts of policy, pragmatism, and expediency.

Having done this, the Court found Welsh "clearly entitled" to C.O. status under its new test for the applicability of section 6(j): "This section exempts from military service all those whose consciences, spurred by deeply held moral, ethical, or religious beliefs, would give no rest or peace if they allowed themselves to become a part of an instrument of war."[26] The Court, in clear violation of the statutory language, held that one whose objection to war is based upon his moral code qualifies for a section 6(j) exemption.

Justice Harlan, in a concurring opinion that detailed the legislative history of section 6(j), maintained that the statutory language was just not that elastic and that the Court must confront the Establishment Clause issue. He asserted that a statute that classifies based on the distinction between religious and nonreligious belief creates a "religious benefit" that offends the Establishment Clause. The only appropriate criterion for exemption as a conscientious objector "must be the intensity of moral conviction with which a belief is held."[27] The Court, however, may choose not to eliminate the unconstitutional provision but rather to build upon it. Thus the justices may rewrite the statute to cure "the defect of underinclusion."[28]

---

[23] *Id.* at 341.
[24] *Id.*
[25] *Id.* at 342-43.
[26] *Id.* at 344.
[27] *Id.* at 358.
[28] *Id.* at 367.

Justice Harlan said the constitutional standard for exemption is "the intensity of moral conviction with which a belief is held." This likewise is the test that those justices endorsing the plurality opinion employed. Such a test does follow logically from *Seeger* and cases that preceded it. Furthermore, it may be the only way for the Court to define religion without itself offending the Establishment Clause; to define religion is to establish what religion is and is not, and to favor or disfavor one set of beliefs against another set of beliefs. No doubt aware of this problem, the Court has never attempted a definition of religion for first amendment purposes. (*Seeger* and *Welsh* are offering a statutory definition.) One tendency, however, is to treat the term "religion" as including as many different types of beliefs as possible. Another tendency is to view religion functionally—not as a set of beliefs but as a role in the life of the believer. This is exactly what *Seeger* did. This approach has resulted in the *Welsh* opinion in a "definition" of religion as virtually equivalent to conscience. We are left with an illogical state of affairs. In order to avoid offense to the Establishment Clause, we define religion broadly as conscience. But if we insert the word "conscience" into the Establishment Clause, it makes little sense; certainly the Framers did not intend to prohibit the establishment of conscience, although perhaps they did intend to prohibit the imposition of the conscience of one person upon other people.

IV. SINCERITY

In *Witmer v. United States*,[29] a 1955 case involving the claim of a Jehovah's Witness for a C.O. exemption, the Supreme Court stated that "the ultimate question in conscientious objector cases is the sincerity of the registrant in objecting, on religious grounds, to participation in war in any form."[30] In *Seeger* the Court said that sincerity was the threshold question. In *Welsh* it may have become the *only* question. When deciding whether a professed follower of an established religion is entitled to a C.O. exemption, the Court first looks at the tenets of that religion to determine whether they dictate pacifism. If they do, the Court then considers the credibility of the registrant. Does he really adhere to the dogma of his church? In *Seeger* the first question is not whether the registrant adheres to a pacifist religion but whether his pacifism is religious. "A belief that plays a role parallel to that of orthodox religion" is one, in part, that is deeply held. The two prongs of the test begin to merge. By *Welsh* one could argue that sincerity (firmly held conviction) is the only question. If one sincerely believes what he professes to believe, he is entitled to a section 6(j) exemption.

One can also see that determining who qualifies for an exemption

---

[29] 348 U.S. 375 (1955).
[30] *Id.* at 381.

becomes more difficult as the test of religion becomes psychological rather than institutional. If, for example, one professes to be a Quaker, the issue of his sincerity is essentially one of his credibility and can be proven by objective means. Does he attend meetings? Does he follow other tenets of the faith? Was he educated or reared as a Quaker? But how do we measure the firmness of one's conviction in a personal and perhaps unique faith?

Using sincerity of one's belief as the sole criterion for exemption creates other problems as well, for the trier-of-fact's belief in the sincerity with which another holds a particular faith is necessarily linked to what ideas the trier-of-fact finds believable. What he finds believable may be limited by what he believes. This was pointed out by Justice Jackson dissenting in *United States v. Ballard.*[31] The Ballards were charged with using the mails to defraud by means of a so-called religious movement. They had claimed *inter alia,* miraculous communication with the spirit world and power to heal the sick. The majority held that the truth of the defendants' beliefs could not be considered by the jury, but that the defendants' sincerity (*i.e.,* whether or not they intentionally misrepresented their powers and connections) could be considered. One can see, however, that their sincerity would be placed in issue only after their professed religious beliefs were found to be false. A judicial finding that a particular religious view is false offends the Establishment Clause. Jackson therefore concluded that misrepresentation of religious experience or belief is not prosecutable. If this reasoning were applied in the conscientious objector cases decided after *Welsh,* the registrant's sincerity could not be questioned by the trier-of-fact and one who professed to fall within the section 6(j) exemption would indeed fall there.

But the Court most certainly has not adopted such an approach. Instead, by emphasizing "sincerity" it has been able to exclude more registrants from section 6(j) exemptions.

V. GILLETTE V. UNITED STATES

Gillette v. United States and *Negre v. Larsen* (decided together)[32] raised the issue of selective conscientious objection. Both defendants objected to participation in the Vietnam War but not to "participation in war in any form" as required by section 6(j). They maintained that the "war in any form" limitation impermissibly discriminates among types of religious belief and affiliation, and that their religious beliefs, which distinguished between just and unjust wars, were as worthy of exemption under section 6(j) and the Establishment Clause as any other religious beliefs.

---

[31] 322 U.S. 78, 92 (1944).
[32] 401 U.S. 437 (1971).

The Court demurred, holding that section 6(j) is neutral on its face, that it "does not single out any religious organization or religious creed for special treatment."[33] To the contention that section 6(j) "works a de facto discrimination among religions," the Court replied that the claimant "must be able to show the absence of a neutral, secular basis for the lines government has drawn."[34] The Court found neutral and secular reasons for the limitation to war in any form. One such secular justification was to assure fair, even-handed and uniform decision-making, for "a program of excusing objectors to particular wars may be impossible to conduct with any hope of reaching fair and consistent results.[35] Why would the extension of the exemption to selective C.O.'s be any harder to administer fairly than exemption of those objecting to participation in all war? It is more difficult because "opposition to a particular war does depend *inter alia* upon particularistic factual beliefs and policy assessments that presumably were overridden by the government that decides to commit lives and resources to a trial of arms."[36] In other words, some consideration of "policy" is involved in the registrant's objection to a particular war, to his determination that it is unjust. The question, under the test enunciated in *Welsh*, then should become: Does his objection rest *solely* on considerations of policy and not at all upon "moral, ethical or religious principle"? It has been suggested by one commentator[37] that *Gillette* answers this question: "In all probability, yes." And that being the case, exemption for selective objectors should be denied. In other words, the Court doubts the sincerity of the selective objector's statement that his belief is "religious," for the Court states that "opposition to a particular war may more likely be political and nonconscientious, than otherwise."[38] Based on the content of the objector's belief the Court is doubting his sincerity. This would seem a violation of the principles established in *Seeger* and *Welsh*, but, states *Gillette*, " 'sincerity' is a concept that can bear only so much adjudicative weight."[39] It is curious that the Court rejects Gillette's and Negre's claims at least in part because it generally doubts the sincerity of those making such claims; nonetheless, it states that no doubt as to the sincerity and religious nature of the claim of either Gillette or Negre exists.

It is also curious that the difficulty of determining sincerity is considered too great in the case of Negre, a devout Catholic. Negre had based his claim on the doctrine of the Catholic church that distinguishes

[33] *Id.* at 451.
[34] *Id.* at 452. Note that this requirement shifts the burden of proof to the claimant.
[35] *Id.* at 456.
[36] *Id.* at 459.
[37] Bowser, *supra* note 19, at 180.
[38] 401 U.S. at 455.
[39] *Id.* at 457.

between just and unjust wars.[40] That his objection was based on institutionalized religion should have simplified the problem of determining sincerity, as pointed out earlier.[41] Yet the Court found the task too difficult.

Petitioners in *Gillette* also argued that the limitation of section 6(j) to those who oppose war in any form interfered with the free exercise of their religion. The majority answered this contention: "Our analysis of § 6(j) for Establishment Clause purposes has revealed governmental interests of a kind and weight sufficient to justify under the Free Exercise Clause the impact of the conscription laws on those who object to particular wars."[42] The free exercise of religion is protected only "when the burden on First Amendment values is not justifiable in terms of the government's valid aims."[43] Here the government's interests—particularly its interest "in procuring the manpower necessary for military purposes"[44]—outweigh the individual's right to freely exercise his religion. The suggestion is that in 1971 if Congress excused from military service all those young men who believed the war in Vietnam was morally wrong, it would be unable to raise an army.

The thrust of the *Gillette* decision seems to be that if one has a right to free exercise of conscience, one has it only so long as few other people wish to exercise that right in the same way, but once many people's consciences clash with the interests of government, their consciences are no longer protected by the Free Exercise Clause. The reasoning in *Gillette* is reminiscent of the "clear and present danger" test that the Court earlier employed in the area of freedom of speech. Dissent is respected as long as it is ineffectual.

VI. FREE EXERCISE

The Court in *Gillette* decides only the narrow issue of whether one has a free exercise right to exemption under section 6(j) for "religious" opposition to a particular war. The majority does not address the broader issue (which remains unanswered) of whether a free exercise right to some type of C.O. exemption exists. As Justice Douglas put it in his

---

[40] *See* 401 U.S. 470 (Douglas, J., dissenting) for a discussion of this idea and the theological authority for it.

[41] A similar situation arose in Clay v. United States, 403 U.S. 698 (1971). Here Mohammed Ali refused to participate in the Vietnam War because his Moslem religion taught that he not "aid the infidels or nonbelievers in Islam." The Court reversed Ali's conviction on procedural grounds. Only the concurring Justice Douglas reached the substantive issue and found a constitutional right to refuse participation in war of a character proscribed by one's religion.

[42] 401 U.S. at 461.

[43] *Id.* at 462.

[44] *Id.*

dissent in *Gillette* "Can a conscientious objector, whether his objection be rooted in 'religion' or in moral values, be required to kill?"[45]

The question was first discussed in *United States v. Macintosh*,[46] where the petitioner was denied naturalization because he would not swear that he would bear arms on behalf of the United States unless he felt a war was morally justified. Macintosh lost the case because of the Court's statutory interpretation of the oath of allegiance, but in dictum the Court said: "Whether any citizen shall be exempt from serving in the armed forces of the nation in time of war is dependent upon the will of Congress and not upon the scruples of the individual, except as Congress provides."[47] *MacIntosh* was later overruled[48] and the force of its dictum dissipated. Although the dissent by Chief Justice Hughes is generally more respected today than the majority opinion, even Hughes did not go so far as to declare a constitutional right to an exemption. Rather he said that the majority's construction of the oath was "directly opposed to the spirit of our institutions and to the historic practice of Congress"; it violated "principles which have long been respected as fundamental."[49]

Why has the Court not clearly ruled[50] on the question of a free exercise right to conscientious exemption?[51] First, were the Court to find a free exercise right, it would be faced with a conflict between the Free Exercise Clause and the Establishment Clause. If the right freely to exercise his religion entitles one to be excused from military duty, in so excusing him the state is favoring his religion over the religion or non-religion of another. One way out of this dilemma was suggested by the separate opinions of Justice Douglas in the three 1971 cases involving conscientious objectors.[52] Douglas equated religion with conscience for purposes of free exercise analysis:

> It is true that the First Amendment speaks of the free exercise of religion, not of the free exercise of conscience or belief. Yet con-

---

[45] *Id.* at 464.

[46] 283 U.S. 605 (1931).

[47] *Id.* at 623.

[48] Girouard v. United States, 328 U.S. 61 (1946).

[49] 283 U.S. at 627. It is interesting to note that Hughes also saw no bar to conscientious exemption on the grounds that Macintosh was a "selective" objector. *Id.* at 629.

[50] There have been cases in which the Court ruled that the state had the right to deny some benefit to those refusing military service, (*see for example* Hamilton v. Board of Regents, 293 U.S. 245 (1934)) but this is different from having the right to compel an individual to kill.

[51] Justice Douglas dissenting in *Gillette* and Ehlert v. United States, 402 U.S. 198 (1971), and concurring in *Clay* stated that such a free exercise exemption does exist. Harlan, in his concurrence in *Welsh*, stated that there is no such free exercise right. The dissenters in *Welsh*—White, Burger, and Stewart—did not decide the issue but wrote *"on the assumption . . .* that the Free Exercise Clause of the First Amendment does not by *its own force* require exempting devout objectors from military service. . . ." [Emphasis added]

[52] *See* notes 41 and 51, supra.

science and belief are the main ingredients of First Amendment rights. They are the bedrock of free speech as well as religion. The implied First Amendment right of "conscience" is certainly as high as the "right of association" which we recognized in Shelton v. Tucker and NAACP v. Alabama. [Citations omitted.] Some indeed have thought it higher.[53]

Thus either by reading "religion" as meaning "conscience" in the Free Exercise Clause and "a particular ideology" in the Establishment Clause or by implying a separate, penumbral right of free exercise of conscience, the right to a conscientious exemption based on conscience could be given constitutional stature without coming into conflict with the Establishment Clause.

But no constitutional right is unqualified. Since 1878 the Court has distinguished between belief and action in the area of free exercise and held that under some circumstances the government may control action.[54] In *Sherbert v. Verner*[55] the Court held that to justify interference with the free exercise of religion, a compelling state interest must exist. In order to find whether a compelling state interest existed that would justify the conscription of pacifists, the Court in *Seeger* and *Welsh* may have had to deal with some issues it preferred not to. For one thing, the state interest in denying exemptions necessarily depends on the number of exemptions sought. To argue that the state's ability to pursue the war in Vietnam would be jeopardized by allowing the exemption would be to acknowledge the amount of dissent there was to the war. Furthermore, it would raise the question of whether the state had a valid interest in pursuing the war, or whether Vietnam was an illegal exercise of the war powers. Could there be a compelling state interest in an undeclared war? A compelling state interest in a peacetime draft? All in all, one understands why the Court preferred to evade these questions.

VII.   1980

If Congress in reenacting draft legislation merely takes the Selective Service Act of 1967 out of deep freeze and leaves section 6(j) unaltered, many of these constitutional questions may never be resolved. If, however, Congress either eliminates the C.O. exemption or narrows it, the Court will no doubt be forced to decide the basic first amendment questions.

If Congress for the first time in the history of the draft provides no exemption for conscientious objectors, will the Court hold that such an

---

[53] 401 U.S. at 465-466.
[54] Reynolds v. United States, 98 U.S. 145 (1878).
[55] 374 U.S. 398 (1963).

exemption is nonetheless inherent in the Free Exercise Clause? If the Court looks to the "compelling state interest" test for its answer, it may find such an interest in the defense of the nation. The result may depend upon whether the Court looks at the state's action in terms of its interest in conscripting soldiers or in terms of its interest in allowing no exemptions from conscription. (This decision would not be wholly severable from one of the breadth required for any exemption to meet the demands of the Establishment Clause.)

Or the Court may look to the balancing test set out in 1972 in *Wisconsin v. Yoder*,[56] which held that the state compulsory education statute violated the free exercise rights of the Amish community. *Yoder* posited that "only those interests of the highest order and those not otherwise served can overbalance legitimate claims to the free exercise of religion."[57] The difficulty in predicting the results of an application of this test in the area of conscientious objection is that it is not clear whether the religion side of the scale always weighs the same and it is the amount of state interest that tips the balance one way or another, or whether the weight assigned to religion may vary with the act being exercised and/or its centrality to the faith of the individual. Does, for example, the religiously based refusal to salute the flag[58] weigh the same as the religiously based refusal to kill a human being? *Yoder* does on the whole suggest that the exercise of religion is a static value. This approach, if applied to the question of conscientious objection, would in all probability result in a finding that one did not have a free exercise right to military exemption,[59] at least not while the United States was lawfully and actively at war. However, consideration of the degree of violation of conscience involved in forcing one to take another's life might yield a result in favor of the C.O. Seemingly, the constitutional approach is not to consider the nature of the act demanded of the individual, for to assign value to the religious practices of individuals is to evaluate the truth of their beliefs in violation of the Establishment Clause.[60]

The suggestion is also present in *Yoder* that the centrality of a religiously-based act to the tenets of one's religion may bear on the value assigned the free exercise thereof. This idea cannot be clearly distinguished in the case from the question of the sincerity of the Amish in contending

---

[56] 406 U.S. 205 (1972).

[57] *Id.* at 215.

[58] *See* West Virginia State Board of Education v. Barnette, 319 U.S. 624 (1943).

[59] A belief that this would be the result is enhanced by the fact that Justice Douglas, now deceased, is the only justice to have declared that such a right exists. Most of the present justices have spoken of the "suggestion" that there is no such right or "on the assumption" that there is none.

[60] United States v. Ballard, 322 U.S. 78 (1944).

that conventional education beyond the eighth grade violated their religious faith and not just their social mores. Perhaps the questions of sincerity and centrality inevitably merge. In any event, *Yoder* looks to the
history of the sect to determine both. If the Court does clearly separate
sincerity from centrality for purposes of free exercise analysis and grants
more weight to practices as they approach the center of belief, the scales
will tip a bit more in favor of a free exercise right to conscientious exemption from conscription.

 Yoder is of interest in the present context for another reason. It makes
clear that the Burger Court is going to define religion narrowly, for "the
very concept of ordered liberty precludes allowing every person to make
his own standards on matters of conduct in which society as a whole has
important interests."[61] To the Chief Justice, a claim by Henry Thoreau
would be "philosophical and personal rather than religious."[62]

 The Burger Court clearly is not about to adopt Justice Douglas's idea
of a right of conscience inherent in the first amendment. If confronted with
a selective service statute that limits the C.O. exemption to members of
established faiths or members of established peace churches or which in
some other way attempts to circumvent the broad interpretation which
the Court has given the concept of religion in section 6(j), the present
Court will probably find it constitutional by finding a secular and neutral
purpose behind the classification, much as it did in *Gillette*.

CONCLUSION

 In conclusion, the relationship between the first amendment and conscientious objection to military service has never been resolved. Furthermore,
attempted resolution may involve a clash between the values embodied in
the Free Exercise Clause and those embodied in the Establishment Clause.
Should Congress restore the draft, but either eliminate or restrict the C.O.
exemption, the Supreme Court would be forced to make a ruling on the
constitutional dimensions of conscientious exemption. Although Justice
Douglas suggested at least a partial solution to the problem when he found
a right to the free exercise of conscience embedded in the first amendment,
the present Supreme Court would not adopt such an analysis. Instead, it
would probably find that there is no free exercise right to C.O. status and
no violation of the Establishment Clause in a statute that limits the exemption to adherents of traditional religions.

GAIL WHITE SWEENEY

---

[61] 406 U.S. at 215, 216.
[62] That Thoreau would be thrown in jail once again, raises the question, "What are you
doing out there, Waldo and Warren?"

Part IV
Towards the Legal Definition
of 'Religion'

[12]

On Legal Definitions of "Religion"

WOJCIECH SADURSKI
Senior Lecturer in Department of Jurisprudence, University of Sydney

The relationship between the State and religion in modern secular nations is regulated by two principles: the principle of non-establishment of any religion through law (henceforth referred to as the Non-Establishment Principle) and the principle of free exercise of any religion (henceforth: the Free Exercise Principle). These two principles, in this order, have been entrenched inter alia both in the Constitution of the United States[1] and in the Constitution of the Commonwealth of Australia.[2] The two principles display some tension in their mutual relationship: while the Free Exercise Principle calls for some degree of governmental accommodation of religion, the Non-Establishment Principle in contrast calls for suspicion towards any such accommodation, and it detects in them impermissible governmental assistance to religion. In other words, the Free Exercise Principle has an expanding dynamic built into it (calling for a positive and active legal attitude towards claims to have one's religious requirements respected through legal accommodation, exemptions and privileges), and this very dynamic threatens to undermine the disengagement of the State from religious matters demanded by the Non-Establishment Principle.

The tension between the two principles outlined above is reflected in the controversy about the legal definition of "religion": the Free Exercise Principle favours a definition of religion which is ultimately unacceptable under the Non-Establishment Principle. Consider, first, the significance of the controversy. Whether a body is religious or not may be decisive in granting or denying certain privileges; for instance, an organisation may want to be considered "religious" in order to qualify for tax exemptions[3] or to protect its practices from regulation by governmental bodies,[4] and conversely, it may wish to be classified as non-religious in order, say, to be able to promote its practices in public schools.[5] But in order to decide about such a classification, the court must first establish what is "religion" — and, in this respect, the Free Exercise Principle and the Non-Establishment Principle point in opposite directions.

The natural tendency built into the principle of the free exercise of religion leans toward an expansive concept of "religion", for any limits upon the concept threaten to leave some putative "religions" (which happen not to match the definer's expectations about what the "religion" is about) outside the category of beliefs deserving protection under the Free Exercise Principle. Any definitional constraint therefore involves the danger of discrimination based on a definitional bias against unknown, or unpopular, religions (precisely those which are in the greatest need of legal protection). But, as we will see, any extension of the concept of "religion" inevitably comes under fire from the Non-Establishment Principle because it undermines the legitimacy of the routine State regulations in the areas previously (that is to say, before the definitional extension)

---

[1] "Congress shall make no law respecting an establishment of religion, or prohibiting the free exercise thereof; ..." (United States Constitution, First Amendment).

[2] "The Commonwealth shall not make any law for establishing any religion, or for imposing any religious observance, or for prohibiting the free exercise of any religion, and no religious test shall be required as a qualification for any office or public trust under the Commonwealth" (Commonwealth Constitution, s 116). While s 116 contains four religion-related clauses, the religious-observance clause and the religious-test clause are clearly derivative from the other two which will be, for the purposes of this article, treated as fundamental.

[3] See *Church of The New Faith v Commissioner for Pay-roll Tax* (1983) 57 ALJR 785.

[4] See *Founding Church of Scientology v United States* (1969) 409 F 2d 1146 (DC Cir) cert denied (1969) 396 US 963.

[5] See *Malnak v Yogi* (1977) 440 F Supp 1284 (DNJ) affd (1979) 592 F 2d 197 (3d Cir).

held "secular". In an expanding era of the social and economic functions of the Welfare State, the Non-Establishment Principle must, it would appear, call for the narrowing down to some extent of the scope of the "religious" classification.

But even apart from the problems raised by the definition of "religion" under the Non-Establishment Principle (a problem to which we will return later), is there any substantive definition of "religion" which could avoid the dangers of discriminatory bias (under the Free Exercise Principle) and at the same time distinguish meaningfully the religious and non-religious beliefs, codes of conduct, and bodies? The history of the religion clauses jurisprudence of the Supreme Court of the United States and of the High Court of Australia warrants a good deal of scepticism about the possibility of an affirmative answer. In their praiseworthy attempts to forge a non-discriminatory concept of "religion", both these Courts bravely rejected a number of conventional notions about what constitutes "religion". First, and least controversially perhaps, both these Courts rejected the legitimacy of judicial inquiry into the "truth" or "falsity" of beliefs claimed to be religious; in a memorable sentence by Justice Douglas of the United States Supreme Court (cited also by the High Court): "Heresy trials are foreign to our Constitution."[6] Second, both Courts rejected confining the concept of "religion" to theistic beliefs only.[7] Significantly, the rejection of such limitation of the concept of religion was accompanied in *Torcaso* by a list of examples of beliefs identified by the Court as religious which included "Buddhism, Taoism, Ethical Culture, *Secular Humanism* and others"[8] [emphasis added].

From this point on, the lines of argument about the definition of "religion" in the two Courts' decisions part company. The United States Supreme Court settled for a fully subjective-functional approach, in which virtually the only indicium of the "religiousness" of a given belief is the sincerity with which it is held, and the function it plays, but not its tenets. This test was set forth in two conscientious-objection cases. In *United States v Seeger*,[9] in interpreting the scope of exemption from military service based on "religious training and belief", the Court extended the exemption upon those who rejected dependence on a Creator for a guide to morality, and concluded that:

"[a] sincere and meaningful belief which occupies in the life of its possessor a place parallel to that filled by the God of those admittedly qualifying for the exemption comes within the statutory definition."[10]

The subjectivity of the test resided in the Court's holding that the only inquiry of the draft board should have been into

"whether the beliefs professed by a registrant are sincerely held and whether they are, *in his own scheme of things*, religious" [emphasis added].[11]

The process was completed by *Welsh v United States*,[12] a case of a conscientious objector who expressly struck the word "religious" from his application and who claimed to ground his anti-war beliefs on readings in history and sociology. A plurality of the Court

[6] *United States v Ballard* (1944) 322 U 78 at 79; quoted approvingly in *Church The New Faith* at 789 (per Mason an Brennan JJ). See also, ibid, at 788: "Th courts are constrained to accord freedom t faith in the supernatural, for there are n means of finding upon evidence whether postulated tenet of supernatural truth erroneous . . . ."
[7] *Torcaso v Watkins* (1961) 367 US 48 *Church of the New Faith* (1983) 57 ALJR 7 at 791 ("To restrict the definition of r ligion to theistic religions is to exclu Theravada Buddhism, an acknowledged r ligion, and perhaps other acknowledge religions. It is too narrow a test").
[8] (1961) 367 US at 495, n 11.
[9] (1965) 380 US 163.
[10] Ibid, at 176.
[11] Ibid, at 185.
[12] (1970) 398 US 333.

nevertheless found him to be religious, and explained the *Seeger's* test (the person's "own scheme of things") as intended

"to indicate that the central consideration in determining whether the registrant's beliefs are religious is whether these beliefs play the role of a religion and function as a religion in the registrant's life".[13]

While under *Seeger* "essentially" non-religious views (for example "political, sociological or economic" beliefs) were still denied exemption,[14] under *Welsh* such a possibility became foreclosed and the exclusion of exemption had been confined to considerations of "policy, pragmatism, or expediency", as contrasted with a "moral, ethical or religious principle".[15]

The High Court of Australia refused to go as far as that, and explicitly rejected the subjectivist-functional approach.[16] Predictably, it found that the subjectivist-functional definition (not labelled in this particular way) had an effect of "expand[ing] the concept of religion beyond its true domain".[17] In its place, the Court stipulated in *Church of The New Faith* that the criteria of religion were twofold: (1) belief in a supernatural Being, Thing or Principle; and (2) the acceptance of canons of conduct in order to give effect to that belief.[18]

One can appreciate why the High Court has not gone all the way along its American counterpart's path of rejecting the content-based definitions. The subjectivist-functional definition may be said to suffer from three important defects. First, it seems to be tautological: in order to know whether certain beliefs "play the role of religion", we need to know what the religion is in the first place, but this is precisely what the subjectivist-functionalist test refuses to tell us. Second, *any* set of beliefs, even those commonly seen as non-religious or anti-religious, may be seen as "playing the role of religion" in a person's own scheme of things; consequently, treating them as "religious" has the effect of diluting the meaningfulness of the word "religion", and cannot account for the privileged status of religion in constitutional texts. If beliefs generally viewed as non-religious obtain protection under constitutionally entrenched rights, why did these constitutions mention "religion" specifically, rather than protecting an individual conscience or individual beliefs in general? Third, the subjectivist-functionalist test, in order to screen off claims which are not serious but merely a hoax[19] (a danger inherent in a situation where the characterisation of a belief as religious is beyond the competence of anyone other than the adherent)[20] necessitates inquiry into the sincerity with which given beliefs are held by a person or a group; but sincerity is notoriously difficult to prove or to disprove before a court.

Later in this article, it will be submitted that the first two "defects" are really the sources of strength of the subjectivist-functionalist definition, and that they can be justified by the overall pattern of freedom of religion moulded, as it is, by the principle of neutrality of law towards religions. About the third defect, it is perhaps sufficient to say that the inquiry into sincerity of religious beliefs is not qualitatively different from any another judicial scrutiny of the individual state of mind, such as in the examination of criminal mens

[13] Ibid, at 339.
[14] (1965) 380 US at 173.
[15] (1970) 398 US at 343.
[16] Curiously enough, as an object of its criticism, the High Court chose a lower American court's interpretation of the *Seeger* and *Welsh* definition, rather than the Supreme Court's opinions directly. See *Church of the New Faith* (1983) 57 ALJR 785 at 790-791 (extensively quoting, and rejecting the approach by, Adams J in *Malnak v Yogi* (1979) 592 F 2d 197).
[17] *Church of the New Faith* (1983) 57 ALJR 785 at 791.
[18] Ibid, at 789.
[19] Ibid, at 796 (Murphy J, dissenting).
[20] See Note, "Toward a Constitutional Definition of Religion" (1978) 91 Harv L Rev 1056 at 1081.

Law and Religion

rea, or of legislative intent for the purpose of statutory interpretation. That this cannot be a serious objection against the subjectivist test of religion is perhaps indicated by the fact that even the critics of such definition rarely raise this particular objection. After all, there are a number of methods of measuring the sincerity of a claim for religious exemption: inter alia, the conformity of this claim with the written or empirically verifiable traditions and proscriptions of the religion or cult, congruence between the professed religious tenets and one's actions,[21] the willingness to undertake alternative duties and burdens, equally onerous but neutral from the point of view of that religion's proscriptions. etc.

Let us, however, grant, arguendo, that the first two defects mentioned above are real, and that a substantive definition of religion is necessary. From this point of view, the effort of the High Court seems to deserve some applause: its substantive definition is arguably so general and non-discriminatory that it seems to avoid successfully the perceived danger of so defining religion

"as to exclude from its ambit minority religions out of the mainstreams of religious thought".[22]

On closer reflection, however, this becomes less certain. The key operative word in the Court's substantive definition of religion is "supernatural": in order to be religious, the belief must be in a supernatural Being, Thing, or Principle. What exactly "the supernatural" means for the Justices is not absolutely clear. True, a judicial opinion is not a philosophical or a theological treatise. Yet, so much hinges upon the concept of "supernatural" in the *Church of the New Faith*, as *the* test for discriminating between religious and non-religious beliefs, that we must have some degree of clarity about what it means, and how it can be used to avoid the Scylla of too narrow definitions (and hence, biased against minorities) and the Charybdis of too broad (and hence, according to the Court, useless) definitions.

A closer reading of the *Church of the New Faith* suggests that the Justices' concept of the "supernatural" encompasses two related philosophical notions: a metaphysical concept of the transcendental order, transcending the bounds of individuals and of the physical world, and an epistemological concept of non-empirical (or extra-empirical) cognition, available to humans by means other than through the mediation of our senses and reason. These two elements are present in this crucial phrase, in which the non-religious approach (as perceived by the Court) is contrasted with the religious one:[23]

"For some, the natural order, known or knowable by use of man's senses and his natural reason, provides a sufficient and exhaustive solution to these great problems [of the existence of the universe, the meaning of human life, and human destiny]; for others, an adequate solution can be found only in the supernatural order, in which man may believe as a matter of faith, but which he cannot demonstrate to others who do not share his faith."

It is not clear how useful the notion of the "supernatural" (as the transcendental order and cognition) can be in defining the scope of

[21] Consider the case in which a court refused to recognise a defendant's right not to have a trial held after sunset on a Friday because the defendant often worked on Saturdays despite his religious tenets forbidding it. See *Dobkin v District of Columbia* (1963) 194 A 2d 657 (DC). See generally, Comment, "'Mind Control' or Intensity of Faith: The Constitutional Protection of Religious Beliefs" (1978) 1 Harv Civil Rights-Civil Liberties L Rev 75 at 763-764.
[22] (1983) 57 ALJR 785 at 787.
[23] Ibid, at 788.

'religion''. For one thing, some modern Protestant theologians have called for the rejection, in the name of authentic Christianity, of the ideas of transcendence and of associated Christian metaphysical statements. John A T Robinson, Bishop of Woolwich, gives in his book an explicitly negative answer to a dramatic question: "Must Christianity be 'Supranaturalist'?"[24] In fact the general thrust of his book is to reject emphatically the notion of a God "out there" and replace it with a view of religion as "ground[ing] all reality ultimately in personal freedom — in Love".[25] To be sure, this view was criticised by the mainstream Christian writers,[26] but surely the High Court would not want to get embroiled in a theological dispute about the ontological status of God. The main thesis of one of the leading modern progressive theologians, Paul Tillich, is that the essence of religious phenomena is in the matters of "the ultimate concern" for an individual: the test of "religiousness" lies therefore, for Tillich, not in the substance of a given experience but in the superior ranking that religious experiences have over all other concerns.[27] For this reason, according to Tillich, every person experiences "the presence of the divine" and "the relation to the holy"[28] and "even he who denies God as a matter of ultimate concern affirms God, because he affirms ultimacy in his concern".[29]

Clearly, whether or not these "concerns" relate to what the Australian Justices would characterise as "supernatural", is of no importance for this theory. Nor is the "supernaturalness" relevant to the test of religiousness employed by some scholars of comparative religions. Mircea Eliade, for one, in his distinction of the sacred and the profane (crucial for his understanding of religions) dispensed with an appeal to the supernatural, as he believed that anything, whether an "object, movement, psychological function, being or even game"[30] may at times be viewed as sacred. As some of the examples of "hierophanies", or manifestations of the sacred, he cited the sacred value attached to stones, or to the mystique of eroticism[31] — arguably not "supernatural" phenomena. Functionalist definitions of religion locate the essence of the religious phenomena in the role they play in the lives of individuals and societies, not in their particular tenets, whether "supernatural" or not. Clifford Geertz's definition is a good example: he defines religion as

"a system of symbols which acts to establish powerful, pervasive and long-lasting moods and motivations in men by formulating conceptions of a general order of existence and clothing these conceptions with such an aura of factuality that the moods and motivations seem uniquely realistic".[32]

Again, a "general order of existence" need not reach the dimension of "transcendence" required by the concept of the supernatural.

Now it is true that neither theology nor the study of comparative religion can be equated with a religion itself, but if some influential theological or scholarly traditions postulate a non-supernatural notion of religion, then this suggests that the judicial definition of "religion" may be under-inclusive, and may simply repeat an earlier error of identifying religions with theism. Indeed, some Eastern religions, such as the so-called "non-dualist" school of Vedantic tradition of Brahmanism, reject a separation between the internal self

[24] See J A T Robinson, *Honest to God* (SCM Press, 1963), p 29.
[25] Ibid, at p 130.
[26] See M E Marty, *Varieties of Unbelief* (Doubleday, 1966), pp 118-121.
[27] P Tillich, *Dynamics of Faith* (Allen & Unwin, 1957), pp 1-4.
[28] Ibid, at p 13
[29] Ibid, at p 46.
[30] M Eliade, *Patterns in Comparative Religion* (Sheed & Ward, 1958), p 11.
[31] Ibid, chs 6 and 9.
[32] C Geertz, *The Interpretation of Cultures* (Doubleday, 1973), p 90.

and the external world: they locate the essence of deity, and the sole reality, *within* the individual. [33]

"The pure Self ... is the only really existing entity, sheer consciousness unlimited by any contents or qualifications ..."; [34]

the "transcendental" ingredient of "the perceived supernatural" is absent there. As far as the second tier of the judicial definition of "religion" is concerned, namely the existence of canons of conduct which give effect to beliefs in a supernatural Being, Thing or Principle, it has been argued that a number of beliefs, for instance the Greco-Oriental mystery cults, prescribed no moral principles to their adherents, and yet the experience they provided was arguably religious. [35]

The above remarks suggest that even the superficially innocuous demand that religions appeal to the supernatural may be under-inclusive and may leave some "religions" outside the limits of judicial protection. But, at the same time, it may prove over-inclusive. The idea of the supernatural, if reducible to the twin components of a transcendental reality and a non-empirical cog-nition, is present in a great number of philosophical and ideological traditions which are not generally viewed as religious, or which are even openly anti-religious. Significantly, some theologians lament that the notion of transcendence has been captured by the agnostic or atheistic ideologies, thus weakening the position of religion. A leading Lutheran theologian in the United States, M E Marty, deplores the rise of "unbelief" in the forms of nationalism, Fascism and Communism, which "supplant[ing] the God of Christian faith" with their own "pantheisms and paganisms of history and power" as new foci of transcendence in a world without God. [36] Also non-theological writers used to characterise (and usually, criticise) movements and ideologies so explicitly atheistic as Marxism-Leninism as religious in their character; [37] others used religious categories to describe Nazism [38] and nationalism in general, [39] arguing that all these ideologies and movements contained clear traces of "transcendence", as a higher order of things beyond the individual and the physical reality. As far as the epistemological indicium of "supernaturalness" is concerned, namely, the notion of non-empirical knowledge, this proposition is again present in a great number of philosophical traditions which are usually not thought of as religious; in fact in all the strands of epistemology which reject empiricism.

Now a possible defence of the High Court's definition against the charge of over-inclusiveness could be that the Court quite deliberately avoided the conventional notions of "religion", and therefore we should not be worried about the inclusion of various traditions of thought and movements which are *not usually thought of* as religious into the judicial definition of religion: the aim is to avoid the majoritarian bias inherent in conventional definitions. Suppose that the court would be willing to recognise as religious any theory which sincerely contains the ideas of transcendental order and non-empirical cognition. But if the court were prepared to extend the ambit of its definition as broadly as that, then its superiority over the subjectivist-functional definition would all but

[33] H Zimmer, *Philosophies of Indi*. (Pantheon, 1951), pp 414-451.
[34] Ibid, at 428.
[35] Note, loc cit, n 20, ante, at 1073.
[36] Marty, op cit, n 26, ante, at p 122, an see, generally, pp 98-144.
[37] See J Bennet, *Christianity and Commu nism* (SCM Press, 1949), pp 33-34.
[38] P Viereck, *Meta-Politics: The Roots* the Nazi Mind (Capricorn, 1961), ch 13.
[39] Marty, op cit, n 26, ante, at pp 15(164.

vanish. The notion of religion would be very importantly diluted in comparison with conventional notions of religiousness. At the same time, the problems with under-inclusiveness, as pointed out earlier, would remain: religions which do not rely on the notion of the supernatural would continue to lie beyond the ambit of constitutional protection.

At this point one can anticipate the protest that we demand the impossible: a definition which is sufficiently narrow (in order to be meaningful) and at the same time broad enough (in order to avoid the bias against unconventional religions). Surely no single definition can satisfy these two conditions. Some writers conclude from this that the quest for a definition of religion (*any* definition) is misconceived, and that religious systems, as we know them, have nothing in common that distinguishes them from all other belief systems: hence "religion" cannot be defined at all. [40] But if this is the case, how can a court decide in real-life cases, which raise the free exercise or non-establishment challenges, whether a given belief, group or purpose is "religious" or not?

The answer to the dilemma can be found, it is suggested, by reflecting upon the over-arching purpose of the Free Exercise Principle and the Non-Establishment Principle. Before attempting this answer, however, let us sum up the earlier discussion by highlighting the divergent pressures exerted upon the definition of religion by the two principles regulating the relationship of law and religion. A built-in tendency of the Free Exercise Principle is to call for as extensive a definition of religion as possible: any definitional limiting factors may discriminate against those religions which are unknown to, or are not approved by, the definer, and result in a denial to them of free exercise, protected from the imposition of State restrictions. It is therefore natural that adherents of *any* system of belief, under the régime of constitutional protection for the free exercise of religion, possess an interest in having their sets of beliefs characterised as "religious". But the more general the concept of religion under the Free Exercise Principle is, the less effective the Non-Establishment Principle becomes in defining the sphere of permissible, secular State action. A distinction between the secular and the religious purposes (and effects) is crucial for the Non-Establishment Principle: the broadening of the scope of "religion" (demanded by the Free Exercise Principle) narrows down the sphere of legitimate State action. Expansive definitions of religion, required by the Free Exercise Principle, may have as their unintended effect the invalidation of a good deal of generally unobjectionable governmental functions.

A solution advocated in this article lies in an appeal to the concept of the State's neutrality between religions, and also between religious and non-religious moral conceptions. [41] Within this unifying scheme, the Free Exercise Principle and the Non-Establishment Principle have equally important but distinct functions. They both serve the aim of securing an equal moral agency of every individual with respect to religious matters, beliefs and conduct. The principle of neutrality means that no legal burden or privilege can attach to an individual's choice, change and pursuit of religious ideals (nor to the choice of non-religious morality). This is the supreme value of a liberal legal order. In a substantiation of this general ideal, the Free Exercise

[40] G C Freeman, "The Misconceived Search for the Constitutional Definition of 'Religion'" (1983) 71 Georgetown LJ 1519. See also, J Weiss, "Privilege, Posture and Protection: 'Religion' in the Law" (1964) 73 Yale LJ 593 at 602-607.

[41] See, further, *Roemer v Board of Public Works* (1976) 426 US 744 at 746; *Everson v Board of Education* (1947) 330 US 1 at 18; J T Valauri, "The Concept of Neutrality in Establishment Clause Doctrine" (1986) 48 Univ of Pittsburgh L Rev 83; W G Katz, "Freedom of Religion and State Neutrality" (1953) 20 Univ of Chicago L Rev 426.

Principle defines a sphere of individual rights (which must not be affected by one's choice of a religion or of non-religious beliefs), while the Non-Establishment Principle describes the institutional structure within which the State disengages itself from religious bodies and groups in order to secure equal moral agency of its citizens. Neither of the two principles needs to prevail over the other because they both serve, in their distinct spheres of application and in their own specific ways, the overall ideal of legal neutrality.

Consider the consequences of these propositions for the definition of religion under the two principles. What matters under the Non-Establishment Principle is the non-interference of the State in the actions of religious bodies and institutions, and making sure that the government-regulated sphere of public life is uncontaminated by religious (or anti-religious) considerations. The principal insight here is that religion must remain a private matter for every individual, and that social life (in this sphere in which it is governmentally regulated) must remain unaffected by religious or anti-religious motivations of the policy-makers and legislators. Consequently, the public decision-makers must know clearly and precisely what is to count as "religion", and how to demarcate the non-religious concerns, in order to screen off the religion-conscious considerations from their decisions. The main evil that the Non-Establishment Principle attacks is a non-neutral merger of secular regulatory concerns and the religious motives.

However, the evil identified by the Free Exercise Principle is quite different: this principle seeks to eliminate not institutional favouritism but rather the coercive pressure imposed upon an individual who is in pursuit of his or her moral (including religious) choices. From this point of view, the distinction between a religion (or what is usually considered religion) and *other moral* beliefs is of no importance, because the wrong committed through illegitimate State coercion consists in restricting one's moral choice. While religious choices constitute an important sub-class of moral choices, the boundaries between them and non-religious moral choices are irrelevant because all these moral choices have to be respected by the government, as long as they are harmless. Once we appreciate this, we need find no contradiction in a somewhat bizarre labelling, in *Torcaso*,[42] of "Secular Humanism" as one of the religious beliefs, for the purposes of the Free Exercise Principle, because from the point of view of this principle the boundaries between secularism and religiosity simply do not matter. Moreover, this also accounts for those judicial pronouncements which enumerate in one breath official religious orthodoxy along with political, national and other "matters of opinion" orthodoxies as all equally unconstitutional.[43] In contrast, the Non-Establishment Principle deals only indirectly with coercion applied against individuals — its main goal is to eliminate institutional favouritism of the State.

This explains why there is no inconsistency in adopting a broad definition of religion for the purposes of the Free Exercise Principle and a narrow one for the purposes of the Non-Establishment Principle. To test this conception, consider the costs involved in adopting a too broad (or, in contrast, too narrow) definition of religion under either of the principles. Under the Free Exercise Principle, as we have seen, the costs of erring on the side of

[42] (1961) 367 US 488 at 495, n 11.
[43] "If there is any fixed star in ou constitutional constellation, it is that no official, high or petty, can prescribe wha shall be orthodox in politics, nationalism religion, or other matters of opinion o force citizens to confess by word or ac their faith therein" (*West Virginia Stat Board of Educn v Barnette* (1943) 319 U 624 at 642).

narrowness are that some religions (which, due to the definitional bias, will not be recognised as such) will not receive legal protection which other more mainstream religions receive. The danger of erring on the side of broadness is rather trivial: it is that some groups will successfully make unjustifiable claims for exemptions from legal burdens. We mentioned that the law has at its disposal some means of minimising such a risk (imposing alternative burdens on persons seeking religious exemptions, etc).

On the other hand, under the Non-Establishment Principle, the consequences of adopting an unduly broad conception of religion are that some legitimate government activities will be delegitimised by virtue of their allegedly "religious" character: a very real and grave danger. But what are the consequences of erring on the side of narrowness? It is that some activities will receive governmental support (thanks to the under-inclusive definition of "religion"), although in fact they are religious in character. Now consider how unlikely it is that such a situation will occur, for it has to be remembered that only these cases of governmental involvement with religion can be said to result from a narrowness of the definition which can be attributed to the law-maker's ignorance about a particular body of thought being a religion. But typical cases under the Non-Establishment Clause have a totally different character: the law-makers well know what beliefs are religious, but they claim that the activity in question has a secular purpose or effect.

Typical examples of the State's illegitimate entanglement with religion do not stem from the mistake of perceiving some religions as being non-religions, but from disagreement about whether secular purposes or effects in a given action prevail over the religious ones. The case of illegitimate favouritism attributable to an excessively narrow definition of religion would occur in the unlikely situation that the legislators had not known that the programme they run favours a religion of which they happen to be ignorant (or which they mistakenly take to be something other than a religion). By the very nature of such a scenario, the (putatively unfair) benefits in question would have to be conferred upon some small, unknown or unorthodox religious groups, and for this reason the governmental support given (by mistake) to such religions obviously cannot have any significant consequences. The real threat perceived by the Non-Establishment Principle is that a powerful group will press the policy-makers to support their religion, or that the policy-makers will attempt to favour their own religion, but in these cases it would be nonsensical to attribute such a favouritism to a mistake stemming from too narrow a range of "religions" included in the official definition of the word.

There is therefore no parallelism in the evils targeted by the two principles, and in the costs of over-broad or under-inclusive definitions of "religion" under the two clauses. In consequence, there is nothing unusual about postulating a "bifurcated" definition of religion,[44] contrary to the numerous critics of such an approach.[45] Legal definitions are devices which serve the purpose of an adequate as possible attainment of certain substantive values and ideals which a given legal rule is supposed to protect. They do not describe an objective reality but form a part of the normative language in which the legally protected values are cast. The specific purpose of any

[44] See Note, loc cit, n 20, ante, at 1056; L Tribe, *American Constitutional Law* (1978), pars 14-16; M Galanter, "Religious Freedoms in the United States: A Turning Point?" (1966) Wisconsin L Rev 217 at 265-268; G Merel, "The Protection of Individual Choice: A Consistent Understanding of Religion Under the First Amendment" (1978) 45 Univ of Chicago L Rev 805 at 834-840; D A J Richards, *Toleration and the Constitution* (OUP, 1986), pp 145-146.

[45] See *Everson v Board of Education* (1947) 330 US 1 at 32 (Rutledge J, dissenting); Note, "Toward a Uniform Valuation of the Religion Guarantees" (1970) 80 Yale LJ 77 at 78; Note, "The Sacred and the Profane: A First Amendment Definition of Religion" (1982) 61 Texas L Rev 139 at 169-170.

given rule is best captured by describing the special problem that the
rule is intended to attack: if a refinement of an accepted meaning of a
particular word or a phrase will help us tailor the rule better to
attack this evil, then this refined meaning should be adopted. Briefly
speaking, legal definitions reflect the values underlying a rule or a
principle in which the defined words appear. Once we decide that
the functions of the two principles regulating relationship between
the State and religion are equally important but operate differently
within a uniform scheme of State neutrality, then there is nothing
odd or improper in reading the same word differently in the two
different clauses.[46]

In the light of these considerations, the stipulation of the meaning
of "religion" by the United States Supreme Court in *Seeger* and
Welsh, ante, exhibits a deep wisdom, and the possible objections
which we mentioned earlier (about "tautology" and "dilution") lose
their validity. Whether the person's beliefs "play the role of
religion" and whether they "function as a religion in the [person's]
life"[47] are all we need to know before we decide about the
presumptive protection of these beliefs against State-imposed burdens (presumptive, because they still have to pass the balancing test).
The "circularity" of this definition is illusory, for it is not a
definition at all: we do not need to draw the line between religion
and non-religion for the purposes of this particular clause. Moreover,
the objection about "dilution" of the specificity of religion is for the
same reason irrelevant: both religious and non-religious beliefs, if
held sincerely by an individual as the motivating grounds of his or
her actions, call for legal protection in a liberal and secular State.

On Legal Definitions of "Religion"

[46] From that point of view, it is of no
relevance that the First Amendment of the
Constitution of the United States actually
uses the word "religion" only once (for this
semantic argument, see sources cited supra,
n 45; D Laycock, "Towards a General
Theory of Religion Clauses: The Case of
Church Labor Relations and the Right to
Church Autonomy" (1981) 81 Columbia L
Rev 1373 at 1414), while s 116 of the
Australian Constitution repeats the word
"religion" in each separate clause.
[47] *Welsh v United States* (1970) 398 US
333 at 339.

[13]

DEFINING "RELIGION" IN THE FIRST AMENDMENT: A FUNCTIONAL APPROACH

> The essence of religion is belief in a relation to God involving duties superior to those arising from any human relation.
> Chief Justice Hughes, 1931.[1]

> Now is a great time for new religions to pop up. There are people who get religious about jogging, they get religious about sex. . . . Health foods have become the basis of a religion. ESP, of course, flying saucers, anything is fertile ground now. There's a new messiah born every day.
> Tom Wolfe, 1980.[2]

The First Amendment provides that "Congress shall make no law respecting an establishment of religion or prohibiting the free exercise thereof."[3] Although the Supreme Court has discussed the concept of "religion" in several cases,[4] it has not provided a specific definition to govern cases arising under the religion clauses. Most courts have approached the question with caution, recognizing that a very rigid judicial definition of religion would implicate the concerns underlying the religion causes.[5] Indeed, one commentator has argued that any judicial definition of religion would violate both the free exercise clause and the establishment clause.[6] Nonetheless, the constitutional command that the government neither promote religion, nor restrain religious liberty, requires an interpretation of the word "religion."

This Note attempts to provide a definition of religion that is generally consistent with Supreme Court precedent, as well as the Court's discussions of the religion clauses, and that will advance the purposes of the religion clauses in both free exercise cases and establishment clause cases. Part I establishes criteria for a constitutional definition of religion in light of the purposes of the religion

---

[1] United States v. McIntosh, 283 U.S. 605, 633-34 (1931).

[2] TWENTY YEARS OF ROLLING STONE: WHAT A LONG STRANGE TRIP IT'S BEEN (J.S. Wenner ed. 1987).

[3] U.S. CONST. amend. I.

[4] See infra notes 24-44 and accompanying text.

[5] See, e.g., Thomas v. Review Board, 450 U.S. 707, 714 (1981) ("The determination of what is a 'religious' belief or practice is more often than not a difficult and delicate task . . . .").

[6] See Weiss, Privilege, Posture and Protection: "Religion" In the Law, 73 YALE L.J. 593 (1964). The author argues that "any definition of religion would seem to violate religious freedom in that it would dictate to religions, present and future, what they must be. . . . Furthermore, an attempt to define religion . . . would run afoul of the 'establishment' clause . . . ." Id. at 604.

clauses and the Supreme Court's general approach to the religion clauses. Part II summarizes the Supreme Court's discussions of the meaning of religion. Part III surveys several approaches to the concept of religion and assesses them in light of the criteria outlined in Part I. Part IV sets forth a proposed definition of religion. Finally, Part V raises several possible objections to this proposal and seeks to defend the proposed definition.

I
THE NEED FOR A UNITARY, FLEXIBLE DEFINITION OF RELIGION

A. The Need For A Specific Definition

Although it has been argued that the courts should, and indeed must avoid defining religion,[7] the plain language of the religion clauses suggests the need for a definition that is specific enough to allow courts to distinguish religious belief or activity from nonreligious belief or activity.[8] Moreover, the Court's modern interpretation of the free exercise clause makes this task unavoidable. Under this interpretation, the free exercise clause, under certain circumstances, entitles persons to an exemption from secular government regulation, where the regulation interferes with a person's religious practices or beliefs.[9] Assessing such free exercise claims requires a definition that is specific enough to enable courts to distinguish between religious beliefs or practices and nonreligious beliefs or practices.[10]

B. A Definition Broad Enough to Account for the Growing Diversity of Religious Belief

The general function of the religion clauses of the First Amendment is to guarantee religious liberty. As Justice Goldberg has stated:

> These two proscriptions are to be read together and in light of the single end which they are designed to serve. [This] basic purpose . . . is to promote and assure the fullest possible scope of religious liberty and tolerance for all and to nurture the conditions which secure the best hope of attainment of that end.[11]

---

   7   *See supra* note 6.
   8   As one commentator put it, "avoiding the task [of defining religion] would seem to violate the principles underlying the [free exercise] clause." L. TRIBE, AMERICAN CONSTITUTIONAL LAW § 14-6, at 1179 (2d ed. 1988).
   9   *See, e.g.,* Wisconsin v. Yoder, 406 U.S. 205 (1972); Sherbert v. Verner, 374 U.S. 398 (1963).
   10   *See generally* Choper, *Defining "Religion" in the First Amendment,* 1982 U. ILL. L. REV. 579, 587.
   11   Abington School Dist. v. Schempp, 374 U.S. 203, 305 (1963) (Goldberg, J., con-

This raises the difficult question of what the concept of "religious liberty" entails. Although the framers probably conceived of religion in a theistic manner,[12] it is not at all clear that they intended the religion clauses to apply only to theistic religions.[13] Moreover, the broad purpose of the religion clauses was not merely to assure the liberty of particular religious denominations, but rather to protect the religious impulses of man from government interference. This purpose is recognized in several Supreme Court opinions. For example, Justice Brennan has observed:

> The constitutional mandate expresses a deliberate and considered judgment that [religious] matters are to be left to the conscience of the citizen and declares as a basic postulate of the relation between the citizen and his government that "the rights of conscience are, in their nature, of peculiar delicacy, and will little bear the gentlest touch of governmental hand . . . ."[14]

Once we recognize that the concept of religious liberty entails protecting matters of conscience from government interference, it becomes clear that a constitutional definition of religion cannot be limited to the theistic religions recognized by the Framers, or even to a broader class of traditional religions. Such a rigid definition of

---

curring). *See also* Merel, *The Protection of Individual Choice: A Consistent Understanding of Religion Under the First Amendment*, 45 U. CHI. L. REV. 805, 810 (1978) ("If there is any single unifying principle underlying the two religion clauses . . . it is that individual choice in matters of religion should be free.") (footnote omitted).

12 *See* Greenawalt, *Religion as a Concept in Constitutional Law*, 72 CAL. L. REV. 753, 757-58 (1984); Note, *Toward a Constitutional Definition of Religion*, 91 HARV. L. REV. 1056, 1060 n.26 (1978) [hereinafter *Definition of Religion*]. James Madison viewed religion as "the duty which we owe to our Creator and the Manner of discharging it." Walz v. Tax Comm'n, 397 U.S. 664, 719 (1970) (Douglas, J., dissenting) (quoting Madison, *Memorial and Remonstrance Against Religious Assessments* in 2 THE WRITINGS OF JAMES MADISON 183-91 (G. Hunt ed. 1901)).

13 *See Definition of Religion, supra* note 12, at 1060. Thomas Jefferson apparently envisioned religious liberty for various faiths. He stated that his Virginia Act for Establishing Religious Freedom "was meant to be universal . . . to comprehend within the mantle of its protection *the Jew and the Gentile, the Christian and Mohometan, the Hindu, and infidel of every denomination." Id.* at 1060 n.27.

14 *Schempp*, 374 U.S. 203, 231 (Brennan, J., concurring) (quoting Representative Daniel Carroll of Maryland, speaking during debate upon the proposed Bill of Rights, August 15, 1789). *See also id.* at 217-18 ("Freedom of conscience and freedom to adhere to such religious organization or form of worship as the individual may choose cannot be restricted by law.") (quoting Cantwell v. Connecticut, 319 U.S. 296, 303-04 (1940)); Gillette v. United States, 401 U.S. 437, 445 (1971) (referring to "the general proposition that fundamental principles of conscience and religious duty may sometimes override the demands of the secular state."). Most commentators have also recognized this fundamental principle. *See, e.g.*, L. TRIBE, *supra* note 6, § 14-3, at 1160 ("The free exercise clause was at the very least designed to guarantee freedom of conscience by preventing any degree of compulsion in matters of belief.") (citations omitted); Clark, *Guidelines for the Free Exercise Clause*, 83 HARV. L. REV. 327, 340 (1969) (arguing "that the principal interest protected by the free exercise clause is the individual's interest in not being forced to violate the compelling requirements of conscience").

religion would be inconsistent with the very concept of religious liberty.[15] Accordingly, any proposed constitutional definition should be broad and flexible enough to include changing concepts of religion, thereby protecting new and unorthodox religious beliefs.

C. A Unitary Definition

Several commentators have argued that in order to provide broad protection under the free exercise clause for the growing diversity of faiths in the United States, without subjecting all government humanitarian programs and activities to establishment clause challenge, "religion" should be defined broadly for free exercise purposes, but narrowly for establishment purposes. For example, Professor Tribe advocated such a dual approach in the first edition of his constitutional law treatise. While arguing for an expansive free exercise definition, Tribe argued that "a less expansive notion of religion was required for establishment clause purposes lest all 'humane' programs of government be deemed constitutionally suspect."[16] In addition to this scholarly support, the dual approach has gained some judicial support.[17]

The dual approach presents two major difficulties. First, it is inconsistent with the language and structure of the First Amendment. Justice Rutledge's comments, in a dissenting opinion, illustrate this point:

> "Religion" appears only once in the Amendment. But the word governs two prohibitions and governs them alike. It does not have two meanings, one narrow to forbid "an establishment," and another, much broader, for securing "the free exercise thereof." "Thereof" brings down "religion" with its entire and exact content, no more and no less, from the first into the second guaranty so that Congress and now the states are as broadly restricted concerning the one as they are regarding the other.[18]

The second problem with a dual approach is that it may result

---

15 *See* L. TRIBE, *supra* note 8, § 14-6, at 1180 ("The idea of religious liberty—combined with the special place of religion in the constitutional order—demands a definition of 'religion' that goes beyond the closely bounded limits of theism, and accounts for the multiplying forms of recognizably legitimate religious exercise.") (citation omitted).

16 L. TRIBE, AMERICAN CONSTITUTIONAL LAW 827-28 (1st ed. 1978). Tribe claimed that anything "arguably religious" should count as religious for free exercise purposes, and that anything "arguably nonreligious" should count as nonreligious for establishment purposes. *Id.* at 828. *See also Definition of Religion, supra* note 10, at 1084 (advocating use of a "bifurcated definition").

17 *See, e.g.,* United States v. Allen, 760 F.2d 447, 450-51 (2d Cir. 1985); Sheldon v. Fannin, 221 F. Supp. 766, 775 (D. Ariz. 1963) ("religion" in the establishment clause looks to majority's concept, while "religion" in the free exercise clause looks to the minority's concept).

18 Everson v. Board of Educ., 330 U.S. 1, 32 (1947) (Rutledge, J., dissenting).

in discriminatory treatment among religions. For example, a dual definition may provide more obscure religions and religious activities with special treatment, by protecting the free exercise of such religions, without placing any establishment clause limits on the government's ability to promote and aid such religions.[19]

A dual approach might be justified in spite of these problems, if it were necessary to reconcile the two religion clauses. However, the conflict does not appear as great as Tribe originally thought. Indeed, Tribe has now rejected the dual approach, stating that it "constitutes a dubious solution to a problem that, on closer inspection, may not exist at all."[20] The establishment clause prohibits government action taken for the sole purpose of advancing religion, or having primarily religious effects, or creating excessive entanglement with religion.[21] It does not, however, prevent the government from taking any action that is consistent with a particular religion or religious tenet.[22] Thus, just as a prohibition on murder is not an establishment of religion merely because it corresponds to one of the Ten Commandments, federal laws promoting equality of opportunity[23] are not establishments of religion, even though a commitment to equality may be a religious command for some.

D. Criteria for a Constitutional Definition of Religion

In light of the preceding discussion, a constitutional definition of religion should meet three main criteria, in addition to the criterion of general compatibility with approaches suggested by the Supreme Court. First, it should be specific enough to circumscribe the concept of religion, and allow courts to distinguish nonreligious from religious beliefs. Second, it should be flexible enough to embrace new and unorthodox forms of religion. Third, it should be applicable to both free exercise clause cases and establishment clause cases.

II
SUPREME COURT APPROACHES TO THE CONCEPT OF RELIGION

The early Supreme Court pronouncements on the meaning of religion generally defined religion very narrowly in terms of a God

---

19   *See generally* Malnak v. Yogi, 592 F.2d 197, 212-13 (3d Cir. 1979) (Adams, J., concurring); Greenawalt, *supra* note 12, at 814.

20   L. TRIBE, *supra* note 8, § 14-6, at 187.

21   Lemon v. Kurtzman, 403 U.S. 602, 612-13 (1971).

22   *See* McGowan v. Maryland, 366 U.S. 420, 442 (1961) ("[T]he Establishment Clause does not ban federal or state regulation of conduct whose reason or effect merely happens to coincide or harmonize with the tenets of some or all religions.").

23   *E.g.*, Title VII of Civil Rights Act of 1964, 42 U.S.C. § 2000e (1982).

or Creator. For example, in 1890 the Court stated that "[t]he term 'religion' has reference to one's views of his relations to his Creator, and to the obligations they impose of reverence for his being and character, and of obedience to his will."[24] In 1961, however, in *Torcaso v. Watkins*,[25] the Supreme Court abandoned the use of a belief in God as the touchstone for religious belief, when it invalidated a Maryland law which required all public office holders to declare a belief in the existence of God.[26] The Court stated that the government may not "aid those religions based on a belief in the existence of God as against those religions founded on different beliefs."[27]

The Court has provided its most extensive discussions of the meaning of religion in cases interpreting the conscientious objector exemption from the selective service. In *United States v. Seeger*,[28] the Court interpreted the Universal Military Training and Service Act which exempted from combat persons who objected to participation "by reason of religious training and belief."[29] The Act defined "religious training and belief" as "an individual's belief in a relation to a Supreme Being involving duties superior to those arising from any human relation, but [excluding] essentially political, sociological or philosophical views or a merely personal moral code."[30] Despite Congress' apparent intent to limit the exemption to objections based on traditional religious beliefs,[31] the Court held that this definition applied to Seeger who had stated that "he preferred to leave the question as to his belief in a Supreme Being open," and that his objection was based on a "belief in and devotion to goodness and virtue for their own sakes, and a religious faith in a purely ethical creed."[32] The Court ruled that "Congress, in using the expression

---

[24]   Davis v. Beason, 133 U.S. 333, 342 (1890). *See also* United States v. MacIntosh, 283 U.S. 605, 633-34 (1931) (Hughes, C.J., dissenting) ("the essence of religion is belief in a relation to God involving duties superior to those arising from any human relation").

[25]   367 U.S. 488 (1961).

[26]   The Court previously had suggested a less rigid approach to the concept of religion, in United States v. Ballard, 322 U.S. 78 (1944), when it observed that "freedom of religious belief . . . embraces the right to maintain theories of life and of death and of the hereafter which are rank heresy to followers of the orthodox faiths." *Id.* at 86-87.

[27]   *Torcaso*, 367 U.S. at 495. The Court then noted that "among religions in this country which do not teach what would generally be considered a belief in the existence of God are Buddhism, Taoism, Ethical Culture, Secular Humanism and others." *Id.* at 495 n.11.

[28]   380 U.S. 163 (1965).

[29]   50 U.S.C. app. § 456(j) (1958).

[30]   *Id.*

[31]   *See* Greenawalt, *supra* note 12, at 759-60. Noting that "Congress had adopted this definition after a dispute in the courts of appeals over how broadly religion should be understood," Professor Greenawalt concludes that "the statutory language rather clearly represented endorsement of a traditional theistic conception of religion." *Id.*

[32]   *Seeger*, 380 U.S. at 166.

'Supreme Being' rather than the designation 'God,' was merely clarifying the meaning of religious training and belief so as to embrace all religions and to exclude essentially political, sociological, or philosophical views."[33] The Court then held that the test for "belief in a relation to a Supreme Being is whether a given belief that is sincere and meaningful occupies a place in the life of its pocessor parallel to that filled by the orthodox belief in God of one who clearly qualifies for the exemption."[34]

Although the Court in *Seeger* was attempting to define religious belief within the meaning of a statute, rather than within the meaning of the First Amendment, its decision was clearly influenced by constitutional considerations. These considerations are evident in the Court's statement that "[t]his construction avoids imputing to Congress an intent to classify different religious beliefs, exempting some and excluding others . . . ."[35] Since a conscientious objector statute distinguishing between different religious beliefs protected by the First Amendment would raise potential establishment clause problems,[36] as well as potential free exercise clause problems,[37] the *Seeger* Court may have viewed its broad interpretation as necessary to avoid finding the statute unconstitutional,[38] or at least as necessary to avoid a difficult constitutional question. Moreover, courts

---

[33]   *Id.* at 165.

[34]   *Id.* at 165-66. In Welsh v. United States, 398 U.S. 333 (1970), a plurality of the Court extended *Seeger* and ruled that:

> if an individual deeply and sincerely holds beliefs which are purely ethical or moral in source and content but that nevertheless impose upon him a duty of conscience to refrain from participating in any war at any time, those beliefs certainly occupy in the life of that individual "a place parallel to that filled by God" in traditionally religious persons.

Id. at 340.

[35]   *Seeger*, 380 U.S. at 176.

[36]   *See* Everson v. Board of Educ., 330 U.S. 1, 15 (1947) ("The [establishment clause] means at least this: Neither a state nor the Federal Government can . . . prefer one religion over another.").

[37]   *See Seeger*, 380 U.S. at 188 (Douglas, J., concurring) (stating that under a more narrow interpretation than the Court's "those who embraced one religious faith rather than another would be subject to penalties; and that kind of discrimination . . . would violate the Free Exercise Clause of the First Amendment"). *See also* Rabin, *When is a Religious Belief Religious: United States v. Seeger and the Scope of Free Exercise*, 51 CORNELL L.Q. 231, 241 (1966) (arguing that "constitutional considerations . . . led the [*Seeger*] Court to construe the statute in the chosen manner.").

[38]   *But cf.* Gillette v. United States, 401 U.S. 437 (1971), in which the Court held that the Congressional decision to protect religious objection to all wars, but not religious objection to a particular war, violated neither the establishment clause nor the free exercise clause. Regarding the establishment clause challenge, the Court found the distinction justified by secular pragmatic considerations, such as "the hopelessness of converting a sincere conscientious objector [apparently meaning an objector to all wars] into an effective fighting man." *Id.* at 453. As for the free exercise claim, the Court, stated that "[t]he incidental burdens felt by [the claimants] are strictly justified by substantial government interests that relate directly to the very impacts questioned." *Id.* at

and commentators have generally interpreted *Seeger* as signaling a broad concept of religion for First Amendment purposes.[39]

The Court's opinion in *Wisconsin v. Yoder*,[40] however, suggests a much more narrow conception of religion. In *Yoder*, the Court held that a group of Amish plaintiffs, who claimed that the state's requirement of compulsory education beyond the eighth grade violated their religion, were entitled to a religious exemption. After observing that "to have the protection of the Religion Clauses, the claims must be rooted in religious belief," the Court emphasized the religious nature of the Amish beliefs, by contrasting these beliefs with philosophical beliefs:

> [I]f the Amish asserted their claims because of their subjective evaluation and rejection of the contemporary secular values accepted by the majority, much as Thoreau rejected the social values of his time and isolated himself at Walden Pond, their claims would not rest on a religious basis. Thoreau's choice was philosophical and personal rather than religious, and such belief does not rise to the demands of the Religion Clauses.[41]

Although this passage seems to cast doubt on the viability of the *Seeger* approach as a constitutional test for religion,[42] it is unclear how much weight *Yoder* carries in determining the scope of "religion." Since the state did not dispute the religious nature of the Amish practices,[43] the definition of religion was not at issue, and the preceding statement was dicta. As a result, *Yoder* should not necessarily be read as a rejection of the *Seeger* approach in constitutional cases.[44]

---

463. The Court left open the question of whether the free exercise clause "would require exemption of any class other than objectors to particular wars." *Id.* at 461 n.23.

[39] *See, e.g.,* Malnak v. Yogi, 592 F.2d 197 (3d Cir. 1979) (Adams, J., concurring). Relying on *Seeger*, Judge Adams concludes that "the modern approach looks to the familiar religions as models in order to ascertain, by comparison, whether the new set of ideas or beliefs is confronting the same concerns, or serving the same purposes, as unquestioned and accepted 'religions.'" *Id.* at 207. *See also* Africa v. Pennsylvania, 662 F.2d 1025, 1030 (3d Cir. 1981); Greenawalt, *supra* note 12, at 760-61 ("the Supreme Court's broad statutory construction of religion [in *Seeger* and *Welsh*] . . . has led other courts and scholars to assume that the constitutional definition of religion is now much more extensive than it once appeared to be").

[40] 406 U.S. 205 (1972).

[41] *Id.* at 216.

[42] In his opinion, dissenting in part, Justice Douglas criticized this passage as a retreat from *Seeger*. *Id.* at 247-48 (Douglas, J., dissenting in part).

[43] 406 U.S. at 219.

[44] *See* Greenawalt, *supra* note 12, at 759 ("[T]he Court did in [*Yoder*] distinguish religious belief from subjective rejection of secular values, but its opinion does not illuminate the lines between religions and nonreligions and is colored by the specific free exercise context of the case. I do not take the passage as representing any retreat from *Torcaso*."). *See also Definition of Religion, supra* note 12, at 1066 n.63, which states that "[t]here is no evidence that the Supreme Court has retreated from *Seeger-Welsh* in recent

III
SOME APPROACHES TO THE PROBLEM AND CRITICISMS

A. The Ultimate Concern Approach

In *Seeger*, the Court relied on the writings of the theologian, Paul Tillach, who argues that God is, for each individual, the source of that individual's "ultimate concern," and "what [one] take[s] seriously without any reservation."[45] One student commentator has argued that this concept of ultimate concern should be the sole criterion for religion under the free exercise clause.[46] The Note argues that ultimate concern represents "the essence of religion."[47] It then explains that " 'concern' denotes the affective or motivational aspect of human experience; the word 'ultimate' signifies that the concern must be of an unconditional, absolute, or unqualified character."[48] Under this view, whatever an individual regards as his ultimate concern, "[e]ven political and social beliefs,"[49] is his religion.

At least in theory, the ultimate concern approach has a number of advantages. By not specifying the content of religious belief, either in terms of the types of questions that religion must address, or the types of answers it must produce, the approach avoids any risk of "religious chauvinism" and ensures tolerance for changing concepts of religion.[50] Moreover, as the Note observes, "what concerns could be more deserving of preferred status than those deemed by the individual to be ultimate?"[51] Finally, since ultimate concerns involve beliefs that "cannot be superseded,"[52] protecting such concerns from government interference would seem to advance the free exercise goal of not subjecting persons to the "hard

---

years." The author argues that the Court's discussion in *Yoder* was simply intended to emphasize that the Amish were "at the core of even a narrow understanding of religion." *Id. But see* L. TRIBE, *supra* note 8, § 14-6, at 1183 ("Although . . . a broad [functional] definition is arguably consistent with the Court's statutory interpretation in the conscientious objector cases, it clashes directly with the constitutional holding in *Wisconsin v. Yoder*.") (citation omitted); Choper, *supra* note 10, at 589 ("the *Seeger* definition's promise for attaining constitutional status has been measurably diminished by the Court's subsequent treatment of the problem in *Sherbert* and *Yoder*").

[45] *Seeger*, 380 U.S. at 187 (quoting, P. TILLICH, THE SHAKING OF THE FOUNDATIONS 57 (1948)).

[46] *See Definition of Religion, supra* note 12. The author would not apply the ultimate concern definition to establishment clause cases, because such an approach "might lead some to conclude that numerous humanitarian government programs should be regarded as unconstitutional." *Id.* at 1084. Accordingly, the author offers a separate definition for purposes of the establishment clause. *See id.* 1086-89. For criticism of such a dual approach to the definition of religion, see *supra* notes 18-23 and accompanying text.

[47] *Definition of Religion, supra* 12, at 1066.

[48] *Id.*

[49] *Id.* at 1071.

[50] *See id.* at 1070, 1076-77.

[51] *Id.* at 1075.

[52] *Id.* at 1075 n.108.

choice between contravening imperatives of religion and conscience or suffering penalties."[53]

Despite these apparent advantages, it is not clear that the concept of ultimate concern would, in practice, perform the function that the Note envisions it performing. First, the ultimate concern approach assumes that "the concerns of any individual can be ranked" and each individual has a single highest concern that "gives meaning and orientation to a person's whole life."[54] However, individuals may have several ultimate concerns, none of which is superior to the rest. As Professor Greenawalt has noted, "[m]any people care a great deal about a number of things—their own happiness, the welfare of their family, their country, perhaps their religion— without any clear ordering among these . . . ."[55] Since the Note assumes that each person has a personal-concern ranking system, it does not explain how we are to determine the ultimate concern of a person having several deep concerns.

A second practical difficulty with the ultimate concern approach is that the concept of ultimate concern may not always coincide with the types of concerns that the religion clauses are intended to protect. The Court has generally recognized that the religion clauses protect persons from government interference with matters of conscience.[56] The Harvard Note does not state that ultimate concern always involves matters of conscience, but it does identify ultimate concern as that which "happens 'in the center of the personal life and includes all its elements.' "[57] And since the Note recognizes the "mandate of inviolability of conscience"[58] as central to the free exercise clause,[59] it apparently assumes that ultimate concerns are always matters of conscience. However, Professor Greenawalt has persuasively argued that what a person views as his ultimate concern, he does not always view as a matter of conscience. For example, "the lives of people addicted to drugs may center around using and obtaining the drug, and they may be willing to do almost anything rather than be deprived of the drug. Yet they may not regard their obsession as one concerning conscience."[60]

---

53   Gillette v. United States, 400 U.S. 437, 445 (1971).
54   *Definition of Religion, supra* note 12, at 1067.
55   Greenawalt, *supra* note 12, at 808.
56   *See supra* note 14 and accompanying text.
57   *Definition of Religion, supra* note 12, at 1076.
58   *Id.* at 1058.
59   *See id.* at 1058, 1074.
60   Greenawalt, *supra* note 12, at 808. This problem might be avoided by claiming that implicit in the ultimate concern approach is that ultimate concerns are equivalent to matters of conscience. Assuming this to be so, Greenawalt's criticism still suggests that "ultimate concern" may be a poor choice of terminology and that a definition in terms

B. A Non-Rational, Transcendent Reality Approach

The concept of religion is often associated with questions facing mankind that are not subject to rational or scientific proof.[61] This view of religion has led some commentators to suggest a definition of religious belief as "faith in something beyond the mundane observable world—faith that some higher or deeper reality exists than that which can be established by ordinary existence or scientific observation."[62] A recent Washington Law Review Note advocates this definition as a modified ultimate concern approach.[63] Under this approach, religion is defined in terms of ultimate concern, which is defined in terms of "questions which science cannot objectively answer."[64] More specifically, the Note states that " '[u]ltimate' refers to all values and 'knowledge' which cannot be proven true, or even tested, by empirical evidence."[65]

This approach presents two related difficulties. First, it seems highly unlikely that an acceptable line could ever be drawn between the realm of scientific demonstrability and the realm of faith. Indeed, it may be persuasively argued that the validity of all claims to scientific truth depend on a leap of faith in accepting the validity of inductive reasoning.[66] Moreover, even if we assume the validity of inductive reasoning, "[n]ot every view is easily classifiable as one that does or does not invoke higher reality since the edges of natural social science, and of rational philosophy, are hardly sharp."[67]

The second problem with the transcendent reality approach is that even if courts could articulate a workable distinction between those beliefs held on faith and those based on scientific proof, the

---

of duties of conscience would be more appropriate. *See infra* notes 134-37 and accompanying text.

61 *See, e.g.*, United States v. Kauten, 133 F.2d 703, 708 (2d Cir. 1943) ("Religious belief arises from a sense of the inadequacy of reason as a means of relating the individual to his fellow-men and to his universe . . . .").

62 Greenawalt, *supra* note 12, at 805. Although Greenawalt rejects the transcendent reality approach, along with all other definitional approaches, (*see infra* notes 94-95 and accompanying text) he claims that "of all the positions that assert some essential core to the constitutional concept of religion, the claim that belief in higher reality constitutes that core is by far the most tenable." *Id.* at 806.

63 Note, *Secular Humanism and the Definition of Religion: Extending a Modified "Ultimate Concern" Test to Mozert v. Hawkins County Public Schools and Smith v. Board of School Commissioners*, 63 WASH. L. REV. 445 (1988) [hereinafter *Modified "Ultimate Concern"*].

64 *Id.* at 457.

65 *Id.* at 456.

66 *See* D. HUME, AN ENQUIRY CONCERNING HUMAN UNDERSTANDING 25-39 (L.A. Silby-Bigge ed. 1893).

67 Greenawalt, *supra* note 12, at 805. *See also* Choper, *supra* note 10, at 603 ("When justifying competing government policies on such varied matters as social welfare, the economy, and military and foreign affairs, there is at bedrock only a gossamer line between 'rational' and 'supernatural' causation—the former really being little more capable of 'scientific proof' than the latter.").

result would almost certainly be an unacceptably overbroad definition of religion. The ability of the government to take action pursuant to particular values would be seriously threatened by an
approach that classified as inherently religious all views not subject
to scientific proof. For example, the teaching of shared societal values in schools would presumably violate the establishment clause.[68]
Furthermore, this approach, at least if strictly construed, would
seem to bring into question criminal prohibitions on murder and
other violent crimes, which are similarly based on shared societal
values.[69]

   The Note claims that while the teaching of values would be prohibited, teaching of science, such as evolution, would be permissible.[70] However, even this is not clear under the transcendent
reality. For example, in *Crowley v. Smithsonian Institution*,[71] the plaintiffs claimed that a Smithsonian exhibit, which allegedly "explain[ed] and advocat[ed] the theory of evolution," inhibited their
free exercise rights, and unconstitutionally established the religion
of Secular Humanism.[72] The plaintiffs argued that evolution is "a
nonobservable and alleged phenomenon which can neither be
proven nor verified by the scientific method" and, therefore, "is not
a true science, but is a *faith* position."[73] The court rejected the challenge, stating: "The fact that religions involve acceptance of some
tenets on faith without scientific proof obviously does not mean that
all beliefs and all theories which rest in whole or in part on faith are
therefore elements of religion as that term is used in the first
amendment."[74] Under the transcendent reality approach, the
evolution exhibit would be an establishment of religion, unless it
could be shown that evolution was subject to scientific proof. Moreover, even if such a showing could be made, the *decision* to advocate,
or even to research, a particular science, arguably reflects non-scien-
tific value judgments, and therefore, might still violate the establishment clause, under this view.[75]

---

   68   *See Modified "Ultimate Concern", supra* note 63, at 459 (Schools may not teach "un-
testable 'ultimate meanings' "), 455 ("Ethical and other value judgments do not have
rational grounds").
   69   The Note seeks to avoid this difficulty by arguing that legislation designed to
advance the majority's non-rational, value-based ends is permissible, so long as the state
is not presenting the "majority values as morally superior to minority values." *Id.* at
461.
   70   *See id.* at 459.
   71   636 F.2d 738 (D.C. Cir. 1980).
   72   *Id.* at 740.
   73   *Id.* at 742.
   74   *Id.*
   75   *See* Choper, *supra* note 10, at 603 ("[A]t the level of final decision, even the most
frankly utilitarian goals depend ultimately on values—such as good or evil, or even the
desirability of human survival—that represent normative preferences rather than ration-

C. An Extratemporal Consequences Approach

In his article, *Defining "Religion" in the First Amendment*,[76] Dean Choper offers a definition of religion that focuses on whether the allegedly religious belief involves "a belief in the phenomenon of 'extratemporal consequences.' "[77] Under this view, a person's beliefs are religious, for First Amendment purposes, if "the effects of action taken pursuant or contrary to the dictates of a person's beliefs extend in some meaningful way beyond his lifetime."[78] Accordingly, the free exercise clause provides protection from government activity that forces a person to face the "cruel choice" between "suffering meaningful temporal disabilities" for violating the government's commands and suffering meaningful extratemporal consequences (or disabilities) for violating commands of one's religion.[79] Choper acknowledges that his definition, like other content-based definitions of religion, "presents the danger of parochialism and intolerance—that judges will include conventional orthodoxy in the definition and exclude new, unfamiliar, or 'dangerous' beliefs." He claims, however, that a definition which focuses on "ultimate supposed effects of beliefs" rather than the substance of the beliefs "is sufficiently flexible and capable of growth to include newly perceived and unconventional values."[80]

A definition that focuses on extratemporal effects has more orthodoxy built into it than Choper seems to recognize. The problem is not so much that it will favor older religions and exclude newer beliefs, but rather that it excludes all religions, new or old, that do not involve an afterlife.[81] As a result, the free exercise clause would provide no protection for religions that do not espouse belief in an afterlife.[82] For example, the beliefs expressed by the persons seeking conscientious objector status in *Seeger* would not be deemed reli-

---

ally compelled choices."). In criticizing the transcendent reality approach, I have focused on the establishment clause difficulties, because they are the most blatant. However, similar overbreadth objections could be made in the free exercise area. Indeed, almost any objection to a legal restriction or obligation could be characterized so as to rest on a nonscientific value judgment.

76   *Id.*

77   *Id.* at 599.

78   *Id.*

79   *Id.* at 597-601.

80   *Id.* at 599.

81   In addition to excluding these religions altogether, the extratemporal consequences approach would recognize the religious beliefs and practices of a religionist who believes in an afterlife, only where the beliefs and practices directly related to the afterlife. Thus, as Professor Greenawalt has observed, the "use of wine for communion" would not be considered a religious practice. *See* Greenawalt, *supra* note 12, at 803.

82   Choper acknowledges that beliefs "associated with the Universalist, Secular Humanism, Deism and Ethical Culture movements" would fall outside his definition. Choper, *supra* note 10, at 600.

gious for First Amendment purposes because none of the claimants in *Seeger* expressed a belief that participation in the war would subject them to eternal damnation or any other extratemporal consequences.[83] Under the extratemporal consequences approach, an objection to military service that "is rooted in a deep-seated faith that [to] voluntarily kill[] another human being [may determine one's] destiny after death" would qualify as a religious objection.[84] But this approach would not recognize the religious nature of objections based on a deep-seated faith in man's spiritual nature and a belief that the "most important religious law [is] that no man ought ever to wilfully sacrifice another man's life as a means to any other end,"[85] or based on "beliefs that taking another's life is a fundamental violation of 'God's law' but causes no afterlife effects."[86]

Choper defends this result by claiming that "the degree of internal trauma on earth for those who have put their souls in jeopardy for eternity can be expected to be markedly greater" than for those who have violated a religious command that does not affect prospects for an after-life.[87] However, the person forced to violate deeply-held convictions of conscience may suffer severe trauma in terms of guilt. It is hardly self-evident that the trauma of one fearing extratemporal consequences is any more severe. Courts and commentators generally recognize the severity of psychological trauma associated with violating one's conscience without considering the effects of the violation.[88] Distinguishing the trauma suffered by one who violates a duty thought to have extratemporal consequences, and that suffered by one who violates some other religious duty, becomes even more difficult when we consider the wide variety of views held by believers in an extratemporal world.[89]

Even if we assume that the religionist who believes his violation will lead to extratemporal consequences will suffer greater trauma

---

[83]   *See* United States v. Seeger, 380 U.S. 163, 166-69, 186-88 (1965).
[84]   Choper, *supra* note 10, at 598.
[85]   *Seeger*, 380 U.S. at 168.
[86]   *See* Choper, *supra* note 10, at 598 n.109.
[87]   *Id.* at 598. Choper refers to those who have violated dictates unrelated to an afterlife, as "those who have only violated a moral scruple." *Id.* This description, however, begs the question by assuming that such dictates are *only* "moral scruples."
[88]   *See, e.g.*, Clark, *supra* note 14, at 337 ("the cost to a principled individual of failing to do his moral duty is generally severe, in terms of supernatural sanction or the loss of moral self respect."). *See also* Gillette v. United States, 401 U.S. 437, 445 (1971) (referring to the "hard choice between contravening imperatives of religion and conscience or suffering penalties"). *See also supra* note 14 and accompanying text.
[89]   *See generally* Greenawalt, *supra* note 12, at 804. Greenawalt concludes that "[w]hen we recognize the wide range of views among persons whose beliefs include faith in some life beyond this one, we will be hesitant to conclude that persons with such faith will generally suffer more torment from violating conscience than will persons who think they have done some terrible wrong in the only life they have to live." *Id.* at 804.

for violating a religious duty than will one who violates his duty of religion, but anticipates no such consequences, Choper's argument remains unpersuasive. The problem is that the argument assumes that the religionist will violate his religious beliefs, rather than the government's command. If, instead, the religionist chooses to disobey the government, then the nonextratemporal believer would appear to face the greater trauma. As Choper notes, "at a psychological level, the identical cost may be more comfortably borne by those religionists who can balance [the punishment suffered for violation of the government's command] against eternal rather than temporal benefits. Indeed, some may believe that martyrdom has independent value in affecting their destiny."[90] Thus, in some cases, the government may be doing the afterlife believer a favor by punishing him.

In response to this, Choper argues that "because the burden of *obeying* the law is so severe for the religious objector [whose objection is based on extratemporal effects], our traditions hold that his noncompliance is not as morally culpable as one [sic] who disobeys for other reasons."[91] This explanation fails for two reasons. First, Choper does not explain why we should focus on the burden of obeying the law, rather than on the burden of disobeying the law, or some combination of these two factors. Second, and perhaps more important, it is not at all clear that the person who disobeys for fear of eternal damnation is less morally culpable than the person who disobeys because of his devotion to God's law, or his deep-seated faith and "devotion to goodness and virtue for their own sake," or his commitment to the "most important religious law . . . that no man ought ever to wilfully sacrifice another man's life as a means to any other end."[92] Indeed, just the opposite would seem true. A person who violates the law in the name of altruistic principles is generally thought of as morally defensible, if not morally commendable. In contrast, a person who violates the law in pursuit of his own self-interest, is generally thought of as the most condemnable violator.[93]

D. A Non-Definitional Analogical Approach

In his article, *Religion as a Concept in Constitutional Law*,[94] Professor Greenawalt rejects both the "ultimate concern" approach,[95] and

---

90 Choper, *supra* note 10, at 598.
91 *Id.*
92 *Seeger*, 380 U.S. at 168.
93 The extratemporal consequences approach also creates difficulties as applied to the establishment clause. *See* Greenawalt, *supra* note 12, at 804.
94 *Id.*
95 *See id.* at 806-11.

the "extratemporal consequences" approach,[96] claiming that these and other "dictionary approach[s] are wholly inadequate to produce acceptable results in a wide range of religion clause cases."[97] Arguing that "any dictionary approach oversimplifies the concept of religion,"[98] Greenawalt proposes that "religion should be determined by the closeness of analogy in the relevant respects between the disputed instance and what is indisputably religion."[99]

Analogizing to other religions is by no means a unique approach. Any approach to religion must begin with a focus on what are the usual features of recognized religions.[100] For example, a focus on ultimate concern reflects the fact that religions traditionally have dealt with questions of ultimate concern.[101] Similarly, a focus on extratemporal consequences reflects the fact that most traditional religions include strong beliefs regarding extratemporal consequences.[102] Indeed, Greenawalt recognizes that the distinctive feature about his approach is not its use of analogical reasoning, but that "it denies that a search for essential conditions is a profitable method for applying the concept of religion."[103]

This denial results in an approach that provides little guidance in determining what qualifies as a religion. While Greenawalt suggests several "indubitably religious" attributes,[104] he does not indicate how many of, or what combination of, these attributes must be present to satisfy the constitutional concept of religion. As a result, the approach presents problems of potential overinclusiveness and underinclusiveness.

By failing to identify any necessary condition for religion, the

---

96   *See id.* at 803-04.

97   *Id.* at 765.

98   *Id.* at 763.

99   *Id.* at 764

100   In this sense my proposal also represents an analogical approach. *See infra* notes 130-34 and accompanying text. It differs from Greenawalt's approach, however, in that it seeks to identify the essential features of commonly recognized religions.

101   *See Definition of Religion, supra* note 12, at 1067 n.68 (suggesting the concept of "God" for traditional religions is equivalent to ultimate concern).

102   *See* Choper, *supra* note 10, at 600 (claiming that Christianity, Islam, most branches of Judaism, Hinduism, and Buddhism all teach a belief in some form of afterlife).

103   Greenawalt, *supra* note 12, at 766.

104   These include:

a belief in God; a comprehensive view of the world and human purposes; a belief in some form of afterlife; communication with God through ritual acts of worship and through corporate and individual prayer; a particular perspective on moral obligations derived from a moral code or from a conception of God's nature; practices involving repentance and forgiveness of sins; "religious" feelings of awe, guilt, and adoration; the use of sacred texts; and organization to facilitate the corporate aspects of religious practice and to promote and perpetuate beliefs and practices.

Id. at 767-68.

analogical approach, if interpreted broadly, presents the risk that organizations or belief systems, which are loosely analogous to previously identified religions, but generally not considered to be religious (even by their followers), will be defined as religion under the First Amendment. The approach does not explain, for example, whether a political philosophy such as Marxism, which has some of the religious attributes set forth by Greenawalt, would qualify as a religion.[105] Greenawalt indicates that Marxism "is usually not considered religious,"[106] but he does not explain how one would reach this conclusion relying solely on his analogical approach.

Conversely, by failing to identify any sufficient condition for religion, the analogical approach is subject to a narrow interpretation that might exclude new and different religions. For example, any emphasis on the structural features of organized religion[107] would result in the exclusion of very personal approaches to religion that do not conform to any particular group or organization.[108] Such a result would be inconsistent with the concept of religious liberty.[109]

One might argue that to criticize the analogical approach for failing to provide necessary or sufficient conditions for whether something is religion misses the point of the approach. After all, Greenawalt's position is that any test based on essential conditions or on a set definition, even if desirable, is unworkable for purposes of the religion clauses.[110] Greenawalt, however, is incorrect in his perception that a definition providing essential features of religion will necessarily oversimplify the concept of religion. I will argue that the definition outlined below, which provides the necessary and sufficient conditions for religion, does provide a workable approach to the religion clauses.[111]

E. An Analogical Approach Based on External Manifestations of Traditional Religions

Another possible method of definition by analogy would be to

---

105 Marxism does present "a comprehensive view of the world and human purposes," it has "a particular perspective on moral obligations derived from a moral code . . .," it arguably makes "use of sacred texts," and at least in some modern manifestations, it has an "organization to facilitate the corporate aspects of [its] practices and to promote and perpetuate beliefs and practices."

106 Greenawalt, *supra* note 21, at 768.

107 In terms of Greenawalt's suggested attributes of religion, structural features would include those features related to "corporate aspects of religious practice," and in some cases "the use of sacred texts." *See supra* note 104.

108 *See infra* notes 116-21 and accompanying text.

109 *See infra* note 122 and accompanying text.

110 *See supra* notes 97-98, 103 and accompanying text.

111 *See infra* notes 131-56 and accompanying text.

focus on the external manifestations that are generally associated with traditional religions. For example, Judge Adams of the Third Circuit has proposed a test for religion consisting of three indicia, the third of which is the presence of "any formal, external, or surface signs that may be analogized to accepted religions."[112] Among the external signs that might be considered in determining whether a belief or practice is part of a religion are, "formal services, ceremonial functions, the existence of clergy, structure and organization, efforts at propagation, observation of holidays and other similar manifestations associated with the traditional religions."[113] The primary advantage of such an approach is that it provides more objective and tangible elements for courts to focus on in assessing whether a belief or practice is religious.

However, any approach that focuses on such external indicia favors organized religion over individualized personal approaches to religion. Thus, it would threaten to exclude religious beliefs that are not held by any group or sect. For example, the religious beliefs asserted in *Seeger* did not involve any organizational or formal trappings.[114] *Bowen v. Roy*[115] presents another example. In that case, Roy asserted a religious belief that the use of a Social Security number for his daughter would "rob [her] spirit . . . and prevent her from attaining greater spiritual power."[116] Although the belief was based on conversations with a tribal chief,[117] Roy's testimony indicated that this was a personal religious belief, rather than one associated with any organized formal group.[118] Under an approach that focuses on external manifestations of religion, these beliefs might be considered nonreligious simply because they were privately held by individuals, rather than by a formal group or organization.

Moreover, an undue focus on organizational elements might exclude religious beliefs of a member of one sect where they conflict with the views of other members of the sect. The Supreme Court recognized this problem in *Thomas v. Review Board*.[119] In *Thomas*, the

---

[112]   Malnak v. Yogi, 592 F.2d 197, 209 (3d Cir. 1979) (Adams, J., concurring). The first two parts of Judge Adams' test are discussed in Part IV. *See infra* notes 131-34 and accompanying text.

[113]   *Malnak*, 592 F.2d at 209 (Adams, J., concurring). Judge Adams' test does not make these signs necessary conditions for religion, but suggests that in light of the Court's dicta in *Yoder* (*see supra* note 41 and accompanying text), "formal and organizational signs may prove to be more important in defining religion than the conscientious objector cases would suggest." *Malnak*, 592 F.2d at 209 n.43 (Adams, J., concurring).

[114]   *See* United States v. Seeger, 380 U.S. 163, 166-69, 186-88 (1965).

[115]   106 S. Ct. 2147 (1986).

[116]   *Id.* at 2150.

[117]   *Id.*

[118]   *See id.* at 2150 n.3.

[119]   450 U.S. 707 (1981).

Court rejected the Indiana Supreme Court's suggestion that a Jehovah's Witness' refusal to participate in the production of war materials was based on personal, rather than religious beliefs.[120] Observing that the Indiana court improperly gave "significant weight to the fact that another Jehovah's Witness had no scruples about working on tank turrets," the Court held that "the guarantee of free exercise is not limited to beliefs which are shared by all the members of a religious sect."[121] The Court also criticized the Indiana Supreme Court for relying on "the facts that Thomas was 'struggling' with his belief and that he was not able to 'articulate' his belief precisely."[122] The Court added that "courts should not undertate to dissect religious beliefs because the believer admits that he is 'struggling' with his position or because his beliefs are not articulated with . . . clarity and precision . . . ."[123]

These examples suggest that any definition that focuses on external signs of traditional religions would recognize the beliefs and practices of institutions as religious more easily than it would recognize the beliefs of individuals as religious. This would be inconsistent with the role of the Bill of Rights to protect the liberty of individuals. As Professor Tribe has argued, definitions which "focus on the externalities of a belief system or organization . . . unduly constrain the concept of religion."[124] Accordingly, courts cannot properly rely on externalities, such as "the belief system's age, its apparent social value, its political elements, the number of its adherents, the sorts of demands it places on those adherents, the consistency of practice among different adherents, and the system's outward trappings—e.g., prayers, holy writings, and hierarchical organizational structures."[125]

That external manifestations should not be relied on in determining whether something is a religion does not mean they are irrelevant to First Amendment analysis. To be entitled to free exercise protection, a claimant must demonstrate the sincerity of his alleged religious beliefs.[126] The fact that a claimant can show that

---

120   See id. at 714-16.
121   Id. at 715-16.
122   Id. at 715. See also In Re Jenison, 375 U.S. 14 (1963) (vacating for reconsideration in light of Sherbert v. Verner, 374 U.S. 398 (1963)) (see infra note 152 and accompanying text), a Minnesota judgment denying exemption for woman opposed to jury duty based on her own (apparently unique) interpretation of the Bible). Cf. Hobie v. Unemployment Appeals Comm., 107 S. Ct. 1046, 1051 (1987) (holding recently adopted religious beliefs are entitled to full free exercise protection).
123   Thomas, 450 U.S. at 715.
124   L. TRIBE, supra note 8, § 14-6, at 1181.
125   Id. at § 14-6, at 1181-82 (citations omitted).
126   See id. at § 14-12, at 1242 ("In order to gain the exemption, the claimant must show . . . a sincerely held religious belief"). See also Wisconsin v. Yoder, 406 U.S. 205,

he has consistently taken part in the ceremonial aspects of an organized religion will certainly be probative as to the sincerity of his beliefs. Nonetheless, the absence of any ceremonial aspects connected with a claimant's asserted religious belief should not have any bearing on whether the belief qualifies as religious.[127]

IV
A FUNCTIONAL APPROACH TO THE CONCEPT OF RELIGION

A. Seeger: A Definition Based on the Role or Function That Recognized Religions Have in the Life of the Adherents

The very concept of religious liberty suggests the inappropriateness of an overly content-based definition.[128] In order to embrace new forms of religion, religion should be defined in a flexible manner that reflects the general purposes of religious liberty rather than the specific practices or beliefs of traditional religions. An approach that focuses on the function of religion in the adherent's life performs this task far better than an approach that focuses on the more tangible physical manifestations of religion. The Supreme Court offered the bare skeleton of such a functional approach in *United States v. Seeger*.[129]

In *Seeger*, the Court held that to qualify for a military service exemption under a statute that required a "belief in relation to a Supreme Being," a claimant must have a "belief that is sincere and meaningful [and] occupies a place in the life of its possessor parallel to that filled by the orthodox belief in God of one who clearly qualifies for the exemption."[130] This definition focuses on the function of belief in God in the life of a traditional religionist. Since the First Amendment protects religious belief rather than "belief in relation to a Supreme Being," the focus should be on the function of religious belief, rather than the function of belief in God. Accordingly, applying the functional approach to the religion clauses, religion might be defined as a set of beliefs that occupies a place in the life of its possessor parallel to that filled by the religious beliefs of an ad-

---

235 (1972) ("the Amish in this case have convincingly demonstrated the sincerity of their religious belief"); Africa v. Pennsylvania, 662 F.2d 1025, 1030 (3d Cir. 1981) (in a free exercise case, "[a] court's task is to decide whether the beliefs avowed are . . . sincerely held").

127 *Cf.* L. TRIBE, *supra* note 8, at 1182 ("To be sure, courts should be wary of sudden births of religions that entitle practitioners to special rights or exemptions. But the proper place for that inquiry is in the assessment of the believer's sincerity, not in any evaluation of the belief's externalities.").

128 *See supra* note 15 and accompanying text.

129 380 U.S. 163 (1965). *Seeger* is discussed more fully *supra* notes 28-39 and accompanying text.

130 *Id.* at 166.

herent to something that would clearly qualify as a religion within the meaning of the First Amendment.[131] However, without an explanation as to what role religious belief usually plays for the follower of a recognized religion, this definition provides little guidance.[132] The next section will attempt to remedy this by providing content to the function of religion in individual's lives.

B. The Religious Function: Addressing The Fundamental Questions of Human Existence and Providing A Guide for Conducting One's Life

Although *Seeger* did not spell out what role religion plays in the life of a traditional religionist, several opinions of the circuit courts shed light on this issue. The most complete discussions of the specific content of *Seeger's* functional approach have appeared in two opinions by Judge Adams of the Third Circuit. The first of these was a concurring opinion in *Malnak v. Yogi*,[133] a case holding that the teaching of Science of Creative Intelligence—Transcendental Meditation in the public schools violates the establishment clause. Explaining his "definition by analogy,"[134] Judge Adams has identified the role of religion in the life of the religionist, as providing a comprehensive belief system that "addresses fundamental and ultimate questions having to do with deep and imponderable matters."[135] Such fundamental questions include "the meaning of life and death, man's role in the Universe, [and] the proper moral code of right and wrong."[136]

---

[131] Although strictly speaking, *Seeger* was a case of statutory interpretation, courts and commentators have commonly used it as a guide to approaching issues raised under the religion clauses. *See supra* note 39 and accompanying text.

[132] *See* Choper, *supra* note 10, at 593 ("One major ambiguity of the *Seeger-Welsh* formulation concerns what 'place' religion occupies in the life of a member of a conventional religious sect.").

[133] 592 F.2d 197 (3d Cir. 1979).

[134] *Id.* at 207 (Adams, J., concurring).

[135] Africa v. Pennsylvania, 662 F.2d 1025, 1032 (3d Cir. 1981); *see also Malnak*, 592 F.2d at 208-09 (Adams, J., concurring). In these opinions, Judge Adams proposes a test for religion consisting of three indicia:

> First a religion addresses fundamental and ultimate questions having to do with deep and imponderable matters. Second, a religion is comprehensive in nature; it consists of a belief system as opposed to an isolated teaching. Third, a religion often can be recognized by the presence of certain formal and external signs.

Africa, 662 F.2d at 1032. *See also Malnak*, 592 F.2d at 207-09. The third element is discussed *supra* notes 112-27 and accompanying text.

[136] *Malnak*, 592 F.2d at 208 (Adams, J., concurring); *see also Africa*, 662 F.2d at 1033 ("Traditional religions consider and attempt to come to terms with what could best be described as 'ultimate' questions—questions having to do with, among other things, life and death, right and wrong, and good and evil."); Founding Church of Scientology v. United States, 409 F.2d 1146, 1160 (D.C. Cir. 1969) (characterizing recognized religions as having "underlying theories of man's nature or his place in the Universe").

The requirement of a comprehensive belief system addressing fundamental questions provides a good first criterion for the concept of religion. Taken alone, however, it fails to capture the generally accepted notion of religion as giving rise to duties of conscience. This notion is captured in the language of the conscientious objector statute which refers to belief "involving duties superior to those arising from any human relation."[137] The fact that religion generally involves a compelling sense of devotion and duty helps explain why the First Amendment singles out the practice of religion for special constitutional protection.[138] As one commentator has noted, this sense of a duty provides a "forceful explanation [and] justification for the free exercise clause" in that it is "particularly cruel for the government to require the believer to choose between violating [the commands of religious belief] and suffering meaningful temporal disabilities."[139] Moreover, the general understanding of the religion clauses as serving to protect the sanctity of conscience reflects this view of religion.[140]

Supplementing Judge Adams' idea of a comprehensive belief system that addresses fundamental questions with the notion of duties of conscience provides a workable definition of religion for purposes of the First Amendment. Taking these two ideas together, religion can be defined as a comprehensive belief system that addresses the fundamental questions of human existence, such as the meaning of life and death, man's role in the universe, and the nature of good and evil, and that gives rise to duties of conscience. The following section suggests a number of possible objections to this definition and attempts to justify the definition by providing responses to these objections.

V

IMPLICATIONS AND POSSIBLE OBJECTIONS

A. Underinclusiveness

One possible criticism of the proposed definition is that it will exclude certain recognized religious beliefs. For example, Dean

---

137 *See Seeger*, 380 U.S. at 165. *See also* United States v. MacIntosh, 283 U.S. 605, 633-34 (1931) (Hughes, C.J., dissenting) ("belief in a relation to God involving duties superior to those arising from any human relation").

138 James Madison's definition of religion suggests the importance of religious duty. Madison viewed religion as "the duty which we owe to our Creator." Walz v. Tax Comm'n, 397 U.S. 664, 719 (1970) (Douglas, J., dissenting) (quoting Madison, *supra* note 12, at 183-91).

139 Choper, *supra* note 10, at 597.

140 *See supra* note 14 and accompanying text. Arguably, this notion of duties of conscience is implicit in Judge Adams' identification of "the proper moral code of right and wrong." *Malnak*, 592 F.2d at 208, as one of the fundamental questions.

Choper argues that a definition focusing on a comprehensive belief system that addresses fundamental questions creates problems of underinclusiveness. He claims that the difficulty "is that at least some traditional religious beliefs would not appear necessarily to be comprehensive."[141]

The claim that not all religious beliefs are comprehensive seems to misunderstand the approach. The comprehensiveness requirement does not mean that each religious belief or practice must be "comprehensive." Rather, it simply recognizes that religions are "not generally confined to one question or moral teaching."[142] Similarly, the fundamental question requirement does not mean that each belief or practice must address or directly relate to a fundamental question to be considered religious.[143] The belief or practice need only be a part of a belief system that addresses fundamental question.[144] Thus, a practice such as the use of wine for communion, which does not necessarily have any comprehensive relation to fundamental questions, but is an integral part of a system meeting the criteria for religion, would be recognized as a religious practice.

B. Overinclusiveness

Dean Choper also argues that "many comprehensive beliefs are not necessarily religious."[145] He illustrates his overinclusiveness argument by suggesting that "atheistic Marxism may be fairly described as comprehensive because it supplies answers to profound questions and denies the significance of other issues."[146] One might apply this overinclusiveness objection to the proposed approach, by further claiming that a philosophy such as Marxism gives rise to duties of conscience in its adherents.

Although Marxism and other comprehensive political philoso-

---

141 Choper, *supra* note 10, at 596 n.104.
142 *Malnak*, 592 F.2d at 209 (Adams, J., concurring).
143 This may be Choper's real concern, as he seems to equate the comprehensive element with the fundamental question element. *See* Choper, *supra* note 10, at 596 n.104 ("Marxism may fairly be described as *comprehensive* because it supplies answers to profound *questions*") (emphasis added).
144 *See Malnak*, 592 F.2d at 197. Judge Adams stated:

It should not be reasoned that those teachings of accepted religious groups that do not address "ultimate" matters are not entitled to religious status. . . . Once a belief-system has been credited as a "religion" through an examination of its "ultimate" nature, its teachings on other matters must also be accepted as religious.

Id. at 208-09 n.40 (Adams, J., concurring).
145 Choper, *supra* note 10, at 596 n.104.
146 *Id.* at 596-97 n.104. *See also* L. TRIBE, *supra* note 8, § 14-6, at 1182-83 ("A generous functional definition would seem to classify any deep-rooted philosophy as religion, Marxism as well as Methodism.").

phies may indeed address profound questions, it is not clear that
they address fundamental questions as defined in the proposed definition.[147] Their concerns tend to be more mundane than the fundamental questions suggested above. For example, rather than
addressing "man's role in the universe," most political philosophies
address man's role in some political community, such as a city-state,
a nation-state, or under a "dictatorship of the proletariat."[148] Moreover, with the possible exception of natural law theories, political
philosophies do not usually address the nature of good and evil in
a normative sense; they generally attempt to define "good" in
a descriptive sense, and then advocate means to obtaining that good
or goods.[149] And few, if any, political philosophies, Marxism included, attempt to explain the meaning of life and death. Thus,
even focusing solely on the first criterion of the fundamental ques-
tion/duties of conscience approach, the approach does not appear
overinclusive.

When we consider the second requirement of the proposed approach, that the belief system give rise to duties of conscience,
strictly political philosophies are even more removed from the definition. Although political philosophies generally provide guides to
action, these guides, for most people, are better characterized as
prudential maxims, than duties of conscience. A duty of conscience
serves as an end in itself, which cannot be compromised to serve
some more mundane duty (such as the duty to obey the law). A duty
arising from one's political philosophy generally serves as a means
to some other end, and lacks the compelling nature of a duty of
conscience. For example, persons who believe strongly in democracy may feel a duty to vote, but few would view this duty as too
compelling to be outweighed by other considerations, such as a family or professional obligation that would make it impossible to vote.

For some people, however, a political philosophy does give rise
to imperative duties of conscience. For example, persons advocat-

---

147   *But see infra* text following note 148.

148   *See, e.g.*, K. MARX, THE COMMUNIST MANIFESTO 92-95 (J. Katz ed. 1964).

149   In so far as natural law theories do address the nature of good and evil, they
often tend to have religious underpinnings. For example, Thomas Hobbes argued that
the laws of nature correlate to the laws of God. *See* Hobbes, *De Cive*, in T. HOBBES, MAN
AND CITIZEN 295 (B. Gert ed. 1972) ("Because the word of God, ruling by nature only, is
supposed to be nothing but right reason . . . it is manifest that the laws of God . . . are
only the natural laws . . . ."). Indeed, the natural law notions of equality embodied in the
Declaration of Independence seem to suggest a divine source: "When in the course of
human events, it becomes necessary for one people . . . to assume among the powers of
earth the separate and equal station to which the laws of nature and of nature's *God*
entitle them. . . . We hold these truths to be self evident; that all men are *created* equal,
that they are *endowed by their creator* with certain unalienable rights . . . ." The Declaration
of Independence para. 1 (U.S. 1776) (emphasis added).

ing civil disobedience often view the duty to disobey unjust laws as a duty of conscience.[150] Under the proposed approach, this would not necessarily make that person's political philosophy a religion. The person would also have to view their political philosophy as addressing the fundamental questions. But if a person views a certain political philosophy as providing imperative duties of conscience, perhaps even duties he would sacrifice his life for, then that person may also view the philosophy as addressing such fundamental questions as man's role in the universe, the nature of good and evil, and perhaps even the meaning of life and death. If a philosophy does play such a role in a person's life, then it should be treated as a religion with regard to that person. Similarly, if a public school were to present philosophical teachings as a comprehensive belief system addressing fundamental questions and creating duties of conscience, it might well violate the establishment clause.[151]

C. Risk of Fraudulent Claims Under The Free Exercise Clause

A strict functional definition that does not include the element of formal religious trappings arguably presents a greater risk of fraudulent claims than a definition that requires or at least considers such trappings. Since a purely functional definition considers only whether the alleged belief or practice relates to the internal religious function of the individual, there will be less opportunity to rely on external evidence in assessing a religious claim. However, as I argue above, any focus on such external manifestations of religion would tend to discriminate against unorthodox religions in a manner inconsistent with the concept of religious liberty.[152] Moreover, the proposed approach does require that the alleged religious belief play a certain role in the claimant's life: it must be part of a comprehensive belief system that addresses certain fundamental questions and gives rise to duties of conscience. Thus, the issue in a free exercise case is not simply whether the claimant sincerely believes that the belief or practice in question is a religious belief, but whether he sincerely believes that it plays the religious role in his life. The definition of that role provides a basis for the factfinder to question the nature of the belief, and to assess the claimant's sincerity, thereby reducing the likelihood of successful fraudulent claims.

---

150 *See, e.g.*, M. L. KING, JR., *Letter From Birmingham Jail*, in WHY WE CAN'T WAIT 82 (1968) ("one has a moral obligation to disobey unjust laws").

151 *Cf.* Malnak v. Yogi, 592 F.2d 197, 209 (3d Cir. 1979) (Adams, J., concurring) ("moral or patriotic views are not by themselves 'religious,' but if they are pressed as divine law or a part of a comprehensive belief-system that presents them as 'truth,' they might well rise to the religious level").

152 *See supra* notes 114-24 and accompanying text.

D. Risk of Undue Interference with Government Activity

In combination with the strict scrutiny test established in *Sherbert v. Verner*,[153] the proposed, relatively broad definition of religion may appear to present a serious obstacle to the government's ability to act on behalf of the general welfare. In *Sherbert*, the Court indicated that in order to justify an infringement on a person's free exercise of religion, the government must demonstrate a "compelling state interest."[154] It is unlikely, however, that the proposed interpretation of religion would pose a serious threat to government activity, even assuming vigorous free exercise protection. First, a successful free exercise claim typically does not lead to invalidation of a statute or of an entire government program; it simply requires an exemption for the claimant.[155] Second, if the sincerity test is taken seriously, and claimants are made to demonstrate the sincerity of their claims,[156] then it will be difficult for persons to simply fabricate a belief in order to avoid a government restriction or obligation.

Even assuming the proposed definition would lead to an unmanageable number of exemptions, this result is more a function of the test set out in *Sherbert* than of the definition. The Court could limit the number of religious exemptions by applying the compelling state interest test only in cases in which the religious belief at issue is central to the claimant's religion.[157] Alternatively, the Court could apply a general balancing approach, under which it would measure the extent of the infringement of the claimant's religion against the impact of an exemption on the state interest.[158]

CONCLUSION

The First Amendment's command that the government "make

---

153   374 U.S. 398 (1963).

154   *See id.* at 406.

155   The Court's recent decision in Lyng v. Northwest Indian Cemetery Ass'n, 108 S. Ct. 1319 (1988) seems to ensure that free exercise claims cannot go further than individual exemptions from government restrictions or obligations. In *Lyng*, the Court held that the free exercise clause does not "require the government to bring forward a compelling justification" for "government programs which may make it more difficult to practice certain religions but which have no tendency to coerce individuals into acting contrary to their religious beliefs." *Id.* at 1326.

156   *See supra* note 126 and text following note 150.

157   Such an approach was proposed in a recent dissenting opinion by Justice Brennan, joined by Justices Blackmun and Marshall. *See Lyng*, 108 S. Ct. at 1338 (Brennan, J., dissenting) ("I believe it appropriate . . . to require some showing of 'centrality' before the Government can be required . . . to come forward with a compelling justification. . . ."). The majority, however, rejected this approach. *Id.* at 1329.

158   Professor Greenawalt advocates a balancing approach and argues that courts already implicitly use this approach. *See* Greenawalt, *supra* note 12, at 781-84, 790.

no law respecting an establishment of religion, or prohibiting the free exercise thereof" requires an interpretation of religion that will allow the courts to distinguish between religious and nonreligious belief. On the other hand, the purpose of the religion clauses—to ensure religious liberty for all—requires an interpretation that will encompass the religious impulses in persons, whether these impulses are expressed in the form of a traditional religion, or in the form of a unique, unstructured, personal religion. These two goals are served by defining religion in terms of the religious function in an individual's life—addressing the fundamental questions of human existence and providing a guide for how to conduct one's life. The proposed definition embodies this religious function and provides a specific, but flexible guide for determining what is religion in both free exercise and establishment clause cases.

Ben Clements

[14]

DEFINING "RELIGION" IN THE FIRST AMENDMENT†

Jesse H. Choper*

I. INTRODUCTION

Giving the concept of "religion" a precise meaning is a formidably complicated task. Although the first clauses of the Bill of Rights designate "religion" as a subject of special constitutional significance—both prohibiting government from granting it undue assistance and at the same time affording it distinct protection from government regulation—the Supreme Court has never seriously discussed how this term should be defined for constitutional purposes.

Moreover, the scope of religious pluralism in the United States alone has resulted in such a multiplicity and diversity of ideas about what is a "religion" or a "religious belief" that no simple formula seems able to accommodate them all. Scholars have written volumes on the subject without reaching anything approaching agreement. Judicial as well as theological efforts to cabin the notion may take on the appearance of exercises in circularity, proposed definitions using as a starting point comparison to groups or beliefs that are stipulated as being religious.[1] Thus, although a constitutional definition of "religious belief" may be expressed as whether the belief "occupies a place in the life of its possessor parallel to that filled by the orthodox belief in God,"[2] or "religion" may be described as "the state of being ultimately concerned,"[3] these formulations may be no more useful when applied to specific cases than the words "religious belief" and "religion" themselves. Further, any definition of religion for constitutional purposes that excludes certain beliefs (or groups) that are reasonably perceived or characterized as being religious by those who hold them (or belong

† *An abbreviated version of this article was delivered at the University of Illinois College of Law, April 15, 1982, as the second 1981-1982 lecture of the David C. Baum Lectures on Civil Rights and Civil Liberties.*

* *Dean and Professor of Law, University of California, Berkeley. B.S. 1957, Wilkes College; LL.B. 1960, University of Pennsylvania; D. Hu. Litt. 1967, Wilkes College. I wish to thank John H. Magee, Class of 1981, University of California, Berkeley, for his exceptionally able assistance in the preparation of this paper. I also wish to express my appreciation to Meir D. Cohen, John E. Coons, Joseph D. Grano, Phillip E. Johnson, John T. Noonan, Donald H. Regan, Michael E. Smith, Stephen D. Sugarman, and William W. Van Alstyne, all of whom, while by no means in agreement with the ideas contained herein, afforded helpful criticisms.*

1. *See, e.g.*, United States v. Seeger, 380 U.S. 163, 184 (1965).
2. *Id.* at 184.
3. *See infra* text accompanying notes 89-105.

580   UNIVERSITY OF ILLINOIS LAW REVIEW   [Vol. 1982

to them) may be fairly viewed as judicial preference of some "religions" over others. Indeed, the very idea of a legal definition of religion may be viewed as an "establishment" of religion in violation of the first amendment.[4] These complexities notwithstanding, the definition of "religion" plays as integral a role in the articulation of any well-developed doctrine governing the constitutional separation of church and state as does the content to be assigned to the religion clauses' two substantive terms—"establishment" and "free exercise."

In my view, an ideal constitutional definition of "religion" should fulfill several criteria. First, it should comprehend those experiences and aspirations of mankind that have been generally thought of as "religious," thus reasonably corresponding to most theological and lay ideas of the term. At the same time, the definition should be sufficiently capable of growth to include new, unusual, and nonconformist sects and beliefs as well as traditional ones.[5] Moreover, application of the definition should avoid intrusive examinations into the private realms of thought and behavior of claimants as much as possible. The crucial task, however, even if it necessarily results in major qualifications of the ideal, is to construct a "legal" definition of religion for a Constitution that frames the structure of our secular government which, although granting "religion" a special place for certain purposes, nonetheless forbids that greater weight in its lawmaking process be accorded to values simply because they have religious origins. More particularly, this "legal" definition of religion should seek to fulfill the several (and sometimes seemingly conflicting) goals of the religion clauses, both contributing and conforming to the proper substantive scope of those provisions. Further, while the broad historical values underlying the religion clauses should furnish an informed perspective for the definition, its ultimate form must serve purposes beyond the specific visions of the framers, even assuming that they may be discerned. In addition to reflecting presently cherished values, the definition, as an operational matter, should not be very abstract or esoteric despite the thoughtful views of sophisticated theologians to the contrary. Rather, the constitutional boundaries should be sufficiently specific and understandable to produce fair and uniform results—even if this creates what may be perceived as only peripheral or superficial differences in some instances on either side of the principled line—thus

---

4. Weiss, *Privilege, Posture and Protection—"Religion" in the Law*, 73 YALE L.J. 593, 604 (1964).

5. The truth is that one man's "bizarre cult" is another's true path to salvation, and the Bill of Rights was designed to safeguard minorities from the man-on-the-street's uncertain capacity for tolerance. . . . [A] man-in-the-street approach would surely have ruled out early Christianity, which seemed both subversive and atheistic to the religious Romans of the day . . . . The new challenge to our pluralism often comes from Oriental religious movements, because their views of religion differ so fundamentally from ours.

Cox, *Playing the Devil's Advocate, as it Were*, N.Y. Times, Feb. 16, 1977, at 25, col. 1. *See also infra* text accompanying note 112.

limiting opportunities for arbitrary decisions by parochial, biased, or intolerant judges and juries, and providing for meaningful appellate review.

II. THE FREE EXERCISE CLAUSE

Virtually all of the Supreme Court's efforts, modest as they have been, to wrestle with the problem of what constitutes a "religion" or a "religious belief" have occurred in cases presenting claims that properly fall under the free exercise clause[6] rather than the establishment clause. Under well developed constitutional principles, however, most free exercise cases either could have been, or were in fact, resolved under constitutional provisions other than either of the religion clauses. As is true of most constitutional doctrine, the precise scope of the first amendment's interdiction—made applicable to the states by the fourteenth amendment[7]—of laws "prohibiting the free exercise" of religion remains somewhat unclear. But several fairly settled propositions describing its reach may be generally stated which demonstrate that most violations of the free exercise protection may be vindicated without reference to the free exercise clause and thus require no constitutional definition of "religion" at all.

A. Belief, Expression, and Worship

First, it is clear that government action which interferes with an individual's right to hold any set of religious beliefs,[8] or that attempts to "force citizens to confess by word or act their faith therein"[9] is flatly forbidden. Further, any government imposition of penal or civil sanctions on, or denial of government benefits to, persons for expounding religious views is invalid unless the judiciary concludes that it is justified by a state interest strong enough to be characterized as "compelling," "substantial," "important," "overriding," or the like.[10]

As the decisions documenting these doctrines make manifest, however, these protections for religious liberty are solidly grounded in the "freedom of speech" provisions of the first and fourteenth amendments and would be readily secured even if there were no free exercise clause in the Constitution. Indeed, many of the Court's most prominent free speech rulings—on such issues as prior restraint,[11] fighting words,[12]

---

6. See infra Sec. II, D.

7. Cantwell v. Connecticut, 310 U.S. 296 (1940).

8. Id. at 303-04, 310.

9. West Va. State Bd. of Educ. v. Barnette, 319 U.S. 624, 642 (1943).

10. Compare Chaplinsky v. New Hampshire, 315 U.S. 568 (1942), with Cantwell v. Connecticut, 310 U.S. 296 (1940).

11. Kunz v. New York, 340 U.S. 290 (1951); Niemotko v. Maryland, 340 U.S. 268 (1951); Saia v. New York, 334 U.S. 558 (1948); Cantwell v. Connecticut, 310 U.S. 296 (1940); Lovell v. Griffin, 303 U.S. 444 (1938).

12. Chaplinsky v. New Hampshire, 315 U.S. 568 (1942).

public forums,[13] time-place-manner rules,[14] and the permissibility of regulating[15] or taxing[16] the distribution of literature—in fact involve religious expression or such traditional religious activities as proselytization or solicitation. Similarly, there is no doubt that most rituals, rites, or ceremonies of religious worship—such as fasting, confessing, or performing a mass—that may be denominated as constituting "action" rather than "belief" or "expression," fall squarely within the protection the Court has afforded to nonverbal "symbolic speech."[17]

B. Discrimination

The constitutional guarantee of religious freedom also has consistently been held to contain an antidiscrimination precept that both complements and overlaps the doctrines described above. This requirement of neutrality in the religious sphere, which is buttressed by the establishment clause's prohibition of governmental preference for one religion over another[18] as well as by the free exercise clause,[19] forbids any government action that deliberately singles out one or more religious groups for adverse treatment[20] or that penalizes or withholds benefits from persons because of their peculiar sectarian beliefs.[21]

Here again, however, modern constitutional developments under other first amendment provisions eliminate the necessity of using the religion clauses to prevent anything resembling or approaching the persecution of religious dissidents that was so abhorred by the Framers.[22] Thus, there is no doubt that just as a law denying privileges to members of the Communist Party or any other group advocating forcible overthrow of the government as an abstract principle would violate the freedom of association guarantee of the first and fourteenth amendments,[23] so, too, the Court could invoke this principle to invalidate a statute, such as that in *Davis v. Beason*,[24] disenfranchising any person

---

13. Widmar v. Vincent, 102 S. Ct. 269 (1981).
14. Heffron v. International Soc'y for Krishna Consciousness, 452 U.S. 640 (1981).
15. Martin v. Struthers, 319 U.S. 141 (1943); Schneider v. Irvington, 308 U.S. 147 (1939).
16. Follett v. McCormick, 321 U.S. 573 (1944); Murdock v. Pennsylvania, 319 U.S. 105 (1943).
17. Spence v. Washington, 418 U.S. 405 (1974); Schacht v. United States, 398 U.S. 58 (1970); Tinker v. Des Moines School Dist., 393 U.S. 503 (1969); Stromberg v. California, 283 U.S. 359 (1931).
18. Everson v. Bd. of Educ, 330 U.S. 1, 15 (1947). *See also* Gillette v. United States, 401 U.S. 437 (1971).
19. The Court's opinions dealing with this phenomenon often fail to carefully distinguish between the establishment clause and the free exercise clause. *See* Torcaso v. Watkins, 367 U.S. 488 (1961); Fowler v. Rhode Island, 345 U.S. 67 (1953).
20. Braunfeld v. Brown, 366 U.S. 599 (1961); Fowler v. Rhode Island, 345 U.S. 67 (1953).
21. Torcaso v. Watkins, 367 U.S. 488 (1961).
22. *See* Letter from John Madison to William Bradford, Jr., (Jan. 24, 1774), *reprinted in* J. MADISON, THE COMPLETE MADISON 298 (S. Padover ed. 1953) [hereinafter THE COMPLETE MADISON]. *See also* Everson v. Bd. of Educ., 330 U.S. 1, 15 (1947).
23. Communist Party v. Whitcomb, 414 U.S. 441 (1974); United States v. Robel, 389 U.S. 258 (1967); Aptheker v. Secretary of State, 378 U.S. 500 (1964).
24. 133 U.S. 333 (1890).

belonging to an organization that encouraged the practice of polygamy. Similarly, freedom of speech doctrine prevents a state from requiring that notaries public declare their belief in the existence of God[25] just as easily as it bars a provision requiring an expression of belief in the virtues of the free enterprise system as a condition of holding public office.[26]

Supplementing the first amendment's freedoms of speech and association, the equal protection clause of the fourteenth amendment (with its fifth amendment counterpart)[27] provides an additional weapon against religious discrimination without any need for a constitutional definition of "religion." Under the "fundamental rights" branch of equal protection doctrine, classifications that inhibit the exercise of a constitutional right—such as association or speech—are subject to strict judicial scrutiny.[28] Although no opinion for a majority of the Court has relied on this axiom in a case involving an alleged preference for certain religious groups or beliefs over others,[29] it is plainly available to invalidate any government attempt to benefit "people whose [religious] views it finds acceptable" or to disadvantage "those wishing to express less favored or more controversial views."[30]

C. Regulations of Conduct

Beyond protecting against government action that interferes with religious beliefs, expression, and rites of worship or that singles out religious beliefs or groups for adverse treatment, the free exercise clause has also been held to apply when a general government regulation, undertaken for truly secular purposes, either penalizes (or otherwise burdens) *conduct* that is dictated by some religious belief or requires (or otherwise encourages) *conduct* that is forbidden by some religious belief. The Court's early response to this conflict between religiously motivated conduct and an otherwise valid law of general application was to hold that under the free exercise clause, Congress "cannot interfere with mere religious beliefs and opinions . . . but was left free to reach actions which were in violation of social duties or subversive of good order."[31] By 1940, however, the Court abandoned this sharp dichotomy between religious beliefs and religiously mandated action (or inac-

---

25. *See* Torcaso v. Watkins, 367 U.S. 488 (1961).
26. *See* Bond v. Floyd, 385 U.S. 116 (1966).
27. *See* W. LOCKHART, Y. KAMISAR & J. CHOPER, CONSTITUTIONAL LAW: CASES-COMMENTS-QUESTIONS 1245 n.a (5th ed. 1980).
28. *See* San Antonio Indep. School Dist. v. Rodriguez, 411 U.S. 1 (1973); Shapiro v. Thompson, 394 U.S. 618 (1969).
29. *But see* Welsh v. United States, 398 U.S. 333, 357 (1970) (Harlan, J., concurring); Fowler v. Rhode Island, 345 U.S. 67, 70 (1953) (Frankfurter, J., concurring); *cf.* Gillette v. United States, 401 U.S. 437, 450-54 (1971) (applying equal protection type analysis under the establishment clause). *See also* United States v. Seeger, 326 F.2d 846 (2d Cir. 1964), *aff'd*, 380 U.S. 163 (1965).
30. Chicago Police Dep't v. Mosley, 408 U.S. 92, 96 (1972).
31. Reynolds v. United States, 98 U.S. 145, 164, 166 (1879).

tion), ruling that the free exercise clause "embraces *two* concepts,—freedom to believe and freedom to act." Although "the first is absolute . . ., in the nature of things, the second cannot be" because "conduct remains subject to regulation for the protection of society." Nonetheless, the government's "power to regulate must be so exercised as not, in attaining a permissible end, unduly to infringe the protected freedom."[32]

It was not until 1963, however, that the Court gave real content to the proposition that, under certain circumstances, the free exercise clause requires an exemption for religiously dictated action (or inaction) that is burdened by a secular government regulation of general applicability. In *Sherbert v. Verner*,[33] a mill worker who was a Seventh Day Adventist was discharged by her employer when she would not work on Saturday, the Sabbath day of her faith, after all the mills in her area adopted a six-day work week. South Carolina denied her unemployment compensation benefits for refusing to accept "suitable work," even though that would require her to work on Saturday. The Court held that this violated the free exercise clause because "to condition the availability of benefits upon [her] willingness to violate a cardinal principle of her religious faith effectively penalizes the free exercise of her constitutional liberties."[34] Nearly a decade passed before the Court expressly employed this doctrine again in *Wisconsin v. Yoder*,[35] which held that the free exercise clause demanded that Amish children be exempted from the state's requirement of school attendance until age sixteen. In 1981, the Court used the doctrine for only the third time in *Thomas v. Review Board*,[36] a case remarkably similar to *Sherbert*.

The *Sherbert* and *Yoder* rulings and rationale are especially significant because the constitutional immunity that they afford, at least under existing precepts, is exclusively for "religion." For example, it is clear that if Sherbert had refused Saturday work because of her deeply felt (but not religiously based) obligation to spend the full weekend with her children, or if the Yoders had resisted sending their teenagers to high school because the family's financial plight required them for farm chores, neither party would have any constitutional right to be excused from the state rules that forbade this conduct. Nor would their actions secure constitutional protection under the free speech guarantee even if undertaken for the sole purpose of communicating an idea. Thus, Sherbert would not be constitutionally entitled to unemployment compensation if she refused a Saturday job specifically to express her disagreement with the South Carolina "suitable work" rule, and the Yoders would have no constitutional defense to a prosecution under

---

32. Cantwell v. Connecticut, 310 U.S. 296, 303-04 (1940).
33. 374 U.S. 398 (1963).
34. *Id.* at 406.
35. 406 U.S. 205 (1972).
36. 450 U.S. 707 (1981).

the Wisconsin compulsory school attendance law if they kept their children home to protest the quality of public education. For the Court has rejected "the view that an apparently limitless variety of conduct can be labelled 'speech' whenever the person engaging in the conduct intends thereby to express an idea"—at least where the governmental interest in regulating such conduct "is unrelated to the suppression of free expression."[37] Indeed, neither the first amendment's freedoms of speech nor association would require that Sherbert receive unemployment compensation even if she declined "suitable work" because she wished to devote at least two days a week to organizing a new political party or allow the Yoders to take their children out of school even if they were desperately needed to work in their mother's campaign for public office. It is true that the Court has reasoned that speech and associational activities may be protected by the first amendment even though the burdensome government action is not directed to suppressing such speech or association (but rather is intended to accomplish some independent regulatory end).[38] Nonetheless, it is quite clear that, despite the fact that such activities are at the core of our democratic system, the standard by which the Court will judge the application of the challenged legal restraint is greatly more relaxed than *Sherbert's* "compelling state interest"[39] or *Yoder's* "interests of the highest order"[40] requirement (with the burden on the state "to demonstrate that no alternative forms of regulation"[41] would suffice).

D. Other Exemptions for "Religion"

Although *Sherbert, Yoder*, and *Thomas* are conventionally regarded as being the only free exercise clause decisions of the Supreme Court that grant a special constitutional immunity for "religion" from secularly based general government regulations of conduct—and which, therefore, cannot be explained under some other constitutional provision securing individual rights—two additional "freedom of religion" problems also properly fall within this category.

1. Fraudulent Solicitation of Funds

In *United States v. Ballard*,[42] the defendant was indicted for using the mails to obtain money by false representations. He had solicited funds for the "I Am" movement, asserting, *inter alia*, that he had been

---

37. United States v. O'Brien, 391 U.S. 367 (1968). *See also* Zemel v. Rusk, 381 U.S. 1, 16-17 (1965).

38. *See* Choper, *Thoughts on State Action: The "Government Function" and "Power Theory" Approaches*, 1979 WASH. U.L.Q. 757, 766.

39. Sherbert v. Verner, 374 U.S. 398, 403 (1963) (quoting NAACP v. Button, 371 U.S. 415, 438 (1963)).

40. Wisconsin v. Yoder, 406 U.S. 205, 215 (1972).

41. *See* Sherbert v. Verner, 374 U.S. 398 (1963).

42. 322 U.S. 78 (1944).

selected as a divine messenger, had used his supernatural powers to heal hundreds of incurable diseases, and had talked and shaken hands with Jesus. The Court held that the free exercise clause barred submitting to the jury the question of whether these religious beliefs were true, reasoning that "religious experiences which are as real as life to some may be incomprehensible to others. . . . If one could be sent to jail because a jury in a hostile environment found those teachings false, little indeed would be left of religious freedom."[43]

The free speech clause has been interpreted to place definite strictures on the state's ability to penalize or award civil damages for the making of false statements,[44] and it may well be that the Court would impose similar constitutional limits on an allegedly deceived political contributor's damages action against a successful candidate for subsequently failing to abide by campaign promises. But, apart from the peculiar nature of "religious" experiences, the Constitution presently requires no analogous ban on adjudicating the truth or falsity of statements as to events, allegedly already having taken place, that are made the basis for a solicitation of funds. Thus, the special rule of the *Ballard* case applies exclusively to "religion" and requires a definition of that term for constitutional purposes.

2. *Internal Ecclesiastical Disputes*

The rule has evolved that, in lawsuits between a local congregation and its church hierarchy over the ownership of church realty, "the First Amendment prohibits civil courts from resolving . . . [such] disputes on the basis of religious doctrine and practice."[45] In such cases, as well as in other ecclesiastical controversies involving such matters as whether a particular individual is a duly constituted church official,[46] the religion clauses require that "civil courts defer to the resolution of issues of religious doctrine or polity by the highest court of a hierarchical church organization."[47]

There is much to be said for interpreting the freedom of association guarantee to mandate an analogous rule of judicial deference for all intra-organizational disputes involving the ideological tenets of the group. But because the Justices have in no way suggested adoption of such a principle, it is only the subject of "religion" that contains this special exemption from ordinary rules of civil adjudication.

---

43. *Id.* at 86-87.

44. *See generally* W. LOCKHART, Y. KAMISAR & J. CHOPER, *supra* note 27, at 867-69.

45. Jones v. Wolf, 443 U.S. 595, 602 (1979). *See also* Presbyterian Church v. Hull Church, 393 U.S. 440 (1969). For a similar approach in contests between factions of a congregational church, see Watson v. Jones, 80 U.S. 679 (1871).

46. Serbian Orthodox Diocese v. Milivojevich, 426 U.S. 696 (1976); Gonzales v. Archbishop, 280 U.S. 1 (1929).

47. Jones v. Wolf, 443 U.S. 595, 602 (1979).

E. Defining "Religion"

It has been forcefully argued that the free exercise clause should not be read to require any special dispensation for religion from general government rules enacted to serve secular goals.[48] If this view had been accepted, there would be no need to construct a definition of "religion" for these purposes.[49] But the series of decisions just described have chosen to grant religion a special privilege under certain circumstances, a position that I endorse—at least when such an exemption does not itself interfere with anyone's religious liberty and is not outweighed by a sufficiently strong government interest.[50] Thus, the question of how the Court should define "religion" for these purposes must be confronted.

1. Evolution in the Supreme Court

The Justices' first real attempt at a definition of religion came at the end of the 19th century in *Davis v. Beason*,[51] sustaining a law of the territory of Idaho that disenfranchised any person belonging to an organization that encouraged the practice of polygamy:

Bigamy and polygamy are crimes by the laws of all civilized and Christian countries . . . . To extend exemption from punishment for such crimes would be to shock the moral judgment of the community. To call their advocacy a tenet of religion is to offend the common sense of mankind. . . . The term "religion" has reference to one's views of his relations to his Creator, and to the obligations they impose of reverence for his being and character, and of obedience to his will.[52]

This passage contains two separate elements. The thrust of its first part—that because the practice of polygamy was (at least then) abhorrent to our culture, it cannot be classified as "a tenet of religion"—confuses the question of what is or is not "religion" (the issue that the Court purported to address) with the question of whether the practice, even if it is a "religious" one, may nonetheless be proscribed by civil authority (the issue that this portion of the Court's rationale in fact resolved). The second part of the Court's discussion, however, directly considers the relevant problem and, echoing James Madison's perception of religion as "the duty which we owe to our Creator,"[53] adopts a

---

48. P. KURLAND, RELIGION AND THE LAW (1962).

49. This is not to say, however, that Professor Kurland's thesis, which forbids all classifications in terms of "religion," would altogether avoid the need for a constitutional definition. See Mansfield, Book Review, 52 CALIF. L. REV. 212, 215-16 (1964).

50. *See* Choper, *The Religion Clauses of the First Amendment: Resolving the Conflict*, 41 U. PITT. L. REV. 673, 686-700 (1980).

51. 133 U.S. 333 (1890).

52. *Id.* at 341-42.

53. J. Madison, *Memorial and Remonstrance Against Religious Establishments, reprinted in* THE COMPLETE MADISON, *supra* note 22, at 302. Compare, however, Jefferson's view that his Virginia Act for Establishing Religious Freedom "was meant to be universal . . . to comprehend

theistic definition conforming to the traditions of western Judeo-Christian thought.

As late as 1931, Chief Justice Hughes, joined by Justices Holmes, Brandeis and Stone, opined that "the essence of religion is belief in a relation to God involving duties superior to those arising from any human relation."[54] But by 1944, the Court stepped back, albeit somewhat ambiguously, from the ukase that "religion" requires a belief in God, stating in *United States v. Ballard* that "freedom of religious belief . . . embraces the right to maintain theories of life and of death and of the hereafter which are rank heresy to followers of the orthodox faiths."[55] And in 1961, in *Torcaso v. Watkins*, in the course of invalidating a Maryland provision requiring a declaration of belief in the existence of God as a test for public office, the Court observed that the religion clauses prohibit government support of "those religions based on a belief in the existence of God as against those religions founded on different beliefs," noting that "among religions in this country which do not teach what would generally be considered a belief in the existence of God are Buddhism, Taoism, Ethical Culture, Secular Humanism and others."[56]

The most generous definition that the Supreme Court has given to religion has been in a statutory, rather than a constitutional, setting. In *United States v. Seeger*,[57] the Court interpreted a provision of the Universal Military Training and Service Act[58] that exempted from military service, "those persons who by reason of their religious training and belief are conscientiously opposed to participation in war in any form."[59] "Religious training and belief," was defined by the statute as "an individual's belief in a relation to a Supreme Being involving duties superior to those arising from any human relation, but does not include essentially political, sociological or philosophical views or a merely personal moral code."[60] Seeger claimed to have a religious opposition to war, although he did not believe in God, asserting rather a religious "belief in and devotion to goodness and virtue for their own sakes, and a religious faith in a purely ethical creed."[61] Rather than

---

within the mantle of its protection *the Jew and the Gentile, the Christian and Mahometan, the Hindoo, and Infidel of every denomination.*" W. BLAKELY, AMERICAN STATE PAPER BEARING ON SUNDAY LEGISLATION 133 n.1 (rev. enl. ed. W. Blakely 1911) (emphasis in original).

54. United States v. MacIntosh, 283 U.S. 605, 633-34 (1931) (Hughes, C.J., dissenting).

55. 322 U.S. at 86-87.

56. 367 U.S. at 495 n.11. *See also* United States v. Seeger, 380 U.S. 163, 182-83 (1965) (describing the writings of "Dr. David Saville Muzzey, a leader of the Ethical Culture Movement" as being among "the views that comprise the broad spectrum of religious beliefs found among us.").

57. 380 U.S. 163 (1965).

58. 50 U.S.C. App. § 456(j) (1958).

59. *Id.*

60. *Id.*

61. 380 U.S. at 166.

reach the merits of Seeger's constitutional challenge, the Court gave the Act a sufficiently expanded construction to include his beliefs:

We have concluded that Congress, in using the expression "Supreme Being" rather than the designation "God," was merely clarifying the meaning of religious training and belief so as to embrace all religions and to exclude essentially political, sociological, or philosophical views. We believe that under this construction, the test of belief "in a relation to a Supreme Being" is *whether a given belief that is sincere and meaningful occupies a place in the life of its possessor parallel to that filled by the orthodox belief in God of one who clearly qualifies for the exemption.* Where such beliefs have parallel positions in the lives of their respective holders we cannot say that one is "in a relation to a Supreme Being" and that the other is not.[62]

The opinion also stated that the statute protected "all sincere religious beliefs which are based upon a power or being, or upon a faith, to which all else is subordinate or upon which all else is ultimately dependent,"[63] referring to the writings of modern theologians such as Paul Tillich in support of the view that the concept of a "Supreme Being" is very broad and need not refer to an anthropomorphic entity "out there."[64]

Although *Seeger* was resolved strictly as a matter of statutory interpretation, the decision appeared to have significant constitutional portents, particularly because the Court's straining of the language of the statute[65]—recently described as "a remarkable feat of linguistic transmutation"[66]—was prompted by its desire to "[avoid] imputing to Congress an intent to classify different religious beliefs, exempting some and excluding others . . . ."[67] The complexities surrounding *Seeger's* "functional" approach to defining religion—in contrast to one that emphasizes the "content" of the beliefs that seek constitutional recognition as being "religious"—will concern us shortly.[68] But the *Seeger* definition's promise for attaining constitutional status has been measurably diminished by the Court's subsequent treatment of the problem in

---

62. *Id.* at 165-66 (emphasis added).
63. *Id.* at 176.
64. *Id.* at 180-83.
65. *See also* Welsh v. United States, 398 U.S. 333 (1970), in which a plurality of the Court extended the statutory exemption even further so as to (1) cover a person who "originally characterized his beliefs as nonreligious" but later "declared that his beliefs were 'certainly religious in the ethical sense of that word,' " and (2) not "exclude those who hold strong beliefs about our domestic and foreign affairs or even those whose conscientious objection to participation in all wars is founded to a substantial extent upon considerations of public policy." *Id.* at 340-44.
66. Note, *Toward a Constitutional Definition of Religion*, 91 HARV. L. REV. 1056, 1065 n.60 (1978) [hereinafter *Definition of Religion*].
67. 380 U.S. at 176. Justice Douglas, in his concurrence, stated explicitly that he believed the Court's construction of the statute necessary to save it from unconstitutionality. 380 U.S. at 188 (Douglas, J., concurring). And in *Welsh*, Justice Harlan characterized *Seeger* as a "distortion to avert an inevitable constitutional collision." 398 U.S. at 354 (Harlan, J., dissenting).
68. *See infra* text accompanying notes 87-88.

Sherbert and *Yoder*, which were necessarily grounded in the free exercise clause rather than an act of Congress.

The seminal decision in *Sherbert* did not discuss at any length the type of claimant who was entitled to assert the newly established exemption from general government regulations nor the sort of a claim that may be raised. At several points, however, the Court's opinion seems to underline that Sherbert's position was based on a clearly recognizable, fairly conventional religious precept. Thus, the Court observed that there was no "doubt that the prohibition against Saturday labor is a basic tenet of the Seventh-Day Adventist creed, based on that religion's interpretation of the Holy Bible";[69] that South Carolina's denial of unemployment compensation burdened "a cardinal principle"[70] of Sherbert's faith; and that "South Carolina may not constitutionally apply the eligibility provisions so as to constrain a worker to abandon his religious convictions respecting the day of rest."[71] All of these declarations have a ring of orthodoxy that is commonly related to worship in the Judeo-Christian tradition.[72]

A more explicitly considered view of religion was expressed in *Yoder*, which emphasized that the free exercise clause's extraordinary exemption was available for only "a 'religious' belief or practice,"[73] and then, without clearly specifying the criteria for a definition, nonetheless articulated a relatively cautious approach:

> A way of life, however virtuous and admirable, may not be interposed as a barrier to reasonable state regulation of education if it is based on purely secular considerations; to have the protection of the Religion Clauses, the claims must be rooted in religious belief. Although a determination of what is a "religious" belief or practice entitled to constitutional protection may present a most delicate question, the very concept of ordered liberty precludes allowing every person to make his own standards on matters of conduct in which society as a whole has important interests. Thus, if the Amish asserted their claims because of their subjective evaluation and rejection of the contemporary secular values accepted by the majority, much as Thoreau rejected the social values of his time and isolated himself at Walden Pond, their claims would not rest on a religious basis. Thoreau's choice was philosophical and personal rather than religious, and such belief does not rise to the demands of the Religion Clauses.[74]

The Court then reviewed the record in detail to demonstrate that "the

---

69.   374 U.S. at 399 n.1.
70.   *Id.* at 406.
71.   *Id.* at 410.
72.   Only Justice Douglas in his concurrence seemed untroubled by the breadth and variety of religious claims for exemption from neutral secular laws that *Sherbert*, read broadly, would seem to authorize. *Id.* at 410-13 (Douglas, J., concurring).
73.   406 U.S. at 215.
74.   *Id.* at 215-16.

traditional way of life of the Amish is not merely a matter of personal preference, but one of deep religious conviction, shared by an organized group, and intimately related to daily living,"[75] stressing that the Amish are an old and established Christian sect, and that their opposition to formal higher education is grounded in Biblical beliefs.[76]

2. The Relationship Between Definition and Scope of Substantive Protection

The Court's seemingly guarded attitude in *Sherbert* and its more openly conservative approach in *Yoder*—both cases involving beliefs that could easily be characterized as religious by reference to conventional ideas of Christian orthodoxy—may well have been influenced by the very generous protection those decisions afforded to claims falling within the Court's conception of religion. Indeed, it is fair to question whether the Court would have reached the same results if the claimants' beliefs had not been reinforced by membership in recognized sects or if the Justices had been less familiar with the content of those beliefs.[77]

There is an obvious relationship between the legal definition of religion and the shaping of substantive doctrine under the free exercise clause. In effect, the definition acts as a screening mechanism that determines what claims will be subjected to the substantive "balancing test" that the Court has developed for judging whether an exemption for religion must be granted. Thus, the more inclusive the legal definition of religion, the greater the number and diversity of claims under the free exercise clause that must be considered on the merits. Indeed, one function of arguments for a broad definition of religion—e.g., "all that is *'arguably religious'* should be considered religious in a free exercise analysis" so that the free exercise clause may "continue to fulfill its 'historic purpose' "[78]—is the creation of an indirect and textually-based method of obtaining meaningful and expanding judicial protection for "rights of privacy and personhood"[79] despite the Court's reluctance to do so under the rubric of substantive due process.

Nevertheless, a spacious judicial definition of religion need not

---

75. *Id.* at 216.
76. Justice Douglas emphasized this point by dissenting from it:
[T]he Court retreats when in reference to Henry Thoreau it says his "choice was philosophical and personal rather than religious, and such belief does not rise to the demands of the Religion Clauses." That is contrary to what we held in *United States v. Seeger* . . . .

. . . .

I adhere to [the *Seeger* and *Welsh* definitions] and see no acceptable alternative to them now that we have become a Nation of many religions and sects.
Id. at 247-48 (Douglas, J., dissenting in part).
77. *But see In re* Jenison, 375 U.S. 14 (1963) (woman opposed to jury service because of her own interpretation of the Bible; vacated and remanded for reconsideration in light of *Sherbert*).
78. L. TRIBE, AMERICAN CONSTITUTIONAL LAW 828 (1978).
79. *Id.* at 886.

necessarily lead to greater protection for religious freedom or for other personal liberty. The ultimate reach of the free exercise clause can be expanded or limited by the Court at either the definitional or substantive steps of the process, and it is unlikely that an extremely broad definition of religion will be permitted to coexist with an extremely generous protection of the claims that fall within that definition. The restrictions that the free exercise clause places on government's power to enact neutral, generally applicable regulations governing health, safety, and welfare are marked exceptions to the plenary nature of that authority. Judicial recognition of the fact that, at least under our present system of values, civil government requires that these exceptions be fairly narrow[80] is obvious from the Court's observation in *Yoder* that "the very concept of ordered liberty precludes allowing every person to make his own standards on matters of conduct in which society as a whole has important interests."[81] Thus, the Court's recognition of all conceivably religious claims as falling within the free exercise clause probably would result in a relatively modest degree of substantive protection for them, whereas a more confined definition of religion more readily permits the quite far-reaching protection that the Court has afforded those beliefs.[82]

---

80. This tension between broad protection under the free exercise clause and the general regulatory power of government may explain the different approaches taken by the Court in *Seeger* and *Welsh* on the one hand and *Sherbert* and *Yoder* on the other. In the former cases, the Court was not dealing with a constitutionally mandated immunity, but rather with a legislatively created exemption whose judicial interpretation could presumably be altered by Congress. (The Court has stated several times that the conscientious objector exemption is not constitutionally required. *E.g.*, Gillette v. United States, 401 U.S. 437, 461 n.23 (1971); United States v. MacIntosh, 283 U.S. 605, 623-24 (1931).) Thus, the Court could more comfortably adopt a broad definition of religion without threatening the legislative scheme, because the legislature had the power to undo the Court's work. In *Sherbert* and *Yoder*, however, the Court was potentially subjecting every state law to a judicially final balancing test on behalf of every religious claimant.

81. 406 U.S. at 215-16. *See also* Galanter, *Religious Freedoms in the United States: A Turning Point?*, 1966 WIS. L. REV. 217, 270-71. It has recently been observed that many of the new religious cults—an estimated 1,300 appearing in the United States since 1965—"often encourage their members to disobey or disregard society's laws in favor of the group's mores." Rudin, *The Cult Phenomenon: Fad or Fact?*, 9 N.Y.U. REV. L. & SOC. CHANGE 17, 18, 31 (1980-81).

82. The discord between a broad definition of religion and vigorous substantive protection under the free exercise clause for those that are encompassed by it would be significantly ameliorated by a proposal that I have advanced elsewhere that seeks to reconcile the conflict between the religion clauses. Under my view, the establishment clause, which was designed as an important guarantor of religious liberty, should be held to forbid special exemptions for religion from uniform secular laws when such exemptions would tend to coerce, compromise, or influence the religious freedom of others. *See* Choper, *supra* note 50. Thus, any religious exemption that involves the expenditure of public funds to aid religion (such as in *Sherbert*) or that places those with particular beliefs at such an advantage that people would be strongly encouraged to alter their religious beliefs so as to qualify (such as with the draft exemption) would be invalid under the establishment clause; such an invalid exemption obviously could not be justified or required by the free exercise clause. As a result, although a very inclusive definition of religion might well bring a particular claimant within it, the exemption sought under the free exercise clause might well be barred by the establishment clause. Moreover, because there would appear to be a direct relationship between the value of the benefit to be obtained by the exemption under the free exercise clause and the degree to which the establishment clause would forbid such special treatment for religion, my thesis would either work to deter many claimants from characterizing their

It should be clear, however, that once a belief is categorized as "religious," it must be accorded the same constitutional refuge as all other such "religious" beliefs; the Court cannot adjust the substantive part of the process to secure the practice of one assertedly "religious" group and reject the same precept of another. For example, in *Yoder*, the Court's grant of an exemption to the Amish but not to those like Thoreau was accomplished on a definitional basis, not on a substantive one. If the Court had defined Thoreau's beliefs as "religious," it would have been faced with the choice of either granting an exemption to all the Thoreaus of the world, as well as to the Amish, or affording no such immunity at all. Indeed, the increased impact on state programs of exempting a wider group might well have led the Court to reach the opposite result on the merits.

3. The Seeger-Welsh *Formulation*

The most thoroughly considered effort by the Supreme Court to define "religion"—albeit, at least technically, in a nonconstitutional context—produced the *Seeger* opinion's standard of "whether a given belief . . . occupies a place in the life of its possessor parallel to that filled by the orthodox belief in God."[83] This guideline as to "whether a conscientious objector's beliefs are religious"[84] was given further content (and elasticity) in *Welsh v. United States*,[85] the opinion announcing the Court's judgment pointing out "that 'intensely personal' convictions which some might find 'incomprehensible' or 'incorrect' come within the meaning of 'religious belief' " if they are "held with the strength of traditional religious convictions."[86] Although the *Seeger* Court expressed the view that this "parallel position" test would be "simple of application,"[87] a probe beneath its veneer—especially as more fully articulated in *Welsh*—discloses substantially greater difficulties than the Court's confident language suggests.

One major ambiguity of the *Seeger-Welsh* formulation concerns precisely what "place" God or religion occupies in the life of a member of a conventional religious sect. In fact, a traditional believer's religion does not play a single, ascertainable role in his existence; rather, it may influence his being in a variety of ways—*e.g.*, morally, spiritually, socially, etc. Nor need its influence remain constant; rather, it may

---

beliefs as "religious" in the first place or render their portrayal inconsequential in any event. Nonetheless, because my proposal would still permit free exercise clause consideration for a substantial number of claims—such as those raised in *Yoder, see id.* at 697, or by Sabbatarians seeking an exemption from a Sunday closing law as in *Braunfeld v. Brown, see id.* at 700—it would not fully resolve the free exercise clause dilemma between definition and substance.

83. 380 U.S. at 166.
84. Welsh v. United States, 398 U.S. 333, 339 (1970).
85. *Id.*
86. *Id.* at 339-340.
87. 380 U.S. at 184.

change over time. Moreover, even within a given sect, religion will fill different functions in the lives of different members.

More importantly, there appears to be no readily observable line of demarcation between those beliefs that are "parallel" to a belief in God or other orthodox religious precepts and those beliefs that are not. It is true that some parallels can be drawn between the beliefs of, for example, Orthodox Jews, Jehovah's Witnesses, and Catholics. All three involve a belief in God, but that is precisely the parallel that *Seeger* rejected as being too narrow. All three also involve membership in a group that propounds certain moral principles, but this is equally true for the Boy Scouts and the American Bar Association, neither of which is either commonly perceived as a religion or thought to be entitled to the special privileges of the free exercise clause.

There are two distinct paths that may be pursued in adding texture to the *Seeger* "parallel position" formulation's uncertain scope. One is a functional approach that seeks equivalence in the intensity of conviction with which beliefs are held. Another is a content-based approach that searches for analogues in subject matter that are both common and exclusive to concededly religious beliefs.[88] In considering these broad alternatives (and their more specific applications) for defining "religion" for the purpose of the free exercise clause's constitutional immunity from secularly based general government regulations of conduct, it is important to attempt to identify various historic and contemporary values underlying the provision that justify this very special protection. Then the alternatives can be evaluated in light of those values as well as the more general criteria for a legal definition of the term discussed earlier.

4. *"Ultimate Concerns": A Functional Criterion*

As a comparison of the *Davis v. Beason* and *Seeger* opinions reveals, judicial efforts to define religion in the legal context have attempted to keep pace with modern theological ideas. Developing concepts of religion within the Christian tradition have tended to move beyond orthodox concepts of God.[89] Some contemporary theologians, with a significant Christian following, urge secularization as the proper path of the church and social change as the just study of theology.[90] Others, while reaffirming the importance of transcendental faith, have departed from an anthropomorphic concept of a deity. Thus, John

---

88. *See* Mansfield, *Conscientious Objection—1964 Term*, in 1965 RELIGION & PUB. ORD. 3, 9.

89. The views of distinguished Christian theologians are particularly relevant for several reasons. First, the Judeo-Christian religious tradition is dominant in our culture and, whether rightly or wrongly, all other beliefs seeking recognition as religious tend to be compared to it. Second, because Christianity is generally a highly theocentric religion, the existence within it of nontheistic currents is especially instructive.

90. *See, e.g.*, H. COX, THE SECULAR CITY (1965).

A.T. Robinson, the Bishop of Woolwich, in his controversial book, *Honest to God*,[91] which was quoted by the Court in *Seeger*,[92] rejects the idea of "a God 'out there,' a God who 'exists' above and beyond the world he made, a God 'to' whom we pray and to whom we 'go' when we die."[93] Paul Tillich identifies faith as "the state of being ultimately concerned,"[94] and God as "the ground of all being."[95] The *Seeger* Court also quoted Tillich's work in support of its holding.[96]

Because of the favorable attention given by the Court to these progressive theologians, several constitutional interpretations of religion have been advocated that are based on the idea of "ultimate concerns,"[97] a phrase taken from the writings of Tillich. These proposals look primarily to the functional aspects of religion—its importance in the believer's scheme of things—rather than to its content. Ultimate concerns are to be protected, no matter how "secular" their subject matter may appear to be.[98]

This approach has several attractive features. First, it fulfills the need for a tolerant definition by its capability of including nonconformist, fringe religions as well as known orthodox sects and by its rejection of judicial determinations of whether some beliefs are inherently more "valuable" than others. Even more importantly, respect for deeply held beliefs is plainly a central value underlying the religion clauses. By focusing on the great significance that the belief holds for the claimant, this approach responds to the aversion, discussed more fully below,[99] of confronting an individual with the especially oppressive choice of either forsaking such precepts or suffering the pains of government sanctions.

The virtues of this definition, however, are outweighed by a series of difficulties. First, although Tillich's views may well be the profound expressions of a radical theologian searching for truth, even today they only marginally comprehend "religion" as that term is understood by most theologians or laymen. Moreover, Tillich's writings occupy volumes and are directed at theologians and lay believers, not lawyers. To extract from them the phrase, "ultimate concerns," and instruct judges to apply it as a legal formula seriously underestimates the subtlety of Tillich's thought and overestimates the theological sophistication of the participants in the legal process. For example, although Tillich recognizes that individuals may have such things as nationalism

---

91. J. ROBINSON, HONEST TO GOD (1963).
92. 380 U.S. at 181.
93. J. ROBINSON, *supra* note 91, at 14.
94. P. TILLICH, DYNAMICS OF FAITH 1 (1957) [hereinafter DYNAMICS OF FAITH].
95. P. TILLICH, THE SHAKING OF THE FOUNDATIONS 63 (1963).
96. 380 U.S. at 180, 187.
97. *See* Clark, *Guidelines for the Free Exercise Clause*, 83 HARV. L. REV. 327, 340-44 (1969); *Definition of Religion, supra* note 66.
98. *Definition of Religion, supra* note 66, at 1075-76.
99. *See infra* text following note 106.

or worldly success as their ultimate concerns,[100] he accords them no special respect, finding them to be idolatrous, because they claim to be ultimate without really being so.[101]

Our experience reveals that ultimate concerns may relate to such matters as science, politics, economics, social welfare, or even recreation—all staples of normal government regulation.[102] For this reason, the "ultimate concerns" approach is at odds with an important historic sentiment that underlies the constitutional protection granted by the religion clauses: that religion comprehends matters with which the government, whose authority is presumptively plenary, is incompetent to interfere.[103] Pursuant to this postulate, religion was to be regarded as a separate realm, to which the first amendment ceded a degree of sovereignty. Because "ultimate concerns," however, pervade virtually all areas of ordinary government involvement, whatever the true importance of such beliefs to the individual or society as a whole, to grant them the special constitutional immunity of the free exercise clause merely because they are strongly held would severely undermine the state's ability to advance the commonweal.[104]

---

100. DYNAMICS OF FAITH, *supra* note 94, at 1-4.

101. *Id.* at 11-12. Moreover, not all religious belief is "ultimate" in the functional sense, although it may deal with "ultimate" subject matter. *See* Welsh v. United States, 398 U.S. 333, 358-59 (1970) (Harlan, J., concurring); Mansfield, *supra* note 88, at 9 n.96.

102. The tenets of various political movements have been directed toward ultimate concerns. *E.g.*, Communism, *see* J. BENNETT, CHRISTIANITY AND COMMUNISM 87-88 (1970), and J. MURRY, THE NECESSITY OF COMMUNISM (1932); Marxism, *see* L. DEWART, THE FUTURE OF BELIEF 56-58 (1966), and J. SCHUMPETER, CAPITALISM, SOCIALISM AND DEMOCRACY 5-8 (5th ed. 1976); Nazism, Italian Fascism and Japanese Militarism, *see* E. SHILLITO, NATIONALISM: MAN'S OTHER RELIGION (1933). *See also* Bellah, *Civil Religion in America*, 96 DAEDALUS I (1967). Moreover, some users of drugs such as LSD do so to achieve a state of ultimate concern. W. BRADEN, THE PRIVATE SEA: LSD AND THE SEARCH FOR GOD 9-10, 89-92 (1967).

103. As Madison wrote in his *Memorial and Remonstrance Against Religious Establishments*: "that the Civil Magistrate is a competent Judge of Religious truth . . . is an arrogant pretension falsified by the contradicting opinions of Rulers in all ages, and throughout the world . . . ." *Reprinted in* THE COMPLETE MADISON, *supra* note 22, at 302.

104. Closely related to the "ultimate concerns" approach is the suggestion that "religion" should be construed to embrace "a comprehensive belief system . . . [that] proffer[s] a systematic series of answers . . . to the questions and doubts that haunt modern man." Malnak v. Yogi, 592 F.2d 197, 209, 214 (3d Cir. 1979) (Adams, J., concurring). *See also* Africa v. Pennsylvania, 662 F.2d 1025, 1035 (3d Cir. 1981). Further, see Judge J. Skelly Wright's emphasis on the fact that a group seeking classification as a religion subscribe to "the underlying theories of man's nature or his place in the Universe which characterize recognized religions." Founding Church of Scientology v. United States, 409 F.2d 1146, 1160 (D.C. Cir.), *cert. denied*, 396 U.S. 963 (1969). Similarly, John Mansfield has suggested that "religious" beliefs are distinguished by "the fundamental character of the truths asserted, and the fact that they address themselves to basic questions about the nature of reality and the meaning of human existence." Mansfield, *supra* note 88, at 10. This position has the theological support of John Haynes Holmes, who defined religion as "the consciousness of some power manifest in nature which helps man in the ordering of his life in harmony with its demands . . . [it] is the supreme expression of human nature; it is man thinking his highest, feeling his deepest, and living his best." *Quoted in* United States v. Seeger, 380 U.S. 163, 166 (1965).

The difficulty, however, is that at least some traditional religious beliefs would not appear necessarily to be comprehensive and, more seriously, that many comprehensive beliefs are not necessarily religious. Clark, *supra* note 97, at 339. For example, atheistic Marxism may be fairly described as comprehensive because it supplies answers to profound questions and denies the

Finally, because of its inherent vagueness, the "ultimate concerns" standard suffers from being based in large measure on psychological factors that are very difficult to administer. The legal process would be confronted with such formidable issues as what an "ultimate concern" really is and how "ultimate" must a concern be in order to qualify as religious. The broad discretion afforded the fact finder, whether judge or jury, poses a significant risk that parochial preconceptions will often prevail to the detriment of claimants with unorthodox principles and that appellate review will be able to correct only the most blatantly arbitrary decisions. Moreover, because the claimant's own characterization of his beliefs will frequently be the sole evidence supporting his position and because success will often depend on the ability to articulate the relationship between deeply held beliefs and a definition whose meaning is only dimly understood, the likely beneficiaries will be both the orthodox believers and those others who are best educated and most articulate.[105]

5. "Extratemporal Consequences": A More Content-Based Criterion

As indicated above,[106] a forceful explanation and pragmatic justification for the free exercise clause's special exemption from otherwise universal governmental regulation is the fact that the commands of religious belief, at least as conventionally perceived, have a unique significance for the believer, thus making it particularly cruel for the government to require the believer to choose between violating those commands and suffering meaningful temporal disabilities.[107] More-

---

significance of other issues. Indeed, it has been urged that Marxism is, at least to some, a religion. See Boyan, Defining Religion in Operational and Institutional Terms, 116 U. PA. L. REV. 479 (1968). See also Dupre, Spiritual Life in a Secular Age, 111 DAEDALUS 21, 22 (1982). However, because its tenets involve economic and social theories squarely within the realm of everyday government concern, Marxism both is and should be generally regarded as a political, not a religious, ideology.

The same problems of under- and over-inclusiveness arise in respect to another basically functional approach. Several courts have attempted to define "religion" (for both constitutional and statutory purposes) by looking to "formal, external, or surface signs that may be analogized to accepted religions." Malnak v. Yogi, 592 F.2d 197, 209 (3d Cir. 1979). Such signs, usually regarded as useful rather than essential, id., "might include formal services, ceremonial functions, the existence of clergy, structure and organization, efforts at propagation, observation of holidays, and other similar manifestations associated with traditional religion." Id. at 209. See also Founding Church of Scientology v. United States, 409 F.2d 1146, 1160 (D.C. Cir. 1969); Washington Ethical Soc'y v. District of Columbia, 249 F.2d 127 (D.C. Cir. 1957); Fellowship of Humanity v. County of Alameda, 153 Cal. App. 2d 673, 315 P.2d 394 (1957).

105. Compare Seeger with Gruca v. Secretary of the Army, 436 F.2d 239 (D.C. Cir. 1970), cert. denied, 401 U.S. 978 (1971). Seeger's correspondence with his draft board is very articulate and filled with references to Kant, Plato, John Stuart Mill, and others. Gruca, on the other hand, "either could not or would not express himself in any way" when examined by his draft board. 436 F.2d at 245 n.2. He stated that "[t]he Supreme Being said that all people was to be created equal and to love thy neighbor," and that "[i]f I am sent someplace where it is called war and I kill someone that is allright, and if I go out on the road and kill someone they call me a murderer." Id. at 247. Seeger was granted his exemption. Gruca was not, although the court was troubled.

106. See supra text accompanying note 99.

107. This policy is reflected in numerous free exercise clause opinions. See, e.g., Gillette v.

over, although the state may—and sometimes must—make many harsh demands on its citizenry—such as serving in the military, paying taxes, and forbearing from various forms of pleasurable behavior—our traditions, informed by both moral and instrumental concerns, have set certain constitutional, statutory, and common law limits on the reach of government power.[108]

The relationship between religion and this tradition may be illustrated by hypothesizing two objectors to military service. One has sincere conscientious scruples against killing, but they are not claimed by anyone, including the draftee, to be religious. The other's objection is rooted in a deep-seated faith that if he voluntarily kills another human being, this will influence or indeed determine his destiny after death. At the extreme, he may believe that if he does so, his immortal soul will be damned for eternity. Clearly, both will experience severe psychic turmoil if required to kill. But, although there is no sure method of proving it scientifically as an empirical matter, intuition and experience affirm that the degree of internal trauma on earth for those who have put their souls in jeopardy for eternity can be expected to be markedly greater than for those who have only violated a moral scruple.[109]

It must be acknowledged, however, that the state is not exclusively responsible for the concededly grave consequences facing the religious objector to military service. The government has simply presented both draftees with the option of either fulfilling their legal obligation or paying the price of fines, imprisonment, or a loss of government benefits. Because these state-imposed consequences are the same for both objectors, it may be said that there is no special cruelty in punishing the latter. Moreover, at a psychological level, the identical cost may be more comfortably borne by those religionists who can balance it against eternal rather than merely temporal benefits. Indeed, some may believe that martyrdom has independent value in affecting their destiny. Nonetheless, because the burden of *obeying* the law is so severe for the religious objector, our traditions hold that his noncompliance is not as morally culpable as one who disobeys for other reasons. This principle is reflected in the defenses of duress and necessity in the criminal law,[110] excusing or justifying violations when the cost of compliance is higher than an individual can reasonably be expected to bear.

United States, 400 U.S. 437, 445 (1971) ("hard choice between contravening imperatives of religion and conscience or suffering penalties"); *id.* at 454 ("painful dilemma"); Braunfeld v. Brown, 366 U.S. 599, 616 (1961) (Stewart, J., dissenting) ("to choose between his religious faith and his economic survival . . . is a cruel choice").

108. *See infra* text accompanying note 110.

109. There is, of course, a third type of conscientious objector, one who deeply believes that taking another's life is a fundamental violation of "God's law" but causes no afterlife effects. Although this person surely would be commonly considered as a "religious" objector, for purposes of the particular discussion here, he should be classified with the nonreligious objector.

110. *See* MODEL PENAL CODE § 2.09, Comment (Tent. Draft No. 10, 1960); MODEL PENAL CODE § 3.02, Comment (Tent. Draft No. 8, 1958).

This "special cruelty" factor—that seeks to draw a line beyond which it is unreasonable for society to expect a person to alter or violate his beliefs—is difficult to measure precisely, because the degrees of importance of various individuals' beliefs obviously form a continuous spectrum. Nonetheless, I believe, as the discussion above suggests, that belief in the phenomenon of "extratemporal consequences"—whether the effects of actions taken pursuant or contrary to the dictates of a person's beliefs extend in some meaningful way beyond his lifetime—is a sensible and desirable criterion (albeit plainly far short of ideal) for determining when the free exercise clause should trigger judicial consideration of whether an exemption from general government regulations of conduct is constitutionally required.

The "extratemporal consequences" criterion, which does not focus on the intensity of conviction with which the beliefs are held but rather on the perceived repercussions of their violation, is somewhat more content-based than functional in approach. By tending toward the subject matter of beliefs in this way, it probably conforms more than the "ultimate concerns" approach with the conventional, average-person conception of religion which, although largely intuitive, would generally conclude that a belief in God is religious but a belief in the Republican party is not, no matter how strongly held either of the beliefs may be.

While this approach thus has the virtue of greater common acceptability, the primary disadvantage of adopting a content-based definition of "religion" for constitutional purposes is the danger of parochialism and intolerance—that judges will include conventional orthodoxy in the definition and exclude new, unfamiliar, or "dangerous" beliefs. This is in fact the course that the Supreme Court took in the polygamy cases.[111] Thus, it has been argued that, "[a]t the very point where [content-based efforts to define religion] say, in effect, that a person must hold certain tenets or focus on certain issues in order to come within the constitutional protection, they demonstrate their incapacity to effectuate that protection. They enshrine an orthodoxy within a Constitution designed in part to protect unorthodoxy."[112]

Several considerations, however, support the "extratemporal consequences" precept. First, unlike content-based approaches that center on the specific substance of beliefs—such as a belief in God—it looks only to the ultimate supposed effects of beliefs whatever their peculiar substance may be. In this sense at least, it is sufficiently flexible and capable of growth to include newly perceived and unconventional values.

Second, to the extent that this criterion "enshrines" beliefs of a particular genre, it must be recalled that the dominant purpose of the

---

111. *See supra* text accompanying notes 51-53.
112. *Definition of Religion, supra* note 66, at 1074-75.

600   UNIVERSITY OF ILLINOIS LAW REVIEW   [Vol. 1982

religion clauses is to single out "religion," as opposed to other systems of belief, and requires that the concept have some minimum content.[113] It should also be remembered that beliefs falling outside this definition (such as those associated with the Universalist, Secular Humanism, Deism and Ethical Culture movements) are not remitted to uncontrolled punishment or persecution. Rather, all individual concerns, opinions, and beliefs receive substantial protection under other constitutional provisions.[114] As a matter of history and necessity, however, the special immunity for *conduct* afforded by the free exercise clause may belong only to a special category of beliefs.[115]

Third, although the content of even the most well-recognized religious belief systems is so varied as to defy any efforts to distill uniform tenets, the extratemporal consequences phenomenon finds support not only in those traditional religions prevalent in our culture but in most of the world's other major sects as well. At present, Christianity, Islam, and most branches of Judaism all believe in some form of divine judgment after death.[116] Various sects of Hinduism and Buddhism teach that each person is to be reincarnated, with the merit accumulated by

---

113. *See supra* text accompanying notes 36-47.

114. *See supra* text accompanying notes 7-30.

115. The extratemporal consequences approach also may be sensibly used in the two other free exercise clause contexts where the Court has carved an immunity for "religion" that is not capable of being vindicated by some other constitutional provision.

First, in respect to the general problem posed by the *Ballard* case, *see supra* text accompanying notes 42-44, the free exercise clause should be held to prohibit a judicial finding that money was obtained under false pretenses because promised extratemporal consequences did not or could not occur, but the Constitution should not bar a judge or jury from concluding that a representation assuring worldly results was fraudulent. The *Ballard* case itself did not involve a promise of extratemporal consequences for contributors, nor is there any indication that defendants would suffer any extratemporal consequences if they were punished by the state for fraudulent solicitation of funds. Rather the Supreme Court treated the case as only involving representations that supernatural events had already taken place (although, in fact, defendants were also charged with pledging that temporal benefits of health and wealth would accrue to those "willing to pay therefor," Ballard v. United States, 138 F.2d 540, 543 (9th Cir. 1943), *rev'd*, 322 U.S. 78 (1944)). In my view, should the Constitution be interpreted (as it apparently was in *Ballard*) to immunize claims of the kinds recited by the Supreme Court from adjudicative scrutiny, then the category should be sufficiently enlarged to encompass other assertions that are similarly not truly verifiable through ordinary experience—including all those grounded in some "transcendental" explanation, *see infra* text accompanying notes 121-27, and probably others which we often uncritically speak of as being subject to "scientific proof," *see* discussion following *infra* note 130. In any event, whatever the precise scope of the exemption, it should not turn on a constitutional definition of "religion."

Second, in respect to the doctrine governing internal ecclesiastical disputes, *see supra* text accompanying notes 45-47, if the first amendment's freedom of association guarantee is not read (as it probably should be) to impose an analogous protection for all intra-organizational disputes involving the ideological tenets of the group, then I find no persuasive reason not to restrict the existing rule to disputed issues whose resolution carries extratemporal consequences for those affected by the adjudication.

116. J. Noss, Man's Religions 557-58, 561, 574, 622 (1963); H. Schoeps, The Religions of Mankind 209, 234-35 (1966); L. Shinn, Abingdon Dictionary of Living Religions 238-39 [hereinafter cited as Abingdon Dictionary]; 5 Hastings Encyclopedia of Religion and Ethics 380-86 (1951) [hereinafter Hastings Encyclopedia]; 2 Historia Religionum 41, 43 (C. Bleeker ed. 1971).

virtuous acts in this life affecting one's status in the next, and with the possibility of eventual entry into heaven or Nirvana.[117] Moreover, this extratemporal consequences concept already has appeared in major Supreme Court decisions. The *Yoder* opinion, for example, notes that the Old Order Amish "believed that by sending their children to high school, they would . . . endanger their own salvation and that of their children."[118] Similarly, Justices Black and Douglas observed in the *Flag Salute Case* that "compelling little children to participate in a ceremony . . . ends in nothing for them but a fear of spiritual condemnation."[119]

Finally, the extratemporal consequences standard is consistent with a primary goal of the religion clauses—to isolate government from matters that it has neither the power nor competence to control.[120] Because the state can neither perceive nor determine what happens after death, it is particularly appropriate that it have minimal legislative authority to affect what may possibly occur in that realm.

6. "Transcendent Reality": A Possible Criterion

Despite the advantages of the extratemporal consequences test for determining when a system of beliefs qualifies for the special constitutional protection of the free exercise clause, it must be admitted that this criterion is not totally congruent with much that theologians and laymen would include in a definition of religion. Even within the Christian tradition, there are many articles of faith that do not relate directly to any rewards or punishments after death. Belief in the possibility of divine intervention on earth is one example: faith healing, retribution, and answered prayers. Another is the precept, which many find in the teachings of such persons as Saint Augustine and John Calvin, that salvation is the gift of God to His chosen, and is not to be earned by such behavior as good works during life.[121] Under beliefs of this nature, one may act under a religious compulsion that is not at all connected to the achievement of redemption.

Other religions, moreover, may ignore the afterlife consequences of one's acts altogether. Many major religions in their "primitive" stages have been far more concerned with the relationship between the

---

117. J. Noss, *supra* note 116, at 123, 145-47, 181-83, 189-90, 206-09.
118. 406 U.S. 205, 209.
119. West Va. State Bd. of Educ. v. Barnette, 319 U.S. 624, 644 (1943) (Black, J., concurring).
   The religious exemption provision of the Selective Service Draft Act of 1917, 40 Stat. 78 (1917), which was the progenitor of this now longstanding national policy, "stressed the peculiar plight of the orthodox theistic pacifist who is forced to disobey his country's law *or suffer eternal damnation*. It was depriving men of the hope of eternal life which was perceived by many in Congress as distinctively and impermissibly cruel." R. MORGAN, THE SUPREME COURT IN RELIGION 180 n.8 (1972).
120. *See supra* text accompanying notes 103-04.
121. J. Noss, *supra* note 116, at 646, 676-77; H. SCHOEPS, *supra* note 116, at 274; ABINGDON DICTIONARY, *supra* note 116, at 580.

living and the world around them than with the fate of the dead.[122] Some religions that do concern themselves with the deceased often have as their aim to propitiate the spirits of the departed or to prevent them from returning,[123] an attitude towards the dead that is still widespread. The indigenous religion of China, for example, is a well-developed system of ancestor worship in which the spirits of dead forebears are regarded as taking an active and continuing role in the well-being of the family.[124] Chinese religion involves strong duties, but does not usually connect them with consequences to follow after death.[125] Thus, although belief in this life as but one phase of existence, with the next phase to be determined by one's actions on earth, is extensive, it is not universal among the world's major religions, nor is it the only important belief of those sects that do hold it.

Admittedly, many beliefs that are generally regarded as religious despite their exclusive bearing on temporal affairs do share a common core with the extratemporal consequences precept. These beliefs are concerned with aspects of reality that are not observable in ordinary experience, but which are assumed to exist at another level. By addressing "basic questions"[126] or perhaps through mystical revelation of the unity of the world, such beliefs tend to infuse reality with transcendent meaning and significance—often through doctrines that explain such phenomena as the creation of the world and the nature of life and death. These aspects of reality may be felt by the believer, but because they cannot be demonstrated as facts, they transcend material experience.

This is confirmed by theological conceptions such as John Robinson's, which substitutes the metaphor of depth for the metaphor of height and views God as "the ultimate depth of all our being, the creative ground and meaning of our existence."[127] Robinson rejects the naturalistic contentions that "God is merely a redundant name for nature or for humanity,"[128] and thus affirms the transcendent nature of religion.[129] Similarly, Paul Tillich has written that "the source of this affirmation of meaning within meaninglessness, or certitude within doubt, is not the God of traditional theism but the 'God above God,' the power of being, which works through those who have no name for

---

122. J. Noss, *supra* note 116, at 14-31; 5 HASTINGS ENCYCLOPEDIA, *supra* note 116, at 380-83.

123. J. Noss, *supra* note 116, at 28-30.

124. *Id.* at 336-41.

125. A Chinese person who betrayed his ancestors, however, might have been considered an outcast by his family, a result that would pursue him after death. J. Noss, *supra* note 116, at 340-44. Further, it is said that the "more pious" Chinese can lessen punishment after death by devout acts. ABINGDON DICTIONARY, *supra* note 116, at 167.

126. Mansfield, *supra* note 88, at 10.

127. J. ROBINSON, *supra* note 91, at 47.

128. *Id.* at 54.

129. See also Tillich's discussion of true and idolatrous faiths. DYNAMICS OF FAITH, *supra* note 94, at 11-12.

it, even the name of God."[130]

It may be persuasively argued that *all* beliefs that invoke a transcendent reality—and especially those that provide their adherents with glimpses of meaning and truth that make them so important and so uncompromisable—should be encompassed by the special constitutional protection granted "religion" by the free exercise clause. Such beliefs not only conform to broadly based theological and lay perceptions of religion, but appear to be distinguishable from those more secularly grounded ideologies (such as humanistic pacifism, socialism, or Marxism) that we think of as being concerned largely with observable facts or ordinary human experience, even though the latter sets of beliefs may be as comprehensive and deeply held.

Systems of belief that are grounded in observable facts, about which evidence can be gathered, experts consulted, empirical conclusions drawn, and policies made, fall squarely within the realm of traditional governmental decisionmaking. While individuals may hold strong views on these matters, presumably there is a demonstrably correct answer that civil authority may decree. On the other hand, facts that are not observable in a conventional sense nor empirically verifiable, but are rather unknowable in the physical world, can only be experienced by the believer or taken on faith. No one, including government, can dictate or deny such experiences. Thus, it may be said that beliefs concerned with transcendent reality are outside the regulatory competence of the state.

In many ways, however, transcendental explanations of worldly realities are essentially no different, even in terms of government regulatory competence, than conventional exegeses for temporal outcomes that are based on such "rational" disciplines as economics, political science, sociology, or psychology, or even such "hard" sciences as biophysics, geophysics, or just plain physics. When justifying competing government policies on such varied matters as social welfare, the economy, and military and foreign affairs, there is at bedrock only a gossamer line between "rational" and "supernatural" causation—the former really being little more capable of "scientific proof" than the latter. Moreover, at the level of final decision, even the most frankly utilitarian goals depend ultimately on values—such as good or evil, or even the desirability of human survival—that represent normative preferences rather than rationally compelled choices. Therefore, if government possesses generally plenary authority to regulate the worldly affairs of society—and it surely does under our historical and contemporary political scheme—then its ability to do so should not be restricted because of the nature of the causes, which are all basically unverifiable, that different groups believe will produce consequences

---

130. P. TILLICH, 2 SYSTEMATIC THEOLOGY 12 (1957), *quoted in* United States v. Seeger, 380 U.S. 163, 180 (1965).

that the state seeks to achieve. In addition, from the standpoint of the need for principled adjudicative standards so vital for constitutional decisionmaking by a nonmajoritarian judiciary, there are several other central factors as to which it appears very difficult, if not impossible, to distinguish transcendental ideologies from those commonly considered to be based on secular premises—the intensity with which the beliefs are held (and the mental anguish resulting from their violation) and the comprehensive scope of the creeds' dogmas. Moreover, from a utilitarian perspective, the intuitive empirical judgment persists that obeying the law at the price of perceived eternal repercussions produces substantially greater psychological suffering than doing so at the cost of compromising scruples with only temporal reactions. Thus, the extreme protection from government power to regulate conduct afforded by the free exercise clause should be reserved for those who believe that departure from certain beliefs will carry uniquely severe consequences extending beyond the grave.

III. THE ESTABLISHMENT CLAUSE

The Supreme Court has developed a three-part test for assessing alleged violations of the establishment clause. In order to pass constitutional muster, government action (1) must have a secular, rather than a religious purpose, (2) may not have the principal or primary effect of advancing or inhibiting religion, and (3) may not involve "excessive entanglement" between government and religion.[131] Although each prong of this formula requires that content be given to the term "religious" or "religion," the Court has rarely even begun to do so and, when it has, its discussion has usually been very brief and quite conclusory.

Problems arising under the establishment clause have generally fallen into three broad categories. The first involves government financial assistance to religiously affiliated institutions—usually educational facilities. Because virtually all the cases have involved schools or colleges operated under the auspices of organized churches, the Court's focus has been on whether "religion" permeated the educational offering and on what sorts of aid were permissible. In none of these decisions was any definitional issue seriously disputed, the Court's discussion plainly assuming that everyone knew what was "religious" and what was not. A second group of decisions concerns regulatory laws allegedly enacted for religious purposes. In the two most prominent cases in this area, the Court again simply assumed a common understanding of the difference between a legislature's acting for "religious" rather than for "secular" reasons. The third major category implicates religious influences in the public schools. In the several in-

---

131. *See, e.g.*, Lemon v. Kurtzman, 403 U.S. 602, 612-13 (1971).

stances here that defenders of the challenged practices claimed that they had a nonsectarian goal, the Court rather summarily rejected the assertions as implausible.

A.   Dual Versus Unitary Definition of "Religion"

In order to accommodate the range of values underlying the religion clauses without subverting the regulatory goals of civil government in modern society, the Court has been urged to adopt a dual definition of religion—an expansive interpretation for the free exercise clause so as to protect "the multiplying forms of recognizably legitimate religious exercise,"[132] but a more confined definition for the establishment clause so as to avoid having "all 'humane' programs of government be deemed constitutionally suspect."[133] For example, even though it may be that "a group of gymnasts proclaiming on their trampolines that physical culture is their religion" should fall within the coverage of the free exercise clause, this should not mean that "if Congress, in a particular Olympic year, appropriated funds to subsidize their calisthenics,"[134] this would be aid to "religion" in violation of the establishment clause. Similarly, the fact that some people regard Transcendental Meditation to be their religion, thus entitling them to the constitutional immunity of the free exercise clause, should not lead to the conclusion that the establishment clause forbids a public school course in meditation that is offered for its psychologically beneficial effects.[135]

Apart from the objection that the text of the first amendment—"Congress shall make no law respecting an establishment of religion, or prohibiting the free exercise thereof"[136]—makes it grammatically difficult to argue that "thereof" has a different meaning than the word "religion" to which it refers,[137] close examination of the operative doctrines for the religion clauses suggests that a dual definition of religion may not be required to avoid the results feared under a unitary version of the term. Although there is considerable overlap in the purpose and operation of the two provisions—the central function of both being to secure religious liberty[138]—each nonetheless has an identifiable empha-

---

132. L. TRIBE, *supra* note 78, at 827.
133. *Id.* at 828.
134. Manning, *The Douglas Concept of God in Government*, 39 WASH. L. REV. 47, 66 (1964).
135. *See* L. TRIBE, *supra* note 78, at 828.
136. U.S. CONST. amend. I.
137. Justice Rutledge made the point in *Everson v. Board of Education*, 330 U.S. 1, 32 (1947) (Rutledge, J., dissenting):

'Religion' appears only once in the [First] Amendment. But the word governs two prohibitions and governs them alike. It does not have two meanings, one narrow to forbid 'an establishment' and another, much broader, for securing 'the free exercise thereof.' 'Thereof' brings down 'religion' with its entire and exact content, no more and no less, from the first into the second guaranty, so that Congress and now the states are as broadly restricted concerning the one as they are regarding the other.

138. Choper, *supra* note 50, at 677.

606   UNIVERSITY OF ILLINOIS LAW REVIEW   [Vol. 1982

sis. In the main, the free exercise clause protects *adherents of religious faiths* from *secularly* motivated government action whose effect imposes burdens on them because of their particular beliefs. When the Court finds a violation of the free exercise clause, this usually means that the law is invalid as applied; all that is required is an exemption for the claimant from the law's otherwise proper operation. In contrast, the principal (although—as we shall see[139]—not the exclusive) thrust of the establishment clause concerns *religiously* motivated government action that poses a danger that *believers and nonbelievers* alike will be required to support their own religious observance or that of others. When the Court finds a violation of the establishment clause, this ordinarily means that the offensive law (or part thereof) is invalid in its entirety and may not be enforced at all.

Under these existing principles, the Court may hold that, on balance, the free exercise clause requires an exemption from a generally valid regulation that happens to impose burdens on what the Court concludes to be the "religion" of Transcendental Meditation. But a public school course in meditation does not violate the establishment clause, despite the fact that this course is very helpful to, or parallels that required by, the Transcendental Meditation faith, unless it is shown that the school board's purpose in instituting the course (or the principal or primary effect of its being offered) is to advance religion.[140] The Court has made clear that the establishment clause does not forbid government action simply because it provides some aid to what is conceded to be a "religion," or because there is a coincidence between a legal command and the dictates of a group that comes within the protective coverage of the free exercise clause. That many conventional religious sects adhere to the Ten Commandments—prohibiting such acts as murder, adultery, perjury, theft, disrespect for one's parents, and Sunday labor—does not alone disable the government from legislating on those subjects. "In many instances, the Congress or state legislatures conclude that the general welfare of society, wholly apart from any religious considerations, demands such regulation."[141]

B.   Identifying Legislative Purpose

The crucial question, of course, is how to determine whether the

---

139. *See infra* text accompanying notes 156-59.

140. The Court's three-part test also states that an establishment clause violation may be found, despite both a secular purpose and a primary secular effect, if the challenged government action fosters "an excessive government entanglement with religion." *See supra* text accompanying note 131. It is unclear whether the Court is using this factor as an independent criterion of constitutionality, as "warning signal," Lemon v. Kurtzman, 403 U.S. 602, 625 (1971), calling for stricter application of other criteria, as a makeweight, or simply as a factor to reinforce its conclusions. I have criticized the use of "excessive entanglement" elsewhere. Choper, *supra* note 50, at 681-85. It is enough here to observe that I do not believe that any separate definitional problems are posed by this element and, if there are, they may be simply solved by its desirable elimination.

141. McGowan v. Maryland, 366 U.S. 420, 442 (1961).

legislative purpose is to further "the general welfare of society" rather than to "advance religion."[142] Just as the free exercise clause should require judicial acceptance of a claimant's bona fide subjective characterization of his beliefs as being "religious"[143] (as that term is defined for constitutional purposes), so, too, this key issue under the establishment clause should ultimately center on the intent of the lawmaking body. Although not dispositive, the crux of this delicate inquiry[144] into why a majority of legislators enacted a particular law is best evidenced by its primary (or independent) effect[145] and should turn not on the fact that some person or group perceives the law's goals or results as being "religious" (which may suffice to afford that person or group the protection of the free exercise clause), but rather on a more general societal perception of the matter. For although there may be occasions when it can be proven that the legislature is consciously pursuing sectarian ends despite a contrary popular understanding, ordinarily the public's perception that "the general welfare of society" is the law's object will powerfully evidence the intent of their elected or appointed representatives.

For example, if a group adopted physical fitness as its religion and believed that practices pursuant thereto had extratemporal consequences, and if an extratemporal consequences definition of religion were accepted for purposes of the free exercise clause, then action (or inaction) dictated by the group's tenets would be comprehended by the free exercise clause. But if this same definition of religion were applied under the establishment clause, the government would not thereby be prohibited from sponsoring physical fitness programs unless it could be shown that the legislative purpose was to advance physical fitness because of its extratemporal consequences. Because, in the absence of unusual evidence to the contrary, most government physical fitness programs are correctly perceived by the public to be directed at health, rather than to extratemporal consequences, no establishment clause problem would be present.

Those few establishment clause decisions of the Supreme Court that consider the issue of how to identify what is "religion" or "religious" are consistent with this approach. As for regulatory laws alleg-

---

142. It is important to note that the "general welfare" goal must be *independent* of any "religious" goal, *i.e.*, it may not be derived from the initial achievement of some religious purpose. The latter dynamic would "employ Religion as an engine of Civil policy," J. MADISON, *Memorial and Remonstrance Against Religious Establishments*, *reprinted in* 5 THE COMPLETE MADISON, *supra* note 22, effectively nullifying the values underlying the establishment clause. *See generally* Choper, *The Establishment Clause and Aid to Parochial Schools*, 56 CALIF. L. REV. 260, 278-79 (1968).

143. *See* United States v. Seeger, 380 U.S. 163, 184-85 (1965); Thomas v. Review Bd., 450 U.S. 707, 713-16 (1981).

144. *See* Village of Arlington Heights v. Metropolitan Hous. Dev. Corp., 429 U.S. 252, 266-68 (1977).

145. For fuller exploration of the matter, see *supra* note 142 and *infra* text accompanying notes 158-59. *See generally* Choper, *supra* note 142, at 277-83.

608   UNIVERSITY OF ILLINOIS LAW REVIEW   [Vol. 1982

edly enacted for religious purposes, in upholding Maryland's Sunday closing law, the Court found that despite the fact that "the original laws which dealt with Sunday labor were motivated by religious forces," their "present purpose and effect" was to further "the general welfare of society."[146] The Court relied on the fact that secular emphases in language and interpretation had come about, that recent "legislation was supported by labor groups and trade associations,"[147] and that "secular justifications have been advanced for making Sunday a day of rest, a day when people may recover from the labors of the week just passed and may physically and mentally prepare for the week's work to come."[148] Thus, even though refraining from work on Sunday is a tenet of major American religious groups, the relevant evidence satisfied the Court that the present legislation was motivated by economic and social considerations. In contrast, in invalidating a state statute prohibiting the teaching of evolution in public schools, the Court concluded that "Arkansas' law selects from the body of knowledge a particular segment which it proscribes for the sole reason that it is deemed to conflict with a particular religious doctrine."[149] Citing newspaper advertisements and letters supporting adoption of the statute in 1928, the Court found it "clear that fundamentalist sectarian conviction was and is the law's reason for existence."[150]

In two of the cases invalidating religious influences in the public schools, the Court—acknowledging the intimate relationship between the Bible and the nation's dominant religious sects—also drew on common understanding of what constitutes "religion" to impeach what it obviously concluded were implausible assertions that there were secular purposes for the challenged practices. In *Abington School District v. Schempp*,[151] the defendant school boards contended that the reading, without comment, of a chapter of the Bible at the opening of the school day served such nonsectarian ends as promoting moral values, inspiring pupil tolerance and discipline, contradicting the materialistic trends of the times, and teaching literature. The Court's brusque reply was that, "surely, the place of the Bible as an instrument of religion cannot be gainsaid."[152] More recently, the Court summarily reversed a decision by the Kentucky Supreme Court which had upheld the practice of posting copies of the Ten Commandments in public school classrooms.[153] The avowed purpose for posting the Ten Commandments was printed at the bottom of each copy: "The secular application of the Ten Commandments is clearly seen in its adoption as the fundamental

---

146. McGowan v. Maryland, 366 U.S. 420, 431-32 (1961).
147. *Id.* at 435.
148. *Id.* at 452.
149. Epperson v. Arkansas, 393 U.S. 97, 103 (1968).
150. *Id.* at 107-08.
151. 374 U.S. 203 (1963).
152. *Id.* at 224.
153. Stone v. Graham, 449 U.S. 39 (1980).

legal code of Western Civilization and the Common Law of the United States."[154] Observing that the Commandments were not integrated into any study of history, ethics, or comparative religion, but could only have the effect, if any, of inducing students to meditate on, revere, or perhaps obey them, the Court quite peremptorily concluded that "the Ten Commandments is undeniably a sacred text in the Jewish and Christian faiths, and no legislative recitation of a supposed secular purpose can blind us to that fact."[155]

C. The Relevance of "Effect"

As noted earlier, the Court's three-part establishment clause test holds that a law is invalid if either its purpose *or* its principal or primary effect is to advance religion.[156] Although the establishment clause decisions in the categories of religious influences in the public schools and regulatory laws with allegedly religious motivation have focused almost exclusively on legislative purpose rather than on effects, some rulings have invalidated financial aid to church-related schools or colleges on the ground that despite their bona fide secular purpose the programs' primary effects advanced religion.[157]

The fact that government action which furthers religious interests serves potentially as an independent ground for invalidating a program rather than simply evidencing the legislature's purpose creates substantial problems of judicial prerogative.[158] Such an approach empowers the Court to assess, by means of an ad hoc balancing process, the multiple impacts of legislation, to isolate those that are religious from those that are secular, and then to determine which are paramount, relying ultimately on the Justices' subjective notions of predominance.[159]

Regardless of the deficiencies of this process, however, it need not influence the issue of a dual versus a unitary definition of religion. The hypothetical physical fitness cult discussed previously again provides an illustration. Despite the fact that a government sponsored bodily health program might assist this group in pursuing its concededly religious goals, just as a Sunday closing law undoubtedly aids those conventional religions that require church attendance on their Sabbath, it

---

154. *Id.* at 41.

155. *Id.*

156. Although the Court's prescription also condemns government action whose principal or primary effect "inhibits" religion, it has never relied on this criterion as such in establishment clause adjudication. To the extent that the Court has discussed this element, it has done so to indicate that religiously motivated programs that it has held violative of the establishment clause pose dangers to individual religious liberty. *See* Choper, *supra* note 50, at 678-79.

157. *See, e.g.*, Committee for Public Educ. v. Nyquist, 413 U.S. 756 (1973); Tilton v. Richardson, 403 U.S. 672 (1971).

158. Elsewhere I have discussed the serious problems that arise from the Court's edict that religious purpose alone results in a violation of the establishment clause. *See* Choper, *supra* note 50.

159. *See* Choper, *supra* note 142, at 279-80, 323-25.

is extremely unlikely that advancement of the physical fitness faith could be found to be either the "principal" or "primary" effect of the program.

D.   The Role of Free Speech and Association

To this point, the question of what specific definition of religion should be adopted for purposes of the establishment clause has not been explored. But if, as prior discussion suggests, there is to be a unitary definition for both religion clauses, and if the "extratemporal consequences" test were to be accepted for the free exercise clause, how would this affect the scope of the establishment clause? If it could be shown that the purpose of government action—whether in the form of financial assistance, general regulatory legislation, or public school practices—was to support individuals or groups in pursuit of their beliefs or practices to achieve extratemporal consequences, then, under the premises stated, the establishment clause would be violated.[160] If this were the full extent of its reach, however, the deficiencies of employing this definition for establishment clause purposes are obvious. A wide variety of activities that are generally regarded as "religious" (despite the absence of any "afterlife" connection) could be aided or sponsored by the state free of the strictures of the anti-establishment precept. For example, the public schools might have voluntary programs of prayers to God seeking only worldly assistance, or state funds might be granted to a modern Protestant sect whose beliefs excluded salvation.

The remedy for this plainly unsatisfactory situation, I believe, lies in pursuing the question of whether, if such actions were immune from attack under the establishment clause, they nonetheless would abridge some other constitutional prohibition. The freedom of expression and association guarantees of the first amendment impose some significant, albeit as yet sketchily defined, limitations on the government's ability to support, or require citizens to support, particular beliefs or groups— whether or not their teachings or tenets are generally considered to be "religious."[161] At least under present doctrine, however, there is no strict constitutional requirement "that government must be ideologically 'neutral.' "[162] It may be assumed that, at a minimum, those who disdain American patriotic symbols have no constitutional right to "prevent government from promoting respect for the flag by proclaim-

---

160. My own approach to the establishment clause would also require that the government action pose the danger of coercing, compromising, or influencing the religious beliefs of persons subject to the program or whose taxes were being used to support it. *See* Choper, *supra* note 50.

161. Wooley v. Maynard, 430 U.S. 705 (1977) (state may not require use of license plates with motto to which vehicle owner is ideologically opposed); Abood v. Detroit Bd. of Educ., 431 U.S. 209 (1977) ("services charges" required of public employees may not be spent by union for ideological causes opposed by employee); West Va. State Bd. of Educ. v. Barnette, 319 U.S. 624 (1943) (public school pupils may not be required to salute flag).

162. L. TRIBE, *supra* note 78, at 588.

ing Flag Day or by using public property to display the flag . . . [or by spending] public funds to subsidize flag production . . . ."[163] Moreover, it may be conceded that the solution to such thorny constitutional problems as the extent to which government may underwrite political speech, artistic expression, or the education of children is exceedingly complicated and still at or beyond the frontiers of developing first amendment principles.[164] Similarly, it must be acknowledged—as earlier discussion reveals[165]—that any effort to draw a principled establishment clause line between "religious" beliefs (that may not be supported by the state) and "nonreligious" ideologies (that may be furthered by the government) is extraordinarily difficult if not impossible. Nonetheless, there is substantial reason to believe that government efforts to subsidize or promote such narrow partisan ideologies as the school prayers to God or the aid to modern Protestant sects hypothesized above—to fund these activities or attempt to indoctrinate its citizens in these views or persuade them to accept these beliefs—would abridge the freedom of association's ban on requiring a person "to contribute to the support of an ideological cause he may oppose"[166] and invade "the sphere of intellect and spirit which it is the purpose of the first amendment to our Constitution to reserve from all official control."[167]

For example, although it would appear to be within a state's constitutional authority to offer a public school program in meditation for the purpose of teaching students psychologically beneficial techniques of concentration and relaxation, this should be contrasted with the recently litigated New Jersey public school course in Transcendental Meditation (and the related "Science of Creative Intelligence"). The federal district court's review of the contents of the textbook found that the "Creative Intelligence" it described was analogous to the broad concept of "God" used by modern theologians.[168] The court also found that the "puja," a ceremony in which each student received a "mantra" with which to meditate,[169] was an invocation of a deified human being.[170] Therefore, the course was "nothing more than an effort to propagate TM, SCI and the views of Maharishi Makesh Yogi"[171]—an attempt by government "to encourage this version of ulti-

---

163. *Id.* at 590.
164. *See generally* Kamenshine, *The First Amendments' Implied Political Establishment Clause*, 67 CALIF. L. REV. 1104 (1979); Shiffrin, *Government Speech*, 27 U.C.L.A. L. REV. 565 (1980); Yudof, *When Governments Speak: Toward a Theory of Government Expression and the First Amendment*, 57 TEX. L. REV. 863 (1979).
165. *See supra* text accompanying notes 101-04 and following note 130.
166. Abood v. Detroit Bd. of Educ., 431 U.S. 209, 235 (1977).
167. West Va. State Bd. of Educ. v. Barnette, 319 U.S. 624, 642 (1943).
168. Malnak v. Yogi, 440 F. Supp. 1284, 1321-22 (D.N.J. 1977), *aff'd*, 592 F.2d 197 (3d Cir. 1979).
169. *Id.* at 1289-1312.
170. *Id.* at 1323.
171. Malnak v. Yogi, 592 F.2d 197, 215 (3d Cir. 1979) (Adams, J., concurring).

mate truth . . . ."[172] Even if the "ultimate truth" promoted by the public school did not invoke any "extratemporal consequences," and thus the program would not violate the establishment clause using that definition of religion, nonetheless, such ideological partisanship by government would readily be held to abridge the broader protections of the first amendment. Similarly, while there is no constitutional difficulty with a public school's offering courses in morality or philosophy—just as "study of the Bible or of religion, when presented objectively as part of a secular program of education,"[173] is fully permissible—for the state (through its schools or otherwise) to attempt to convince its people (through either its regulatory or fiscal powers) of the "ultimate truth" of the teachings of Dewey or Hegel—or Keynes or Friedman, or Luther or Christ—should be unconstitutional wholly apart from the establishment clause. Although government may undoubtedly regulate the *conduct* of its citizens to promote society's perception of the public welfare despite such programs having emanated from dogmatic ideological roots (whether religious or otherwise), it is an entirely different matter constitutionally for the state to commit its collective resources to persuade its people to *believe* in the validity of those ideas. Ultimately, the solution to the constitutional problem— and the challenge to first amendment theorists—is development of a coherent doctrine that meaningfully distinguishes what I have loosely described as "narrow partisan ideologies" (which government may not subsidize or promote) from what may be conclusorily labeled as "widely shared and basically noncontroversial public values"—such as the inherent dignity of the individual and the essential equality of all human beings—(which the state may aid or sponsor).

IV. CONCLUSION

In considering the issue of how "religion" should be defined in the first amendment, I have in no way attempted to catalogue all of the systems of belief that have been (or may be) reasonably (or unreasonably) comprehended by that term. Nor have I even begun to explore the profound and subtle theological lines that have (or may be) drawn. In a word, this article is not primarily about "religion." Rather, its guiding impulse has been an effort to resolve the problem of a constitutional definition for religion in a way that sensibly and usefully accounts for the substantive content that has been (and should be) given to the free exercise and establishment clauses. Thus, it has focused on constitutional doctrines, primarily under the religion clauses and other parts of the first amendment, to suggest that the seemingly intractable abstract question of what constitutes a "religion" need be answered in only a very limited way for constitutional purposes. Embedded interpreta-

---

172. *Id.* at 214.
173. Abington School Dist. v. Schempp, 374 U.S. 203, 225 (1963).

tions of the "freedom of speech" provision in fact dispose of almost all problems fairly considered under the free exercise clause, and I have proposed a relatively narrow definition of religion—surely imperfect, but grounded in certain functional considerations and some historic values—for purposes of the unique and very limited immunity from general government regulations of conduct that the free exercise clause has been held to provide. Authoritative interpretations of the freedom of expression and association precepts less readily handle the issues that have been traditionally considered under the establishment clause. But the core of recent doctrinal developments reflected in *Wooley v. Maynard*[174] and *Abood v. Detroit Board of Education*[175] (as well as their progenitor, *West Virginia State Board of Education v. Barnette*[176])—of which I approve—strongly indicate the very limited significance, if any, of using this same relatively narrow definition of religion for purposes of the establishment clause.

174. 430 U.S. 705 (1977).
175. 431 U.S. 209 (1977).
176. 319 U.S. 624 (1943).

Name Index